Law and Critique in Central Europe
Questioning the Past, Resisting the Present

During the period of actually existing socialism, Central Europe was simultaneously the eastern periphery of the capitalist world-system and the western periphery of the Soviet bloc. Following the transition, it transformed itself into a unique amalgam of postcolonialism (vis-à-vis the former Soviet power) and neocolonialism (vis-à-vis the West). This double peripherality means Central Europe's geopolitical situation is both problematic and traumatic. It is a space that conveys fantasies of conquest and normalization as well as reluctance and rejection. The present collection of essays brings together both established and emerging legal scholars from Central Europe to explore the sources and potentialities of critical legal scholarship in a Central European setting, the heritage of an authoritarian past and its influence over Central European law and politics, and the strategies of challenging the present legal status quo.

Rafał Mańko is external fellow at the Centre for the Study of European Contract Law (University of Amsterdam).

Cosmin Cercel is Assistant Professor in Law (University of Nottingham).

Adam Sulikowski is full Professor of Legal Theory (University of Wrocław) and Head of the Department of Legal Theory at the University of Opole.

Law and Critique in Central Europe

Questioning the Past, Resisting the Present

Edited by

Rafał Mańko, Cosmin Cercel,
and Adam Sulikowski

COUNTERPRESS
OXFORD

First published 2016
Counterpress, Oxford
http://counterpress.org.uk

© 2016 Rafał Mańko, Cosmin Cercel, and Adam Sulikowski

REVIEWERS
prof. dr hab. Paweł Chmielnicki
dr hab. Przemysław Kaczmarek

Rights to publish and sell this book in print, electronic and all other forms and media are exclusively licensed to Counterpress Limited. All other rights are reserved by the authors. An electronic version of this book is available under a Creative Commons Attribution-NonCommercial (CC-BY-NC 4.0) International license via the Counterpress website: http://counterpress.org.uk

ISBN: 978-1-910761-01-4 (paperback)

Typeset in 10 on 12 pt Sabon
Cover by SUGAHTANK design
www.behance.net/SUGAHTANK

Global print and distribution by Ingram

Contents

Contributors ix

Foreword: On a Recent Change of Tone
in Politics and Law xii
Costas Douzinas

Introduction: Law and Critique in Central Europe:
Laying the Cornerstone 1
Rafał Mańko, Cosmin Cercel, Adam Sulikowski

Chartering Central Europe as a Legal Space 1
Giving Voice to Europe's 'Central' Periphery 4
Sources of legal Critique in Central Europe 7
Challenging the Present 10
Overview of the Chapters 11

1. Government of Judges and Neoliberal Ideology:
   The Polish Case 16
   Adam Sulikowski

   1.1 Introduction 16
   1.2 A Genealogy of the Polish Constitutional Court 17
   1.3 The Affirmative Amnesia of Polish Constitutionalists .. 23
   1.4 Postmodern Conditions *à la Polonaise* 27

2. The Importance of Being a Linguist:
   Critical Legal Thought in Central Europe 32
   Martin Škop

   2.1 The Confusion of Tongues 32
   2.2 The Importance of Being a Linguist 35
   2.3 The Critical Tradition in Central Europe:
       Spectres of the Forgotten 37
   2.4 Introduction of Critical Ideas 40
       2.4.1 *Preferred Reading* 40
       2.4.2 *Cultural Hegemony* 42

vi CONTENTS

3. **Law out of Bounds: Legal Picnolepsy, Intellectual Austerity, and Romania's Legal Past** 44
   COSMIN SEBASTIAN CERCEL

   3.1 Introduction 44
   3.2 Picnolepsy, Experience and Exception:
       Forgetting in the World of Late Capitalism 45
   3.3 From a History to Forget to the Forgetting of History 51
   3.4 The Material of Forgetting: Law's Unconscious 60

4. **Demons of the Past? Legal Survivals of the Socialist Legal Tradition in Contemporary Polish Private Law** 66
   RAFAŁ MAŃKO

   4.1 Introduction 66
   4.2 A Blackout only Worth Forgetting: Narratives of the
       State socialist Past 68
   4.3 Examples of State Socialist Legal Survivals
       in Polish Private Law 74
       4.3.1 *Introduction* 74
       4.3.2 *Perpetual Usufruct* 75
       4.3.3 *Cultivation Contract* 78
       4.3.4 *Prosecutor's Standing in Civil Proceedings* 80
       4.3.5 *Preliminary References to the Supreme Court* 84
   4.4 Conclusions: Demons of the Past
       or Useful Legal Institutions? 85

5. **Feminist Legal Education in Croatia: A Question of Fundamentalism or a Fundamental Question?** 90
   IVANA RADAČIĆ

   5.1 Introduction 90
   5.2 Feminist Approaches to Law and Legal Education 91
   5.3 Approach to Law and Legal Education in Croatia 93
   5.4 Marginalization of Feminist Perspectives
       in Croatian Legal Academia 98
   5.5 First Year Introductory Subjects 98
   5.6 Subjects Introducing Legal and Political Orders 100
   5.7 Courses with a Subject Area of a Specific
       Relevance to Women 100
   5.8 Exclusion of Feminist Perspectives
       from Scholarly Production 102
   5.9 Conclusion: The Way forward 103

6. **The Social Construction of Femininity in the Discourse of the Polish Constitutional Court** 106
   HANNA DĘBSKA & TOMASZ WARCZOK

   6.1 Introduction 106
   6.2 The Social Construction of Reality—Towards Material Anthropology 107
   6.3 Fields and the Production of Meaning 110
   6.4 Social Changes after Political Transformation in 1989 114
   6.5 Femininity as Constructed Judgment in the Case Law of the TK 118
   6.6 Conclusions 128

7. **Structural Violence and its Gender Dimension in Polish Law** 131
   LIDIA RODAK

   7.1 Introduction 131
   7.2 Structural violence in law and its gender dimension 133
   7.3 Official/Unofficial Law 136
   7.4 Informal Rules and Gender Violence 138
   7.5 Structural Violence in Polish Law 141
   7.6 (In)formal Rules and Structural Gender Violence 147
   7.7 Conclusions 153

8. **A Technicist Perspective and the Contemporary Perception of the Role of Lawyers in Polish Society** 154
   JACEK SROKOSZ

   8.1 Introduction 154
   8.2 The Technicist Approach in Social Sciences 154
      8.2.1 *The Meaning and Genesis of Technicism* 154
      8.2.2 *Factors Reinforcing the Technicist Approach* 157
      8.2.3 *The Technicization of University Studies in Poland* ... 161
   8.3 Technicism in Law 163
      8.3.1 *Technicist Law Teaching* 163
      8.3.2 *Legal Policy and the Technicist Approach* 165
      8.3.3 *Legal Positivism and the Technicist Approach* 166
      8.3.4 *The Technicist Approach in Polish Legal Practice* 169
      8.3.5 *Advantages and Disadvantges of the Technicist Approach in Legal Practice* 172
   8.4 Conclusions 174

9. From Sublimation to Naturalization:
   Constructing Ideological Hegemony
   on the Shoulders of Roman Jurists 176
   PAULINA ŚWIĘCICKA

9.1 Introduction 176
9.2 Monumental Roman Law and the Ideology of Continuity 180
9.3 The Dominant Historical Narrative about Roman Law
    and Roman Legal Tradition: The Sacralization of the
    Legal Source and the Narrative Concerning the
    Roman Roots of Institutions of Contemporary Law 187
9.4 Impacts of the Ideology of Continuity of the Common Legal
    Tradition on Legal Practice—the Polish Example 193
9.5 Conclusions 203

10. The Role of Václav Havel in Czech Critical Legal Thought 206
    MARKÉTA KLUSOŇOVÁ

10.1 Introduction 206
10.2 Legal Critique in the Czech Republic 206
10.3 Critical Legal Thought and the CLS movement 208
10.4 Václav Havel as the Main Figure of Czech Dissent 210
10.5 Havel's texts 211
     10.5.1 *Český úděl? (The Czech Lot?)* 211
     10.5.2 *Plays* 212
10.6 Dissidents 215
10.7 Living in Truth 216

Afterword: Law Between the Specters of the Past
and the Impossible Object of Desire 219
LESZEK KOCZANOWICZ

Index 223

Contributors

Dr Cosmin Sebastian Cercel is Assistant Professor at the University of Nottingham (United Kingdom). He completed his doctorate in Comparative Legal Studies at the University Panthéon Sorbonne (Paris I) in 2012 with a thesis dedicated to the analysis of the nexus between law, politics, and culture in communist Romania. His main research focuses on genealogies of law and politics with specific reference to 20th century continental legal history. His current research aims to put under a critical scrutiny the dissolution of classical concepts of legality and constitutionalism in the historical context of the rise of authoritarianism during the interwar in Europe. His recent publications include several articles on the relation between law and authoritarianism as well as a psychoanalytical reading of the historiographical intricacies of the authoritarian past. He is now writing a monograph analyzing the jurisprudential aspects of state communism.

Dr Hanna Dębska is a lawyer and sociologist specializing in critical sociology of law and constitutionalism. She is Assistant Professor at the Institute of Political Science of the Pedagogical University in Cracow where she teaches law, and a PhD candidate in sociology at the University of Warsaw. She is the author of numerous articles in peer-reviewed Polish journals and a monograph (in Polish) on the symbolic power of the Polish constitutional courts, recently published by the Polish Parliament's publishing house (Wydawnictwo Sejmowe). She was awarded the First Prize for her PhD in law by the Polish Academy of Sciences (2015) and a 'START' Scholarship for Young Scholars by the Foundation for Polish Science (2016). Her current research focuses on a sociology of knowledge approach to Polish legal academia.

Dr Rafał Mańko received his master's degree in law from the University of Warsaw (2003) and his PhD in law from the University of Amsterdam (2014). He is external fellow at the Centre for the Study of European Contract Law at the University of Amsterdam and policy analyst at the European Parliamentary Research Service in Brussels. His research focuses on three main areas: the interplay between socioeconomic transformation and law; the theory and practice of legal interpretation; and, within the sphere of doctrinal research, private law (especially consumer contract law) and its Europeanization. He is the author of over 50 scholarly publications in peer-reviewed journals and edited volumes.

Dr Markéta Klusoňová received her PhD degree in legal theory at the Masaryk University, Brno, Czech Republic in 2016. She currently works as assistant professor at the Department of Legal Theory of the same university. Her research focuses on the use of fiction literature as an argument in judicial decisions. She is also studying towards a bachelor's degree in theatrology at Masaryk University, focusing, inter alia, on law as a form of ritual theatre, the role of theatre in legal education, as well as legal aspects of street art performances.

Dr Ivana Radačić is a senior research associate at the Ivo Pilar Institute of Social Sciences in Zagreb, and a part-time lecturer at the University of Zagreb and the University of Osijek. She was a visiting lecturer at UCL, European Inter-University Centre for Human Rights and Democratisation, UN University for Peace (Costa Rica), and a research fellow at the University of Kent and the University of Melbourne. Her research interests are feminism and human rights, and gender, sexuality, and the law. She has published widely in these areas. She is a member of the EU COST Action Comparing European Prostitution Polices and a founding co-chair of the ESIL interest group on International Human Rights. She worked at the European Court of Human Rights and is the CoE expert on human rights.

Dr Lidia Rodak is an assistant professor of legal theory at the University of Silesia Faculty of Law (Katowice, Poland). She holds an LLM from the European Academy of Legal Theory in Brussels and a PhD from the University of Ghent. She conducted her post-doctoral research at the University in Palermo working on the topic of objectivity in law. Her current research focuses on objectivity and subjectivity in law, with a focus on feminist jurisprudence and gender studies. Her monograph on Discursive Objectivity is forthcoming with Peter Lang.

Dr Jacek Srokosz is an associate professor of legal philosophy at the University of Opole, Poland. He holds a master's degree and a PhD in law from the University of Wrocław. His research interests cover legal education (including critical legal education), the social role of lawyers, solidarism, communitarianism, as well as the legal and political philosophy of the authoritarian regime in Poland in the 1920s and 1930s. He is the author of a monograph *W stronę silnego państwa. Koncepcje ustrojowe prawników obozu rządzącego w Polsce 1926–1939* [Towards Strong State. The legal system in thought of the lawyers associated with the governing camp in Poland 1926–1939] and of numerous articles in peer-reviewed Polish academic journals.

Dr Martin Škop is a lawyer and a sociologist. He is an assistant professor in the Department of Legal Theory (Faculty of Law), Masaryk University, Brno, Czech Republic. His research is concerned with general theoretical problems of law, jurisprudence, legal sociology and legal methodology, with a main focus on law and literature, as well as law and language. He has published four books (in Czech): *Law and Violence; Law in Postmodern Situation; Law and Passion; Law, Language, and Story*. He holds the position of a vice dean at the University of Brno Faculty of Law and is becoming a promising pianist.

Prof. Dr Adam Sulikowski is full professor of legal theory at the University of Wrocław (Poland) and head of the Legal Theory Department at the University of Opole (Poland). His research focuses on applications of postmodern critical theory within the legal field. His most recent monographs (all in Polish) include *Post-humanism and Jurisprudence* (2013), *Constitutional Discourse: The Triumph and Crisis of Modern Episteme* (2011), and *The Contemporary Paradigm of Constitutional Justice and the Crisis of Modernity* (2008).

Dr Paulina Święcicka is Assistant Professor in the Chair of Roman Law at the Jagiellonian University in Kraków, Poland. She is the author of over 30 articles in Polish and international peer-reviewed academic journals and collective monographs. Her research focuses on Roman law and the classical tradition, philosophy of law (with a particular focus on the legal argumentation of Roman jurisprudence), sociology of law, as well as rhetoric in its ancient and modern dimensions.

Dr Tomasz Warczok is a sociologist, currently Assistant Professor at the Institute of Philosophy and Sociology of the Pedagogical University in Kraków and researcher at the Institute for Social Studies at the University of Warsaw, Poland. He was a visiting scholar at the University of California, Berkeley (2016). He has published a number of articles in peer-reviewed Polish and international journals, including *Current Sociology, Polish Sociological Review, Studia Socjologiczne* and *Kultura i Społeczeństwo*. His current research focuses on the sociology of social sciences.

Foreword

On a Recent Change of Tone in Politics and Law

Costas Douzinas

I AM WRITING THIS PREFACE in the Chamber of Hellenic Parliament a little after giving my maiden speech as a newly elected Member of Parliament for Syriza, the radical left party and current government of Greece. It is only a short six weeks since I gave the opening address at the amazing Critical Legal Conference ('CLC') on 5 September 2015 in Wrocław, Poland, the first CLC in Central Europe.

The change in my life since this historic meeting in Wrocław is momentous. I was asked to stand for the Greek Parliament on September 6th in my Wrocław hotel room. I had no desire or preparation to become a politician. I wanted to help Syriza at a difficult time—it had won handsomely the January 2015 elections and the July 2015 referendum on an anti-austerity programme. But after it was blackmailed into accepting a further bailout and accompanying memorandum of recessionary measures, its popularity with the Greek people seemed to be on the wane. I believe that the Left must experience the difficult and almost impossible task of government. I believe that we do not have any recipes or textbooks about the meaning of the radical Left in the 21st century. I believe therefore that Syriza, wounded after the defeat, should stay in power and try to work out through experimentation, imagination, and risk-taking what left govern-mentality and democratic socialism mean today.

I accepted to run for Syriza in the September 20th elections—less than three weeks away—that strange day in Wrocław when I was assured that my chances of getting elected were slim. I was elected, however, and the change in my life is quite dramatic. It is also characteristic of the wider change taking place all over Europe. An arc of virtue started emerging in Europe since the beginning of 2015. From Turkey to Greece and Spain, from Portugal to Ireland and Scotland, the dominant neoliberal ideology of the European Union is on the retreat. And the first CLC in Central Europe is a natural extension of this trend.

Being critical and radical in law or in any other area of intellectual activity has not been an easy task. When the first CLC took place in

1985 at the University of Kent, being critical was not conducive to career advancement. Using deconstruction, rhetoric, psychoanalysis, postcolonial, or queer theory in the reading of legal texts was considered at best exotically irrelevant and at worse ideologically suspect. In 1985, an article I wrote with Ronnie Warrington with the title 'The deconstruction of jurisprudence' was rejected because it included words that could not be found in the Oxford English Dictionary. 'Deconstruction,' 'logocentrism,' and 'logonomocentrism' offended the word police. It was not just the words. Our learned friends did not consider that deconstructing legal doctrine and theory was proper. How things have changed! Nowadays mainstream legal journals have articles on the 'deconstruction' of this or that doctrine, the 'legal aesthetics' of Shakespeare, or law and dance. Legal scholarship has experienced a renaissance in the last thirty years. The CLC has been at the forefront. Coming to Central and Eastern Europe is a natural extension.

But what is critique? Kant's *Critiques* start by posing the question '*quid iuris*'—by what legal right.[1] The link between law and critique is a central feature of modernity.

> In the eighteenth century, history as a whole was unwittingly transformed into a sort of legal process ... the tribunal of reason, with whose natural members the rising elite confidently ranked itself, involved all spheres of activity in varying stages of its development. Theology, art, history, the law, the State and politics, eventually reason itself—sooner or later all were called upon to answer for themselves.'[2]

Critique brings reason, its faculties and disciplines to a legal tribunal and asks them to justify themselves according to legal protocols. In the original Kantian sense, critique means the exploration of the transcendental presuppositions, the inescapable conditions of possibility of a discourse or practice. To use human rights as an example, we could say that an examination of the transhistorical conditions of the emergence of human rights requires a critical appreciation of concept of humanism and the practice of rights in the Western legal tradition.

The aim of critique is to introduce a limit attitude, to 'dare people to know', but also to delineate what ought to remain off limits to knowledge because it does not belong to its kingdom. Critique is therefore a policing operation too; its judgment establishes boundaries while its border guards police the line between inside and outside, a function that appeared from the beginning to be excessively and essentially negative. Critique's business is to prohibit and exclude, to keep ideas safe and protected. Critique comes before the law and is shaped according to legal protocols, peculiarities, and

---

[1] Cf. Immanuel Kant, *Critique of Pure Reason*, A84/B116.
[2] Reinhart Koselleck, *Critique and Crisis* (Cambridge, Mass.: MIT Press, 1988), 9–10.

procedures. It finds in law its essence and form, it becomes law-like, the critic a judge or a guard, something not far removed from the Freudian conception of the law-like character of conscience or the superego. The critic is either the judge who makes distinctions, passes judgment, and sets limits, or the policeman who guards those limits and ensures that the judicial fiat is translated into daily practice. We are well aware of these two positions in intellectual life and their expressions in the legal academy. Critique takes its severe and austere stance from the protocols of legal propriety and sobriety.

Κρίνειν (*krinein*) however means also to cut; critique is a cutting force. It aims to distinguish between true manifestations and inauthentic counterparts of a phenomenon. Marx's critique undercut 'bourgeois' philosophy arguing that the categories and suppositions of bourgeois thought conceal the true operations. The critical gaze saw the effects of inequality and power where philosophy had seen reason or the unproblematic development of tradition. To return to the example of human rights, the classic Marxist tradition would see these ideas as a fiction of a particular political order that attempts to preserve its hold on power by offering minor concessions, or blinding people with ideologies of the 'rights of man'; for a Marxist, the rights of man include the rights of some to live in luxury, and the rights of the many to starve. The key to just social organization was imagined not as catalogues of rights, but as collective control over the state mechanisms that had been used to oppress them. Marxism is irreducibly marked by a utopian moment. The later manifestations of the tradition, for instance the celebrated Frankfurt School, continued and intensified both the analytical and utopian elements. In post-Marxist theory, the critic places much greater importance on the social imaginary and bears witness to the gaping cleavage between real and its idealized, ideological representations.

The British 'Crits' see themselves as a counter-movement with a practical and an ideational moment.[3] We are radicals who do not discard the possibility of taking power. But at the same time we are demanding the impossible. The social has to be re-imagined. Notions such as the 'intersubjective zap' of the early American critical legal studies or the 'momentary principle of justice' in the British ethical period represent the intense moment when people perceive there is a possibility that coming together can be both a provocation and a utopian urge for a better world. Its Marxist loans are apparent in its theories of ideology and alienation. The legitimacy of the

---

[3] On the British critical legal movement see Costas Douzinas, 'A Short History of the British Critical Legal Conference or, the Responsibility of the Critic,' *Law and Critique* 25/2 (2014), 187–198. For a Polish translation see Douzinas, 'Krótka historia brytyjskiej Krytycznej Konferencji Prawniczej albo o odpowiedzialności krytyka' *Archiwum Filozofii Prawa i Filozofii Społecznej*, 8/1 (2014), 5–17, accessed 4 January 2016, http://archiwum.ivr.org.pl/wp-content/uploads/2014/09/afp_2014_01_005.pdf.

social world is sustained by 'overpowering' symbols that extend over the whole operation of the law.

In this sense, critical legal theory is intimately associated with philosophy and with emancipatory and radical politics. In equal measure, a critical movement is theoretical and political and a critical legal movement addresses the institutional and doctrinal politics of law and the politics of law's self-understanding in the form of jurisprudence and legal theory. If one is not aware that legal concepts are reified and abstracted, they appear to have some kind of foundational substance, a kind of autonomy or independent being. Law presents the social order as if resting upon itself. This loses sight of the fact that the law manufactures its own conditions of legitimacy and then attempts to legislate them as *a priori* universals that have a legitimizing effect through their appeal to reason. Reification is a corruption of the very process of reasoning in that it passes off one thing as another: it gives coherence and substance to things that can have no independent being, like those fetishes that attribute human powers and capacities to objects and constructs. No social organization is a 'given'—it is a cultural construction where ideas have gone into action. Over time, these ideas take a solid form, and the sheer contingency of the events that have constituted an order become forgotten. Behind every social organization there is thus a philosophy, even if this has become fetishized, unquestioned common sense, forgotten.

These are the issues and challenges that lawyers from Central Europe face. As this volume amply demonstrates, critical lawyers in this part of the world are doubly marginalized. First, they are seen as irrelevant and peripheral at best and as unacceptably disobedient and seditious at worst. Secondly, Eastern European comrades have suffered a kind of 'symbolic violence' in the hands of their Western European counterparts. The invigoration of critique in the East must combine the 'left-right division with the centre-periphery dichotomy.'

The first challenge is not dissimilar to what Western critics experience. Being critical in the West always invited a suspicion of bad faith a kind of *trahison des clercs*. Hadn't the West triumphed over the 'evil empire' by showing its commitment to the rule of law and human rights? Isn't the critique of these hallowed institutions an expression of concealed communism? This type of suspicion accompanied too my encounters with dissident lawyers before 1989. In unintended alliance with the most reactionary parts of the Western legal establishment, Eastern dissidents thought that all critique of the Western legal system was part of an attempt to overturn it in favour of some unclear version of socialist legality.

Nothing was further from our mind. Our defensive strategy tried to keep the law honest, by making it deliver on its own promises of fairness, limited equality before the law, and a vague sense of care for people, something fatally undermined by the recent neoliberal turn. The more aggressive stance, associated with the utopian moment, attempted to conceptualize the alternative society and law at the bar of which current state law has to give an account and be held accountable. This alternative law is not something for the future. It is implicit in the here and now of legality from which we can tease out liberatory and future-oriented principles. In this sense, all critical legal scholarship is in effect paradoxical: it serves principles central to a legality of social justice while at the same time advocating a wholesale change of the law. Critical lawyers suffer from a kind of identity crisis, a mild schizophrenia. As lawyers, we use legal methods and procedures to defend the poor, the disadvantaged, the refugees, and migrants who are the contemporary face of exclusion and destitution. But as critics, we know that every victory for the oppressed and exploited offers legitimacy to a system that upholds its weak and weakened principles only exceptionally.

But I am a resolute optimist. Seeing a radical left party in government would have sounded a short and cruel joke before 2015. Seeing the CLC in Wrocław would have sounded an unreal pipedream of a few dreamers: several Central European lawyers (most of them present in this volume) and a few Crits in the West. They both happened in that extraordinary 2015. As I try to combine academic and political work, commuting every week from Athens to London to teach my class at the University I can only smile in the midst of great difficulties. We leftists have been used to intellectual failure and political defeat. Perhaps this is the time that things start changing and what was always an impossible dream, indeed what was the definition of impossibility, can become possible. Wrocław meets Athens and a novel tonality enters politics and law. This is hope and reality.

Athens/London, 5 November 2015

Introduction

Law and Critique in Central Europe: Laying the Cornerstone

Rafał Mańko, Cosmin Cercel, Adam Sulikowski

Chartering Central Europe as a Legal Space

Central Europe—here understood as the former state-socialist countries, which joined the EU between 2004 and 2013[1]—remains, to a large extent, unchartered territory for (Western) critical lawyers and comparatists-at-law. In order to fill this lacuna this collection of essays aims at exploring the background, the state of the art, and new perspectives on critical legal thought in this part of Europe. The idea of the book originates in a stream 'Reconstruction, Return or Revolution? The Phenomenon of Critical Legal Thought in European Post-Communist Countries' convened by Adam Sulikowski at the 2013 Critical Legal Conference in Belfast. However, this book is not a simple volume of conference proceedings, but a collective research monograph in its own right, given that the scope of the chapters goes beyond the initial theoretical and hermeneutical engagement of the presented papers. Rather, the first Central European stream at the CLC should be understood as an Event which gave rise to the emergence of the critical legal community of Central Europe, for which this very first collective volume is the cornerstone. We shall return to our engagement with the British Critical Legal Conference in section III where we explore the variegated and multifaceted sources of legal critique in our region.

Whilst the geographical, cultural, and political setting of our plural engagement with law and critical theory is one of the topics informing the background of this book, it is not the only point of juncture. Our contributions aim to critically explore the status of law in national and regional contexts by asking three crucial and interconnected questions.

---

[1] These are, in alphabetical order: Bulgaria, Croatia, the Czech Republic, Estonia, Hungary, Latvia, Lithuania, Poland, Romania, Slovakia and Slovenia. For a similar approach, see Michal Bobek, 'Conclusions: Of Form and Substance in Central European Judicial Transitions' in *Central European Judges Under the European Influence: The Transformative Power of the EU Revisited*, ed. Michal Bobek (Oxford: Hart Publishing, 2015), 391.

We are interested, first of all, in exploring the sources and potentialities of critical legal scholarship in a Central European setting, secondly, the heritage of an authoritarian past and its influence over law and politics in Central Europe, and thirdly, the strategies of challenging the present legal status quo.

The notion of 'Central Europe' is certainly a problematic one. While before World War I, *Mitteleuropa* doubtlessly encompassed the Austro-Hungarian Empire and, plausibly, eastern parts of the German Reich, the situation changed after 1918 with the emergence of numerous newly independent states, such as Poland, Czechoslovakia, Hungary, or the Baltic republics. The rise of authoritarianism during the last years of the 1930s, the outcome of World War II, and more specifically the politico-symbolic erection of the Iron Curtain, temporarily erased Central Europe from maps, substituting a strictly bipolar East/West division in its place. The fall of the Berlin Wall in 1989 immediately brought about a resurrection of Central Europe as a spatial concept and as a region understood either in geopolitical or cultural terms.[2] The subsequent integration of former Soviet bloc countries within the European Union justifies a pragmatic notion of Central Europe as pointing to this part of the former Soviet bloc which is now within the EU, as such including so-called new Member States.[3] As Zdeněk Kühn has pointed out, the countries of the former Austro-Hungarian Empire (including Poland, the Czech and Slovak Republics, Slovenia, Hungary, and Croatia) share a common legal past with regard to legal culture, even if Hungarian law differed from Austrian law.[4] Furthermore, all Central European countries—this time including the Baltic states (Lithuania, Latvia, and Estonia),[5] as well as Romania and Bulgaria—share the same legal past of actually existing socialism which lasted 45 years, until the fall of the Soviet bloc.[6] Moreover, they all—this time in contrast to Eastern Europe—share similar experiences of transformation and preparation for EU membership. These three factors militate

---

[2] A poignant example of 'Central Europe' as a spatial concept is the denomination of 'Central European University' in Budapest. On the ways in which Central and Eastern Europe has become an object of a discourse fashioned in terms of 'region' and 'culture' and the politics inherent to this reading, see Alex Cistelecan, 'From Region to Culture, from Culture to Class,' *Journal of Contemporary Central and Eastern Europe* 23/1 (2015), 45–60.

[3] The notion of Eastern Europe would include post-Soviet countries to the east of Central Europe, such as Ukraine, Belarus, Moldova, or even the Caucasic countries (Bobek, 'Conclusions,' 393).

[4] Zdeněk Kühn, *The Judiciary in Central and Eastern Europe: Mechanical Jurisprudence in Transformation?* (Leiden-Boston: Martinus Nijhoff, 2011), ch. I.

[5] Cf. Peter van Elsuwege, From Soviet Republics to EU Member States: A Legal and Political Assessment of the Baltic states' accession to the EU (Leiden and Boston: Martinus Nijhoff, 2008).

[6] Kühn, *The Judiciary*, ch. II.

in favour of treating Central Europe, in terms of legal culture informed by legal tradition *and* by their present condition of being a periphery of the EU,[7] as one bloc for many research purposes, including the present endeavour.

The term 'Central Europe' readily used by Central European scholars, but often giving way to terms such as 'Eastern Europe,' 'East-Central Europe,' or 'Central and Eastern Europe' in the vocabularies of our Western European observers, is slightly misleading. This is because in terms of the centre/periphery dichotomy, *de nomine* Central Europe is *de facto* peripheral Europe.[8] What is more, during the period of actually existing socialism, apart from being the eastern periphery of the Western centre of the capitalist world-system (in Wallersteinian terms), Central Europe was simultaneously the western periphery of the Soviet Union (in geopolitical terms).[9] This experience of being a *peripheria duplex* is nothing short of a traumatic event in the region's collective consciousness, including that of the legal community. Following the transition, the situation did not become much better, transforming itself into a unique amalgamation of postcolonialism (vis-à-vis the former Soviet power) and neocolonialism (vis-à-vis the West). A *peripheria duplex*—a simultaneous postcolonial and neocolonial area with extraordinarily liquid political boundaries turning the region into a buffer zone between East and West—indicates Central Europe's geopolitical situation could not have been more problematic.[10]

We contend that Central Europe is a cultural, political, and social construct which owes much to the civilizing gaze of Western Enlightenment as much as it owes to the imperial cartographers of late 18th century, ethnologists of the 19th century, and constitutional engineers of the post-1989

---

[7] Cf. the outcome of Tomasz Giaro's monumental research project on legal transfers and modernization of law in Central Europe in the form of two volumes: Tomasz Giaro, ed., *Rechtskulturen des Modernen Osteuropa. Traditionen und Transfers* (Frankfurt am Main: Vittorio Klostermann, 2006/7).

[8] Cf. Damjan Kukovec, 'Law and the Periphery,' *European Law Journal* 21/3 (2015), 406–28, 409.

[9] For an explicit application of Wallerstein's world-system analysis to Central Europe (*in casu* Poland) see Jakub Majmurek, 'PRL jako projekt modernizacji peryferyjnej (perspektywa systemu-świata)' [The Polish People's Republic as Periphery Modernisation Project (A World-System Perspective)], in *PRL bez uprzedzeń* [*An Unbiased Perspective on the Polish People's Republic*], ed. Jakub Majmurek & Piotr Szumlewicz (Warszawa: Książka i Prasa, 2010).

[10] With respect to political boundaries, the examples of Poland and Hungary are perhaps most instructive here. Poland, which emerged on the political map of Europe in 1918 and had its boundaries fixed only as from 1922, suffered from a forced displacement of territory and population to the West in 1945, losing its eastern lands (Wilno region, Polesie region, Wołyń, Eastern Galicia) and gaining formerly German lands in exchange (Warmia and Mazury, Pomerania, Silesia). Likewise Hungary, which in the former Habsburg Empire covered today's Slovakia, Transylvania (in today's Romania), Voivodina (now in Serbia), and Slavonia (now in Croatia) saw its borders shrink after World War I.

transition.¹¹ As such it is a space which conveyed fantasies of conquest and normalization as well as reluctance and rejection. Constructed as Western Europe's half-Other, it is already in the discourse while occupying a place of paradoxes and ambiguities, covering symbolically the space between the familiarity of Western rationality and radical otherness of the East. In this very specific sense, Central Europe conveys the idea of Freud's *das Unheimliche*, the unfamiliar which nests at the core of familiarity.¹²

This historical trajectory did not fail to significantly influence the region's legal cultures. For more than a decade now a new trend of thinking and understanding the law has insinuated itself into law's empire, once it was reconstructed from the debris of actually existing socialism. Eclectic, controversial, polemic, and to some extent marginal, this trend shares with the cultural space from which it emerged the same unfamiliarity that usually troubles the keepers of the gate in imperial settings. For, to be sure, the law in Central Europe pertains to the world of contemporary 'empire' as much as it builds upon a patchwork of historical imperial reminiscences. Central Europe is, legally speaking, an extraordinary place (in the sense used by Örücü),¹³ that is a place where things 'out of the ordinary' are happening and where lawyers are questioning once again the tenets of the order.

Giving Voice to Europe's 'Central' Periphery

In a recent paper, a Slovenian legal scholar connected to the critical legal circles at Harvard, Damjan Kukovec, emphasized the need to introduce the centre-periphery dichotomy to the legal discourse of European law.¹⁴ We fully agree with Kukovec's stance, and indeed share his view that the lack of a centre-periphery concept in European legal discourse is a form of symbolic violence towards Central Europe, aimed at ideologically stifling our legal communities and preventing them from articulating our— specifically Central European—point of view on contentious issues of EU law such as those, inter alia, of public economic law.¹⁵ A general conclusion

---

¹¹ For a seminal work exploring, from a Foucauldian/Saïdian standpoint, Eastern Europe's construction as an intellectual object of knowledge, see Larry Wolff, *Inventing Eastern Europe: The Map of Civilization on the Mind of the Enlightenment* (Stanford: Stanford University Press), 1994.

¹² Sigmund Freud, 'The Uncanny,' in *The Standard Edition of the Complete Psychological Works of Sigmund Freud*, ed. James Starchey (London: Hogarth, 1955), 217–56.

¹³ Esin Örücü, 'Comparatists and Extraordinary Places,' in *Comparative Legal Studies: Traditions and Transitions*, ed. Pierre Legrand and Roderick Munday (Cambridge: CUP, 2003).

¹⁴ Kukovec, 'Law and the Periphery,' 410.

¹⁵ Kukovec, 'Law and the Periphery,' 411–15.

from Kukovec's paper is highly pessimistic and it points to the fact that lawyers from peripheral Central Europe are marginalized within European legal discourse as a result of symbolic violence inflicted by lawyers from the Western European centre, and this despite the (purely) formal possibility of participating in this discourse on an equal footing, e.g. before the CJEU.

Therefore, one of the aims of this collection of essays is to revindicate the space for Central European legal discourse and give voice to the periphery and its legal critique. However, we also take the view that a simple transplant of Western critical legal thinking to Central Europe would constitute, *mutatis mutandis*, the same form of symbolic violence as occurs in mainstream legal discourse, where lawyers are expected to take the views of the centre.[16] Different socio-economic and political dynamics within the centre and peripheries of Europe require different legal tools for their articulation. We believe that this applies par excellence to legal critique. Being therefore keen on creating a space for centre-periphery (*in casu*, West-East) dialogue of critical legal communities, we are far from advocating a wholesale and mechanical reception (transplantation) of the British or American school of critical legal thought. Such a move would amount to yet another act of symbolic violence inflicted by the (Western) centre upon the (Central European) periphery. Whilst the same set of values (such as the belief in the need for emancipation of any oppressed subjects) and fundamental philosophical inspirations (such as French theory or more recently Žižekian Lacano-Marxism) may be adequate, the practically applicable *sul campo* tools of legal critique will not necessarily be the same. The ideological superstructure of critical legal thinking must correspond to its base if it is to be an effective tool for destabilizing hegemony and opposing oppression. The left-right division must be combined with the centre-periphery dichotomy, as Kukovec insists, lest it become perverted and distorted, serving the opposite interests from those it was initially conceived to further.[17]

Furthermore, apart from the need for devising adequate methodological tools (some of which may be of use outside the region), we must address, in our concrete historical, socio-economic and geo-political context, a number of issues which are, due to objective circumstances, of little or no significance to our Western counterparts. These include, in particular, the following: the need to build a critical transitional justice scholarship, with particular reference to a critique of the ideology of the 'rule of law'; a critical analysis of lustration and decommunization practices; and a critical analysis of post-communist privatization and its ideological

---

[16] Kukovec, 'Law and the Periphery,' 427.
[17] Kukovec, 'Law and the Periphery,' 424.

underpinnings.[18] A critical school of transitional justice studies would be conceived as a remedy against the hegemonic liberal variant of this field of study, based on (neo)liberal dogmas and ideological underpinnings.

Secondly, we need a critical analysis of judicial formalism (hyper-positivism) in its Central European, peripheral version.[19] A peripheral variant of formalism, distinct from its Western equivalent, requires a different, socio-legally conscious form of critique.

Thirdly, on a more general level, we need to employ throughout the critical legal discourse full awareness of the centre/periphery dynamic between the (peripheral) Central Europe and the (Western) centre, both within and beyond the EU).[20]

Furthermore, the legacy of the socialist legal tradition, a phenomenon idiosyncratic of Central (and Eastern) Europe mandates a critical study of legal survivals of actually existing socialism and the on-going influence, from the grave, of the former socialist legal tradition.[21]

Obviously, not all of these topics can be addressed in this volume. Furthermore, a number of topics analyzed in the chapters of this research

---

[18] For a seminal work see Liviu Damşa, 'The Incomprehensible Post-Communist Privatisation,' *Global Journal of Comparative Law* 3 (2014), 137–85. An earlier version of Damşa's paper, although not published in this volume, was presented at the Central European stream convened by Adam Sulikowski at the CLC 2013 in Belfast. In his paper Damşa argues that the injunction to privatize state property, which was one of the key assumptions of the post-1989 transformation, was actually rooted in a series of false assumptions concerning the nature of state property under actually existing socialism. These false assumptions led to a series of failures for the privatization project, in particular the enrichment of the economic *nomenklatura* of communist managers. However, with regard to privatization in general it is, due to the domination of neoliberal ideology, a topic of legal critique common to Western and Eastern authors.

[19] See especially Kühn, *The Judiciary* and, with specific reference to Poland and its legal culture, Marcin Matczak, *Summa iniuria. Błąd formalizmu w stosowaniu prawa* [Summa Iniuira: On the error of formalism in the application of law] (Warsaw: Scholar, 2007).

[20] For a seminal paper on the legal field in the peripheries, see Hanna Dębska, 'Strategia wielopozycyjności w półperyferyjnym polu prawnym. Homo academicus na rynku' [Strategy of Multipositionality in a Semiperipheral Legal Field: Homo Academicus on the Market], in *Polska jako peryferie* [Poland as a Periphery], ed. Tomasz Zarycki (Warszawa: Scholar, 2016 forthcoming).

[21] See, e.g. Rafał Mańko, 'Legal Survivals: A Conceptual Tool for Analysing Post-Transformation Continuity of Legal Culture' in *Tiesību efektivitāte postmodernā sabiedrībā* [Effectiveness of Law in Post-Modern Society], ed. Jānis Rozenfelds et al. (Riga: Latvia University Press, 2015). See also, e.g. Rafał Mańko, 'Is the Socialist Legal Tradition "Dead and Buried"? The Continuity of Certain Elements of Socialist Legal Culture in Polish Civil Procedure,' in *Private Law and the Many Cultures of Europe*, ed. Thomas Wilhelmsson et al. (Alphen aan den Rijn: Kluwer Law International, 2007); Alan Uzelac, 'Survival of the Third Legal Tradition?,' *Supreme Court Law Review* 49 (2010) 377–96; Rafał Mańko, 'Survival of the Socialist Legal Tradition? A Polish Perspective,' *Comparative Law Review* 4/2 (2013); Rafał Mańko, '"We Do Not Recognize Anything »Private«": Public Interest and Private Law Under the Socialist Legal Tradition and Beyond,' in *Private Interest and Public Interest in European Legal Tradition*, ed. Bronisław Sitek et al. (Olsztyn: WPiA UWM, 2015).

monograph have a relevance reaching beyond the Central European periphery, such as the critique of *gouvernment de juges (constitionelles)* in chapters one and six, the contributions to the stream on Feminist Jurisprudence (in chapters five, six, and seven), or the critique of a technocratic vision of lawyership (in chapter eight). But even those topics which are of a universal value, are addressed here with regard to their Central European context.

Sources of legal Critique in Central Europe

The emergence of critical scholarship in the field of law in the Central European context places itself also under the sign of paradox. This is because it produces an effective break with the prevailing post-ideological consensus specific to the continental tradition of treating law as (written) law and nothing beyond. From this vantage point it defines itself as a contrarian movement which opposes not only a strong tradition of legal formalism inherited from the French and Austrian schools of 'exegesis' as well as the formalist German 'conceptual jurisprudence' (*Begriffsjurisprudenz*)—significantly strengthened during the period of actually existing socialism—but also mainstream 'soft positivism,' which still insists on law's autonomy and rationality.[22] The strong component of ultra-formalism can even be said to form an *objet petit a* differentiating the Central European periphery from the Western European centre, perhaps even warranting the existence of a 'Central European legal family' alongside the conventionally accepted Romanic, Germanic, Common Law, and

[22] On the sources and condition of Central European formalism, see especially Kühn, *The Judiciary* and, with specific reference to Poland and its legal culture, Matczak, *Summa iniuria*; Tomasz Milej, 'Europejska kultura prawna a kraje Europy Środkowej i Wschodniej' [European Legal Culture and Central Eastern European Countries], *Przegląd Legislacyjny* 15/1 (2008), 60–74; Rafał Mańko, 'Weeds in the Gardens of Justice? The Survival of Hyperpositivism in Polish Legal Culture as a Symptom/Sinthome,' *Pólemos: Journal of Law, Literature and Culture* 7/2 (2013), 207–33. However, the view that hyperpositivsm is a specifically Central European phenomenon has been question by Peter Cserne, 'Formalism in Judicial Reasoning: Is Central and Eastern Europe a Special Case?' in Bobek, *Central European Judges*. On the basis of his analysis, Cserne concludes that whilst Central and Eastern Europe is 'a special case,' he 'seriously doubt[s]' that this *differentia specifica* of our region is judicial formalism. He argues that the 'distinctiveness-of-formalism thesis,' as he calls it, 'is misguided because it leads to an exclusive focus on the region in isolation,' which is a flawed approach (Cserne, 'Formalism,' 41). In our view, a promising way out of the controversy as between Peter Cserne and inter alia Zdeněk Kühn, Rafał Mańko, or Tomasz Milej regarding the idiosyncrasy of Central European formalism could be the introduction of the centre/periphery dynamic into the analytical toolbox, as suggested recently by Damjan Kukovec. In this optic, Central European formalism is a *peripheral* formalism, and this feature could explain, inter alia, its 'crude' features, lamented by Kühn, Mańko, Matczak, Milej, and others. The issue definitely requires further empirical socio-legal research.

Scandinavian ones in Europe.[23]

Legal critique in Central Europe also expresses an alternative gesture of renewing links to a tradition of critique well rooted in the Central European ethos and cultural heritage. Psychoanalysis, the critique of ideology, the Frankfurt School as well as the dissident counter-culture of actually existing socialism all come to mind as historical sources of legitimation and strategies of critically reading legal texts.

But critique is not, of course, a purely Central European phenomenon. Caught within the dynamics of the global present, legal cultures of Central Europe cannot escape law's recent history of contestation and intellectual struggle. French theory, the tradition of critical legal studies, feminist theory, and postcolonial studies are other sites of articulating strategies of dissent and resistance as well as places of deconstructing law's pretence of founding the truth. As such, the praxis of legal critique in the Central European context defines itself as eclectic and resolute in the struggle for voicing its disapproval of the legal and political status quo.

An important building block of legal critique in Central Europe has been the inspiration drawn from the British critical legal community, informally known as the 'BritCrits.'[24] The links between the two communities have been gradually emerging since 2012, when the first group of Central European legal scholars (Cosmin Cercel, Rafał Mańko, and Jakub Łakomy) attended the Critical Legal Conference ('CLC') on 'Gardens of Justice' at the University of Technology in Stockholm. Since then, the Central European presence at the CLC has strengthened year by year.

In 2013, at the CLC in Belfast devoted to 'Reconciliation and Reconstruction' where some of the papers in this volume originate from, Adam Sulikowski and Bartosz Greczner convened a stream on 'Reconstruction, Return, or Revolution? The Phenomenon of Critical Legal Thought in European Post-Communist Countries.' The stream proved to be very successful and was attended by critical legal scholars from Poland,

---

[23] For a preliminary formulation of this argument, see Rafał Mańko, 'Survival of the Socialist Legal Tradition? A Polish Perspective,' *Comparative Law Review* 4/2 (2013). Cf. Alan Uzelac, 'Survival of the Third Legal Tradition?,' *Supreme Court Law Review* 49 (2010), 377–96; Jaakko Husa, *A New Introduction to Comparative Law* (Oxford: Hart-Bloomsbury, 2015), 219–20; H. Patrick Glenn, *Legal Traditions of the World: Sustainable Diversity in Law*, 5th ed. (Oxford: OUP, 2014), 347; Alan Uzelac, 'Mixed Blessing of Judicial Specialisation: the Devil is in the Detail,' *Russian Law Journal* 2/4 (2014), 162.

[24] For a historical account see Costas Douzinas, 'A Short History of the British Critical Legal Conference or, the Responsibility of the Critic,' *Law and Critique* 25/2 (2014), 187–98. A Polish translation of this text appeared earlier as Costas Douzinas, 'Krótka historia brytyjskiej Krytycznej Konferencji Prawniczej albo o odpowiedzialności krytyka' [A short history of the British Critical Legal Conference or the responsibility of the critic], trans. Rafał Mańko, *Archiwum Filozofii Prawa i Filozofii Społecznej* 1/8 (2014), 5–17.

Romania, the Czech Republic, as well as Croatia.[25] It was in Belfast that, following a suggestion made by Costas Douzinas earlier during the year, the University of Wrocław officially submitted its bid to organize the 30th Critical Legal Conference, to be held for the first time on Central European territory in 2015.

During the 2014 Critical Legal Conference held at the University of Sussex at Brighton, Wrocław's bid was officially accepted, by acclamation, by the critical legal community. CLC 2014, devoted to 'Power, Capital, Chaos,' saw an ever stronger presence of Central European scholars, with two streams convened by Central Europeans.[26] In the meantime, we witnessed the publication of a special 'critical' issue of *Archiwum Filozofii Prawa i Filozofii Społecznej*, the official academic journal of the Polish section of the International Association for the Philosophy of Law and Social Philosophy ('IVR'), with texts by Polish critical legal scholars and a translation of Costas Douzinas's article on the history of the CLC.[27] In parallel, Michał Stambulski, Michał Paździora, and Rafał Mańko developed the idea of holding annual international workshops on law and ideology,

---

[25] For a detailed report from CLC 2013, focusing on the Central European stream, see Jakub Łakomy and Rafał Mańko, 'Critical Legal Conference, Belfast, Irlandia Północna, 5–7.09.2013 r.,' *Archiwum Filozofii Prawa i Filozofii Społecznej* 8 (2014), 88–91.

[26] Romanian crits Cosmin Cercel and Alex Cistelecan convened a stream on 'Beyond the Law: State of Exception and Powers of Capital'; Polish crits Adam Sulikowski, Rafał Mańko and Jakub Łakomy convened a stream on 'Ideology, Hegemony and Law: An East/West Perspective,' attended by some two dozen critical legal scholars from Poland, the Czech Republic, Romania, Russia, and Japan. Furthermore, the Ukrainian critical legal scholar based in Ireland, Ekaterina Krivenko, convened a stream on 'Thinking Resistance Beyond Power, Violence... and Law?' A conference report (in Polish) from CLC 2014 by Paweł Snopek is forthcoming in the *Archiwum Filozofii Prawa i Filozofii Społecznej*.

[27] The special issue encompasses the following papers: Costas Douzinas, 'Krótka historia brytyjskiej Krytycznej Konferencji Prawniczej albo o odpowiedzialności krytyka' [A short history of the British Critical Legal Conference or the responsibility of the critic]; Hanna Dębska, 'W okowach prawniczego sensus communis. O trudnościach uprawiania krytycznie zorientowanej socjologii prawa' [Shackled by the legal sensus communis. On the difficulties of a critically oriented sociology of law]; Karol Kuźmicz, 'Dlaczego kooperatyzm Edwarda Abramowskiego może nie być utopią?' [Why Edward Abramowski's cooperativism may be not the utopia?], Rafał Mańko, 'Koncepcja interpelacji ideologicznej a krytyczny dyskurs o prawie' [The Notion of Ideological Interpellation and Critical Discourse on Law]; Michał Paździora and Michał Stambulski' 'Co może dać nauce prawa polityczność? Przyczynek do przyszłych badań' [What 'The Political' Can Bring to The Polish Theory of Law. Toward a Further Investigation]; Lidia Rodak, 'Are we all feminists now? Wyzwania ze strony Feministycznej Jurysprudencji wobec tradycyjnej teorii prawa' [Are we all feminists now? The Challenge of Feminist Jurisprudence to Traditional Legal Theory'; Adam Sulikowski, 'Afirmatywna amnezja i konserwatywni crits. Kilka uwag o kondycji krytycznej myśli prawniczej w Europie Środkowej i Wschodniej' [Affirmative amnesia and conservative crits. Some remarks on the condition of critical legal thought in Central and Eastern Europe]. The volume also contained two conference reports: from the CLC 2013 in Belfast (by Jakub Łakomy and Rafał Mańko) and from the 1st International Workshop on Law and Ideology, Wrocław, 29–30 March 2014 r. (by Wojciech Kauczor and Wojciech Zomerski).

which have a clear critical legal inspiration. The first exploratory one was held in Wrocław in May 2014,[28] followed by a second one in Sarajevo, held in May 2015, which was devoted to a critical exploration of issues of transitional justice under the title 'Memories of Struggles, Struggles of Memories,' convened jointly by Samir Forić, Rafał Mańko, and Michał Stambulski.[29] The third workshop, devoted to a critical exploration of the 'rule of law' rhetoric took place in May 2016 in Tbilisi, Georgia.

A turning point in the history of Western and Central European critical legal thought was the 30th Critical Legal Conference held in 2015 at the University of Wrocław, devoted to the topic of 'Law, Space, and the Political' (convenors: Adam Sulikowski, Rafał Mańko and Jakub Łakomy). The conference was a huge success, and was attended by over 200 delegates from the Czech Republic, Ireland, Romania, Slovakia, Slovenia, Sweden, and the UK, as well as from Australia, Brazil, Canada, China, India, South Africa, Taiwan and Turkey. Plenary talks were given both by scholars belonging to the core of the 'BritCrit' community (Costas Douzinas, Illan Rua Wall, Stewart Motha) or closely connected with it (Andreas Philippopoulos-Mihalopoulos), scholars critical of the current neoliberal status quo but not necessarily applying the classical toolbox of BritCrit research (Marija Bartl, Harm Schepel), as well as Central and Eastern European academics directly engaging in critical legal scholarship (Marija Bartl, Cosmin Sebastian Cercel) or sympathizing with the critical legal movement (Jiří Přibáň, Monika Płatek, Ekaterina Krivenko).

As Costas Douzinas mentioned in one of his emails to the organizers of CLC 2015, it was destined from the outset to become 'the beginning of a beautiful friendship' between the British critical legal community and the emerging critical legal groups in Central Europe.

Challenging the Present

The legal and political changes brought by 1989 were followed by major social upheavals which kept most Central European countries under the label of post-communism and their respective constitutional laws under the scrutiny of theorists of democracy. The legal present of Central Europe finds its roots in the confused theoretical enthusiasm of the 1990s linking, unwittingly, democracy and capitalism in a convincing narrative specific to the 'end of history' mindset. It also follows the social practices of excluding

---

[28] Rafał Mańko, Wojciech Kauczor and Wojciech Zomerski, 'Conference Report: 1st International Workshop on Law and Ideology (Wrocław, 29–30 May 2014),' *Wrocław Review of Law, Administration and Economics* 3/2 (2015), 84–7.

[29] A conference report from this workshop, by Filip Rakoczy, is forthcoming at the *Wrocław Review of Law, Administration and Economics*.

otherness (and transforming it into a Schmittian enemy) and implementing economic 'shock therapy.'

Western Europe's reunifications with its peripheral half-Other, the ongoing crisis of capitalism and the growing concern with Europe's future have significantly influenced the emergence of new forms of critique inside the legal field. Critical legal scholarship thus tries to question the existing hierarchies in public space, to open new fora for debate at the interstices of law and politics and ultimately to challenge the monolinguism of existing discourses of power.

Overview of the Chapters

To address these issues, this collection brings together both emerging and established scholars engaged in the field of critical legal scholarship in Central Europe. It aims to provide a unique range of perspectives on this topic, providing both system-specific theoretical analysis and broader critical engagement with the deeper significance of legal thought and praxis in Central Europe.

The chapters are preceded by a foreword by Costas Douzinas, which has strong symbolic value. Through his gesture Douzinas, a founder of the British school of critical legal thought and of the Critical Legal Conference, creates a bridge between the BritCrits and the emergent Critical legal communities of Central Europe.

The first chapter by Adam Sulikowski (Professor of Legal Philosophy, University of Wrocław) is entitled 'Government of Judges and Neoliberal Ideology: The Polish Case.' The main purpose of Sulikowski's contribution is to formulate a diagnosis of Polish discourse on the constitutional court, using selected critical tools inspired by the Frankfurt School and by French Theory. He argues that the Court has enjoyed immunity from legal critique due to its perceived role in the post-communist transformation and makes a sustained attempt at piercing the protective veil of mainstream legal ideology and opening up a space for critique of the government of (constitutional) judges.

In the second chapter entitled 'The Importance of Being a Linguist: Critical Legal Thought in Central Europe,' Martin Škop (Reader in Legal Theory, Masaryk University in Brno) points to the challenges created by the hegemony of the English language in critical legal theory and its development in Central Europe.

The third chapter by Cosmin Cercel on 'Law Out of Bounds: Legal Picnolepsy, Intellectual Austerity and Romania's Legal Past' points out that law in Central Europe resists acknowledging its own past, which—in the author's view—not only has implications for historical scholarship and collective memory but also, and above all, for politics. With these assumptions in mind, Cercel aims at subjecting this collective oblivion to a critique. For this purpose, he draws on Paul Virilio's concept of 'picnolepsy,' that is a momentary lapse of consciousness, after which the interrupted narrative and action are picked up again as if they had never been subject to the interruption in question. The author argues that the metaphor of picnolepsy aptly describes the Romanian legal community's approach to its communist past, it was simply a momentary lapse of consciousness (which never took place), and after 1989 Romanian legal discourse allegedly emerged from the point where communism was just about to start. Drawing also on the theoretical framework of Walter Benjamin and Giorgio Agamben, Cercel analyses the contemporary constitutional discourse in Romania as regards its dealing with the communist past, where he detects the presence of 'intellectual austerity.' In conclusion, the author advocates the redemption from law's amnesia, which in his view is instrumental towards destabilizing the grip of its authority under conditions of late capitalist state of exception.

In the fourth chapter entitled 'Demons of the Past? Legal Survivals of the Socialist Legal Tradition in Contemporary Polish Private Law,' Rafał Mańko (External Fellow at the University of Amsterdam) discusses the phenomenon of legal institutions which had been introduced under Actually existing socialism and which, in certain cases, were subject to a change in social function rather than removed following the transformation of 1989. Mańko's critical methodology is inspired by Marxist theorists, Karl Renner and Hugh Collins, and attempts to give a socio-legal account of the dynamics of legal continuity and the tensions created by the pressure on law's adaptation to the new circumstances of (neoliberal) capitalism. The thrust of Mańko's critique is directed at the stereotypical picture of Actually existing socialism being merely a 'black hole' or 'blackout' in the legal development in the region. This chapter represents an example of a locally important topic, which is specific for Central European scholarship due to its post-communist condition, but has not yet been sufficiently accounted for, either in Western scholarship (where the problem of post-communist legal survivals is not present) or in Central and Eastern Europe (where the centre-periphery dynamic has resulted in a repression of the traumatic communist legal past from mainstream discourse).[30]

Three following chapters touch upon feminist jurisprudence. In chapter five, entitled 'Feminist Legal Education in Croatia: A Question of Fundamentalism or a Fundamental Question?' Ivana Radačić (Ivo Pilar Institute, Zagreb) contends that legal education in Croatia is gendered both in its conceptualization of legal education as the transmission of

[30] Cf. Mańko, 'Weeds.'

technical apolitical knowledge and in its exclusion or insufficient attention to feminist (or even gender) issues. She argues that the exclusion of feminist (and other critical) perspectives in legal education has a significant negative impact as it maintains and perpetuates the patriarchal nature of law and the legal profession in Croatia.

The thread of gender-sensitive legal critique is picked up by Hanna Dębska and Tomasz Warczok (both assistant professors at the Pedagogical University in Kraków, Poland) in their chapter on 'The Social Construction of Femininity in the Discourse of the Polish Constitutional Court.' Dębska and Warczok apply the tools of Pierre Bourdieu's critical sociology, combining them with Norman Fairclough's critical discourse analysis as well as with Berger and Luckmanns's sociology of knowledge to show how the Polish constitutional court perpetuates patriarchal ideological visions of the female subject. This chapter not only critiques the patriarchate in the discourse of the Polish constitutional court, it also offers an innovative methodological proposal. It was Warczok who, in a seminal text published in 2013, suggested the possibility of combining Bourdieu's critical sociology with Fairclough's critical discourse analysis.[31] Warczok's methodological blueprint was applied to the legal field for the first time by Dębska,[32] who further enriched the toolbox by adding to it Berger and Luckmann's sociology of knowledge. Indeed, we believe that the toolbox they have jointly put forward, i.e. an original combination of critical sociology, critical discourse analysis and sociology of knowledge has immense potential for bringing forward applied critical legal theory. Dębska and Warczoks' input constitutes an important and universally relevant contribution of Central European scholarship to legal critique, as it can be perfectly applied to any other courts in Europe and elsewhere to unmask their latent ideological entanglements. Their methodological *instrumentarium* can also be deployed as a tool for destabilizing the currently hegemonic and highly formalistic systems theory approach which, we contend, lacks the critical potential of Bourdieu's and Fairclough's toolbox.[33] In chapter seven,

---

[31] See especially Tomasz Warczok, 'Dyskurs Ucieleśniony—dyskurs skontekstualizowany' [Embodied Discourse—Contextualised Discourse], *Qualitative Sociology Review* 9/1 (2013), 32–47, accessed 8 September 2015, http://www.qualitativesociologyreview.org/PL/Volume21/PSJ_9_1_Warczok.pdf .

[32] Hanna Dębska, 'Legal Doxa as a Form of Neutralization of Values in the Law. The Case of Constitutional Tribunal Judgments' in *Neutralization of Values in Law*, ed. Krzysztof Pałecki (Warsaw: Wolters Kluwer 2013). For a large-scale application of this methodology, see Dębska, *Władza, symbol, prawo. Społeczne tworzenie Trybunału Konstytucyjnego* [Power, Symbol, Law: The Social Construction of the Constitutional Court] (Warszawa: Wydawnictwo Sejmowe, 2015).

[33] Obviously, this introductory chapter is not an appropriate place to put forward a sustained critique of the systems theory approach. However, it is worth pointing out that Luhmann's highly formalist and abstract sociology of law is fully subservient to affirmative

Lidia Rodak (Lecturer in Legal Theory, University of Silesia, Katowice) investigates the central forms of structural violence perpetrated within law against women in the Polish socio-legal context. She concludes that gender not only differentiates but also discriminates, dominates, and excludes, leading to a hierarchical submission of women in both official and non-official law. These findings allow Rodak to unmask the notion of so-called 'objectivity' of/in law which—as she argues—is nothing more than a 'masculine narrative' that underpins structural violence.

Following the chapters on feminist jurisprudence, the book moves to a focus on the legal profession. Jacek Srokosz (Lecturer in Legal Theory, University of Opole) discusses 'a technicist perspective and the contemporary perception of the role of lawyers in Polish society,' focusing on the impact of neoliberal capitalism upon legal education in Poland. He argues that a technicist approach to law in Poland is becoming increasingly hegemonic. In his view, this situation results from the positivist programme of neatly separating law from the spheres of politics and morality. For him, law is perceived as 'being clear, strict, precise, predictable and easily justifiable.' This, in turn, leads to the proliferation of a formalist paradigm of interpretation, whereby lawyers are seen as merely applying the linguistic sense of legal rules. On a more sociological note, Srokosz points out that the technicist approach to law is reinforced by the capitalist 'market' which perceives legal practice as a form of service provision, rather than as a socially responsible mission driven by the desire to deliver justice. Srokosz is critical of this technicist approach which 'constitutes a threat to the proper functioning of law in society, because it makes it narrow, shallow, schematic, and overly technical.'

The penultimate chapter comes from a legal historian whose research focuses on applying contemporary legal theory/philosophy of law tools to the legacy of the *ius Romanum*. In her chapter entitled 'From Sublimation to Naturalisation: Constructing Ideological Hegemony on the Shoulders of Roman Jurists,' Paulina Święcicka (Jagiellonian University, Kraków) looks at the role of Roman law in the ideological construction of reality within legal discourse. An analysis of a number of cases from the Polish Supreme Court leads Święcicka to the conclusion that Roman law is instrumentalized to produce and sustain the hegemonic ideology of legal continuity which,

---

positivism (and opposed to any form of legal critique), as it 'insists that law is a separate subsystem of society, differentiated from politics as well as from morality. Only the law, and not politics or morality or any other system of communication, determines what the law is.' (Hugh Baxter, 'Niklas Luhmann's Theory of Autopoietic Legal Systems,' *Annual Review of Law and Social Science 9* (2013), 174). As Baxter further points out, Luhmann's sociology of law neatly coincides with the mainstream legal philosophy of Herbert Hart, situating itself at odds with the critical legal tradition, focusing on laying bare the true (class) interests and ideological entanglements of the legal enterprise.

as she points out, directly serves the interests of neoliberal governmentality. Święcicka's chapter is a valuable engagement of legal history with legal critique, a link which can be instrumental to enlarging the space for the critique of ideology within the legal field.

The final chapter by young Czech critical legal scholar, Markéta Klusoňová, explores 'The role of Václav Havel in the Czech critical legal thought.' Václav Havel was not only a politician and playwright, but—as Klusoňová persuasively shows—his literary work had 'a crucial influence over civic legal consciousness during the era of actually existing socialism.' Klusoňová points out that by resorting to the form of literature, Havel actually 'subverted the communist ban of any form on resistance to the law' and remains a central figure to Czech legal critique.

Leszek Koczanowicz, philosopher and social psychologist from the University of Social Sciences, concludes this volume with an afterword.

1

Government of Judges and Neoliberal Ideology: The Polish Case

Adam Sulikowski

1.1 Introduction

The main purpose of this text is to formulate a diagnosis of Polish discourse on the constitutional court (*Trybunał Konstytucyjny*, hereinafter: 'the TK') by applying certain critical methods in the spirit of the Frankfurt School and so-called French Theory.

Social and economic factors resulting from the political transformation in Poland produced a very interesting intellectual phenomenon. The TK became a spokesperson for neoliberal elites and a chief engineer of transformation, making a lot of political decisions that did not have much in common with controlling the constitutionality of laws. Despite a very activist style, the TK was never strongly criticized by the political mainstream. It was also under the strong protection of constitutionalists. Allegations of political bias elicited sharp reactions from politicians and legal scholars, always ready to justify even the most activist decisions of constitutional judges.[1] Of course, some critical views of the TK can be found in studies in the field of constitutional law, but they are rather cautious. To undermine the legitimacy of the tribunal would spark allegations of supporting 'the dark side.' The mainstream saw the activism of the 'engineers of the constitution' as a consequence of the need to modernize the country, while criticism of the TK was seen as an act against modernization.[2]

The discursive environment of the TK has changed in recent years. In

---

[1] Wojciech Sadurski, *Rights Before Courts: A Study of Constitutional Courts in Post-communist States of Central and Eastern Europe* (Dordrecht: Springer, 2005), XV.

[2] For a detailed account of the building of the TK's social legitimacy and symbolic power see recently Hanna Dębska, *Władza, symbol, prawo. Społeczne tworzenie Trybunału Konstytucyjnego* [Power, Symbol, Law: The Social Construction of the Constitutional Court in Poland] (Warszawa: Wydawnictwo Sejmowe, 2015). See also Hanna Dębska and Tomasz Warczok, 'Sacred Law and Profane Politics: The Symbolic Construction of the Constitutional Tribunal,' *Polish Sociological Review* 188/4 (2014), 465–78.

my view, this is mainly related to the breakdown of a political consensus concerning the country's modernization. The radical postmodern left and strong populist and anti-modern right wing forces appeared in Poland. Criticism of the TK has intensified both in political journalism, as well as among legal scholars. At the same time other external and internal factors complicated constitutional engineering. Poland, after a brief but intense phase of modernization, became a typical postmodern state with radical contradictions, ideological conflicts, and unsolvable problems.

The explanation of the above-mentioned processes requires the examination of three phenomena. Firstly, the origins of the TK. Secondly, the so-called 'affirmative amnesia' of Polish constitutionalists. Thirdly, the postmodern conditions in which the TK and its political and social environment currently operate.

1.2 A Genealogy of the Polish Constitutional Court

The beginning of constitutional courts is the evident consequence of the modernist, bourgeois scientist view—found in the constitutional ideas of Plato—asserting the superiority of the government of wise men over other options. This idea was accurately stated by Zygmunt Bauman in his famous maxim, which affirms that the government of intellect must denote the government of its engineers. In my view, constitutional courts exist in order to control the rationality of lawmakers' activity. The constitution is only a pretext to ensure the conformity of laws with bourgeois 'meta-reason': the principles of formal justice, the spirit of capitalism, and the concept of the rule of law built on a modern economy.[3]

The idea of creating a constitutional court was discussed in Poland before World War II, however the authoritarian landscape (after the 1926 coup) was not the best in which to realize it.[4] Most constitutionalists were against the control of constitutionality, as it could weaken the position of the president.[5] This position of the head of state, especially under the second inter-war constitution (called the April Constitution of 1935),[6] was

---

[3] I have written about this extensively in my other works. See Adam Sulikowski, W*spółczesny paradygmat sądownictwa konstytucyjnego wobec kryzysu nowoczesności* [Contemporary constitutional judiciary paradigm towards the crisis of modernity] (Wrocław: Wydawnictwo Uniwersytetu Wrocławskiego, 2008); Adam Sulikowski, *Konstytucjonalizm a nowoczesność. Dyskurs konstytucyjny wobec tryumfu i kryzysu nowoczesności* [Constitutionalism and Modernity: Constitutional Discourse and the Triumph and Crisis of Modern Episteme] (Wrocław: Wydawnictwo Uniwersytetu Wrocławskiego, 2012).

[4] Cf. Dębska, *Władza, symbol, prawo*, 106–8.

[5] Dębska, *Władza, symbol, prawo*, 108 (with further references).

[6] Constitutional Act of 23 April 1935 (Dz.U. no. 30, item 227) (hereinafter 'April Constitution').

exceptional. The president was not only the most important executive power, but he also had extensive legislative and control powers,[7] and enjoyed a right of veto with regard to acts of Parliament.[8]

After the war, Poland was occupied by the Soviet Union and the debate on issues of constitutionality had not even started.[9] According to the Soviet perspective, constitutional courts were drawing back societies towards capitalism. Judges could potentially restrain the revolutionary processes relying on old-fashioned, petrified norms, even if law could not hold back historical necessity.[10] According to socialist constitutional theory, people's democracy requires the power of the parliament to be unlimited. Of course, the parliament was a rather decorative body since the real power was in the hands of communist party committees. The situation changed in the 1960s and some inconspicuous discussions emerged within constitutional discourse. Poland in the sixties was the era in which the intelligentsia was trying to emancipate itself. The culmination of this process was the revolt of the universities in 1968. Due to the lack of support in the ranks of workers and peasants, the 'academic revolution' was quite easily suppressed by the government. One had to wait until the 1970s for a constitutional court to be finally conceived and it quickly becoming extremely popular among legal scholars for the following main reasons:

1. The opening towards the West. The policy of the First Secretary of the Communist Party (*Polska Zjednoczona Partia Robotnicza*, 'PZPR') Edward Gierek limited criticism of the Western model of life. Also the media started to describe Western countries in a positive manner. Polish elites were travelling abroad more often than before. Western models of society and political organization of the country started to be discussed across Poland.

2. Legal scholars became more independent from the ruling party. This partial autonomy of Polish constitutionalists appeared to stimulate brave new ideas and constitutional scholars soon understood that they could join the winning side in the struggle for hegemony if they helped to establish constitutional courts.

3. After several years of economic growth a huge crisis struck. Between 1976 and 1980 there were a significant number or massive strikes. Despite being effectively suppressed it resulted in a downturn in the legitimacy

---

[7] See especially Art. 2 (4) of the April Constitution: 'Unitary and indivisible state power is vested in His [the President's—A.S.] hands.' Art. 3 (1) provided that the executive, legislative and judicial powers are 'under the control of the President of the Republic.'

[8] Art. 54 of the April Constitution.

[9] See, e.g. Dębska, *Władza, symbol, prawo*, 112–13.

[10] Михаил Абрамович Нудель [Mikhail Abramovich Nudyel'], *Конституционный контроль в капиталистических государствах* [Control of Constitutionality in Capitalist States] (Москва: Юрид. лит., 1968), 14.

of the authorities. As a consequence, the authorities tried to base their legitimacy on experts and to strengthen law and order. This appeared to be the best ground to implement a constitutional court.[11]

The Gierek era (1970–80) had changed the cultural position of the intelligentsia. Even in popular culture (books, movies), poor and uneducated but loyal workers and peasants gave way to new role models: certified engineers who by working efficiently received relatively high salaries; directors of companies who got rich legally by developing companies managed by them for the good of the country's economy. One of the most popular movies of the time is the series '*Czterdziestolatek*' ['The Forty-year-old']. The protagonist of the series is an engineer whose wife had a degree in chemistry, and his best friend was a doctor. At the opposite end, the working class was represented by Maliniak who was nothing short of a careerist simpleton. Even the detective stories had changed. Lieutenant Borewicz, the most popular Polish detective of the era was an educated psychologist (who liked women and cars) and the criminals hunted by him where not, as was the case before, imperialist agents or remnants of pre-war bourgeoisie, but peasants and workers. The positive hero (of secondary importance) of one of the episodes was a Polish millionaire who lived in a house with a swimming pool and a tennis court. In one of the last episodes of the series, Borewicz even cooperated with an American policeman.

This change in popular culture, albeit controlled by the regime, was a promise from party administration to share power with the middle class. In exchange for loyal participation in governing the country, the communists promised the intelligentsia to introduce into Poland the otherwise bourgeois modern power control mechanisms. In short, the constitutional court had to belong to professionals. It was thought to become a symbol of the new era, when the dictatorship of the proletariat would be replaced by the socialism of experts and lawyers. For their part, the experts had to help the government to restrain the workers.[12] At this juncture, it is worth noting that the riots against the government in the 1970s were organized mainly by workers and the 1968 protest was the last one in which the intelligentsia took part. The implementation of new solutions became even more urgent when strikes in 1980 forced the government to accept the existence of the independent trade union *Solidarność* [Solidarity]. In a short space of time, no less than 10 million people joined the union. Interestingly enough, Solidarity supported the proposals for the establishment of the constitutional court.

---

[11] See Dębska, *Władza, symbol, prawo*, 114–25.
[12] Jadwiga Staniszkis, *Samoograniczająca się rewolucja. Historia Solidarności* [A Self-limiting Revolution: History of the Solidarity Movement] (Gdańsk: Europejskie Centrum Solidarności, 2010), 195.

The impulse to start work on the constitutional court was a resolution from July 1981 enacted during the extraordinary convention of the PZPR. On 13 December 1981 martial law was introduced in Poland as an overt form of state war against Solidarity.[13] As a consequence, all democratic processes were suspended. After calming the situation in the country, a constitutional reform was enacted in March 1982 which entered into force in April 1982.[14] Besides the TK, the Tribunal of State (*Trybunał Stanu*, a special court for those who breach the law while holding the highest offices) and the Supreme Chamber of Control (*Najwyższa Izba Kontroli*, a part-independent body that controls spending of public money) were created. After a long period, the TK Act was enacted on 29 April 1985 as a result of a political compromise.[15] Accordingly, the TK had limited powers and its judgments could be vetoed by the parliament. According to official justifications, the TK was intended to strengthen rights and freedoms of the citizens and to ensure the observance of principles of equality and social justice. As a theoretical basis for the TK, the lawmakers thus adopted a model based on the following assumptions and which one could easily label Kelsenian:

1. the structure based on professional judges, well-educated, and trained in the field of the interpretation of law (both statutes and the constitution);

2. judgements which were based on and formally separate with objective content from constitution;

3. proceeding under an abstract form of control, based on the comparison of the objective content of constitutional norms and the norms of statutes, a position which ultimately amounts to judicial self-restraint;

4. the effect of a negative decision (deeming a specific norm invalid), leading to a derogation that determines the prospective character of the judgement.

The TK started work on 1 January 1986. During the first years of its existence it was rather reserved and passive, and undertook numerous but cautious decisions to strengthen the rule of law institutions in Poland.[16]

Although the government failed to convince the intelligentsia of the need to cooperate with the regime, the new control bodies were not attacked by

---

[13] Decree of 12 December 1981 on the martial law (Dz.U. no. 29, item 154); Resolution of the Council of State of 12 December 1981 regarding the introduction of martial law for reasons of state security (Dz.U. no. 29, item 155).

[14] Act of 26 March 1982 amending the Constitution of the Polish People's Republic (Dz.U. no 11, item 83).

[15] Act of 29 April 1985 on the Constitutional Court (Dz.U. no. 22, item 98).

[16] Sadurski, *Rights Before Courts*, 1; Rafał Mańko, '"War of Courts" as a Clash of Legal Cultures: Rethinking the Conflict between the Polish Constitutional Tribunal and the Supreme Court Over "Interpretive Judgments",' in *Law, Politics, and the Constitution: New Perspectives from Legal and Political Theory*, ed. Michael Hein, Antonia Geisler and Siri Hummel (Frankfurt am Main: Peter Lang, 2014), 83.

the opposition, which was at that time both informal and illegal. The creation of the TK and other new bodies was regarded as a sign of the progress of democratization. Their expert nature and ideological independence had thus been recognized. Solidarity (illegal since 1981) treated the TK as a body which, in the future, after the victory of the revolution, would be able to adapt the old law to the new political creeds.

In the late 1980s, the socialist system in Poland suffered economic collapse. Rampant inflation and shortages made life difficult. The TK continued to operate safely and was not blamed for the country's disastrous condition. The court was ultimately able to convince the legal community that it functioned separately from power and politics while slowly securing for itself the status of a 'sacred cow.' However, the best times for the TK came with the revolution of 1989, a period of time when Western solutions where implemented very fast. The reforms resulted in the emergence of many contradictions between the old socialist legislation and new legal arrangements and economic practice.[17] Undoubtedly, the situation favoured judicial activism. Moreover, the April 1989 amendment of the Polish constitution vested new powers in the TK,[18] namely to provide universally binding interpretations of statutes and *a priori* review of constitutionality of acts of Parliament (the President of Poland—the new head of state who replaced the collective Council of State—obtained the right to request the TK ensure laws conform with the constitution before signing them). Equipped with the new tools, the TK adopted measures incompatible with Kelsenian principles:

1. *The completion of the constitution*: As Würtemberger rightly formulates, this technique is based on a statement that 'rules implicate from the constitution and they are not connected with the text of the act' while required as a form of control (for example, in order to remove unneeded law) or as an abstract principle (a new rule which is effective *erga omnes*).[19] The TK 'discovered' in the constitution many unwritten rules such as: the presumption of innocence, the right to justice, the right to life, the right to privacy, the principle of proportionality (the prohibition of excessive interference in the rights of individuals), the rule of law, the principle of social justice, the principle of loyalty to the state of the citizen,

---

[17] A number of examples of such institutions (in the area of private law) was analysed by Rafał Mańko, '"We Do Not Recognise Anything »Private«": Public Interest and Private Law Under the Socialist Legal Tradition and Beyond,' in *Private Interest and Public Interest in European Legal Tradition*, ed. Bronisław Sitek et al. (Olsztyn: Wydział Prawa i Administracji Uniwersytetu Warmińsko-Mazurskiego w Olsztynie, 2015), 31–65.

[18] Act of 7 April 1989 amending the Constitution of the Polish People's Republic (Dz.U. no. 19, item 101).

[19] Thomas Würtemberger, 'Current Trends In German Legal Methodology,' 7 *Ukrainian Law Review* 5 (2004), 5–6.

the non-retroactivity of law (*lex retro non agit*), the principle of *lex severior non agit*, the protection of acquired rights, the principle of legal clarity, etc. Of course, the names of these principles sound pretty. Most of them can be considered important for democracy—in the new constitution in 1997 they were included in written form.[20] However, during the transition, unwritten rules were often used to invalidate the laws passed by a democratically elected parliament. In addition, understanding the principles did not always chime with their names. The devil is always in the details. For example, from the unwritten principle of the protection of human life the TK deduced a partial prohibition of abortion.[21]

2. Postponing the decision of unconstitutionality: This technique is based on a very simple action which provides a kind of *vacatio legis* for a judicial decision. During the *vacatio legis*, the law declared unconstitutional remains in the system and is still applicable. The main idea of this instrument is quite easy to grasp. By controlling the activity of the parliament, the TK can 'fix' the latter's mistakes thus preventing the chaos that would be caused by the elimination of a rule from the legal system. This institution, however, is not so common across constitutional courts.[22] It is also sometimes restricted by other rules, for instance, on the 'avoidance of causing serious damage' or 'common good or legal safety.'[23]

3. Interpretational decisions: These are decisions about the conditional conformity of law with the constitution. The court acknowledges in such decisions that the analyzed rule is consistent with the constitution but only under a specific meaning. Usually the interpretation given by the courts is not consistent with accepted rules of interpretation of both constitution and statutes. This technique can also be used in order to keep in force controversial laws. So if the court wants to keep the law, judges create a special interpretation according to which the law is legal and still valid. This type of legal action is called sometimes 'the interpretation of the constitution in conformity with the law.'[24]

The TK took up the role of chief engineer of transformation and made numerous and controversial political decisions. This is especially true in

---

[20] Constitution of the Republic of Poland of 2 April 1997 (Dz.U. no. 78, item 483). Non-binding English translation: *Sejm*, accessed 10 February 2016, http://www.sejm.gov.pl/prawo/konst/angielski/konse.htm.

[21] Judgment of 28 May 1997, Case K 26/96.

[22] Bogusław Banaszak, *Porównawcze prawo konstytucyjne współczesnych państw demokratycznych* [Comparative constitutional law of modern democratic states] (Kraków: Zakamycze, 2004), 597.

[23] Jerzy Porowski, *Skutki orzeczeń o niekonstytucyjności ustaw w prawie i orzecznictwie sądów konstytucyjnych* [The effects of decisions on the unconstitutionality of laws in the law and case law of constitutional courts] *Państwo i Prawo* 11 (1984), 34.

[24] Leszek Garlicki, *Sądownictwo konstytucyjne w Europie Zachodniej* [Constitutional Court in Western Europe] (Warszawa: Państwowe Wydawnictwo Naukowe, 1987), 217.

the case of the 'signalling orders' (*postanowienia sygnalizacyjne*). These decisions may be issued by the TK of its own motion and are designed to induce the legislature into certain activities under the pretext of the liquidation of gaps in the legal system. I analyzed these judgments in detail and almost none of them concerned the objective gaps (in the sense that the theory of law gives to this term).[25] The political reforms from 1997 ended the parliament's control over the TK so it started to be completely independent. Its position became even stronger thanks to the apologetic attitude of legal scholars towards activist decisions, the faith in the objective truthfulness of the political conceptions transplanted from the West, and the specific position (prestige) of the intelligentsia (professors and experts) present in the TK.[26]

The court had been given significant power. Thanks to the dominant view that the court is neutral and apolitical, constitutional judges were able to universalize their particular ideology.[27] The effectiveness of the court was on the highest level while it was considered a representative of rational knowledge and an embodiment of universal values which might serve everyone. In fact, the court took very brave political decisions which were turned into law. Allegedly, those decisions were taken from a neutral place devoid of politics and power struggles. They were considered neutral and objective, keeping the power of the tribunal 'invisible.'[28]

1.3 The Affirmative Amnesia of Polish Constitutionalists

The specific 'atmosphere' around the TK may also be explained by a phenomenon specific to Polish legal scholars of 'affirmative amnesia.'[29] In order to clarify this phenomenon I would like to start with a quote from a popular constitutional law textbook published in 1964:

---

[25] Adam Sulikowski, 'Postanowienia sygnalizacyjne Trybunału Konstytucyjnego. Założenia instytucjonalne, praktyka, wykonywanie' [The signaling orders of the Constitutional Court. Institutional assumptions, practice, enforcement], in *Wykonywanie orzeczeń Trybunału konstytucyjnego w praktyce konstytucyjnej organów państwa* [Enforcement of judgments of the Constitutional Court by the constitutional authorities of the State], ed. Kazimierz Działocha and Sylwia Jarosz-Żukowska (Warszawa: Wydawnictwo Sejmowe, 2013), 257–60.

[26] Dębska, *Władza, symbol, prawo*, 216*ff*.

[27] Cf. Hanna Dębska, 'Legal Doxa as a Form of Neutralization of Values in the Law. The Case of Constitution Tribunal Judgments,' in *Neutralization of Values in Law*, ed. Krzysztof Pałecki (Warszawa: Wolters Kluwer, 2013).

[28] Cf. Dębska, *Władza, symbol, prawo*, 294*f*.

[29] Adam Sulikowski, 'Afirmatywna amnezja i konserwatywni crits. Kilka uwag o kondycji krytycznej myśli prawniczej w Europie Środkowej i Wschodniej' [Affirmative Amsnesia and Conservative Crits: Some Remarks on the Condition of Critical Legal Thought in Central and Eastern Europe], *Archiwum Filozofii Prawa i Filozofii Społecznej* 8 (2014), 77–87.

Polish constitutionalism does not conceal its class character. It openly admits that it serves the interests of a particular social class. Bourgeois legal scholars are also class oriented—they serve the interests of the propertied classes. The difference between Western and the Polish constitutionalism lies in the fact that the former hides its character and presents itself as 'apolitical,' 'objective,' and 'uninvolved.'[30]

After 1989 the author of the above quote—still active and a prominent professor of constitutional law—did not write a word about the class character of the law despite his institutional relationship with the left. Experienced former 'crits' came apologists without any explanation. This is characteristic of the intellectual position of Polish legal scholars.

Poland in the sixties and seventies has become more open to the West. Polish intellectuals (with the exception of the real and alleged opposition) started to travel abroad. Western books, especially left-wing books were translated and are well known in Poland. The views that founded critical theory were widely discussed, but of course only in accordance with the official doctrine of the Communist Party.[31] To be sure, the main function of official Marxism was the legitimization of Communist Party rule. Out of the three founding fathers of critical theory—Marx, Nietzsche, and Freud—only Marx was officially promoted in Poland in a form that was compatible with the resolutions of the Central Committee. Honesty and freedom of expression were partially limited. However, the Party allowed criticism of law, at least the law in force in capitalist countries. This criticism was present in the works of Polish legal scholars. The authors excavated the relation of constitutional law, civil law, and even criminal law with class interests and the ideology of the ruling classes. Some of these studies were undoubtedly sincere and honest in their criticism of the dominant ideology. In some books those authors used irony to show (in the spirit of critical theory) the involvement of Polish socialist legal practice. At the same time, under more or less the discrete control of the special services, Polish legal scholars organized numerous discussions on post-Marxism and the moral revolution in the West. There were also organized illegal leftist debates in books that were not officially available. No one denied the claim that the

---

[30] Stanisław Gebethner in *Prawo państwowe PRL* [The state law of Popular Republic of Poland], ed. Janina Zakrzewsk (Warszawa: Państwowe Wydawnictwo Naukowe, 1964), 14. This and all other translations from Polish texts into English are my own.

[31] See, e.g. Grzegorz Leopold Seidler, *Doktryny prawne imperializmu* [Legal doctrines of imperialism] (Kraków: Wydawnictwo Literackie, 1979); Kazimierz Opałek and Jerzy. Wróblewski, *Współczesna teoria i socjologia prawa w Stanach Zjednoczonych* [Contemporary theory and sociology of law in the United States] (Warszawa: Państwowe Wydawnictwo Naukowe, 1963), Maria Borucka-Arctowa, 'Socjologia a współczesne koncepcje prawnonaturalne,' *Państwo i Prawo* 10 (1954); Jerzy Kowalski, *Funkcjonalizm w prawie amerykańskim: studium z zakresu pojęcia prawa* [Functionalism in Americal Law: A Study on the Concept of Law] (Warszawa: Państwowe Wydawnictwo Naukowe, 1960).

law was built on economic relations and that it was ideologically involved with and determined by social factors.

It is clear that some socialist legal scholars in Poland had unofficially liberal and free-market views while at the same time being aware of the fact that the law and its interpretation were strongly related to politics and economics. In spite of all this, after 1989 the criticism of the 'bourgeois' law had become almost taboo. Western neoliberal standards had been recognized by the official legal discourse as normal, universal, and the only correct approach in legal studies. The political transformation determined the activism of judges, so even the most creative interpretation of the law was considered necessary and free of ideology. Polish postmodern rightists, whom I will detail later, explained the disappearance of legal criticism as a result of a conspiracy between post-communists and neoliberal elites. According to this narrative, the revolution in Poland had not been made by (and for) the people, but was a result of an informal agreement between the communists, the opposition, and the criminal underworld to gain control of national assets. Lech Wałęsa was a communist agent constantly controlled by the communist secret services, etc. In reality, legal education in Poland was deprived of pluralism and criticism. Poles freed from one cultural colonization were quickly and without reflection subjected to subsequent neoliberal colonization.

After 1989 the Polish elite had become part of the neoliberal Western world and accepted the imported economic system as universally true. Polish legal scholars from the era of socialism tacitly accepted their role in the new system. Perhaps unsurprisingly, their role was similar to the old days—legitimization of the status quo, silencing doubts, and protecting the system. Legal scholars fulfilled this role willingly because as a group they clearly benefited from the transition. Looking at the situation from the perspective of the critical sociology of Pierre Bourdieu, we can see the 'interest in disinterestedness' in legal practice and legal studies.[32] Legal scholars became apologists not only for selfish reasons—and contrary to their beliefs—but according to the 'logic of the social universe.' Their views were readily cited by the courts, which facilitated the career of their authors and guaranteed them a sense of impact on the system. The comfortable position and the belief that every alternative was worse, both

---

[32] Pierre Bourdieu, 'Genesis and Structure of the Religious Field,' *Comparative Social Research* 13 (1991), 1–44; Pierre Bourdieu, 'The Force of Law: Toward a Sociology of the Juridical Field,' *Hastings Law Journal* 38 (1986), 805–53. Cf. Hanna Dębska and Tomasz Warczok, 'Iluzje prawniczego Rozumu. O społecznych warunkach praktyk (bez)refleksyjnych' [Illusions of the Legal Mind. On the Social Conditions of Non-reflexive Practices], *Studia Prawno-Ekonomiczne* 92 (2014), 11–23; Hanna Dębska and Tomasz Warczok, 'Hidden Influences. Some Remarks On the Social Constraints of the Autonomy of Law,' *Przegląd Prawa Publicznego* 5 (2015), 9–15.

for lawyers and for the country, reduced the possible doubts of prominent law professors. A critique of the law was regarded as something useless or even dangerous, something that only impedes the correct development of the country, something that might provoke those people who are irrational and do not understand the *raison d'état*. The special sense of mission and a fear of the irrationality of the people was typical of the elites in peripheral countries.[33] Moreover, critical thinking drawn from Marxism was considered to be discredited and obsolete.

It is not surprising that the new Polish neoliberal law was not criticized by legal scholars, even though Polish lawyers were trained for years in a critical approach and applied it successfully to the study of Western law. Former legal 'crits' of the western legal system were ready, under the new conditions, to justify any creative interpretation of the laws made by the TK as a necessary 'import' of western *acquis constitutionnel*. 'Acquis' was defined as a set of rules for the functioning of the state: non-controversial, free of ideology, and tested in practice. As I mentioned, the affirmative consensus among legal scholars was compatible with the unity of the political establishment. In the first years of transition in Poland, intellectual differences between left and right on fundamental issues were illusory. All major political parties supported the pro-Western, neoliberal reform orientations. Besides, it can be said that the 'left' did not exist at all as institutionalized political power.

The official left-wing party, *Sojusz Lewicy Demokratycznej* ('Democratic Left Alliance,' hereinafter 'SLD'), represented mainly the post-communist establishment and supported the neoliberal reforms. The government of SLD liberalised the labour code, setting standards of worker protection worse than those that existed in the European Union. The advantage of right-wing thinking in the mainstream was evident. The mainstream formed an alliance with the church, which was regarded as the main hero of the 'war' against communism in Poland. The TK had become not only a voice of the pro-Western political elites but also the guardian of Catholic influence. It took controversial decisions on reproductive rights and European integration (treaties of the European Union have been declared compatible with the constitution in a rather creative manner to avoid any formal constitutional amendments under the uncertain support of a majority of the population). This system was strongly supported by the constitutionalists and other legal scholars. Krzysztof Wojtyczek, professor of constitutional law at the Jagiellonian University in Kraków, wrote in his

---

[33] On Poland's (semi-)peripherality from the perspective of the legal community see Hanna Dębska, 'Strategia wielopozycyjności w półperyferyjnym polu prawnym. Homo academicus na rynku' [Multipositioning Strategy in a Semiperipheral Legal Field: Homo Academicus on the Market] in *Polska jako peryferie* [Poland as a Pheriphery], ed. Tomasz Zarycki (Warszawa: Scholar, 2016).

report on the state of constitutional scholarship in Poland:

> The contemporary Polish intelligentsia is under a strong influence of liberalism, and this influence is also evident in constitutional law scholarship. This discourse generally supports liberal and market-oriented economic and political reforms. The analyzed discipline is more skeptical about the critical currents of contemporary social philosophy that treat the state and law as an instrument of domination and exploitation, providing for certain social groups a share in the national income disproportionate to their contribution to the creation of the income. Polish constitutional law scholarship accepted the Western model of liberal constitutional democracy, limiting its criticism of the rationality of imported solutions, and providing suggestions for their improvement. Polish constitutionalists avoid critical reflection on the social function of legal institutions and on the idea of a constitutional democracy.[34]

The Polish mainstream 'knowledge-power complex' was formed around the belief that 'universal Western liberal modernity' was all we needed in Poland. Interestingly, among the most active defenders of the status quo were former leading Marxists (now also officially affiliated with left-wing parties). When a few years ago I started to criticize the constitutional discourse in Poland in the most well known Polish journal 'State and Law,'[35] my most active adversary was Jerzy Jaskiernia, former secretary of the Communist Party and minister of justice in the government of the left. Jaskiernia argued in his essays that socially engaged post-Marxist criticism of the law was 'unscientific' and can only impair constitutional discourse.[36]

1.4 Postmodern Conditions *à la Polonaise*

To recap, the pro-Western 'revolution' in Poland brought about a very specific intellectual climate. The spirit of modernization had become ubiquitous. The criticism of law almost disappeared. Western intellectuals in the 1960s criticized modern politics and economics and all systems based on them. These critical opinions were also seen in Poland. During real socialism in Poland people were discussing the works of Max Horkheimer, Theodor Adorno, Michel Foucault and/or Jacques Derrida. Of course, it

---

[34] Krzysztof Wojtyczek, 'Polska nauka prawa konstytucyjnego na przełomie wieków' [Polish Constitutional Law Scholarship at the Turn of the Century] in *Dwadzieścia lat transformacji ustrojowej w Polsce* [Twenty Years of Systemic Transformation in Poland], ed. Marek Zubik (Warszawa: Wydawnictwo Sejmowe, 2010), 36–7.

[35] Adam Sulikowski, 'O możliwościach postmodernizacji nauki prawa konstytucyjnego' [On the possibility of post-modernization of constitutional law scholarship], 12 *Państwo i Prawo* (2010), 3–12.

[36] Jerzy Jaskiernia, 'O znaczeniu postmodernizmu dla nauki prawa konstytucyjnego' [The significance of postmodernism for the study of constitutional law], 4 *Państwo i Prawo* (2011), 35–45.

was quite hard to criticize Marxism, but it was not prohibited to criticize Western culture and its philosophical or intellectual mainstream. Ten years after the revolution all critics of the West disappeared. There appeared instead a strange belief that Poland must be modernized and that there should be created one universal 'public reason' as a mix of Western ideas with the small addition of catholic conservatism. The Polish tribunal was very successful in supporting this change. The difference between the political left and right on fundamental topics was very small. This could be seen as an advantage for the right because of their alliance with the church which was considered the main opponent of communism. The radical left (with a Western spirit) was considered politically insignificant and ignored by the real and official left—the communist parties.

This situation has been changing over the past several years with the reception of the Western radical left, which influenced legal discourse. Legal scholars started writing more and more works influenced by postcolonial theory, gender studies, queer theory, post-structuralism, or post-humanism, which turned out to be very popular. The constitutional tribunal and its neutrality started to be criticized as the new Polish 'crits' asked uneasy questions posed by Michel Foucault and later by Jean-Francois Lyotard, 'Who decides what is reasonable and who knows how to decide?'

We can also see in Poland the process of radicalization of the 'postmodern right.' According to its followers, secularization and demythologization brought by the Enlightenment and modernism were considered a temporary mistake of humanity. This mistake should be rectified by an anti-modern revolution. Supporters of anti-modernist right-wingers see in the constitutional court the priest-usurper, who in the service of Western, anti-Polish, atheistic neocolonialism seeks to violently change the last bastion of Catholic premodern traditions.[37]

The consensus around Polish modernization began to weaken and broke down both in politics and at the universities. Polish rightists encouraged a wider discussion about the constitutional courts. In 2006, the following comment was made by the leader of PiS (*Prawo i Sprawiedliwość*—Law and Justice Party) during an interview: 'there are no undeniable rules on the interpretation of law.' He also mentioned that the constitutional judges were not entirely neutral.[38] This controversial interview was commented

---

[37] Dorota Majka-Rostek, 'Tolerancja jako wartość i jako zagrożenie—oświeceniowe pojęcie w polskim współczesnym dyskursie narodowo-katolickim' [Tolerance as a Value and as a Danger: The Enlightenement Concept in Contemporary Polish National-Catholic Discourse] in *Dogmatyzm, rozum, emancypacja* [Dogmatism, Reason, Emancipation], ed. Piotr Żuk (Warszawa: Scholar, 2005), 212.

[38] Press release: 'Kaczyński chce dyskutować o TK' [Kaczynski wants to discuss the constitutional Court], *Wprost*, 23 March 2006, accessed 1 February 2016 http://www.wprost.pl/ar/88219/Kaczynski-chce-dyskutowac-o-TK/.

on by the president of the tribunal at that time, Marek Safjan, who replied: 'after sixteen years of freedom and with Poland being a democratic country, we should ask for obvious truth and recall a banal thesis. If Kaczyński's statement is true, every constitutional judge should retire on the spot.'[39] Safjan's overreaction was supported by some constitutionalists. But this 'defence' is not convincing and the neutrality of the Polish tribunal is being discussed at the moment.[40] The weakening of the 'force field' around the tribunal also encourages other authorities to confront the constitutional engineers. The Supreme Court (*Sąd Najwyższy*, 'SN'), which has long been skeptical about the activism of the constitutional court, attacked it quite heavily.[41] In December 2010, the SN ruled that an interpretative decision taken by the TK could not serve as a basis for the resumption of the proceedings before the ordinary courts. In turn, the Supreme Administrative Court (*Naczelny Sąd Administracyjny*, 'NSA') refused the approval of another invention of the TK—the privilege of benefits. This solution (invented by the TK) lies in the fact that during the *vacatio legis* of the TK's decision on the unconstitutionality of an act of Parliament, the person who initiated the proceedings may effectively raise the claim of unconstitutionality, while others have no such powers, even if they are in a very similar factual situation.

The situation of the TK is further complicated by its unsteady relationship with the judicial authorities of the European Union and the Council of Europe. European integration involves the polycentric creation of law. Constitutional courts are connected with the logics of their national countries while also having to face problems that take into account European norms.[42] It seems that on this ground it will be much harder to foster old myths and to continue old habits and illusions of neutrality as well as to administer law on the basis of objective knowledge. A new era for constitutional engineers is on its way. It will be difficult to defend the 'fairy tales' about rational and a priori constitutional programmes coming

---

[39] Marek Safjan, 'Nie wikłajmy Trybunału do polityki PiS' [We cannot become entangled in politics of PiS], text no longer available on the official website of the TK, previously accessed 1 October 2014, http://www.trybunal.gov.pl/wiadom/Prezes/gw.pdf.

[40] Issue No 4 (93) / 2009 of *Przegląd Sejmowy*—the official scholarly journal of the Polish parliament—is devoted entirely to a discussion about the legitimacy of the constitutional court in the new conditions. The following are some of the titles of texts included in this issue: Włodzimierz Gromski, 'Legitimacy of Constitutional Courts and the Legislative Power;' Marek Zubik, Marcin Wiącek, 'The Competencies of a Constitutional Court and the Limits of Judicial Discretion of the Judges of the Constitutional Tribunal;' Lech Morawski, 'The Tripartite Division of Powers Principle. The Constitutional Tribunal and Judicial Activism;' Bogusław Banaszak, 'Judicial Activism of the Constitutional Tribunal;' Leszek Garlicki, 'New Phenomena in the Constitutionality Review of Laws (A Contribution to the Discussion on the Legitimacy of Constitutional Courts).'

[41] See, e.g. Mańko, 'War of Courts,' 83*ff*.

[42] Cf. Mańko, 'War of Courts,' 89.

out of neutral readings of the constitution. The so-called radiation of the constitution is losing its power with the collision with other competitive radiations. Those collisions are getting more and more harmful and painful. As Bator has noted, 'from one point of view, postmodernity (as a social state of things) determines a multicentre but, from another point of view, postmodernism as a fundamental power of a particular intellectual attitude creates problems with meta-regulation insofar as they are privileged conceptions.' Postmodernism shows lawyers that the 'constitutional rule is not the highest in a hierarchy of rules within the same idiom (commonly understood and accepted pragmatic idea) but refers to a specific doctrinal narration, the language of unwritten constitutional values which always has its author.'[43]

The modern way of thinking shows one and only one solution, the reconstruction of a hierarchic system, finding relations, determining the 'enthronisation of a new king,' a philosopher who has entire power in his hand, who can create a set of rules which may—as Lyotard would say—turn constitutional *différends* into *litiges*. Obviously this system would be supranational. It is hard to believe, but today there is also a strong view among constitutionalists that globalization simple transfers national reliance to a higher level, that we should still build a system based on Kelsen's and Weber's pyramidal ideas, a homogenizing course based on supranational constitutions. The Court of Justice of the European Union is considered to be at the hierarchical apex of Europe.[44] But some go even further. Maus, one of the most influential French constitutionalists, argued that it may be possible to impose total order on the world if the International Court of Justice used all its powers.[45] Maybe so, however, fortunately, the lack of legitimacy of today's 'philosophers kings' together with the postmodern plurality of views on the law are not conducive to homogenization. Postmodern perspectives undermine the mechanisms that lead to harmonization and reveal them to be a sign of violence. Today, social engineering is something almost impossible to imagine. The philosophy of law is dominated by the view that the era of the purely technical use of law has passed. Contemporary law is created by many entities whose mutual

---

[43] Andrzej Bator, 'Debaty prawnicze. Rozmowa bez konsensu' [Lawyers' Debates: A Conversation without Consensus], in *Z zagadnień teorii i filozofii prawa. Ponowoczesność* [Issues of Theory and Philosophy of Law: Postmodernity], ed. Michał Błachut (Wrocław: Kolonia Limited 2007), 47.

[44] Koen Lenaerts and Marlies Desomer, 'New Models of Constitution-Making in Europe: the Quest for Legitimacy,' *Common Market Law Review* 39 (2002), 1217, 1247–50.

[45] Didier Maus, 'Sur la mondialisation du droit constitutionnel' [Globalization wof Constitutional Law], in *Instytucje prawa konstytucyjnego w dobie integracji europejskiej. Księga jubileuszowa dedykowana prof. Marii Kruk-Jarosz* [The Institutions of Constitutional Law in the Era of European Integration. Liber Amicorum Professor Maria Kruk-Jarosz], ed. Jan Wawrzyniak and Marzena Laskowska (Warszawa: Wydawnictwo Sejmowe, 2009), 92.

relationships are highly complex. On the other hand, the triumph of liberal thinking, distrustful towards centralized power, undermines the legitimacy of the paternalistic or pastoral idea of social control within and through the law. According to Jürgen Habermas's well known diagnosis, the future of law is linked to its use as a communication tool for dispute resolution, so the role of constitutional courts must change. In the postmodern era of pluralism, if the TK can be guided by the idea of realizing 'common' norms or values, it can be easily transformed into an authoritarian agency.[46]

New times have come for constitutional engineers in Poland. New times call for reform of the TK and new justifications for its activity.

---

[46] Jürgen Habermas, *Between Facts and Norms: Contributions to a Discourse Theory of Law and Democracy*, trans. William Rehg (Massachussets: MIT Press, 1996), 258.

2

The Importance of Being a Linguist: Critical Legal Thought in Central Europe

Martin Škop

2.1 The Confusion of Tongues

It can be argued, not only from a linguistic or legal perspective, that law is neither a neutral tool for promoting the goals of those in power nor a tool free from ideology. In society, law is connected with a certain style of thinking. However, there is no objective natural connection between law and any particular and determined style of thinking.[1] Law cannot be objectively connected with any particular style of speaking or writing. It follows that a certain selection and use of a particular language in the analysis of law (for example, the English language in relation to Czech law) may result in emphasizing or suppressing certain facts.

There are two groups of persons who participate in legal discourse, those who are excluded and those who are given the stage. By means of language, they may be ascribed a certain status, regardless of whether they consent to it or not. Improper use of language may result in what Elisabeth Noelle-Neumann calls the 'spiral of silence.'[2] Those who fail to use language in the correct way or use unusual terms or the language of another (non-dominant) environment become increasingly isolated and ultimately silenced. Legal Language has the capacity to stigmatize and is one of the tools by which social inequality is maintained. This need to be properly analyzed, the strategies generating this injustice further explored. As Přibáň points out, we should reveal how general language or its formal structures and the apparent impersonality created by language entrench social and political inequality and unfairness.[3]

From the standpoint of classical legal theory, there is one objective universal legal-linguistic project which includes the possible language of

---

[1] David M. Trubek, 'Where the Action Is: Critical Legal Studies and Empiricism,' *Stanford Law Review* 34 (1984), 576.

[2] Elisabeth Noelle-Neumann, *The Spiral of Silence: Public Opinion, Our Social Skin* (Chicago: University of Chicago Press, 1993).

[3] Jiří Přibáň, 'Kritická právní věda a sociologie práva' [Critical Legal Science and Sociology of Law], *Právník* 140 (2001), 1224.

legal theory. Differences between national languages are not essential. Theoretical terminology tends towards universalization, which itself tends to have unforeseen global effects. In this vision there is only one picture of law, which claims to provide content for all law in different cultures. Consequently, one has the impression that the single word 'law,' which may be translated into any language, has the same meaning across all languages, as if there were a material, linguistic, and contextual determination to the word. This can be seen in several sources of general jurisprudence and specifically applies to the English language, which is becoming the universal international language of legal studies.[4] The same could be said of modern critical theory, which is often dominated by the English language.

The particular cause of the linguistic and contextual dominance of English may be found in its influence over global judicial systems. Leading judicial institutions, such as, for example, the European Court of Human Rights makes decisions which apply to general legal issues and since their daily work language is English,[5] one might expect they derive inspiration from many sources written in English, irrespective of their context. As for critical theory, it is mainly the decisions of American and British courts that are used as an example of the covert impact of ideology. Despite the many languages of the world, English appears as the universal language specific to law, but it need not be this way. Clifford Geertz's thesis on the 'skeletonization of facts' may be invoked analogically, although we would refer to skeletonization of a particular legal system because only the mental object capable of being expressed in a universal general language is relevant.[6] The particular world of law is submitted to the universal and globally shared vision of ideal law.

The regulation of (legal) science and criteria of academic excellence may

---

[4] H. L. A. Hart, *The Concept of Law* (Oxford: OUP, 2012); Ronald *Dworkin, Taking Rights Seriously* (London: Bloomsbury Academic, 2013); Ronald Dworkin, Law's Empire (Cambridge: Harvard University Press, 1986); Ronald Dworkin, *A Matter of Principle* (Oxford: OUP, 1985). A certain hint may be found, despite the limitations given by the sample on which the measurements were carried out, in an article by Fred R. Shapiro quoted below. Although his article takes into consideration other sources, it is relevant for our purposes. Fred R. Shapiro, 'The Most-Cited Legal Books Published since 1978,' *The Journal of Legal Studies* 29 (2000), 39–405; or Fred R. Shapiro, 'The Most-Cited Law Review Articles Revisited,' *Chicago-Kent Law Review*, 71 (1996), 751–79. Fred R. Shapiro and Michelle Pearse's article 'The most Cited Law Review Articles of All Time' is the most relevant for our purposes because it contains data obtained from databases which are not limited to only American or British journals. See Fred R. Shapiro and Michelle Pearse, 'The Most Cited Law Review Articles of All Time,' *Michigan Law Review*, 110 (2012), 1483–520.

[5] Olga Łachacz and Rafał Mańko, 'Multilingualism at the Court of Justice of the European Union: Theoretical and Practical Aspects, '*Studies in Logic, Grammar and Rhetoric* 34 (2013), 80.

[6] Clifford Geertz, *Local Knowledge: Further Essays in Interpretive Anthropology* (New York: Basic Books, 1983), 172.

also be influencing factors in this context. In order to meet the quantitative criteria used for various evaluations of research outputs (existing in Central Europe and beyond), one has to publish his or her work in scientific journals, preferably the journals with so-called impact factor. The most significant scholarly publications tend to be American journals.[7] To publish in them, the author has to provide insights into the object of research to American readers. However, it is likely that these readers will not be familiar with either Czech law or the judicial decisions of Czech courts. It is therefore common to find that authors submitting to such journals focus only on the context familiar to reviewers. To secure publication, they have to adapt their use of universal English language when explaining and discussing domestic legal issues. They also have to take into consideration all kinds of possible limitations that may arise due to such translation. They may also use the artificial language of mathematics or logic.

The idea of a universal language into which a particular legal experience may be translated, may in a paradoxical manner lead to efforts to find the basis of law in linguistic structures that are often created and maintained by law. The move towards structuralist and neostructuralist approaches shows how law failed in the attempt to solve universal social challenges. As Garry Minda states:

> The structuralist approach depicted law as resting upon an underlying structure of meaning, which is neither objective nor fixed but rather dependent on the relationship law shares with the dominant cultural and social patterns of society.[8]

This approach is based on the belief that legal doctrine creates a system of features that represents the meaning of law. Discovering these features and symbols gave rise to legal semiotics,[9] which constitutes the foundation for the literary analysis of legal writings and attempts to detect the real meaning of the terms used.[10]

Accordingly, law and law's status in society are inextricably intertwined with the broader framework structuring social reality. As David M. Trubek states: 'Law creates society and society creates law.'[11] In this particular context, the term 'society' may be easily replaced with 'culture,' in the

---

[7] See, e.g. 'Law Journals: Submissions and Ranking, 2006–13,' Washington and Lee University, School of Law, accessed 24 February 2016, http://lawlib.wlu.edu/LJ/index.aspx.

[8] Garry Minda, *Postmodern Legal Movements—Law and Jurisprudence at Century's End* (New York: New York University Press, 1995), 114.

[9] See, e.g. Duncan, Kennedy, 'A Semiotics of Critique,' *Cardozo Law Review* 22 (2001), 1147–90 or Duncan Kennedy, 'A Semiotics of Legal Argument,' *Syracuse Law Review* 75 (1991), 75–116.

[10] Minda, *Postmodern Legal Movements*, 150.

[11] Trubek, 'Where the Action Is,' 609.

sense understood by Geertz. Hence culture can be understood as a pattern of meanings that has evolved throughout history, i.e. meanings which are included in symbols connected with the means of communication by which people reflect on their life in the broadest sense.[12] Culture links the meanings, language or means of communication, and the way of how one understands oneself and one's surroundings. Manipulating language may result in changes not only to law as a symbolic system, but also to society. In contrast to the classical 'confusion of tongues,' we witness a shift from the multiple languages through which law is described, to a unified form. This failed universalistic project comes to dominate the life of the law.

2.2 The Importance of Being a Linguist

The objectives of the above mentioned semiotic and structuralist approaches consist in analyzing the speech and the language of law in order to reveal their legitimizing function for existing social practices. The main goal is to disclose practices which strictly separate the 'self' from 'others.' As again pointed out by Minda:

> [T]he more sophisticated a person became in the law, the more likely he or she would understand that all issues within any particular doctrinal field are reduced to a single dilemma or fundamental contradiction between the self and others, the individual and the collective.[13]

A reasoned use of these disciplines lead us to the conclusion that the legal interpretation of texts privileges one meaning over all other possible meanings. The hierarchy of meanings whose only goal is to justify existing legal doctrine is thus considered to be statically defined in order to differentiate those who support it (self) from the others. The hierarchy is self-fulfilling in that certain doctrine privilege certain interpretations which retrospectively prove that the doctrine is correct. The existing hierarchy of legal thought may be challenged only when deconstructed. There is here an evident adherence to one of the characteristics of postmodernism, namely the struggle against logocentrism in thinking and, in this case, legal thought. Moreover, the hierarchy of meanings used in legal studies needs to be understood in order to uncover an attempt to establish objective universal linguistic method in which and through which law is described.

The assumption of a so-called universal language of (English) legal discourse should be resisted. Not because it cannot exist—it evidently

---

[12] Clifford Geertz, *The Interpretation of Cultures: Selected Essays* (New York: Basic Books, 1973), 89.
[13] Minda, *Postmodern Legal Movements*, 115.

does—but because this 'correct naming' is connected with connotations that are associated with a particular language or a particular legal system. Any form of naming based on translation seems ridiculous, or is at least incorrect. In translation it is 'impossible to preserve original meaning without modification.'[14] As Walter Benjamin observed, even though there can be the same object in both languages, modes of their intentions will be different.[15] If we connect thinking with a certain linguistic expression, it could be concluded that such a change in language would be reflected in thinking and the modeling of surrounding environment. As Mark Kelman states:

> We think in prepackaged categories, clusters, reified systems. We forged the degree to which we invent the social world. We come to think that rules make us act impersonally; we often forget that we must continually choose to act impersonally.[16]

Such focus on the universal language of (English) translation results in reification not only of speech, but also of the speaking actors. According to Michel Foucault, the supposedly universal features linked to language represent a certain force which we apply towards things. In our case, a force that we apply to legal issues and phenomena that have to be translated not only so that we can discuss them in an international/transnational context but also to criticize them. It is a practice which we force upon things, legal phenomena, and upon the legal environment. We impose justice on them through their subjection to discourse.[17] Novalis describes the something similar in the short story *The Novices of Sais*:

> The broad, echoing halls stood empty and bright, and the wondrous colloquy continued in innumerable languages among the thousandfold natures, which had been gathered together in these halls and arranged in various orders. Their inner forces played one against other. They strove back towards their freedom, their old relations. Some few stayed in their proper place and calmly watched the multiform stirrings about them. The others complained of dire pains and torments and bemoaned the glorious old life in the heart of nature, where a common freedom joined them together and each spontaneously obtained what he needed.[18]

---

[14] Rafał Mańko, 'Multilingualism, Divergent Authentic Versions of a Legal Rule and Legitimate Expectations of Individuals, 'forthcoming in *Studies in Logic, Grammar and Rhetoric* (2016), accessed 24 February 2016, http://ssrn.com/abstract=2729725.

[15] Walter Benjamin, 'The Task of the Translator,' in Benjamin, W. *Illuminations* (New York: Random House, 1988), 74.

[16] Mark Kelman, *A Guide to Critical Legal Studies* (Cambridge: Harvard University Press, 1987), 294.

[17] Michel Foucault, 'The Order of Discourse,' in *Untying the text: A Post-Structuralist Reader*, ed. R. Young (Boston: Routledge & Kegan Paul, 1982), 67.

[18] Novalis, *Novices of Sais* (New York: Archipelago Books, 2005), 69.

In our case, it applies to a game with language; the language that decides what is right and what is wrong.[19] The things themselves are not going to change, only the words are, including their meaning. With no words, the things would make no sense to us. This actually leads to a change in the world, while simultaneously challenging the possibilities of science.[20] Otherwise said, a problem which cannot be translated is not a problem.

We are tending towards the ideological comprehension of language in the same sense that literary critic Mikhail Mikhailovich Bakhtin perceived it:

> We are taking language not as a system of abstract grammatical categories, but rather language conceived as ideologically saturated, language as a world view, even as a concrete opinion, insuring a maximum of mutual understanding in all spheres of ideological life.[21]

By using a universal language we accept its semantic preferences and its domination over the surrounding world. The translation of the legal features specific to national law erodes different perceptions of the world and different legal traditions. Universal language stimulates forces working towards the unification of legal problems regardless of its specific contextual meaning.

2.3 The Critical Tradition in Central Europe: Spectres of the Forgotten

Contemporary critical legal discourse in Central Europe—especially in the Czech Republic—usually draws on the critical traditions developed in the US or the UK. This is problematic because the procedures and examples discussed by these critical traditions are not easy to apply to the continental (Czech) system of law. The context marking the Anglophone sources is hard to transfer to the Czech context and vice versa. The Czech experience as well as other post-socialist experiences may strongly relate to examples of the total influence of ideology or the absolute subordination of law and legal language to power. However, such valuable experiences may not be taken into account because they are hard to translate into other cultural spheres. They become reduced to mere spectres devoid of bonds to any experience. Due to the necessity of translation, it may be hard to apply the critical thought born of another culture to the post-socialist experience.

---

[19] See Gianni Vattimo, *Nihilism and Emancipation. Ethics, Politics and Law* (New York: Columbia University Press, 2004), 136.
[20] Richard Rorty, 'The Banality of Pragmatism and Poetry of Justice,' *Southern California Law Review* 63 (1990), 1813.
[21] Mikhail Mikhailovich Bakhtin, *The Dialogic Imaginaton* (Austin: University of Texas Press, 1981), 271.

The approach to socialist legal reality may be usefully described by drawing on Milan Kundera's novel *The Joke*.[22] Kundera helps us to understand that not only legal tradition, interpretation, or the practice of law are very closely connected with law's history and its specific meanings. In the novel, there was one sentence which turned out to be questionable and which sparked a chain of events: 'Optimism is the opium of the people! A healthy atmosphere stinks of stupidity! Long live Trotsky! Ludvik.'

These few words on a postcard that Ludvik addressed to his girlfriend, who was attending a training session on the strategy and tactics of the revolutionary movement, meant a lot despite it being intended as an ironic joke. They meant being expelled from university, having to find a job, being in conflict with the admired party, etc. Although Ludvik found himself in the end, this does not mean his fate was not altered—these few words had a significant and unforgiving impact. Sending them pushed him into the cogs of a machine, a machine intended to maintain a system that was quickly losing its legitimacy. A way to legitimate it was to create stories whose real substance was completely transformed. Ludvik's clumsy joke became an attack on the socialist system.

The past presents itself in law. Law is linked to the past as it necessarily requires a continuum for its existence and meaning. To understand law authentically we need to explore both its continuity and its moments of rupture. We need a visible continuity also to maintain stories that we link to law and to compose stories through which we create law. Narratives about law have a source in the past; a story or a narrative can help maintain continuity. The philosopher Jean Baudrillard argues: 'We require a visible past, a visible continuum, a visible myth of origin, which reassures us about our end.'[23] The past—and this is also true for a legal system—enables us to trace the trajectory of our movement. It shows us where we can get to with the help of law. As Baudrillard notes, the past serves our future. This not only involves a symbolic dimension but also one of content and form. The symbolic dimension manifests itself in the possibility of legitimating a legal order with the help of history. When exploring legitimate domination (authority), Max Weber identifies the reasons sustaining its legitimation, for instance when he writes, 'grounds resting on an established belief in the sanctity of immemorial traditions and the legitimacy of those exercising authority under them.'[24]

Content also links to the past as does the process of interpretation. The value associated with the content of a normative text does not stem merely

---

[22] Milan Kundera, *The Joke* (London: Penguin Books, 1982).

[23] Jean Baudrillard, *Simulacra and Simulation* (Ann Arbor: The University of Michigan Press, 1994), 10.

[24] Max Weber, *Economy and Society* (University of California Press, 1978), 215.

from an author or a story devoid of historical context. Michel Foucault suggests that up until the seventeenth century the scientific value of a work, its plausibility and integrity, stemmed from the author.[25] Today, we are probably in the same situation. The author is the one who carries prestige,[26] which is itself a product of social premises and expectations that are both in the past and in the present. The value that we associate with an author in the present and which we associate with his past has a significant impact on the value of the content that we work with in the present.

When we explore the intentions of the creator of a legal norm at the time of its creation, we also analyse the historical context of the creation of a normative text. A frequent criticism of originalism (in law as well as literature) involves methodological difficulties (how to identify relevant topics for the norm creator in his or her own time) and inadequacies in attempts to understand an author from a different social and cultural milieu (what was and is a *different* world). The arguments that this approach utilizes,

> face not only the problem of explaining why intentions of long-dead people from a different social world should influence us, but also, perhaps more importantly, the problem of extracting intentions from the collectivity of individuals and institutions necessary to give legal validity to the Constitution.[27]

These difficulties significantly undermine such a pious approach to a text. The rigorous attachment to the author's intentions is too constraining and so is the attachment to historical circumstances and conditions. It is very difficult to objectify the author's original intentions or indeed the context in which the normative text came into being.[28]

Returning to Kundera, we note that Ludvik is suspended from the Communist Party, forced to quit his studies at university and make a living in ways that he has not been used to. All these consequences are perhaps really due to the words on his postcard. But this is possible only in the given historical context, otherwise it is frighteningly absurd. Can we—without knowing the context—actually understand Ludvik's infantile joke?

Although this is an example from literature, one can sense the context

---

[25] Michel Foucault, *Diskurs Autor Genealogie. Tři studie* [Discourse Author Genealogy: Three Studies] (Praha: Svoboda, 1994), 16.
[26] Roland Barthes, *Image Music Text* (London: Fontana Press, 1977), 142–3.
[27] Sanford Levinson, 'Law as Literature,' *Texas Law Review* 60 (1982), 379.
[28] Fiction represents a useful tool when uncovering the past and exploring the possible context of a norm's creation. Although it neither detects exactly what was happening at the time a norm was established nor uncovers the exact circumstances of its reception, fiction nonetheless represents a visible continuum. It describes a past situation that could have been. It also enables us to comprehend how we saw the events subsequently and how we view them now. The aforementioned continuum forms part of literature that can help us understand realities that are important for the interpretation of the text of a legal norm.

which connects the particular social experience with the language by which, for instance, legal examples may be communicated. This context should not be ignored, especially if we admit that much of it resides in something that we do not have to be necessarily aware of and that it may remain secretly present in discourse. It is a past that does not have to be uttered, a presence that does not need to be realized, but they can serve as a base for some critical work.

2.4 Introduction of Critical Ideas

Although 'trafficking' critical ideas into the legal thought of Central Europe should be welcomed, one should also be aware of the special influence of language in this context. Are the things we observe not the mere hegemonic influence of the English critical tradition? The terms and concepts come from this tradition, they are applied to domestic phenomena, and their description within international forums has to comply with the experience of the recipients of the message (e.g. an article).

2.4.1 Preferred Reading

One example of the hegemonic influence of a dominant (English) meaning to domestic concepts is 'preferred reading,' a term coined by the cultural theorist Stuart Hall in the 1970s.[29] The effects of this phenomenon show that, in the process of interpretation, some meanings that correspond with everyday experience, everyday knowledge, or a dominant ideology prevail against ones that are new, novel, deemed dangerous or unusual. The author's particular intentions have no effect as the standard meaning ascribed by the preferred reading is imposed on the writings.[30] It is a sign of the presence of the dominant discourse which subordinates any possible interpretation to its own. The result of this dominant interpretation is that one hears in a discussion what he or she wants to hear while the preferences of the particular speakers may vary.[31] Similarly, a person interpreting writings (the interpreter) 'adjusts' them (by interpretation) to fit with his or her expectations. Clearly, if some deep-rooted frameworks of interpretation are imported from another legal culture, it will influence the manner in which the original legal terms are understood.

---

[29] Stuart, Hall, 'Encoding/Decoding,' in *Culture, Media, Language*, ed. S. Hall, D. Hobson, A. Lowe, and P. Willis (London: Routledge, 2005), 123.

[30] David Moorley, 'Texts, Readers, Subjects,' in *Culture, Media, Language*, ed. S. Hall, D. Hobson, A. Lowe, and P. Willis (London: Routledge, 2005), 158.

[31] Frank H. Easterbrook, 'Text, History, and Structure in Statutory Interpretation,' *Harvard Journal of Law and Public* Policy 17 (1994), 61.

Given the role of politics and ideology in legal interpretation, it can be said that interpretation is, on the one hand, characterized by an absence of objective determination, while on the other hand, fully determined by exposure to power struggles.[32] Interpretation is thus limited, not absolute.[33] Its framework is predetermined, but this determination cannot be absolute. If we apply concepts from other cultural environments, this application may be interpreted in accordance with the imported context. Duncan Kennedy describes the limitation as something that does not depend on the interpreter, but is rather an unquestionable base of a norm, something like the veracity of a legal norm.[34] It may seem that a norm itself, or its expression, includes something unquestionable that restricts interpretation. He disagrees with this approach. Kennedy argues that the determination of interpretation suits only very simple cases and that legal work should be understood as an activity led in a strategic way:

> Legal work, as I am using the term, whether aimed at cores or frames or at penumbras or conflicts or gaps, is undertaken 'strategically.' The worker aims to transform an initial apprehension of what the system of norms requires, given the facts, so that a new apprehension of the system, as it applies to the case, will correspond to the extra-juristic preferences of the interpretive worker.[35]

This applies to both the description of legal thinking and the efforts to seize control over meta-legal discourse. Despite the cultural determination of discourse, certain shifts in interpretation induced by the strategic character of legal work may be found here.

This represents the foundation of the power game of interpretation into which the interpreter is dragged. This game is very similar to Hall's description in that

> meaning, once it is problematized, must be the result, not of a functional reproduction of the world in language, but of a social struggle a struggle for mastery in discourse—over which kind of social accenting is to prevail and to win credibility.[36]

---

[32] Allan C. Hutchinson and Patrick J. Monahan, 'Law, Politics, and the Critical Legal Scholars: The Unfolding Drama of American Legal Thought,' *Stanford Law Review* 36 (1984), 206.

[33] See, e.g. Hans Kelsen, 'On the Theory of Legal Interpretation,' *Legal Studies* 10 (1990), 127-35.

[34] Duncan Kennedy, 'A Left Phenomenological Critique of the Hart/Kelsen Theory of Legal Interpretation,' in *Problemas contemporáneos de la filosofía del derecho*, ed. E. Cáceres (Ciudad de México: Universidad Nacional Autónoma de México, 2005), 372.

[35] Kennedy, 'A Left Phenomenological Critique,' 374.

[36] Stuart Hall, 'The Rediscovery of "Ideology": Return of the Repressed in Media Studies,' in *Culture, Society and Media*, ed. M. Gurevitch, T. Benett, J Curran, and J. Woollacott (London: Routledge, 2005), 75.

If one tries to translate a particular experience into English, it is obvious that the experience will be dominated by the discourse that stems from the translator's language.

The interpreter tries to change the framework set by the meta-legal discourse or to alter this discourse. The interpreter may want to open it to new spheres by means of interpretation.[37] While studying interpretation, we should not focus on what the standard source of law is, but instead look for what is capable of leading a subject to real interpretation.[38] With shifts in discourse, law itself is being changed. Recognizing an interpretation as 'correct' will be subject to perceived success in this dialogue, one in which, to reiterate, there is a tendency to seize control over the field of power and to monopolize the legitimate application of the correct procedures of interpretation.[39]

2.4.2 Cultural Hegemony

As previously mentioned, language is crucial for law and its position in society. One cannot observe law apart from language, which imbues the law with presence, past, and future. When a joke (*The Joke*) can become a crime, we can relate this to a critique of law. Its connection with one linguistic scheme makes it an element of cultural domination or an element of cultural hegemony.[40] Anyone who wants to understand another (legal) system or to successfully translate from one system to another has to comprehend the other system. This does not mean to accept the other system unconditionally, but to understand its essence and to grasp the elements connected with that system. This understanding, however, would be in the other's language because it is not possible to fully translate meaning. Not working in the other's language would mean imprisoning the other in a system which is mine ('I'). It would simultaneously mean a force (violence) in the form of a translation by means of which the uniqueness of the case in hand is covered and by which the uniqueness of the other is interrupted. The same result would be achieved if we tried to reduce all—including 'our' system—to a common denominator. Postmodernism builds a clear barrier against this by what Lyotard called 'the end of grand narratives.'[41] There is no meta-narration or a super-discourse which would

---

[37] Kennedy, 'A Left Phenomenological Critique,' 375.

[38] Vattimo, *Nihilism and Emancipation*, 136.

[39] On the 'field of power,' see Pierre Bourdieu, 'The Force of Law: Toward a Sociology of Juridical Field,' *The Hastings Law Journal* 38 (1987), 814–53; see also Pierre Bourdieu, *Language and Symbolic Power* (Cambridge: Polity Press, 1991), 189.

[40] Antonio Gramsci, *Prison Noteboks*, Volume III (New York: Columbia University Press, 2007), 30.

[41] Jean-François Lyotard, *The Postmodern Condition: A Report on Knowledge* (Minne-

be able to justify each small story, each institution.

Insisting on one universal legal language entails violence of form. The form of discourse in law is limited and it does not fully correspond with the natural language on which it is merely based. It is however inseparably connected with this language. It is difficult for anyone who fails to respect this special mode of natural language to grasp law and to use it. Law forcibly rejects them or forces them to subordinate to someone who acts according to a legal code. This situation may be as linguistically complicated as it was for Meursault in Albert Camus' *Stranger*.[42] The stranger did not suit any category and he neither understood his crime nor the following proceedings. He is aware of what had happened, but he does not understand the language used. It is difficult to resist the dominance of privileged universal language if one does not want to marginalize individualized problems.

We are thus witnesses of cultural hegemony. The language of critical legal thought creates strong bars behind which the criticism should stay. If an ideological problem is brought before an international forum and if the authors want to continue with their academic and scientific career, they have to accept these bars and respect the vocabulary connected with it. They also have to accept its context and to sacrifice their own. Their problems become someone else's problems. These are some of the core challenges that the critical theory of Central Europe deals with.

---

apolis: University of Minnesota Press, 1984).

[42] Albert Camus, *The Stranger* (New York: Alfred A. Knopf, 1946).

3

Law out of Bounds: Legal Picnolepsy, Intellectual Austerity, and Romania's Legal Past

Cosmin Sebastian Cercel

> But in the smallest and greatest happiness there is always one thing that makes it happiness: the power of forgetting, or, in more learned phrase, the capacity of feeling 'unhistorically' throughout its duration.
> — F. Nietzsche

3.1 Introduction

Law in Central Europe seems to express an obstinate resistance to acknowledging its own past and origins. In this chapter I defend the idea that this status of the law entails not only obvious historical and memorial consequences but also significant political implications. I thus affirm that this status should be criticized and contested. I intend to analyze the sources of this politics of forgetting embedded in both constitutional discourse and legal theory and sustained by a series of established cultural tropes defending the understanding of law as a normative system devoid of history and therefore situated above change and contingency. Subsequently, my intention is to explore the potentialities of a critical and historical engagement with the law in order to counter the dominant narrative and to open the possibilities of taking into account law's historical existence. I intend to do so by turning towards Romanian constitutional law and its strategies of selectively erasing or reconstructing the past. This investigation thus aims at unearthing the fragile status of the law within the Romanian context by scrutinizing its repressed history of suspension and erasure during its modern unfolding. It tries to recuperate the unstated and unassumed lost experience of the legal subject by focusing on the symbolic texture of the legal text and the ways in which it relates to historical context.

This endeavour consists of three topical interventions that try to bridge the continuum of our seemingly ahistorical present with the disruptions of the authoritarian past as well as with its putative modern origins. In the first part my focus consists in devising a theoretical framework able to map the core processes of the dissolution of experience in late modernity by drawing on the work of Paul Virilio, Walter Benjamin, and Giorgio Agamben. While picnolepsy and the paradigm of the state of exception shall serve as a guide in this reading, psychoanalysis, understood here as tool of social semiotics, will also provide a conceptual framework to approach law's sublated experience. In the second part, I turn towards Romanian constitutional history in order to situate the process of forgetting and its contemporary legal embodiments with a focus on the constitutional definition of the state. Thirdly, I move further in seeking explanations to this status of the law in the historical origins of legal modernity in Romania. In this way I intend to assess the political and memorial outcomes of the concealment of law's past by highlighting the possible historical and intellectual origins of law's destitution in the modern Romanian context.

3.2 Picnolepsy, Experience and Exception: Forgetting in the World of Late Capitalism

In his *Aesthetics of Disappearance*, Paul Virilio introduces into cultural studies the concept of picnolepsy, which he devised in order to explore the status of the modern subject through the scrutinizing of the rhetorical, anthropological, and political significance of the disappearance of the object in visual arts and modern culture under the expansion of technology.[1] According to Virilio, hypermodernity brings with it a 'nihilism of speed,'[2] one which radically disturbs the symbolic construction of reality and places the subject in the impossibility of articulating material history within the frameworks of a meaningful narrative. In what could be seen as a rather gloomy prophecy, he writes,

> soon the only thing left will be to forget the specious distinction between the propagation of images or waves and that of objects and bodies, since from now on all duration will be measured in intensity.[3]

Under the dynamics of the modern, experience is dissolved in the continuum of a formless maelstrom of intensities with no beginning or end, in which time becomes resistant to any form of imaginary or symbolic rendering.[4] The picnoleptic is as such the subject of a new zeitgeist, in which

---

[1] Paul Virilio, *Aesthetics of Disappearance*, trans. Phillip Beitchmann (Los Angeles: Semiotext[e], 1991 [1980]).
[2] Virilio, *Aesthetics*, 69.
[3] Virilio, *Aesthetics*, 74.
[4] I use the symbolic and imaginary by referring to two of the three orders of signification present in Lacanian psychoanalysis, namely the Real, Symbolic, and Imaginary. The Symbolic stands for meaning production and integration within language and the Law, whereas

the bridges and railings of the symbolic have fallen into the waves of speed brought by late capitalism. It is a time where distinctions are swallowed up by the continuous movement of a flow of velocity and acceleration,[5] for which time and space are just another by-product of the coupling between the eye and the motor, both capturing the ruin of the image under the nexus relating the machinery of war to technological progress.[6] Picnolepsy, understood as both a symptom of our times and as a new subjective status, stands for 'a momentary lapse of consciousness ... which acclimatizes us to the production of continuities where there are none.'[7]

For the picnoleptic, 'the absence lasts a few seconds ... the arrested word and action are picked up again where they have been interrupted,' just as 'nothing really has happened, the missing time never existed.'[8] It is the frequent disappearance of experience, of a time which vanishes because it has no signification for the subject anymore. But this absence of a meaningful time is doubled by a form of paradoxical hypermnesia, for the picnoleptic 'needs constantly to stretch the limits of his memory' by recreating the past through invention, fabrication, or slips into fantasy.[9] The double of such a strategy is the free float of signification as such, for 'everything certain will become suspect' and the picnoleptic will soon be caught in the maze of her own imagined recollections of a time that she has seemingly never experienced. Consequently for the picnoleptic 'nothing really exists ...; even if there is existence, it cannot be described, and even if it cannot be described, it could certainly not be communicated or explained to others.'[10]

The picnoleptic's state seems to be illuminating for the pathologies and the construction of memory in contemporaneity insofar as it captures the specific strain raised by late capitalism over the symbolic framing of experience. Virilio's poignant description of picnolepsy, a syndrome of a time out of bounds seems to recall closely Walter Benjamin's insights into the end of the narrative.[11] Indeed, in a different context, Benjamin, an attentive

---

the Imaginary determines the subject's self-identification in relation to the 'Ideal-I.' See Alan Sheridan, 'Translator's Note,' in *The Seminar. Book XI: The Four Fundamental Concepts of Psychoanalysis*, Jacques Lacan, ed. Jacques-Alain Miller, trans. Alan Sheridan (New York: Norton and Company, 1978), 279; see also Jacques Lacan, *Écrits*, vol. II (Paris: Le Seuil, 1966 [1958]), 9–61 ; see also Jacques Lacan 'Le Séminaire R.S.I,' *Ornicar?* 4 (1975), 91–106.

[5] Virilio, *Aesthetics*, 60.
[6] Virilio, *Aesthetics*, 56
[7] Sean Cubitt, 'Virilio and New Media,' in *Paul Virillio: From Modernism to Hypermodernism and Beyond*, ed. John Armitage (London: Sage, 2000), 128.
[8] Virilio, *Aesthetics*, 9 and 10.
[9] Virilio, *Aesthetics*, 10.
[10] Virilio, *Aesthetics*, 10.
[11] Jakki Spicer, 'The Author Is Dead, Long Live the Author: Autobiography and the Individual,' *Criticism* 47 (2005), 387–403; see also Richard Harvey Brown, 'The Position of the Narrative in Contemporary Society,' *New Literary History* 11 (1980), 545 where the

observer of modernity, noted with regard to the traumatic heritage of the Great War and of the years following it that 'never has experience been contradicted more thoroughly than strategic experience by tactical warfare, economic experience by inflation, bodily experience by mechanical warfare, moral experience by those in power.'[12] In a world in which the first waves of total war have occurred, experience itself 'has fallen in value and it looks as if to fall into bottomless abyss.'[13] With it, the power of narrative which could before link community together is effaced:

Every glance at a newspaper demonstrates that it has reached a new low, that our picture, not only of the external world but of *the moral world as well*, overnight has undergone changes which were never thought possible.[14]

In the wake of the Great War something in the very way one relates to the world has changed dramatically, to such an extent that many aspects of reality have become expressionless.[15] As Benjamin points out:

With the [First] World War a process began to become apparent which has not halted since then. Was it not noticeable at the end of the war that men returned from the battlefield grown silent—not richer, but poorer in communicable experience?[16]

Accordingly, what we are facing in the interwar period is the radical and violent transformation which befell a whole generation that had to struggle with the unbearable legacy of the conflict. It is the trauma faced by 'a generation that had gone to school on a horse-drawn streetcar' and who, under the pressure of war, 'stood under the open sky in a countryside in which nothing remained unchanged but the clouds, and beneath these clouds, in a field of force of destructive torrents and explosions, was the tiny, fragile human body.'[17] It is thus in the fundamental affirmation of the primacy of technology over the human, which became apparent in the

---

author synthesizes vividly the concept: 'Traditional narrative is dead.'

[12] Walter Benjamin, 'The Storyteller,' in *illuminations*, ed. Hannah Arendt, trans. Harry Zohn (New York: Shocken Books, 1969 [1936]), 84.

[13] Rather than using the German word '*Erlebnis*' for experience, Benjamin makes use of '*Erfahrung*.' As Spicer notes, '*Erfahrung* ... is experience that is ongoing, in that it is not only something that has taken place, but it is also something that is continually taking place—it restructures cognition, or even the experience of experience, thus allowing for a new understanding of old experiences and an openness to new experiences.' Spicer, 'The Author Is Dead,' 394 [original emphasis].

[14] Spicer, 'The Author Is Dead,' 394 [emphasis added].

[15] On the relevance of the concept of the expressionless for the law see Pannu Minkkinen, 'The Expressionless: Law, Ethics and the Imagery of Suffering' *Law & Critique* (2008), 19, 65–85; Shoshanna Felman, *The Juridical Unconscious: Trials and Traumas in the Twentieth Century* (Cambridge, MA: Harvard University Press, 2002), 184–5.

[16] Benjamin, 'The Storyteller,' 84.

[17] Benjamin, 'The Storyteller,' 84.

machinery of the Great War, that the body politic of the interwar will be forged. In the wake of the catastrophe, a new subjectivity emerges, that of the new man 'who is supposed to say a wildly joyful Yes to everything; that says No to the "individuality" of "individuals".'[18] It is this subjectivity which gives way to the ultimate aporia of death and representation raised by the killing machine of the extermination camps and which continues to haunt from within our legal systems.[19]

The traumatic moment of rupture induced by the wars of the twentieth century as well as by the authoritarian takeovers and regimes preceding or following them seems to find itself only on the exoteric side of a deeper change which has undermined from within the modern project of Enlightenment. As Agamben notes in what could be read as a re-joinder to Virilio's concept of picnolepsy, 'today ... we know that the destruction of experience no longer necessitates a catastrophe.'[20] It seems that insofar as we are modern, we are subjected to 'a non-translatability into experience that now makes our everyday experience intolerable.'[21] Just as with Virilio's picnoleptic, we, the moderns, seem to have lost the ability to understand what is happening or has happened with and around us up to the point where 'nothing has really happened.'

Yet while the picnoleptic seems to err forever in the dream-like continuum of a timeless present, subjected to the authorless drive towards speed and progress, Agamben hints that the core of this dissolution of experience lies elsewhere rather than in the self-referential deployment of velocity in late capitalism. Accordingly, the dissolution of experience is the result of a decrease in the power of narrative and in the structure of authority. As he writes, 'experience has its necessary correlation not in knowledge but in authority—that is to say, the power of words and narration.'[22] The modern is thus equivalent to a decoupling of narrative and experience: 'it is the character of the present time that all authority is founded on what cannot be experienced and nobody would be inclined to accept the validity of an authority whose sole claim to legitimation was experience.'[23] This peculiar form of estrangement, through which one is

---

[18] Peter Sloterdijk, *Critique of Cynical Reason*, Michael Eldred trans. (Minneapolis: University of Minnesota Press, 1987 [1983]), 446.

[19] 'The ethical question and the legal question, before and after Auschwitz, the question of a legal semiotics of extermination is a simple one. What is the role of the witness, of testimony in this testament to humanity which is the embodied destruction of humanity and of the human.' David Fraser, 'Dead Man Walking: Law and Ethics after Giorgio Agamben's Auschwitz,' *International Journal for the Semiotics of Law* 12 (1999), 402.

[20] Giorgio Agamben, *Infancy and History: The Destruction of Experience*, trans. Liz Heron (London: Verso, 1993 [1978]), 13.

[21] Agamben, *Infancy*, 14.

[22] Agamben, *Infancy*, 14.

[23] Agamben, *Infancy*, 14.

barred access to the realm of the symbolic is itself revelatory not only for the aesthetics of disappearance, but also for its underlying politics. As Brown rightly observes,
the authority structure that once unified author and auditor has been replaced by a new unification authored by the military, the corporation, the party. As things fall apart on the human level, they are transformed, reintegrated, and reproduced on the bureaucratic level.[24]

Picnolepsy, a subjective status signalling the disappearance of the Object as well as the dissolution of experience is a new stage in the process of alienation inasmuch as it furthers the estrangement of the human subject from within a symbolically crumbling reality. As Marx already observed, capitalism entails through its inherent modes of production, a specific form of separation which marks and interpellates the subject as alienated: 'realization appears as a *loss of reality* to the worker, objectification as loss and bondage to the object and appropriation as estrangement.'[25] While there is an apparent intellectual and material thread linking the destruction of experience to the logic of alienation, one needs to underline their historical situation. Following this line, it is worth noting along with Lukács that alienation is a historical condition inescapably related to specific social configurations.[26]

This position becomes even more apparent in Marx's later theory of commodity fetishism which pushes even further the disquieting traits of alienation by stressing that under the conditions of capitalism social relations take the 'fantastic form of a relation between things.'[27] With the disappearance of experience a new threshold is left behind by the dissolving forces of capital. It is the point where the symbolic erupts and where meaning escapes to the subject. In Lacanian terms, picnolepsy might as well be doubled by anxiety, insofar as the disappearance of the Object rests upon an inability to represent it.[28] If we were to follow Lacan, in anxiety 'the lack lacks,' otherwise the basic separation between the symbolic order which sustains the *psyche* and translates the Real into a meaningful reality fades away.[29] The result is a continuous repetition of a constant failure to represent, a process through which anxiety is conjured to disappear through the stable structure of an empty ritual.[30]

---

[24] Brown, 'The Position of the Narrative,' 549.
[25] Karl Marx, *Early Writings* (Harmondsworth: Penguin, 1975), 324.
[26] György Lukács, *The Young Hegel* (London: Merlin Press, 1975), 549.
[27] Karl Marx, *Capital I*, trans. S. Moore and E. Aveling (Moscow: Foreign Languages Publishing House, 1961), 72.
[28] Mladen Dolar, 'I Shall Be with You on Your Wedding-Night: Lacan and the Uncanny,' October 58 (1991), 7.
[29] Jacques Lacan, *Le séminaire, vol. X: l'angoisse* (Paris, Le Seuil, 2004 [1963]), 53.
[30] Joan Copjec, 'Vampires, Breast-Feeding, and Anxiety,' October 58 (1991), 28 where the author writes: 'It should be evident right away that this negation of the real by the symbolic

The political and memorial significance of the concept of picnolepsy should thus become apparent inasmuch as picnolepsy hints to the field of the limits of representation and the articulation of power. Read through these lenses, picnolepsy might shed a new light over the role of law in our contemporary setting. Indeed, Agamben's indictment of modernity for its dissolution of experience points to his later work in which he directly engages with the politico-juridical consequences of this destitution of the symbolic order and of political authority by addressing directly the status of law. For Agamben, 'the state of exception "in which we live"'[31] bears witness to the disappearance of classical concepts of legality and constitutionalism under the ultimate unfolding of biopolitics. Through the proliferation of exceptional measures, of security dispositives and biopolitical technologies,[32] law does not only suspend itself by a complete effacement of the normative, of the authority of the written word and of the narrative founding a stable polity, but also exposes somehow its inner truth, that of not being anything other than an exception. In his own words:

> Law is made of nothing but what manages to capture inside itself through the inclusive exclusion of the *exceptio*: it nourishes itself on this exception and is a dead letter without it.[33]

In this sense, law under the state of exception is reduced to being a mere reproduction of 'law-preserving violence' which defends the mythical powers of the status quo.[34] It presents itself as a force of law out of the bounds of the demos, a 'mythical violence' which only subjects and colonizes the multitude.[35] Under the strain of the state of exception, force and form, violence and narrative are separated, and law seems to approach the limits of articulating power in a meaningful symbolic construction. Thus, picnolepsy might prove a serviceable conceptual device aimed at highlighting the status of our legal present. In this sense, picnolepsy is understood here as the erratic status of a destitute law which can no longer

---

presents a special problem. The real that is to be negated cannot be represented by a signifier, since the real is, by definition, that which has no adequate signifier. How, then, can this negation take place within the symbolic ...? The answer is: through repetition, through the signifier's repeated attempt—and failure—to designate itself.'

[31] Giorgio Agamben, *State of Exception*, trans. Kevin Attell (Chicago: University of Chicago Press, 2005 [2003]), 86.

[32] Agamben, *State of Exception*, 2.

[33] Giorgio Agamben, *Homo Sacer I: Sovereign Power and Bare Life*, trans. Daniel Heller-Roazen (Stanford: Stanford University Press, 1998 [1995]), 22.

[34] Walter Benjamin 'Critique of Violence,' in *Selected Writings*, vol. 1, ed. Marcus Bullock and Michael W. Jennings (Cambridge: Harvard University Press, 1996 [1921]), 285.

[35] 'The mythical manifestation of immediate violence shows itself identical with all legal violence.' Benjamin, 'Critique of Violence,' 296.

found authority nor exercise it unless in its adulterated forms, as debased force, or 'the "law" of the police.'[36] It is the spectral residue of a legal subject which has become nothing short of a 'monument of its own disappearance,'[37] the ruined image of the 'guarantee of foundations,'[38] which precisely as destitute governs the multitude through its empty utterances. Picnolepsy is, as such, the status of a law under the rule of exception.

3.3 From a History to Forget to the Forgetting of History

However, this structural defect of law is not ahistorical as the Agambenian archaeological intervention linking the state of exception to Roman law and ancient rituals might suggest.[39] It is inscribed in the change befalling European polities with the advent of modernity and it takes a specific form under the globalizing forces of capital and the rise of the bourgeoisie. It might thus not be a surprise that the first modern instantiations of the state of exception appear in the context of the French revolution,[40] paralleled by the general mobilization and the gradual militarization of public life.[41] Nor should it be a surprise that the legal framing of the state of siege paving the way for the authoritarian—rightist and leftist alike—takeovers in Europe were paradigmatically accomplished in the wake of the June uprising of 1848.[42] The state of exception and

---

[36] 'The "law" of the police really marks the point at which the state, whether from impotence or because of the immanent connections within any legal system, can no longer guarantee through the legal system the empirical end that it desires at any price to attain.' Benjamin, 'Critique of Violence,' 287.

[37] Anton Schütz, 'The Fading Memory of Homo non Sacer' in *The Work of Giorgio Agamben: Law, Literature, Life*, ed. Justin Clemens, Nicholas Heron and Alex Murray (Edinburgh: Edinburgh University Press, 2008), 127.

[38] Pierre Legendre, 'The Other Dimension of Law,' *Cardozo Law Review* 4 (1995), 952.

[39] 'There is an institution of Roman law that can in some ways be considered the archetype of the modern *Ausnahmezustand* ...: the *iustitium*.' Agamben, *State of Exception*, 41.

[40] 'Loi du 10 juillet 1791 sur la conservation et le classement des places de guerre et postes militaires,' in *Bulletin des lois depuis le mois du juin 1789 jusqu'au mois d'août 1830*, Vol. II (Paris: Paul Dupont, 1834), 235.

[41] See Daniele Conversi 'Homogenisation, Nationalism and War: Should We Still Read Ernest Gellner?' *Nations and Nationalism* 13 (2007), 371–94. The line of argument inextricably linking modernity to the military experience of the French revolutionary wars and the Napoleonic adventure was also defended by George Mosse who was expressly relating this process to the emergence of fascism, see George L. Mosse, *The Nationalization of the Masses: Political Symbolism and Mass Movements in Germany from the Napoleonic Wars Through the Third Reich* (New York: Howard Fertig, 1975). For the legal origins of this process, see Decree of 23 August 1793 determining the drafting of French citizens against the enemies of France, *Collection complète des lois, décrets, ordonnances, réglements*, ed. Jean Baptiste Duverger, Vol. VI, 2nd edition (Paris: A. Guizot, 1834), 107–8.

[42] Loi du 9 août 1849 sur l'Etat de siège, *Bulletin des lois*, no. 186, 146. See also, Louis-Joseph Gabriel de Chénier, *De l'État de siège, de son utilité et de ses effets* (Paris:

the picnoleptic status of the legal subject are thus part of a history of disappearances that the epigrammatic text of the law archives and documents in its interstices. It is perhaps in this gleaming light of the past, which is the ruining image of the law, that a critical reading of history can find its dwelling. Its aim is to wake from oblivion the disturbing forgotten time that law has erased from its own memory.

Romania's case is intriguing for the legal historian and theorist alike insofar as its constitutional history documents a series of seemingly traumatic breaks throughout the short twentieth century which have been miraculously effaced under the 'white mythology' of neoliberal constitutionalism.[43] Indeed, from 1938 to 1989 Romania found itself under five formally explicit dictatorships and under a legally more diffuse one as set up by the constitution of 1965.

While historians of the interwar period describe the unstable state of the Romanian polity by using the accurate though euphemistic term 'semi-authoritarianism,'[44] the constitution of February 1938 by which Carol II asserted full powers did not leave any doubts about the true nature of the regime which suspended traditional constitutional guarantees in order to legally create and fight the enemies of the nation.[45] The decree of September 1940 by which the King invested Marshall Antonescu with full powers before his own abdication opened the way to the National Legionary State founded on an alliance between the fascist movement and the conservative authoritarian branch of the military.[46] The repression of the fascist rebellion in January 1941 established the National and

Librairie Militaire de J. Dumaine, 1849).

[43] This has been for a long time considered to be the almost mythical endpoint of an otherwise sinuous and confused transition to democracy. The features of this political utopia would be 'liberal democratic politics, capitalist economics, both undergirded by the rule of law.' Adam Czarnota, Martin Krygier and Wojceh Sadurski, *Rethinking the Rule of Law after Communism* (Budapest: Central European University Press, 2005), 1; re 'white mythology,' see Jacques Derrida, *Marges* (Paris: Minuit, 1972), 254: 'White mythology—metaphysics which has effaced in itself that fabulous scene which brought it into being, and which yet remains, active and stirring, inscribed in white ink, an invisible drawing covered over in the palimpsest.'

[44] Michael Mann, *Fascists* (Cambridge, CUP, 2004), 44.

[45] The Romanian Constitution of 1938, M. Of., 27 February 1938. By virtue of its section 100, the Romanian Constitution was brought to the 'good knowledge and consent' of the nation.

[46] Decree no. 3072 of 6 September 1940 investing the President of the Council of Ministers with Full Powers and regarding the Royal Prerogatives, M. Of., 6 September 1940. See, 'King Carol II's Manifesto to the Romanians of 6 September 1940,' in Ioan Scurtu, *România și marile puteri* (1933–1940): Documente (Bucharest: Editura Fundației România de Mâine, 2000), 232. See also Statute no. 550 of 14 September through which the Romanian state becomes a national legionary state, M. Of., 14 September 1940. See also Mann, *Fascists*, 297; Aristotle A. Kallis, *Genocide and Fascism: The Eliminationist Drive in Fascist Europe* (London: Routledge, 2009), 221–2 and 251–5.

Social State under Antonescu's sole rule, a military genocidal enterprise allied to Nazi Germany. The ousting of Antonescu as a consequence of the insurrection of August 1944 was steered by the democratic forces grouped around King Michael conservatives, liberals, social democrats, and communists and restored for a short time and in a limited manner the constitutional monarchy of the interwar period.[47]

However, the King's abdication in 1947 and the proclamation of the people's republic brought with them the constitutions of 1948 and 1952 which were explicitly described as being forms of the 'dictatorship of the proletariat.'[48] For its part, the constitution of 1965, even before the introduction of the office of president and the overall ideological turn towards national communism, was formally identifying the sole party as the 'leading political force of the whole society.'[49]

Read against this background, the core of our constitutional present appears both in historical and memorial terms at least problematic. Art. 1 (3) Romanian Constitution 2003 represents a point of departure for my investigation:

> Romania is a democratic and social state under the rule of law, where human dignity, citizens' freedoms and rights, the free development of human personality, justice and political pluralism constitute supreme values which are guaranteed, in the spirit of Romanian people's democratic traditions and the ideals of the revolution of December 1989.[50]

As a preliminary note, it should be mentioned that the introduction of the new text is strongly related to the political context of early 2000s, one marked by Romania's close accession to NATO and the future closure of the negotiations for EU accession, which both took place in 2004.[51]

---

[47] Richard J. Crampton, *Eastern Europe in the XXth Century and After*, 2nd ed. (London: Routledge, 1997, 228–31); Joseph Rothschild and Nancy M. Wingfield, *Return to Diversity: A Political History of East Central Europe Since World War II*, 3rd ed. (Oxford: OUP, 2000), 105–6; Vlad Georgescu, *The Romanians: A History*, trans. Alexandra Bley-Vorman (Columbus: Ohio State University Press, 1991), 220; High Royal Decree no. 1626 concerning the establishment of the rights of Romanians within the frame of the constitution of 1866 as modified by the constitution of 1923, 31 August 1944, *M. Of.*, 2 September 1944, no. 202, 694.

[48] Constitution of the People's Republic of Romania of 13 April 1948, *M. Of.*, 13 April 1948, No 87 bis.; Constitution of the People's Republic of Romania of 27 September 1952, *B. Of.*, 27 September 1952, No 1; See Tudor Drăgan, *Curs de Drept de Stat al Republicii Populare Romîne* (Bucharest: Tipografia Învățămîntului, 1956), 22 where the author writes that 'the essence of the state is the dictatorship of the proletariat.'

[49] Constitution of the Socialist Republic of Romanian of 21 August, in *B. Of.*, 21 august 1965, no. 1.

[50] Section 1 § 3 of the Constitution of Romania as appended by Statute modifying the Constitution no. 429 of 2003, *M. Of.*, 31 October 2003, no. 767.

[51] See Treaty concerning the accession of the Republic of Bulgaria and Romania to the

The reference to the 'Romanian people's democratic traditions' is of course the point where history and law seem to tread different paths. This sudden slip in wording seems more ambiguous than a mere inaccuracy or just sheer wishful thinking induced by the Euro-Atlantic enthusiasm that, at the time, consumed public opinion and political elites alike.[52] From a purely positivist standpoint, this paragraph is not a recital or a preamble, somehow guiding from outside the legal framework the interpretation of the text. It is formally part of the constitution and as such has binding value inasmuch as it refers to a series of core values of liberal democracy such as pluralism, citizen freedoms, and rights, which are explicitly by virtue of the same text binding.[53] It is not my intention to further explore this formalist approach, but it certainly points towards the fact that the reference to tradition is part of the legal framework that lawyers are to interpret and enforce. In short, this historical reference is part of the law. Its presence in the first article gives it a great deal of semiotic weight inasmuch as it is placed at the core of the legal definition of the Romanian state. The present values of today are guaranteed 'in the spirit' of the past. So much the worse for the present, if the history of the law which now pledges its allegiance to democracy has been marked by its complicity with anti-democracy.

At this juncture, one can legitimately ask where the instantiations of these democratic traditions are to be sought insofar as the constitutional definition of the state relies foremostly on their assertion. A close examination of modern Romanian constitutional history seems to render problematic the state's self-perception as a guarantee of an authentic democratic *nomos*. To be sure, the birth of the modern state under the protection of the six Great Powers in the wake of the Crimean War was doubled by a takeover of the constitutional powers by the prince in a local mimicry of Louis Napoleon's Eighteenth Brumaire.[54] The ousting

European Union, OJ L 157, 21 September 2005, 11–27.

[52] The Eurobarometer of September 2004 indicated an unprecedented level of trust in the EU among Romanian citizens of nothing short of 74% of the respondents. See *Eurobarometer 62*: 'Public Opinion in the European Union, Romania: National Report and Executive Summary' (2004).

[53] The text is referred to unambiguously by the constitutional court in its judgment of 9 July 2012 declaring unconstitutional the provisions of a statute aimed at limiting its prerogatives by placing outside the control of constitutionality decisions taken by the plenum of the Chamber of Representatives, the plenum of the Senate or the plenum of the reunited Chambers of the Parliament. In its analysis, the court reads paragraph 3 together with paragraph 4, stating the principle of the separation of powers in order to strengthen the thesis that 'constitutional justice is a dimension of the Romanian state.' The Constitutional Court of Romania, Judgment no. 727, 9 July 2012, in *M. Of.*, no. 477, 12 July 2012.

[54] The moment was May 1864, when in retaliation to the Assembly's opposition to the agrarian and electoral reform, Alexandru Cuza dissolved it and passed a new constitutional act which enabled him to rule by decree. As historians note with specific reference to the regime put in place by Cuza: 'the essence of Romanian constitutionalism lay in the person of

of the prince and the institution of constitutional monarchy marking the years up to the Great War, a very dear period to the Romanian intellectual establishment, have nonetheless known the use of the state of siege and its most dire consequences under the guise of shelling peasant villages.[55] The authoritarian era opened in the interwar period, with its ultranationalist pledges, followed by the Stalinist dictatorship of the 1950s seem to be far from embodying democratic traditions. For its part, Ceaușescu's rule with its turn towards national communism could hardly be labelled as democratic insofar as the party continued to be an entity acting *supra-legem*.[56]

However, it is worth noting the reference to the ambiguous democratic tradition is further qualified by another reference to the values of the revolution of 1989. Within the rhetorical economy of the text, this latter reference acts contrapuntally as focusing the way in which the past should be read. Whereas these values are still debatable, their instantiations offer a better image of what the state pledges to stand for. The tension at work stays, of course, apparent as it marks a point where declarations such as the Proclamation to the Country of the Council of the National Salvation Front or, arguably, the Timișoara Proclamation are uncannily related to a history of usurpations or at least misunderstandings of democracy.[57]

The revolution is rendered as the moment of rupture with the past which opens up the way to its rephrasing. In an almost Hegelian twist of history, the democratic tradition emerges precisely as a result of the break. If the foundational myth of post-communist societies rests on the demise of their

---

the prince.' Keith Hitchins, *Rumania 1866–947* (Oxford: OUP, 1994), 7. Re the birth of the modern state under the protection of the six Great Powers in the wake of the Crimean War, see Georgescu, *The Romanians*, 146–7.

[55] Such is the case of the peasant revolt of 1907. Keith Hitchins sets a number of 11,000 as the death toll ensuing from the army's intervention, see Hitchins, *Rumania*, 114–5 and 176–8. One of the heroes of the day in the quelling of rebellion was none other than a young captain named Ion Antonescu who was to become Romania's infamous military dictator between 1940 and 1944, see Vladimir Solonari, *Purifying the Nation: Population Exchange and Ethnic Cleansing in Nazi-Allied Romania* (Baltimore: Johns Hopkins University Press, 2010), 117.

[56] Daniel Barbu, *Republica absentă* (Bucharest: Nemira, 1999), 157.

[57] Re Proclamation to the Country of the Council of the National Salvation Front: Issued on the 22 December by the provisional government grouping 'all the healthy forces of the country ... who have bravely and strongly raised in defending freedom and dignity during the years of totalitarian tyranny,' the text was programmaticaly declaring the end of one party rule as well as upholding the protection of human rights, see the Council of the National Salvation Front, *Proclamation to the Country*, M. Of., 25 December 1989, no. 2; Re Timișoara Proclamation: Issued on the 11 March by the representatives of a mass rally in response to a coal mine worker's intervention in Bucharest, the text proclaimed the need to break with the communist past while nonetheless stating in its point 10 that 'although we militate for the re-Europeanisation of Romania, we do not favour copying the Western capitalist systems which have their own flaws and inequities.' See Victor Neuman, *Ideologie și fantasmagorie: Perspective comparative asupra istoriei gîndirii politice în Europa Est-Centrală* (Iasi: Polirom, 2001), 190–6.

past politico-juridical regimes, this disappearance of authoritarianism takes the form of a representational elimination. As Girard points out, foundational myths require a symbolic rupture which is narratively construed as effacement or as sacrifice insofar as 'something like a "radical elimination" does really constitute the high point in the mythical drama and it is supposed to play a crucial role in the establishment of the cultural order.'[58]

While the illocutionary force of such an utterance can be questioned, as the material past continues to stay unaffected by present normativity, the paragraph nonetheless manages ideologically to create a fragile link with an imagined tradition. The political implications of such a strategy are manifold, but the fundamental consequence is that of effacing the past. The gain in legitimacy seemingly justifies such a selective reading of history.

One could of course also concede to this legal slip into a mythical construction of the past. After all, most constitutions would indulge themselves in selectively reading historical reality and adjusting it through the magic powers of legal language. One could also largely interpret the text by referring to a counter-history of struggles going back to the Wallachian uprising of 1821, to the revolution of 1848, or to the workers' movement in the early twentieth century in order to find effective forms for the construction of democracy. But this would be futile inasmuch as democracy in its substantial and procedural form has been constantly negated by political and constitutional practice in Romanian legal history.

One could also believe that what we are dealing with is an ideological construction retroactively creating the past of an imagined community deemed to be democratic once the state renewed its pledges of being a 'liberal and civilized state.'[59] And here one may not be wrong. The constitutional subject recognizes itself as democratic through the gaze of the Western world. It may as well project the phantasm of democracy over the shadows of the past. That is because if one is something at a moment in time, it might as well have been like this ever since its beginnings. And after all, law is there to enact and confirm this phantasm.

In order to counter this strategy devised by the constitutional subject, perhaps the constitutional present should be read under the category of 'tainted law,' that is precisely as 'law that appears to have been produced, or absorbed and "sanitized," by a democratic order but which is connected, explicitly or implicitly, with the anti-democratic past.'[60]

---

[58] René Girard, 'Violence and Representation in the Mythical Text,' *Comparative Literature* 92 (1977), 924.

[59] Résolution [de l'Assemblée parlementaire du Conseil de l'Europe] no. 1096 relative aux mesures de démantèlement de l'héritage des anciens régimes totalitaires communistes du 21 juin 1996, in *Annuaire de la Convention européenne des droits de l'homme*, vol. 39 (La Haye, Martinus Nijhoff, 1988), 580–4, para 1.

[60] Stephen Skinner, '"Tainted Law"? The Italian Penal Code, Fascism and Democracy,'

The most extensive engagement to this day with the recent past directed by the state was the Report on the Communist Dictatorship in Romania, approved by the Parliament in December 2006.[61] A strange indictment of the communist terror, halfway between a legal instrument, political statement, and historical analysis,[62] the report hardly gave any serious attention to the judicial apparatus or the legal discourse during the communist years, let alone the fact of not engaging with the various meanings of communism. With respect to the law, it strikingly and unwittingly concluded that 'the reality of the communist legislation is that of a legislation which, beneath oscillating between pompous formulations and regulations of terror, was that of a state without a legal system.'[63]

Such brusque philistinism may be very much a feature of the prevalent anti-communism, an ideology, which manifested itself principally *post-factum*,[64] that has effectively dominated the cultural spectrum and prevented any serious attempt in critically approaching the content of the communist terror and of the social consensus underlying it. But as the old civil law maxim goes, *nemo auditur propria turpitudinem allegans* (no one can be heard to invoke his own turpitude). In fact this statement, which is ostensibly false in terms of positive law, is to be taken at its face value. According to today's ideological consensus, communist Romania did not have a legal system.

This position suits everyone very well, lawyers, spectacular politicians, activists, and public intellectuals alike, as the problem is closed. There is nothing to be changed, as the system was a legal no-man's land for the previous five decades. There are no questions to be asked, and not much to be criticized either on the left or on the right. While the moral condemnation of communism from the superficial standpoint of contesting a 'criminal regime'[65] based on a criminal ideology placed on a par with other totalitarianisms of the 20th century finds a good venue amongst the cultural right and prevents any questioning of the material history of communism, the left is also quite accommodating, by eschewing the intricate problems of the communist revolution turning awry.[66] This especially suits

---

International Journal of Law in Context 7 (2011), 440, 423–46.

[61] Presidential Commission for the Study of the Communist Dictatorship in Romania, *Raport final* [Final Report] (Bucharest: Humanitas, 2006), accessed 20 October 2014, http://www.presidency.ro/static/ordine/RAPORT_FINAL_CPADCR.pdf; Re 'tainted law,' see 440.

[62] See, Daniel Barbu, 'O istorie naturală a comunismului românesc,' in *Iluzia anticomunismului*, ed. Vasile Ernu et al. (Chișinău : Cartier, 2008), 71–104. At page 72 the author speaks of an 'ethico-scientific condemnation of communism.'

[63] See *Raport final*, 403–6.

[64] Daniel Barbu, 'Prefață,' in Ruxandra Ivan (ed.), *Transformarea Socialistă* (Iassy: Polirom, 2008), 16.

[65] *Raport final*, 628.

[66] Re 'criminal regime,' see *Raport final*, 628. Re totalitarianisms of the 20th century see,

the state's ideology with regards to its own representation. Communism was an accident, an 'exotic import' from the east bestowed upon the country by the Stalinist terror and the dire situation of the last war.[67] And this is how the picnoleptic state resolves itself as 'the arrested word and action are picked up again where they have been interrupted.'[68]

But was this interruption real? Was the constitutional subject arrested by its connivance with politics during the communist 'nightmare?'[69] Has this nightmare ended? Or rather was there no interruption at all, as one dictatorship easily changed guises from one to another and law never ceased to be law whether under the fascist marches, the massacres in Ukraine, the red terror of the 1950s, or Ceaușescu's 'sultanism'?[70]

In 1930, one of the most influential Romanian legal theorists of the time, Mircea Djuvara, Chair of Legal Theory at the University of Bucharest and one of the authors of the Code, did not find any theoretical impediment whatsoever in writing in his *Treatise of General Theory of Law* that the law 'seeks to find preventive measures in order to eliminate evil through special measures of social hygiene.'[71] Such utterances, as strange as they may sound now coming from a celebrated neo-Kantian philosopher and member of the liberal party of the time, do indeed echo the pre-eminence granted to the state, the social collective, and biopolitics in Romanian legal thought of that period. Indeed, as the same author ventures to decree: 'society ... and thus the State ... constitutes the material from which the fundamental reality of each of us is woven into our soul.'[72]

Moreover, another prominent figure of the Romanian public law, Paul Negulescu, argued in the midst of the authoritarian era that law is founded on nothing but pure, unregulated force:

> It necessarily has to be a coercive force, it necessarily has to be a great *physical* power, which has to be irresistible, that is it cannot be fought against by somebody within society, it has to be above everything, to be so superior (*sic*) that no resistance would be possible.[73]

---

e.g. Vladimir Tismăneanu, *The Devil in History: Communism, Fascism and Some Lessons of the Twentieth Century* (Berkeley: University of California Press, 2012), 220–6.

[67] Vladimir Tismăneanu, *Stalinism for all Seasons*, (Berkeley: University of California Press, 2003), 37.

[68] Virilio, *Aesthetics*, 9.

[69] Tismăneanu, *The Devil in History*, 49.

[70] See Houchang E. Chehabi and Juan J. Linz, 'A Theory of Sultanism: A Type of Non-democratic Regime,' in *Sultanistic Regimes*, ed. Houchang E. Chehabi and Juan J. Linz (Baltimore: Johns Hopkins University Press, 1998), 3–26.

[71] Mircea Djuvara, *Teoria generală a dreptului* (Bucharest, All Beck, 1999 [1930]), 106.

[72] Djuvara, *Teoria generală*, 73.

[73] Paul Negulescu, *Curs de drept constituțional român* (Bucharest: Ion I. Borșan, 1939), 11.

If the picnoleptic state resolves itself through a recollection of an imagined time when the actions of the subject have been arrested by the continuous movement of modernity, the ongoing re-enactment of the interwar has all the ominous signs of a return of the repressed. That is because, as these texts suggest, fascist ideological tropes were already a common currency among lawyers of those troubled times before the turn towards overt authoritarianism. Thus, a selective reading of the past which forgets the authoritarian drive in modern times cannot but be misguiding with regards to law's deeper history.

To be sure, the fascination of lawyers with unregulated force is not only a sign of fascism or right-wing authoritarianism. As Stalinist lawyers from the time of the 'obsessive decade' would argue, law is an instrument of power, one which is devised to 'liquidate all the capitalist traces in the economy, in social relations and in the attitude of citizens,' to 'vitalize socialist discipline' and to 'activate the fight for defense.'[74] In the times of national communism, law would not only be imbued with life, but also endowed with the uncanny ability of being 'real,' that is 'adapted to the conditions of life,' unlike the law of other countries.[75] It is thus in a continuous relation with the movements of the unregulated *bios*, inasmuch as the constitution is called to 'give a legal form to the realities imposed by life.'[76]

These statements mark the moments punctuating the picnoleptic state. They are what the legal subject forgets while returning to the aseptic realm of formal rationality which apparently has always been there. They represent the material of forgetting, that excess in law's framework which the legal subject will sever from itself as its other, arrested by the powers of horror.[77] What is indeed uncanny in these theoretical slips now effectively foreclosed as a consummated past, is the ways in which they enclose the tension between form and force, between law and violence. By bringing to the fore this relation of exception (*ex-capere*), the authoritarian definitional spectrum of legality constitutes a form of law's self-reflexivity with regards to the relation legal discourse entertains with the reality it tries to regulate, the relation between law and the history it attempts to formalize. As such, the picnoleptic state presents itself as a symptom, as a structure concealing

---

[74] Tudor Drăgan, *Curs de Drept de Stat al Republicii Populare Romîne* (Bucarest: Tipografia Învățămîntului, 1956), 5.

[75] Tudor Drăganu, *Drept constituțional* (Bucharest: Editura. Didactică și Pedagogică, 1972), 21.

[76] Nicolae Ceaușescu, *România pe drumul construirii societății multilateral dezvoltate*, vol. VI (Bucharest : Meridiane, 1972), 203.

[77] 'The abject is the violence of mourning for an object that has always already been forever lost.' Julia Kristeva, *Pouvoirs de l'horreur* (Paris, Le Seuil, 1980), 22. In English: Julia Kristeva, *Powers of Horror*, Leon S. Roudiez trans. (New York, Columbia University Press, 1982), 15.

the ways in which law/the subject enjoys its unconscious,[78] but also as a limit-case of recognition in which the law encounters its own unconscious and posits it *as* other.

3.4 The Material of Forgetting: Law's Unconscious

Picnolepsy is thus not only the sign of a trauma, though it is related to it. It is not the remainder of that which has not been able to be integrated into the narrative constituting the subject.[79] Rather, it is through the picnoleptic symptom that we are able to understand trauma as the moment enabling this very remainder of experience to posit itself as unconscious. In the Romanian case—thus it is not authoritarian history blurring or irrupting into the otherwise 'normal' life of law—it is not the excess which is concealed and forgotten, which is responsible for repression, but, in a sense, the excess that has always been there. Law's tension with violence and illegality is structural to the very process of formalization of the law, inasmuch as positing a law is to do violence to reality. Of course, legal outbursts of violence rendering visible the necropolitical dimensions of law are not the rule of legal dynamics, yet they are the other side in which law's real becomes apparent. The traumatic authoritarian experience just brought to the fore what had already been there in the depths of the juridical unconscious since its origins.

Modern law's emergence in Romania is inescapably related to the advent of capitalism. Indeed, the drafting of the first constitutions for the Danubian principalities started while the first French ships set sail for the port of Braila in the early 1830s to charge up with grain. As a result of the Ottoman defeat in the Russo-Ottoman war of 1829, the Danube was opened to free trade, while the principalities were placed under a Russian protectorate. Modern institutions, such as Parliament, the autonomy of the judiciary, or the army would find their origins in this opening event which involved the principalities in the globalizing economy.[80]

The status of the principalities was strongly connected to the new network of relations to territory and trade, while their shifting sovereignty

---

[78] 'The symptom cannot be defined otherwise than by the ways in which one enjoys the unconscious in as much as the unconscious determines them.' Jacques Lacan, 'La lecture du 17 décembre 1974,' *Ornicar?* 2 (1975), 100.

[79] Slavoj Žižek, *Quatre variations philosophiques sur un thème cartésien* (Paris: Germina, 2010), 182.

[80] See, Vlad Georgescu, *The Romanians*, 100–4 ; Barbara Jelavich, *Russia and the Formation of the Romanian National State* (Cambridge: CUP, 1984); Angela Jianu, *A Circle of Friends: Romanian Political Exile, 1840–1859* (Leiden: Brill, 2011); Keith Hitchins, *Rumania 1866–1947*, 11.

depended on the flows of merchandise and the arrival of fluid modernity. Power relations and old hierarchies were thus formalized and the whole legal landscape moved toward a thorough integration of Western institutions through a tremendous work of translation directed by the state and the elites. Or, at least, this is how the story goes. These legal, political, and cultural dynamics took place mainly at a symbolic level. Ottoman subjects were turned into Romanian citizens in less than five decades; the old medieval world embraced rising capital.

But one should be attentive to the background movement which is obscured by the textual structure of legal modernity. As Gáspár Miklós Tamás argues:

> Old Eastern Europe under the four empires (Hohenzollern, Habsburg, Romanov and Ottoman) in spite of all the half-hearted or simply bogus reforms after 1848 remained, with the exception of the Western fringe and a few other pockets of modernity, an agrarian caste society where the overwhelming majority of the population lived in personal servitude, humility, deference, illiteracy, corvée and scurvy, not to speak of an ecclesiastical reign and brutal terror by the gendarmerie and feudal flunkeys.[81]

What is apparent at this stage is the very tension between the postulate of modernity and the darker undertones of 'real' life. This, however, should not be read as an argument for a simple rift between politico-legal promises or mere constitutional window dressing and the true social reality specific to a backward society. Modernity emerges in Romania through and, I would say, precisely because of this tension. From the marriage between the aristocracy of the land and the aristocracy of the letter, the old order restates itself as an illegitimate excrescence of modern legality. The *ancien régime* posits itself as old by being re-included in the dynamics of the modern. Inasmuch as law formalizes power relations, and in its modern guise aims at controlling and rationalizing the circulation of power, it produces in this context its very Otherness. Modernity is thus the postulation of the legal unconscious.

It is not by chance that the state of exception under the form of the state of siege is for the first time framed and construed in Romanian law together with the Civil Code and the Criminal Code and *before* the constitution.[82] The old discretionary powers of the prince are thus reintroduced into the framework of the law. Citizens may enjoy equal rights and freedoms, but these rights can always be suspended. Law may protect individuals and

---

[81] Gáspár Miklós Tamás, 'A Capitalism Pure and Simple,' *Left Curve* 32 (2008), 68.
[82] 'Lege pentru starea de asediu din 10 decembrie 1864' [Statute for the State of Siege of 10 December 1864], in *Starea de asediu: doctrină, jurisprudență și legislație*, V. Pantelimonescu (Bucharest: Cartea Românească, 1939), 30–1. The first modern formal constitution was adopted only in 1866.

communities, but first of all it has to assert the possibility of instituting itself as a force, by creating the possibility of its own suspension. Exception is thus at the core of the nexus between law, modernity, and capitalism in the Romanian case. The relation between legal and illegal, between the law's rational façade and its unconscious underside thus becomes apparent through the system of separation held in place by the juristic institution. That is to say, that inasmuch as law separates the real of contingent life from the symbolic of its legal logic, thus acting as religion, it also produces its own unconscious, the excess which constitutes law's exteriority.[83]

Intellectual austerity in Romania's legal world may be also a sign of our times, but its historical roots lie elsewhere. The prominence of legal exegesis during the long 19th century, of legal positivism throughout the 20th, and of the epithelial doctrinal dogmatic sustaining our present legal ideology, are not only epistemological modes which came with the French imports of early modernity, but also a constitutive part of the Romanian modern nomos with far-reaching political consequences. Indeed, the enthusiastic reception of the French Civil Code in the early 1860s was widely perceived as 'a great step towards civilization' insofar as 'French law is the best, the most accomplished ... adopted by most of the civilized States.'[84] Steered by the former revolutionaries of 1848—most of whom had by that time become conservative nationalists—and supported by an enlightened aristocracy which saw the law as nothing short of a means of defending 'property and family ... against barbarian ideas fostered at the core of non-knowledge,'[85] the new legal system also borrowed the style and the fascination with form and science prevalent in the French tradition.[86] As Constantin Dissescu, a prominent Romanian constitutionalist of the early 20th century, argued, the originality of Romanian public law 'is almost null as it contains no national or historic law.'[87] The law seems to be that of a community avidly to break with its origins, as its legists, 'disciples of the schools of law of France, of Belgium and London (*sic*), have made a *tabula*

---

[83] 'Religion can be defined as that which removes things, places, animals, or people from common use and transfers them to a separate sphere. Not only there is no religion without separation, but every separation also contains and preserves within itself a genuinely religious core.' Giorgio Agamben, *Profanations*, trans. Jeff Fort (New York, Zone Books, 2007), 74.

[84] Andrei Rădulescu, Șaizeci *de ani de Cod civil* (Bucharest: Cultura națională, 1926), 13.

[85] The words have been uttered by Prince Bibescu, the last Wallachian Prince before the Crimean war, on the occasion of the graduation ceremony at the Law Faculty in 1852. See Andrei Rădulescu, *Cercetări asupra învățământului dreptului în Țara Românească până la anul 1865*, (Bucharest: Institutul de editură și arte grafice 'Flacăra,' 1912), 48.

[86] See Pierre Legrand, *Pour la relevance des droits étrangers* (Paris : IRJS, 2014), 170–98.

[87] Constantin Dissescu, 'L'évolution du droit public roumain' in *Les transformations du droit dans les principaux pays depuis cinquante ans, 1869–1919: livre du cinquantenaire de la Société de législation comparée*, Collectif, vol. II (Paris: L.G.D.J, 1922), 297.

rasa out of the institutions of the past.'[88] What is sure, the division between the written, official law, taught in universities and practised by the courts and the experience of law within the communities could not have been starker. As such, it has been stated that 'our written law is almost entirely the law of Western Europe.'[89]

This trend of disregarding history and experience is not specific only to the troubled times of the early twentieth century. It finds its continuity even during the times of actually existing socialism, when in open contradistinction to the ideological pledges of effectively sustaining popular democracy, legal discourse was constitutively sustained by a thorough formalism. As one of the embodiments of the constitutional 'doctrinal entity' of the time argued, 'a norm always presupposes a form.'[90] To be sure, according to the national communist turn of the time such forms were deemed far from being empty as they were only 'a reflection of the path taken by working men in building and the multilateral development of socialism.'[91]

The regime change of 1989 did not change much in the ways legal and state ideology were framed in their mutual support. As such, up to this day law is prominently conceived as a system of norms sustaining the state, which for its part is considered a reflection of the natural order. The leading treatise of constitutional law nowadays reads that the 'state ... expresses the natural order, it copies it, it reproduces it.'[92] On the other hand the law is 'a systematic organization of legal norms.'[93] While the Kelsenian tropes are of course present in this framework, they are supplemented by a strange slip which supports the primacy of state conceived as the place of sovereignty.[94] We are thus compelled to understand the law as a 'structure of rules secured and guaranteed by the state which aim at organizing and disciplining human conduct.'[95] Although 'when one says "law," one says "rule" or "norm",' the ultimate function of the legal system is to 'realize

---

[88] See Dissesco, 'L'évolution.' Obviously Dissescu was not willing to admit the logic at work in the process of national unification and modernization in another context as wittingly synthesized by Lampedusa in *The Leopard* through the words of Tancredi: 'If we want things to stay as they are, things will have to change.'

[89] Constantin Dissesco, *Les origines du droit roumain* (Paris: Chamerot et Renouard, 1899), 70–1.

[90] Tudor Drăganu, *Drept constituțional*, (Bucharest: Editura Didactică și Pedagogică, 1972), 19.

[91] Drăganu, *Drept constituțional*, 21.

[92] Ioan Muraru and Simina-Elena Tănăsescu, *Drept constituțional și instituții politice*, 13th ed. (Bucharest: CH Beck, 2008), 3.

[93] Muraru and Tănăsescu, *Drept constituțional*, 10.

[94] Hans Kelsen, *General Theory of Law and State*, trans. Anders Wedberg (Cambridge: Harvard University Press, 1949 [1934]), p. 110, where the author writes: 'The legal order is a system of legal norms.'

[95] Nicolae Popa, *Teoria generală a dreptului* (Bucharest: CH Beck, 2008), 70.

the organization of a *concrete social order*.'⁹⁶ According to Romanian's legal theoretical discourse, behind the systematic façade of the law one finds the brute force of the state. In this theoretical staging Carl Schmitt paradoxically rejoins Kelsen and constructs the myth of a law and a state without history or struggle, yet founded on the sovereign decision. In mutual support, law and politics come together in creating the mystique of a state whose force has the qualities of an Aristotelian form.

The opposition between a formalized and structured language and the formless forces which come to sustain it recalls at the same time the paradigmatic division in psychoanalytical discourse between reality as a symbolically constructed domain instituted through language, and the real, which is either an unnameable 'out-there' waiting to be colonized by the symbolic,⁹⁷ or a surplus, an excrescence of the symbolic order itself,⁹⁸ which relates to the subject through the unconscious. In this sense, perhaps it is apt to say that the paucity of legal knowledge within the dominant discourse celebrating the law as a form is rather a strategy in the production and repression of the legal unconscious.

As long as law's ostensible part keeps its coherent appearance, as long as repression functions, the unconscious excess is deemed kept at bay. After all, as a form of social magic, the law has not ceased to be placed on the side of the Symbolic.⁹⁹ The authoritative style and stubborn philistinism marking most Romanian legal textbooks insisting on law's autonomy, its technicity, and scientificity are part of a strategy sustaining life separate from law on the one hand, while refusing the articulation of experience within the legal sphere on the other. They instil forgetting of the past and keep the separation between law and life possible to the extent that law is a system of norms devoid of factual signification, which as an empty form governs the polity nonetheless. As Dissescu argued, this law 'is a law which is not lived, it is not the result of facts. Rather, it created them.'¹⁰⁰

---

⁹⁶ Dan Claudiu Dănișor, Ion Dogaru and Gheorghe Dănișor, *Teoria generală a dreptului* (Bucharest: CH Beck, 2006), 28 and 3 [emphasis added]. This concept echoes Carl Schmitt's view that 'every general norm demands a normal, every day frame of life to which it can be factually applied and which is subjected to its regulations.' Carl Schmitt, *Political Theology*, trans. George Schwab (Cambridge: MIT Press), 13.

⁹⁷ 'Cancelling out the real, the symbolic creates reality, reality as that which is named by language and can thus be thought and talked about.' Bruce Fink, *The Lacanian Subject: Between Language and Jouissance* (Princeton: Princeton University Press, 1995), 25.

⁹⁸ The post-symbolic Real 'is a product of the symbolic order, a residue or surplus-effect that exists or comes into being only as a result of the symbolic operation that excludes it.' Charles Shepherdson, *Lacan and the Limits of Language* (New York: Fordham University Press, 2008), 27.

⁹⁹ As Lacan writes, 'it is there [in law schools] where the existence of codes renders apparent the fact that language keeps itself apart, being constituted through ages.' Jacques Lacan, *Le séminaire XX. Encore* (Paris: Le Seuil, 1975), 10.

¹⁰⁰ Dissesco, 'L'évolution,' 297.

Intellectual austerity keeps the law and its unconscious in a state of continual *jouissance*. This foreclosure of the real finds itself at the core of what renders the legal unconscious possible, law's real can thus be celebrated as such, as the very extimate of the order vanquishing life. Through its policies of forgetting the past and erasing law's mythical origins, it celebrates law's underside, it exposes it as a carnival of public transgressions, that of a law which is rendered as pure semblance, as a free floating signifier, devoid of reality and altogether more real.

The path to be taken by the critical lawyer in relation to this constant erasure of the past is one of an attempt at recalling to the destitute law its own fragility, which is that of being inscribed in history. It is, otherwise said, a way of identifying the legal subject with its own enmeshed symptoms and unearthing its own symbolic limits. The aim is perhaps not to restate the classical relation between word and authority, nor that of fully recuperating experience as the founder of knowledge and guarantor of the polity. Under the changes befalling law and politics in the last century these are mere utopian phantasms or perhaps illusions of a return to an embellished past in which law was still law. The more modest and perhaps more difficult task is to recount law's history in relation to what it archives and documents without recognizing it as part of its structure. That is because the law not only founds and found itself at the core of countless forms of oppression, but in its historical dimension it also signals negatively its relation to a history of struggle.

As Benjamin notes in his *Theses on the Philosophy of History*, 'not man or men, but the struggling, oppressed class itself are the depository of historical knowledge.'[101] A critical historical engagement with law's picnoleptic state is therefore a focus on the repressed memory of the law, that which articulates through negation and repression the inner history of struggle from which the law has emerged. Redeeming the law's amnesia through recalling its material history is thus breaking with its own mythical authority and reading its past from the margins it constantly negates.

---

[101] Walter Benjamin, 'Theses on the Philosophy of History' in *Illuminations*, ed. Hannah Arendt, Harry Zohn trans. (Schocken Books: New York, 1969 [1940]), 260.

4

Demons of the Past? Legal Survivals of the Socialist Legal Tradition in Contemporary Polish Private Law

Rafał Mańko

> According to a stereotype ... 'the real socialism' was ... a kind of blackout of European legal history.[1]
>
> —Tomasz Giaro

4.1 Introduction

The radical socio-economic transformation from capitalism to actually existing socialism, which occurred in Poland after World War II, was caused by external factors—firstly, the liberation of Polish territories from German occupation by the Red Army, and secondly, the macro-political decisions taken by the victorious powers as to Poland's subjection to Soviet tutelage as part of the 'Eastern bloc.'[2] Polish Communists were fully aware that social support for their rule was low, and therefore never dared to organize truly free elections or referenda. Regardless of the successes of Communist rule in Poland in the fields of social progress and economic development,[3] this notorious lack of democratic legitimacy and the consciousness of external imposition of the Communist government have been weighing heavily on commonly held views about the period of actually existing socialism. The stifling lack of political choice (with

---

[1] Tomasz Giaro, 'Some Prejudices about the Legal Tradition of Eastern Europe,' in *Comparative Law in Eastern and Central Europe*, ed. Bronisław Sitek, Jakub Szczerbowski and Aleksander Bauknecht (Newcastle-upon-Tyne: Cambridge Scholars Publishing, 2013), 26–50, 45.

[2] Jerzy J. Wiatr, 'PZPR w pojałtańskiej rzeczywistości' [The Polish United Workers' Party in the Post-Yalta Reality] in *Polska pod rządami PZPR* [Poland under PZPR Rule], ed. Mieczysław F. Rakowski (Warszawa: PROFI, 2000), 293.

[3] Cf. Jan Sowa, 'An Unexpected Twist of Ideology. Neoliberalism and the Collapse of the Soviet Block,' *Praktyka Teoretyczna* 5 (2012), 153–80, 172–3.

systematically falsified elections) and the constant repression of the freedom of expression by preventive censorship, both features enduring throughout the period, have left an overall negative impression of People's Poland even on intellectuals of a sincerely left-wing orientation. If we add to this the widely felt symptoms of Poland's long-term economic crisis which began at the end of the 1970s and spread over the subsequent decade, limiting consumer access to even the most basic goods, it will not come as a surprise that the need for a transformation from actually existing socialism to a market economy was widely accepted. This background well explains why actually existing socialism does not enjoy a particular prestige, also among legal elites, which has led to the adoption of a dominant narrative aimed at downplaying the role of state socialist legal survivals in Polish legal culture.

The purpose of the present chapter is to critically reflect on the dominant narrative of discontinuity with the state socialist past within legal culture. To this end, the chapter will focus on legal survivals of the period of actually existing socialism in private law. Due to the large number of such survivals, the chapter will analyze only four selected examples, two from substantive civil law and two from civil procedure. What is characteristic for the four legal institutions which will be discussed in more detail is that despite their state socialist origin (they date, respectively, from 1950, 1953, 1961, and 1964), they are still being resorted to in practice after the transformation of 1989. This patent fact will serve as a basis to destabilize the dominant anti-communist narrative about discontinuity in Polish legal culture: if legal institutions created under communist rule in Poland are still useful after the transformation, this period cannot be treated as a 'legal black hole' or 'blackout' of Polish legal history. To the contrary, any historical narrative of Polish legal culture should take the period of actually existing socialism (1944–89) into account, treating it *al pari* with any other period of reduced national sovereignty, such as the period of the Duchy of Warsaw (1807–14) or the period of the semi-sovereign Kingdom of Poland (1815–31) created by the Congress of Vienna.[4] Despite the radically different foundations of the socio-economic system (actually existing socialism vs. capitalism), institutions of private law developed during the socialist period have proven to be useful today. This paradoxical feature of legal survivals—their capability of surviving a radical transformation from one system to another—leads me to draw more general conclusions on legal survivals and legal culture, claiming that they are a normal, physiological feature of legal culture, rather than its pathology.

The present chapter is structured as follows: the present chapter begins with a presentation of the dominant narrative about the state socialist

---

[4] Cf. Andrzej Leon Sowa, *Historia polityczna Polski 1944–1991* (Kraków: Wydawnictwo Literackie, 2011), s. 719.

past. This is followed by a discussion of four examples of post-socialist legal survivals in Polish private law. The final section makes more general, concluding remarks about legal survivals and legal culture.

4.2 A Blackout only Worth Forgetting: Narratives of the State socialist Past

As Polish legal historian Tomasz Giaro recently pointed out:

> According to a stereotype ... 'the real socialism' was a historical regression; indeed, a kind of blackout of European legal history. ... [T]he law of real socialism aligns neither with the preceding nor with the following system and should be forgotten straight away.[5]

This approach to the period of actually existing socialism as a 'blackout' applies not only to the legal community, but to the public discourse in Poland in general. A 'discourse of transformation,' which remains dominant, structures the narrative of the past and the interpretation of historic events. Doubtlessly, Poland's history during the last century was marked by perplexing discontinuity. These radical changes affected all aspects of social life—from property regimes to state boundaries, from organization of the workplace to the overall economic system, and from procedural rights of the parties to the organization of judiciary. Such radical changes, undermining the feeling of sense and purpose, need to be built into a broader narrative structure, lending them a feeling of order and teleology. In the general discourse of the past in post-1989 Poland this function has been played by a figure which I have elsewhere proposed referring to as the 'RETURN TO EUROPE schema.'[6] This schema is composed in the same way as any classical narrative structure (from the old Russian fairy tale to a scholarly paper), in that it is based on three compositional elements—a SOURCE, a PATH, and a GOAL.[7] The narrative commences with the SOURCE, then progresses along the PATH in order to reach the GOAL.

In the RETURN TO EUROPE schema the three compositional elements can be identified as follows. First is the initial stage (i.e. the SOURCE), during which Poland is presented as belonging to the (prestige lending) West. This stage corresponds to the period of the Second Republic (1918–39).

---

[5] Giaro, 'Some Prejudices,' 45.

[6] Rafał Mańko, 'Weeds in the Gardens of Justice? The Survival of Hyperpositivism in Polish Legal Culture as Symptom/*Sinthome*,' *Pólemos: Journal of Law, Literature and Culture* 7/2 (2013), 207–33, 210–12.

[7] On narratives and their compositional structures, see, e.g. Steven L. Winter, *A Clearing in the Forest: Law, Life and Mind* (Chicago-London: University of Chicago Press, 2001), 108–11.

The SOURCE is a point of reference for the entire narrative, and therefore the Second Republic is heavily idealized both in popular media and in historiography.[8]

The second stage in the narrative is the PATH, a transitory period, characterized by a lack and imbalance. In the RETURN TO EUROPE schema, the PATH is what is presented as Poland's submission to Soviet domination, which—in contrast to the previous period (the SOURCE) is shown as her 'kidnapping *away from* Europe.' The narrative structure thus detracts away from facts pointing to the development and progress of the nation's society and economy during actually existing socialism,[9] but focuses exclusively on moments of anti-regime revolt and struggle (1956, 1968, 1970, 1976, 1980–81 and subsequent repressions),[10] even structuring the periodization of Poland's post-War history by reference to those events. Important as they undoubtedly are, the predominant focus on those moments of struggle under the RETURN TO EUROPE schema makes the narrative of Polish history one-sided.

The PATH in line with its compositional function obviously leads to the GOAL or *agon* that is the third and final stage of the narrative, lending sense to the previous compositional elements. Therefore, if Poland's initial balanced starting point was in the West (SOURCE) and this balance was distorted by subjection to the East (PATH), the GOAL is Poland's RETURN TO EUROPE. This corresponds to what Polish constitutional lawyer Wojciech Sadurski identified as the 'discourse of "normalcy",' typical of post-transition Central European countries, which boils down to the wish to have

> no experiments; [the wish] to build a normal country, a normal economy, a normal constitutional rule-of-law [where 'normal' refers] invariably ... to a situation corresponding to the (real or imagined) state of affairs in Western Europe or North America.[11]

---

[8] See Agnieszka Mrozik, 'II RP—raj utracony, raj odzyskany' [The Second Republic: Paradise Lost, Paradise Regained], *Bez dogmatu* 93 (2012).

[9] An attempt to revindicate those positive aspects of actually existing socialism have been recently made by the authors of two collective works: Piotr Szumlewicz and Jakub Majmurek, ed., *PRL bez uprzedzeń* [The Polish People's Republic Without Prejudices] (Warszawa: Książka i Prasa, 2010) and Wiesław Żółtkowski, ed., *Zrozumieć PRL* [Understanding the Polish People's Republic] (Warszawa: Muza, 2012).

[10] In June 1956 workers organized riots in Poznań; in March 1968 students protested against excessive censorship in the field of culture; in December 1970 workers protested against rises in the prices of heavily subsidized meat; in June 1976 workers once again protested against attempts to reduce the subsidizing of foodstuff prices; in 1980 workers went on strike for the same reason, but this time the weakened Communist government entered into a social contract (August 1980), broken the next year (December 1981) by the introduction of Martial Law.

[11] Wojciech Sadurski, 'Transitional Constitutionalism: Simplistic and Fancy Theories,' in *Rethinking the Rule of Law After Communism*, ed. Adam Czarnota et al. (Budapest: CEU Press, 2005), 9–24, 9.

In the Polish context, let us add that 'normal' also refers on various occasions to the idealized period of the Second Republic.[12]

Any narrative has a certain agenda and political consequences. The RETURN TO EUROPE schema is no exception here. The most important consequence of adopting this narrative is the view of the transformation of 1989 as a historical necessity, the outcome of a 45-year-long struggle for freedom and independence from foreign occupation rather than a conscious, reflected upon, and informed choice of society.[13] If the transformation of 1989, especially the Shock Therapy,[14] is presented in this teleological way, this allows concealment of the fact that the Polish reformers could have chosen between different varieties of a market economy, instead of opting for the most neoliberal one, as they did. Furthermore, the RETURN TO EUROPE schema also disempowers Polish society, depriving it of the status of conscious subject of historical change, and transforming it into a mass, subjected to destiny or to choices made by enlightened elites.

A further consequence of the dominant narrative is the representation of actually existing socialism as, to use Giaro's expression cited above, a 'blackout' in Polish history,[15] a period tainted with only negative features, an utterly illegitimate regime.[16] This delegitimization has of course the other side of the coin—an unqualified legitimization of the imposition of neoliberal governance after 1989.[17] Under such circumstances, any form of continuity or even semblance with the period of actually existing socialism becomes, therefore, problematic, and can be employed as a delegitimizing argument.[18] This allows neoliberals and neoconservatives to discard any proposals aiming at ensuring greater social justice solely on the premise that this or that solution bears a similarity to a certain solution known during the period of actually existing socialism. An example of this approach is a paper by Polish private lawyer and ECJ judge Marek Safjan, in which

---

[12] See Mrozik, 'II RP.'

[13] Marta Trawińska, 'Współczesne polskie feministki o możliwościach upodmiotowienia kobiet w okresie PRL-u' [Contemporary Polish Feminists on the Possibilities of Female Empowerment in the Period of the Polish People's Republic], in Szumlewicz and Majmurek, *PRL bez uprzedzeń*, 185; Mańko, 'Weeds,' 211.

[14] On which see especially: Jane Hardy, *Poland's New Capitalism* (London-New York: Pluto Press, 2009), ch. 3 and Tadeusz Kowalik, *From Solidarity to Sellout: The Restoration of Capitalism in Poland* (New York: Monthly Review Press, 2011), part 1.

[15] Giaro, 'Some Prejudices,' 45.

[16] Jakub Majmurek and Piotr Szumlewicz, 'Fakty i mity o PRL-u' [Facts and Myths About the Polish People's Republic], in *PRL bez uprzedzeń...*, p. 8–9. Cf. David Ost, 'Wstęp' [Introduction] in *Prywatyzując Polskę. O bobofrutach, wielkim biznesie i restrukturyzacji pracy* [Privatizing Poland: Baby Food, Big Business and the Remaking of Labor], Elizabeth C. Dunn, trans. Przemysław Sadura (Warszawa: Wydawnictwo Krytyki Politycznej, 2008), 5–12, 11.

[17] Majmurek and Szumlewicz, 'Fakty i mity,' 15.

[18] Majmurek and Szumlewicz, 'Fakty i mity,' 16.

he expresses his scepticism with regard to the promotion of social justice in private law, preferring the liberal paradigm of autonomy, and treating social justice as the 'publicization' of private law. Among the arguments raised is a historical one—placed in a section symptomatically entitled 'Socialist Lesson'—where he writes:

> The tendencies to publicize private law, which seem to question its autonomous goals and values and to blur the division between private and public law, are nothing new in the history of the twentieth century. Being aware of all the differences, *we must not forget an experiment carried out for decades in Eastern and Central Europe* which systematically undermined the idea of private law and its status as a branch of law independent from public law. ... [T]o some extent the lesson learnt from that 'experiment' may be useful and instructive in as much as it shows that there is an impassable border to the interference with private law, beyond which there is a risk of damaging the core of its structures.[19]

The above passage confirms the view that the Polish legal community is imbued in the same RETURN TO EUROPE narrative which is applicable in general political and historical discourse. Whereas the general compositional structure remains the same, with the idealization of the period of the Second Republic and, in particular, its legal output such as the Code of Obligations,[20] and a negative evaluation of the period of actually existing socialism, there are some interesting specific conceptual figures in the legal narrative which I would like to draw attention to. I have labelled them elsewhere as the CONTAINER schema, the SUBMISSION metaphor, the PURIFICATION metaphor, and the RECONSTRUCTION metaphor.[21]

The CONTAINER schema is used to stress the fact that Poland was always part of the Western legal tradition, the 'West' is metaphorically pictured as a 'container.' and Poland is 'inside' this 'container.'[22] Thus for instance Polish lawyer Rafał T. Stroiński, writing for a Western audience about Polish company law, started his paper by making the following assertion:

> Polish law *belongs* to the western legal tradition, its laws for historical and cultural reasons *belonging* to the Germanic and Romanist legal families. This influence survives strongly until now.'[23] (Emphasis added)

---

[19] Marek Safjan, 'European Law versus Private Law: Transformation or Deformation of the Paradigm?,' in *General Principles of EU Law and European Private Law*, ed. Ulf Bernitz et al. (Alphen aan den Rijn: Kluwer Law International, 2013), 155–169, 159.

[20] Regulation of the President of the Republic of 27 October 1933—Code of Obligations (kodeks zobowiązań) (Dz.U. no. 82 item 598).

[21] Mańko, 'Weeds,' 212–14.

[22] On the 'container' schema from a cognitive perspective, see Winter, *A Clearing in the Forest*, 62–3.

[23] Rafał T. Stroiński, 'Report from Poland,' *European Company Law* 3/1 (2006), 39.

If, in line with the CONTAINER schema, Poland was always part of the Western legal tradition, its exposure to Soviet legal influence (1944–89) cannot be treated otherwise than as a form of submission. As I noted above, the period of actually existing socialism is presented in the dominant discourse as something unwanted and forced upon Poland. This is expressed, in the legal discourse, by the SUBMISSION metaphor. Lawyers write therefore about 'a fifty-year-long period of *submission* to the so called "socialist family",'[24] (emphasis added) or indicate that 'the development of the civil law codification [in Poland] was *stopped* ... during the Communist regime, again *imposed by force*.'[25]

The way towards the *agon* or GOAL of the RETURN TO EUROPE narrative, that is the final return to 'normalcy,' is presented in legal texts by two metaphors—one of PURIFICATION and another of RECONSTRUCTION.[26] I will focus on the first one here, under which Polish legal culture is metaphorically presented as being 'contaminated' by (the dirt of) Soviet influence which must be cleaned (purified) after 1989. A good example of this metaphorical way of portraying the post-socialist changes in Polish legal culture is the following passage from a paper written by Judge Marek Safjan in co-authorship with an official from the Polish Ministry of Justice:

> 'the Polish private law system ... survived the communist times *buried under the cover* of ideology ... the classic civil law basic constructions remained, sometimes *hidden under the surface* of the ideological ornament [therefore] [w]hen the ideological *implant is removed* [private-law treatises written under actually existing socialism can] serve as a source of great inspiration.[27]

Also for Polish comparative lawyer Jerzy Rajski, the post-1989 legal reforms 'were greatly facilitated by the possibility of *returning* to Poland's pre-war *traditions* [and were] aimed at *eliminating* "socialist" *distortions* to civil law.'[28]

In the same vein, the authors of a textbook on civil procedure write about legal survivals of actually existing socialism as '*accretions* imported from the East' which, after 1989, 'began to be gradually *removed*.'[29] Many

---

[24] Stroiński, 'Report from Poland,' 39.

[25] Jerzy Rajski, 'European Initiatives and Reform of Civil Law in Poland,' *Juridica International* 14 (2008), 151–155, 152.

[26] Mańko, 'Weeds,' 213–4.

[27] Marek Safjan and Aneta Wiewiórowska-Domagalska, 'Political Foundations of European Private Law: Rethinking the East-West Division Lines,' in *The Foundations of European Private Law*, ed. R. Brownsword et al. (Oxford-Portland OR: Hart, 2011), 278. Emphasis added.

[28] Rajski, 'European Initiatives,' 152. Emphasis added.

[29] Jerzy Jodłowski, Zbigniew Resich, Jerzy Lapierre and Teresa Misiuk-Jodłowska, *Postępowanie cywilne* [Civil Procedure] (3rd ed., Warszawa: LexisNexis 2003), 33. Emphasis added.

more examples could be mentioned.[30]

The dominant legal narrative, based on the RETURN TO EUROPE schema, treats therefore any interaction of Polish legal culture with the socialist legal tradition in terms of pollution and impurity, which must be cleaned. This interaction is not interpreted as a stage in the development of Polish legal culture, but rather as something unnatural, imposed by force, whose traces must be removed. The RETURN TO EUROPE schema serves therefore to prevent an evolutionary/teleological account of Polish legal history, which would see the period of actually existing socialism as yet another stage of purpose-oriented development, leading to the current outcome. To the contrary, to quote Giaro once again, the state socialist period is presented as: 'a historical regression ... a kind of blackout,' and therefore the law of that period 'aligns neither with the preceding nor with the following system and should be forgotten straight away.'[31]

This constant disavowal of the state socialist past can be illustrated by the way in which a leading textbook on civil procedure deals with one of the survivals of the socialist legal tradition analyzed in 3.4 below, namely the prosecutor's *locus standi* in civil proceedings. Whilst the 1983 edition of that textbook openly admitted (if not boasted) the Soviet origins of the institution in question,[32] its post-transformation edition tried to conceal them, mentioning that the 'fatherland of the institution of the prosecutor is France,'[33] but symptomatically failing to mention that the Polish model of prosecutorial intervention is a direct (and forced) reception of Soviet law.

A similar approach was taken by the authors of an article-by-article commentary to the Code of Civil Procedure published in 1996,[34] directly after the reintroduction—after 46 years—of 'appeal' (*apelacja*) and 'cassation' (*kasacja*) to Polish civil procedure, which displaced the appelate proceedings of the socialist period, namely the 'revision' (*rewizja*) and the 'extraordinary revision' (*rewizja nadzwyczajna*). The commentary to the articles on *apelacja* and *kasacja* referred exclusively to literature pre-dating the introduction of *rewizja* and *rewizja nadzwyczajna*, and tried to create an impression that the entire period of 46 years (1950–96) was being erased, as if Polish civil procedure made a journey in a time machine back to the pre-1950 period. In fact, the commentary was at pains to underline the origins of *apelacja* in ancient Rome(!), but upon arriving at 1950

---

[30] See Mańko, 'Weeds,' 213 n. 31.
[31] Giaro, 'Some Prejudices,' 45.
[32] Witold Broniewicz, *Postępowanie cywilne w zarysie* [Civil Procedure in Outline] (3rd ed., Warszawa: Państwowe Wydawnictwo Naukowe, 1983), 63–4.
[33] Witold Broniewicz, *Postępowanie cywilne w zarysie* [Civil Procedure in Outline] (8th ed., Warszawa: Lexis Nexis, 2005), 66.
[34] Kazimierz Piasecki in *Kodeks postępowania cywilnego. Komentarz* (Warszawa: C.H. Beck, 1996), Vol. I, 1098–101.

it made an abrupt jump and immediately referred to 1996.[35] The same approach was taken towards the reintroduced *kasacja* which replaced the former *rewizja nadzwyczajna*. Again, the commentary looked for distant historical references, tracing the Polish *kasacja* back to a French *loi* of 1790, but found it totally irrelevant to discuss the *rewizja nadzwyczajna*.

These examples demonstrate that both local and foreign scholars display a manifest preference for a discontinuity-focused approach, treating the period of actually existing socialism as a 'blackout' in local legal history (as Giaro calls it), which should be 'leaped over' rather than analyzed. One is tempted to see here a reversal of what Monateri showed with regard to the Roman law tradition:[36] instead of a bias for continuity, there is a strong bias of discontinuity, and the current impact of the socialist legal tradition is being systemically overlooked, downplayed, and minimized.

Is the period of actually existing socialism really a complete 'blackout' as the stereotype has it, or can existing legal survivals of that period be said to undermine such a view? The instances of legal continuity after 1989, analyzed in the following section, will challenge the stereotype, and allow us to put forward (in the conclusions of the dissertation) a counter-intuitive explanation of the issue.

4.3 Examples of State Socialist Legal Survivals in Polish Private Law

4.3.1 *Introduction*

The notion of 'legal survivals' denotes legal institutions introduced under one historically existing socio-economic and political system (here: actually existing socialism), which were functional towards that system, and which were not removed following a transformation to a different system (here: post-socialist neoliberal capitalism).[37] In contemporary

---

[35] Piasecki in *Kodeks*, 1145–50.

[36] Pier Giuseppe Monateri, 'Black Gaius: A Quest for the Multicultural Origins of the "Western Legal Tradition".' *Hastings Law Journal* 50 (2000), 479–555.

[37] 'Survivals' as a theoretical concept originated not in legal scholarship, but in anthropology and sociology. See, e.g. Bronisław Malinowski, *A Scientific Theory of Culture and Other Essays* [1944] (New York: OUP, 1961), 29; Max Weber, *Economy and Society: An Outline of Interpretive Sociology* (Berkeley-Los Angeles: University of California Press, 1978), 25, 69–71. Probably the first legal scholar to analyze survivals in law in a systematic way was the Austrian sociologist of law Karl Renner, who devoted an entire monograph to the topic (Karl Renner, *The Institutions of Private Law and Their Social Functions* [1904], trans. Agnes Schwarzschild [London-Boston: Routledge and Kegan Paul, 1976]). The theoretical concept of survivals was further developed by British legal philosopher and private lawyer Hugh Collins (Hugh Collins, *Marxism and Law* [1982] [Oxford-New York: OUP, 1988]), 52–55. See also Mańko, 'Weeds?,' 215–16; Rafał Mańko, 'Relikty w kulturze prawnej. Uwagi metodologiczne na tle pozostałości epoki socjalizmu realnego w polskim prawie prywatnym'

Polish private law, understood as encompassing both substantive civil law and civil procedure, there are a number of legal survivals of the socialist period. For the purposes of this chapter, I will draw closer attention to four of them: the right of perpetual usufruct (4.3.2), the cultivation contract (4.3.3), the prosecutor's standing in civil proceedings (4.3.4), and the preliminary references to the Supreme Court (4.3.5).

4.3.2 Perpetual Usufruct

State socialist property law was based on a dogmatic belief in the need to expand and preserve state property, which was understood as a direct implementation of Marx and Engels' views expressed in the *Communist Manifesto*, where they declare that 'the theory of the Communists may be summed up in the single sentence: Abolition of private property.'[38]

Faithful to this mandate, upon seizing power Bolsheviks ensured inter alia the abolition of private ownership of land.[39] Under such circumstances, private individuals wishing to erect a house or another building, which necessarily must be placed on a plot of land, could not acquire the right of ownership of the soil below the building, but had to satisfy themselves with a weaker title. Whilst individuals could acquire, in the guise of 'personal property,' a house of a limited surface for their private use,[40] the land had to remain state-owned.

After the transformation to actually existing socialism, Polish law had to accommodate to the same needs of preserving the state fund of land property. The final legal solution to this conundrum in the form of the 'right of perpetual usufruct' (*prawo użytkowania wieczystego*) was finally devised

---

[Survivals in Legal Culture: Methodological Remarks in the Light of the Remnants of Real Socialism in Polish Private Law] 102 *Przegląd Prawa i Administracji* (2015), 185; Rafał Mańko, 'Legal Survivals: A Conceptual Tool for Analysing Post-Transformation Continuity of Legal Culture' in *The Effectiveness of Law in Post-modern Society = Tiesību efektivitāte postmodernā sabiedrībā*, ed. Jānis Rozenfelds (Riga: Latvia University Press, 2015); Rafał Mańko, 'Transformacja ustrojowa a ciągłość instytucji prawnychuwagi teoretyczne' [Systemic Transformation and the Continuity of Legal Institutions: Theoretical Remarks], 16/2 *Zeszyty Prawnicze* (2016), 5.

[38] Karl Marx and Friedrich Engels, *The Communist Manifesto* [1848] (London: Penguin, 2002), 235.

[39] Lityński, *Prawo Rosji i ZSRR 1917–1991 czyli historia wszechzwiązkowego komunistycznego prawa (bolszewików). Krótki kurs* [The Law of Russia and the USSR between 1917 and 1991 or a History of the All-Union Communist Law (of Bolsheviks): a Short Course] (Warszawa: C.H. Beck, 2012), 216–19.

[40] Michel Lesage, *Le droit soviétique* (Paris: PUF, 1975), 79–80; William E. Butler, *Soviet Law* (London: Butterworths, 1983), 173.

in 1961.[41] Perpetual usufruct was defined in a similar way to ownership,[42] in the sense that the holder of the right could use the land 'with the exclusion of other persons and to dispose of it within the limits prescribed by statute.' Perpetual usufruct could be granted only with regard to urban land, i.e. either land within the boundaries of towns and settlements or lying outside such boundaries but nevertheless included in urban land management plans. The beneficiaries of the right of perpetual usufruct (perpetual usufructuaries) could be natural persons and legal persons, with the exclusion of state and socialized legal persons. Initially, housing cooperatives could not obtain land under this title, but the limitation was later lifted. Perpetual usufruct was established for a period of 99 years (in exceptional cases for a shorter period but not less than 40 years). Furthermore, the prolongation of the right for another period of up to 99 years was a standard and a refusal had to be justified by 'an important public interest.'

The right was established by way of a contract between the beneficiary and the local authority, however the contract had to be preceded by an administrative decision of the competent authority specifying its details, such as the destination of the land. If it was destined for construction, the contract should specify all the details regarding the buildings. Perpetual usufruct was established against a yearly fee determined unilaterally by the competent authority which corresponded to the infrastructural quality and location of the plot of land. The competent authority was entitled to terminate the contract unilaterally and repossess the land if the perpetual usufructuary used the land in a way manifestly contrary to the destination laid down in the contract or if he did not erect buildings which he was supposed to erect according to the contract.

When the Civil Code was enacted in 1964, the rules on perpetual usufruct were split between that Code (of private law) and the (public law) Land Management Act.[43] The standard duration of perpetual usufruct was set at 99 years and the minimum duration at 40 years, with possibilities for an unlimited number of extensions.[44] The legal framework of perpetual usufruct remained a hybrid one throughout the period of actually existing socialism in the sense that private law aspects of the institution in question were regulated in the Civil Code, but there were also numerous rules to be found in administrative law.[45] In particular, the creation, extinction,

---

[41] Act of 14 July 1961 on land management in towns and settlements (Dz.U. no. 32, item 159, hereinafter 'Urban Land Management Act 1961').

[42] The notion of ‚ownership' is used here in the strict Civilian sense of *dominium / Eigentum / propriété*.

[43] Winiarz, *Prawo*, 22–3.

[44] Art. 236 Polish Civil Code [*kodeks cywilny*] (1964).

[45] Cisek, 'Użytkowanie,' 144. In fact, it was difficult to separate the private law aspects

and modification of the right was always preceded by an appropriate administrative decision issued by the competent authority.[46]

After 1990, the legal framework of perpetual usufruct underwent a characteristic evolution, in that the administrative law aspects were gradually removed, and the institution became regulated almost exclusively by private law. At present, the main form in which the right is created is by way of a contract between the state or a local government and an individual or a legal person.[47] The conclusion of such a contract must be, in principle, preceded by a call for tenders.[48] As under actually existing socialism, the perpetual usufructuary may be obliged to construct a building or make other use of the land.[49] Most limitations inherent in the original legal framework have been lifted. First of all, under the Civil Code,[50] both the state and local government (municipal, district, regional) may encumber their land with the right of perpetual usufruct. Secondly, the said right may be established in favour of any natural or legal persons, without any limits as to their character (such as the requirement, that the legal person in question be a housing cooperative). The requirement that the land be within the boundaries of a town or be covered by an urban development plan has been removed, thus creating the possibility of establishing the right of perpetual usufruct on any land held by the State Treasury or a unit of local government for the benefit of any private party, individual, or body corporate.[51]

The right of perpetual usufruct is an absolute property right and is protected by an action to recover property (*rei vindicatio*) and a negatory action (action to stop violation of property—*actio negatoria*) in analogy to the right of ownership.[52] If the perpetual usufructuary uses the land in violation of the contract, the owner of the land (the State Treasury or the local municipality) may file an action in a civil court demanding the dissolution of the tenancy.[53] However, in contrast to the socialist period, since 1998 the tenancy may no longer be ended by a (unilateral)

---

of the institution from its public law aspects, and the elements of state *dominium* from elements of state *imperium* (Wierzbowski, 'O przydatności,' 618–19).

[46] Cisek, 'Użytkowanie,' 144.
[47] Cisek, 'Użytkowanie,' 151.
[48] Cisek, 'Użytkowanie,' 152–3.
[49] Cisek, 'Użytkowanie,' 157.
[50] Art. 232 Polish Civil Code [*kodeks cywilny*] (1964).
[51] Gerard Bieniek, 'W sprawie przyszłości użytkowania wieczystego' [Regarding the Future of Perpetual Usufruct] in *Ars et usus. Księga pamiątkowa ku czci Sędziego Stanisława Rudnickiego* [Ars et Usus: a Collection of Essays Dedicated to the Memory of Judge Stanisław Rudnicki] (Warszawa: LexisNexis, 2005), 54.
[52] Cisek, 'Użytkowanie,' 179.
[53] Cisek, 'Użytkowanie,' 180.

administrative decision of the land owner.[54]

The perpetual usufructuary is under a duty to pay a fee, expressed as a percentage of the market value of the land. A first one-off fee of 15–25% is due at the beginning of the tenancy, and then fees of 0.3%, 1%, 2%, or the standard 3% of the value of the land are due every year, depending on the use to which the land is put.[55]

The legal framework of perpetual usufruct has been frequently resorted to in practice both under actually existing socialism and after the transformation. Scholars underline that after many decades of its existence it has gained social acceptance.[56] Statistical data also witness a rich practice making use of the socialist legal framework. Thus out of all transactions regarding real estates in any one year, contracts for the creation of a right of perpetual usufruct represent 2.9%, while contracts for the sale of such a right (between private parties) represent 1.5% of all real estate transactions.[57] Out of the entire stock of municipally-owned land in Poland (1,012,503 ha) almost 8% is held by private parties under a perpetual usufruct title (79,828 ha).[58] Within the stock of land held under perpetual usufruct, 30% is held by individuals (23,670.20 ha) and the remaining 70% by legal persons. Income from fees paid by perpetual usufructuaries constitute, together with income for fees paid by ordinary usufructuaries and from remuneration for management of real estates by local government, 9% of the income of Polish towns and cities.[59]

4.3.3 *Cultivation Contract*

A cultivation contract (*umowa kontraktacji*) is a typified contract whereby a farmer undertakes to produce and sell a determined quantity of agricultural produce in exchange for a fixed price. Such a typified contract

---

[54] Cisek, 'Użytkowanie,' 180.

[55] Cisek, 'Użytkowanie,' 173. Act of 21 August 1997 on the management of immovables (Dz.U. no. 115, item 741).

[56] Zdzisław Gawlik, 'Użytkowanie wieczyste de lege ferenda' [Perpetual Usufruct De Lege Ferenda] in Czterdzieści lat kodeksu cywilnego [Forty Years of the Civil Code], ed. Mieczysław Sawczuk (Kraków: WoltersKluwer, 2006),115–125, 116.

[57] Data for 2011. Source: Central Statistical Office, Real Estate Turnover in 2011 (Warszawa 2012), 11, accessed 10 November 2013, http://www.stat.gov.pl/cps/rde/xbcr/gus/IK_obrot_nieruchomosciamii_2011.pdf.

[58] Data for stock of municipally-owned land in Poland from 2012. Source: 'Powierzchnia gruntów komunalnych wg prawnych form użytkowania' *Sejmometr*, accessed 10 November 2013, http://sejmometr.pl/bdl_wskazniki/838.

[59] Data for 2009. Source: Główny Urząd Statystyczny (Central Statistical Office), *Budżety jednostek samorządu terytorialnego* [Budges of Entitites of Local Government] (Warszawa 2010), 67, accessed 10 November 2013, http://www.stat.gov.pl/cps/rde/xbcr/gus/PUBL_rn_budz_jedn_sam_teryt_lata_2003-2009.pdf. The notion of 'cities' covers cities having the legal form of districts, that is usually above 100,000 population.

was unknown under the pre-War Code of Obligations, although cultivation contracts were concluded in practice also during that period.[60] However, the codification of the contract within the Civil Code of 1964 seems to have been a direct Soviet inspiration. This is because, on the one hand, in Soviet law, the cultivation contract (договор контрактации, *dogovor kontraktatsii*) was codified in Arts 51 and 52 Fundamentals of Civil Legislation of the USSR and Union Republics,[61] and, on the other hand, the contract is not codified in any Western civil codes which are known to have influenced Polish private law (e.g. French, Austrian, German, or Swiss).

The legal framework of the cultivation contract, as codified in 1964,[62] has undergone only a slight textual change after 1989. Whereas under the original rules from the procuring side it could be concluded only by a unit of socialized economy, duly authorized to perform the function of agricultural procurement,[63] this limitation was removed in 1990 allowing private sector economic operators to procure agricultural produce under the cultivation contract.

The legal framework of the contract was and is distinct both from sales and from the contract to perform a specific service (*umowa o dzieło*).[64] A characteristic feature of a cultivation contract is that the agricultural product must be produced by the farmer who is party to the contract, who cannot perform by buying the same crop on the market; this creates an essential difference between a cultivation contract and the sale of a future object, that is 'purchase of a hope' (*emptio spei*) and the 'purchase of a hoped-for-thing' (*emptio rei speratae*).[65]

---

[60] Juliusz Krzyżanowski, in *Kodeks cywilny. Komentarz*, vol. 2 (Warszawa: Wydawnictwo Prawnicze, 1972), 1348; Andrzej Stelmachowski, 'Kontraktacja' [The Cultivation Contract], in *System prawa prywatnego* [The System of Private Law], ed. Jerzy Rajski, vol. 7 of *Prawo zobowiązań—część szczegółowa* [Law of Obligations: General Part] (2nd ed., Warszawa: C.H. Beck, 2004), 249–52.

[61] Art. 51 Fundamentals of Civil Legislation of the USSR and Union Republics: 'State purchase of agricultural produce from collective and state farms shall be made by contracts for delivery of agricultural produce, which are concluded on the basis of plans for state purchases of agricultural produce and plans for the development of agricultural production in collective and state farms.'

[62] The cultivation contract is regulated in a detailed manner in Arts 613–26 Polish Civil Code [*kodeks cywilny*] (1964).

[63] Andrzej Stelmachowski, 'Kontraktacja' [The Cultivation Contract], in System prawa prywatnego [The System of Private Law], vol. 7 of Prawo zobowiązań—część szczegółowa [Law of Obligations: General Part], ed. J. Rajski (2nd ed., Warszawa: C.H. Beck, 2004), 262; Witold Czachórski, *Prawo zobowiązań w zarysie* (Warszawa: Państwowe Wydawnictwo Naukowe, 1968), 473. Krzyżanowski indicates that in practice the Minister of Agriculture decided which units could act as agricultural contractors (Krzyżanowski, *Kodeks*, 1352).

[64] Stelmachowski, 'Kontraktacja,' 259.

[65] This aspect was identified as an essential element of the cultivation contract, differentiating it from sale already in 1957, see SN resolution of 22 October 1957, Case II CO 10/57, LEX no. 119339; it was introduced to the Civil Code and is underlined in modern

During the state socialist period, cultivation contracts were concluded usually by municipal cooperatives acting as agents for central procurement entities.[66] Cultivation contracts were concluded for a wide range of crops, including potatoes, barley, wicker, flax, herbs, poppy, peas, beans, and onions.[67] They were also concluded for pigs, cattle, sheep, wheat, hops,[68] cabbage,[69] and turkeys.[70] After 1989 the role of the cultivation contract decreased, nevertheless they are still in use, in particular for the procurement of sugar beet and tobacco leaves,[71] as well as canola,[72] wheat,[73] turkeys,[74] duck and goose eggs,[75] and strawberries and raspberries.[76]

On a macro-social level, the cultivation contract played a distinct function under actually existing socialism. In the absence of collectivization of farms in Poland, its function was to integrate private family holdings into the centrally planned economy.[77] On a micro-social level, the contract was simply a way of guaranteeing farmers a secure demand for their products at a fixed price, regardless of the market situation. After 1989, the former macro-social function of cultivation contracts disappeared, together with the planned economy of state socialism.[78] Nevertheless, the micro-social function remained in place, although now the role of the procuring party has been taken over by private sector economic operators.

4.3.4 Prosecutor's Standing in Civil Proceedings

Under pre-1939 Polish civil procedure, the powers of the prosecutor (*prokurator*) to intervene in civil proceedings were extremely narrow even for Western European standards of the period (such as French law).[79] In

---

case law too: see, e.g. SN judgment of 18 March 1998, Case I CKN 576/97, LEX no. 746161; SA/Poznań judgment of 19 August 2009, Case I ACa 507/09, LEX no. 756625 citing Case II CO 10/57, supra).

[66] Stelmachowski, 'Kontraktacja.,' 252.
[67] Stelmachowski, 'Kontraktacja.,' 252.
[68] Czachórski, *Prawo*, 473.
[69] SN judgment of 28 January 1967, Case I CR 45/67, LEX no. 6109.
[70] SN judgment of 18 May 1983, Case I CR 124/83, LEX no. 2900.
[71] Stelmachowski, 'Kontraktacja,' 255–7.
[72] SN judgment of 18 March 1998, Case I CKN 576/97, LEX no. 746161.
[73] SN judgment of 27 June 2002, Case IV CKN 1165/00, LEX no. 80264.
[74] SN judgment of 17 December 2003, Case IV CK 303/02, LEX no. 599555.
[75] SN judgment of 19 February 2009, Case III SK 31/08, LEX no. 503413.
[76] WSA/Gdańsk judgment of 20 October 2009, Case I SA/Gd 465/09, LEX no. 571204.
[77] Stelmachowski, 'Kontraktacja,' 252–3; Czachórski, *Prawo*, 473; Krzyżanowski, in: *Kodeks* vol. 2, 1348; SN judgment of 7 August 1975, Case III CRN 179/75, LEX no. 7732; SN judgment of 25 May 1988, Case II CR 129/88, LEX no. 8884.
[78] Stelmachowski, 'Kontraktacja,' 253.
[79] See, e.g. Kazimierz Stefko, *Udział prokuratora w postępowaniu cywilnym* [The Participation of the Prosecutor in Civil Proceedings] (Warszawa: Wydawnictwo Prawnicze, 1956), 33–40; Halina Zięba-Załucka, *Instytucja prokuratury w Polsce* [The Institution of

contrast, under the Soviet model, the Prosecution Service (прокуратура, *prokuratura*) was conceived of as an independent, hierarchical agency of government entrusted with the task of controlling all other powers, defending 'socialist legality' and enjoying, for this purpose, the powers of protest, proposal, and prosecution.[80]

In 1950, the Soviet model of the prosecution service became the object of a legal transfer to Polish law,[81] which was part of an overhaul of the entire procedural law and organization of the judiciary.[82] Under the Polish legal framework introduced in 1950, prosecutors enjoyed a general and unlimited standing to join or initiate any civil proceedings as well as to challenge any judicial decision. These powers were thoroughly independent from the will or interest of any private party to the civil proceedings and from the will of the court; however, they had full legal effects vis-à-vis the litigants. A judicial decision handed down in such a procedure was binding on the parties (unlike, for instance, in the French cassation 'in the interest of the law'[83]).

This legal transfer, first codified in 1950, was carried over into the new socialist Code of Civil Procedure enacted in 1964, where the prosecutor's standing was raised to the level of a fundamental principle of civil

---

the Prosecution Service in Poland] (Warszawa: LexisNexis 2003), 14.

[80] William E. Butler, *Russian Law* (3rd ed. Oxford: OUP, 2009), 192; Adam Lityński, *Prawo Rosji i ZSRR 1917–1991 czyli historia wszechzwiązkowego komunistycznego prawa (bolszewików). Krótki kurs* [The Law of Russia and the USSR between 1917 and 1991 or a History of the All-Union Communist Law (of Bolsheviks): A Short Course] (Warszawa: C.H. Beck, 2012), 317–18.

[81] Andrzej Jakubecki, 'Naczelne zasady postępowania cywilnego w świetle nowelizacji kodeksu postępowania cywilnego' [Fundamentals Principles of Civil Procedure in the Light of an Amendment of the Code of Civil Procedure], in Czterdziestolecie kodeksu postępowania cywilnego [Forty Years of the Code of Civil Procedure], ed. Izabela Ratusińska (Kraków: Zakamycze, 2006), 356. Despite certain prima facie similarities between the role of the prosecutor in civil proceedings in Poland and in France, there is no doubt that the Polish model of prosecutor's standing in civil proceedings is a legal transfer from the Soviet Union, whereas the French is not. It should also be kept in mind that in Poland a prosecutor who joins civil proceedings has all the powers of a party to the proceedings (e.g. may bring an appeal or petition for cassation) and is not limited only to giving non-binding advice to the court, as is the case in France. In the latter, the prosecutor may challenge a judicial decision only if he initiated the proceedings himself, but not if he joined proceedings already in motion. On French law see, e.g. Gerard Couchez, Xavier Lagarde, *Procédure civile* (16th ed., Paris: Dalloz, 2011), 146–53, 282–5; John Bell, Sophie Boyron, and Simon Whittaker, *Principles of French Law* (2nd ed., Oxford: OUP, 2008), 60–1, 89–90, 112.

[82] For details see Rafał Mańko, 'Is the Socialist Legal Tradition "Dead and Buried"? The Continuity of Certain Elements of Socialist Legal Culture in Polish Civil Procedure,' in *Private Law and the Many Cultures of Europe*, ed. Thomas Wilhemsson et al. (The Hague: Kluwer Law International, 2007), 88–91.

[83] The '*pourvoi dans l'intérêt de la loi*' which can be filed by a *procureur général* attached to the *Cour de Cassation* 'has no effect on the parties' to the proceedings (Bell et al., *Principles*, 112–13; see also Couchez and Lagard, *Procédure*, 508).

procedure.[84] Scholars emphasized its role in making Polish civil procedure truly socialist.[85] The only exception to the prosecutor's standing obtained since 1965 was the exclusion of the right to file for divorce.

After 1989, numerous scholars began to criticize the generalized prosecutorial standing.[86] Some of them even argued that such an institution actually violates the right to an impartial court as guaranteed by international human rights instruments.[87] It was also pointed out that in this respect Polish civil procedure differs from other European countries.[88] Nevertheless, despite numerous amendments to the Code of Civil Procedure, the prosecutor's standing has remained unaffected. The only change which occurred was the removal of the notion of 'protection of social property' from the list of very broadly framed grounds for a prosecutor's intervention (the others being: protection of the rule of law, protection of citizens' rights and protection of the social interest).[89]

The Internal Rules of the Prosecution Service (2010; hereinafter 'Internal Rules') currently in force specify the types of civil cases in which a prosecutor's participation in civil proceedings 'desirable.'[90] These include, for instance, cases of simulated declarations of will, declarations of will made to hide a different legal act or circumvent the law, cases for the annulment of a legal act whose effect is the transfer or encumbrance of an immovable, cases regarding protection of cultural property and

---

[84] Art. 7 Code of Civil Procedure [*kodeks postępowania cywilnego*] (1964).

[85] Albert Meszorer, *Stanowisko i czynności procesowe prokuratora w postępowaniu cywilnym* [The Position and Procedural Acts of the Prosecutor in Civil Proceedings] (Warszawa: PWN, 1957), 75; Jerzy Smoleński, *Prokuratura Polskiej Rzeczypospolitej Ludowej. Komentarz do ustawy o prokuraturze PRL i innych przepisów dotyczących prokuratury* [Prosecution Service of the Polish People's Republic: A Commentary to the Act on the Prosecution Service of the Polish People's Republic and other Provisions Concerning the Prosecution Service] (2nd ed., Warszawa: Wydawnictwo Prawnicze, 1981) 127.

[86] Tadeusz Ereciński, 'O potrzebie nowego kodeksu postępowania cywilnego' [On the Need of a New Code of Civil Procedure], *Państwo i Prawo* 59.4 (2004), 3–10, 8; Piotr Pogonowski, *Realizacja prawa do sądu w postępowaniu cywilnym* [The Realisation of the Right to a Court in Civil Proceedings] (Warszawa: C.H. Beck, 2005), 73; Adam Zieliński, in *Kodeks postępowania cywilnego. Komentarz do artykułów 1–50514* [Code of Civil Procedure. Commentary to Article 1 to 505–14] (2nd ed., Warszawa: C.H. Beck, 2006), 71.

[87] Feliks Zedler, 'Glosa do wyroku SN z dnia 14 września 2005 r. III CZP 58/05' [Case-note on Supreme Court judgment of 14 September 2005 in Case III CZP 58/05], *Orzecznictwo Sądów Polskich* 50/1 (2006), 518.

[88] Andrzej Oklejak, 'Co dalej z kodeksem postępowania cywilnego w czterdziestolecie jego istnienia?' [What Should be Done with the Code of Civil Procedure on the Fortieth Anniversary of Its Existence?' in Ratusińska ed., *Czterdziestolecie*, 13.

[89] See Art. 7 Code of Civil Procedure (1964), as modified by Act of 13 July 1990 (Dz.U. no. 55, item 318).

[90] Regulation of the Minister of Justice of 24 March 2010—the Internal Rules of the Common Organisational Units of the Prosecution Service (consolidated version: Dz.U. 2014, item 144, hereinafter: 'Internal Rules 2010'); Re types of civil cases in which a prosecutor's participation in civil proceedings is 'desirable,' see §§ 374, 378–9 Internal Rules 2010.

protection of copyright, cases regarding the protection of the family and environmental protection. Furthermore, within family law the Internal Rules make it 'desirable' for prosecutors to intervene in cases regarding the annulment of marriage, a declaration of its existence or inexistence, negation of paternity or maternity, adoption of foreigners or Polish citizens who are non-residents, dissolution of adoption, removal of a person subject to parental authority or guardianship, deprivation of parental authority and injunctions prohibiting contacts with a child. Finally, within labour law, the Internal Rules urge prosecutors to bring actions inter alia whenever workers' rights have been flagrantly violated and in cases of termination of employment due to discrimination.

The legal practice applying the principle of prosecutor's participation in civil proceedings continues to be rich.[91] In 2012 prosecutors filed a total of 3,872 actions in litigious civil cases (*powództwa*) and 18,603 actions in non-litigious civil cases (*wnioski wszczynające postępowanie nieprocesowe*) which gives a total of 22,475 civil lawsuits filed altogether.

The subject matter of the lawsuits in litigious civil cases included delict (261 actions), confiscation of consideration provided for in exchange for the commission of a criminal act (183 actions), actions in labour law (7 actions), actions for determination of paternity (79 actions), actions for negation of paternity (1,117 actions), actions for annulment of recognition of paternity (129 cases), as well as actions for alimony or for the increase of alimony (275 cases). The subject matter of the actions in non-litigious proceedings concentrated on actions for compulsory anti-alcoholism treatment (11,399 actions),[92] actions for incapacitation (2,038 actions) and actions regarding family relationships (3,682 actions). The rate of success of the Prosecution Service in non-litigious civil cases was also high, and in 2012 amounted to 85.8% (in 2011, 84.2%).

As regards appellate proceedings, in 2012 prosecutors filed 95 appeals (in 2011, 121 appeals). The success rate was much lower than at trial level, amounting to only 57.8%. Apart from regular appeals, prosecutors also filed 261 petitions for reopening of proceedings (in 2011, 215 petitions). The success rate for those petitions was 87%.

---

[91] The following description of this activity is based on vol. I of *Sprawozdanie Prokuratora Generalnego z rocznej działalności prokuratury w 2012 roku* [Prosecutor General's Report on the Annual Activity of the Prosecution Service in 2012, hereinafter 'Prosecutor General's Report 2012'] (Warszawa: Prokuratura Generalna, 2013), 250–8, accessed 9 July 2013, http://www.pg.gov.pl/upload_doc/000003717.pdf.

[92] A civil (family) court may impose upon an individual the duty to undergo anti-alcoholism treatment upon request by a prosecutor or the competent Municipal Commission for the Solution of Problems Posed by Alcoholism (*gminna komisja rozwiązywania problemów alkoholowych*). See Art. 26 of the Act of 26 October 1982 on educating society in sobriety and combating alcoholism (consolidated version published in Dz. U. 2012, item 1356). The alcoholic's family or neighbours do not enjoy standing to file such an action.

Apart from filing actions, appeals, and petitions for reopening of proceedings themselves, prosecutors also joined civil proceedings initiated by private parties. In 2012 prosecutors participated in 19,999 civil cases initiated by other parties (in 2011, in 18,913 cases). The *Yearly Report* of the Prosecutor General underlines a growth of prosecutors' participation in labour cases.[93] In 2012 prosecutors intervened in 117 cases concerning the protection of workers' rights.

4.3.5 *Preliminary References to the Supreme Court*

Preliminary reference rulings are most widely known in the context of EU law as well as constitutional law in certain countries, but what is less known to the international legal community is the fact that such a system of judicial dialogue was introduced in Poland after World War II—in 1949 in criminal proceedings and in 1953 in civil proceedings. Under the Code of Civil Procedure, as amended, if a regional court deciding upon a revision encountered a 'legal question giving rise to serious doubts,' it could stay proceedings and 'refer that question to the Supreme Court for decision.'[94] The Supreme Court could still, if it wished to, decide the case by itself.[95] The new rule stated explicitly that a resolution of the Supreme Court (the preliminary ruling) is binding on lower courts in the case.[96] The new Code of Civil Procedure of socialist Poland, enacted in 1964, contained an identical rule on preliminary reference proceedings combined with the procedure of taking over the case.[97]

This legal framework survived the demise of actually existing socialism almost unmodified. It has been constantly made use of by the courts since its inception. In fact, the number of references submitted yearly has been roughly similar over the last 60 years of the functioning of the institution, and therefore the transition from actually existing socialism to a market economy was not a significant threshold in this respect. Thus, as regards the socialist period, for instance in 1962, 88 questions were submitted and the average number of questions between 1971 and 1974 amounted to 185 annually,[98] whilst in 1977 there were 103 preliminary references in

---

[93] Prosecutor General's Report 2012, 255.

[94] Art. 388 § 1 sentence 1 Code of Civil Procedure (1930) as amended by Decree of 23 April 1953 (Dz.U. 23 item 90).

[95] Art. 388 § 1 sentence 2 Code of Civil Procedure (1930) as amended by Decree of 23 April 1953.

[96] Art. 388 § 2 Code of Civil Procedure (1930) as amended by Decree of 23 April 1953.

[97] Art. 391 Code of Civil Procedure (1964).

[98] Stanisław Włodyka, 'Specjalne środki nadzoru judykacyjnego Sądu Najwyższego' [Special Means of the Supreme Court's Supervision over Adjudication] in *Sąd Najwyższy w PRL* [The Supreme Court in the Polish People's Republic], ed. M. Rybicki (Wrocław et al.: Zakład Narodowy im. Ossolińskich, 1983), 274.

the Civil Chamber.[99] Currently, the number of references stays comparable, oscillating within the Civil Chamber around 100 (e.g. 141 in 2010, 96 in 2011, 110 in 2012),[100] and in the Labour Chamber around 20 (e.g. 16 in 2012, 26 in 2011).[101] Although the preliminary references are, in statistical terms, only a small fraction (0.2%) of the Supreme Court's business (in 2012 the number of incoming cases in the Civil Chamber amounted to 4,866, with only 110 of these being preliminary references),[102] their actual importance is much greater, and many of the most important decisions of the Supreme Court are actually rendered within this procedure.[103] This is because of a double filter of selection on the merits: first of all, a second instance court must identify an issue as being legally controversial, and secondly, before the Supreme Court decides to issue a formally binding answer (in the form of a so-called 'resolution') it also analyzes whether the issue is of significant legal importance. This ensures that only the most legally significant and vexed issues are decided upon in this procedure.

4.4 Conclusions: Demons of the Past or Useful Legal Institutions?

The four examples of legal survivals briefly presented in the previous section beg the question whether they should be classified as 'demons of the past,' haunting modern Polish private law, which should be removed in the name of its 'purification,' or whether they can be legitimately referred to as

---

[99] Zbigniew Resich, 'Właściwość i zasady postępowania przed Sądem Najwyższym.' in Sąd Najwyższy w PRL [The Supreme Court in the Polish People's Republic], ed. Marian Rybicki (Wrocław et al.: Zakład Narodowy im. Ossolińskich, 1983), 142. The 103 preliminary references were, statistically, a minor fraction of 2,449 cases incoming to the Civil Chamber in 1977. Most of its activity was concentrated on being a court of second instance in ordinary proceedings (1,541 revisions, 429 interlocutory appeals), on top of which it heard 348 extraordinary revisions and 28 other cases.

[100] Sąd Najwyższy Rzeczypospolitej Polskiej (Supreme Court of the Republic of Poland), *Informacja o działalności Sądu Najwyższego w 2012 r.* [Information on the Activity of the Supreme Court in 2013] (Warszawa, 2013), 152, accessed 17 March 2014, http://www.sn.pl/_layouts/SPZWebParts/download.aspx?id=71&ListName=Dzialalnosc_SN (hereinafter: 'SN report for 2012'). The number of 'legal questions' covers not only preliminary references, but also a very limited number of requests for abstract resolutions.

[101] The full name of the chamber is currently 'Labour, Social Security and Public Issues Chamber.' Labour and social security cases are civil cases in the technical sense, and hence the Code of Civil Procedure is applied to them. Re number of references, see SN report for 2012, p. 69. In 2011 the Supreme Court rejected 10 preliminary references, but in 2012 it did not reject any one.

[102] SN report for 2012, 152. The proportion in 2012 within the Labour Chamber is 26 out of 2,987. However, the number of 'legal questions' covers not only preliminary references, but also requests for abstract resolution.

[103] As evidenced by the role given to preliminary rulings in the Supreme Court's yearly reports, see SN report for 2012, 5, 17–40.

useful legal institutions, which have proven their utility also after the 1989 transformation. The mere fact that local administration still establishes perpetual usufruct titles, that private parties enter into cultivation contracts, that prosecutors intervene in a considerable number of civil lawsuits yearly, and that courts of second instance continue to submit preliminary references on important legal questions to the Supreme Court militate in favour of the second option. Although the examples of four legal survivals of actually existing socialism, analyzed in the previous section, were only selected case studies of a broader phenomenon, they already in themselves allow one to draw certain conclusions on the assumption that these would be confirmed by a broader analysis of other legal survivals.

First of all, I stipulate that legal survivals are a normal (physiological) feature of legal culture, rather than its pathology. Any radical socio-economic transformation, such as Poland's passage from actually existing socialism to a neoliberal market economy in 1989, can be compared to a shift of paradigm in science.[104] Just like in science, different theoretical constructions can be superimposed on the same set of data,[105] so the socio-economic relationships of a given society can be governed by very different (legal) systems, guided by radically different principles or paradigms. But the rupture, however radical in its fundamental premises, is never total: there is always a certain space of continuity. In the domain of science:

> Since new paradigms are born from old ones, they ordinarily incorporate much of the vocabulary and apparatus, both conceptual and manipulative, that the traditional paradigm had previously employed. But they seldom employ these borrowed paradigms in quite the traditional way. Within the new paradigm, old terms, concepts, and experiments fall into new relationships with each other.[106]

The same happens after a 'change of paradigm' of the legal system,[107] that is its transition from, for instance, state socialist law to market economy law. Just like scientists, lawyers do not discard those elements from their professional toolbox which, although used in new ways, can

---

[104] For the source domain of this metaphor see Thomas S. Kuhn, *The Structure of Scientific Revolutions* [1962] (3rd ed., Chicago: University of Chicago Press, 1996).
[105] Kuhn, *Scientific Revolutions*, 76.
[106] Kuhn, *Scientific Revolutions*, 149.
[107] Cf. Jürgen Habermas, *Between Facts and Norms: Contributions to a Discourse Theory of Law and Democracy*, transl. by W. Rehg (Massachussets: MIT Press, 1996), 388–404. Habermas understands a paradigm in law as 'the *judge's* implicit image of society' and links it with a specific 'social ideal' ('social model,' 'social vision') (392). The change of paradigm analyzed by Habermas was a shift from the liberal to the social model of private law, which occurred *via* a re-interpretation of general clauses (404), a constitutionalization of private law (403), as well as by explicit legislative intervention (403).

still be fruitfully deployed under the new paradigm. What varies, though, is the degree of adaptation necessary, or—to use the metaphor drawn from science—the way that the old apparatus will be employed. Furthermore, in the domain of science:

> The new paradigm must promise to preserve a relatively large part of the concrete problem-solving ability that has accrued to science through its predecessors. *Novelty for its own sake is not a desideratum in the sciences.* … As a result … new paradigms … usually preserve a great deal of the most concrete parts of past achievement and they always permit additional concrete problem-solutions besides.[108] (Emphasis added)

Law—like science—is above all, a practical enterprise, and the test of viability that legal institutions must pass is their concrete problem-solving ability, the capacity for effectively regulating socio-economic interests and resolving conflicts. In law—like in science—'novelty for its own sake is not a desideratum.'

Secondly, on a critical note, I wish to return to the narrative about the state socialist legal past which prevails among the contemporary Polish legal community discussed in section two above. As I indicated, the legal survivals of actually existing socialism persistent in Polish private law certainly cause irritation among those who insist on 'purging' the legal order from any traces of the *ancien régime*. The story of adaptation of legal survival clearly indicates that the dominant narrative overlooks the fact that law is above all a practical enterprise, and if legal survivals (when necessary, adapted) are capable of fulfilling their social functions within the legal system, there is no need to get rid of them in the name of historical policy or ideological purism.

Thirdly, on a normative note, I wish to insist on the positive aspects of legal survivals for the legal community and society at large. Whilst at first blush legal survivals might seem synonymous to 'relics' (outdated legal institutions opposed to new, more 'rational' legal phenomena,[109] introduced consciously after a transformation), this is not the case. I contend that the legal community's willingness to retain 'traditional' causes of action (in the Weberian sense),[110] that is, old institutions, rules, or concepts (of course adequately adapted to the requirements of the new socio-economic order) is deeply rational and should be supported. This is because it allows the saving of time, effort, and other resources, which would have to be expended if a new legal framework were created from scratch, be it by the

---

[108] Kuhn, *Scientific Revolutions*, 169.
[109] Cf. Piotr Sztompka, *Socjologia. Analiza społeczeństwa* [Sociology: The Analysis of Society] (Kraków: Znak, 2007), 61.
[110] Weber, *Economy*, s. 25.

legislature or by the courts. One could remark that the legal system has a tendency to 'lag behind' social change; however, this 'lagging behind' does not occur for the sake of an unthinking, dogmatic conservatism, but for the sake of preserving the concrete problem-solving ability of the law despite a change of paradigm.

What is perhaps most characteristic, is that even after the October Revolution, when the Bolsheviks officially abolished all pre-revolutionary legal texts in one blow,[111] the post-revolutionary law-makers nevertheless returned to the laws of the *ancien régime* when seeking inspiration for the codification of state socialist law.[112] From a purely symbolic point of view this must not have been a welcome move, but from the perspective of the institutional world of law it logically followed.

Exactly the same mechanism seems to be at work in today's Poland. The efforts of numerous academics to draft a new Polish Civil Code,[113] with the intention of effecting a definitive break from the state socialist past (represented to them by the current Code of 1964), have been heavily criticized by judges of the Supreme Court (incidentally, many of them academics).[114] I agree with their criticism. The judges are perfectly right in that they see nothing wrong in continuing to use the Civil Code of the socialist period, adequately adapted to the new circumstances.

Finally, the story of legal survivals of actually existing socialism allows one to draw more general conclusions about the significance of this period for Polish legal culture. Contrary to common wisdom, criticized by Tomasz Giaro, whereby the socialist period in Polish legal culture is but a 'blackout,' which must be 'forgotten straight away,' the post-War period, albeit characterized by Soviet tutelage and Poland's unprecedented exposure to the socialist legal tradition, still has something to offer to modern legal culture. The preliminary reference procedure, today a commonplace tool in EU law and constitutional law in many European countries, was introduced in Poland already in 1953. The right of perpetual usufruct, giving local administration additional private law instruments to ensure land is used

---

[111] Adam Lityński, *Prawo Rosji*, 197.

[112] A case in point is the Civil Code of the Russian Federal Socialist Soviet Republic of 1922, whose drafters relied on Western European models and, according to some researchers, even on the draft of Russian Civil Code prepared between 1905 and 1913. See Lityński, *Prawo Rosji*, 203.

[113] Komisja Kodyfikacyjna Prawa Cywilnego działająca przy Ministrze Sprawiedliwości [Codification Commission for Civil Law attached to the Minster of Justice], *Księga pierwsza Kodeksu cywilnego. Projekt z uzasadnieniem* [First Book of the Civil Code: Draft with Motives] (Warszawa: C.H. Beck, 2009).

[114] 'Projekt Kodeksu cywilnego. Księga pierwsza. Sprawozdanie z dyskusji przeprowadzonbej w Izbie Cywilnej Sądu Najwyższego' [Draft Civil Code. Book One. Report from a Discussion Held at the Civil Chamber of the Supreme Court], *Przegląd Sądowy* 2 (2010).

in the public interest, was created in 1961. The cultivation contract, a useful legal form unknown to Western European civil codes, was codified in the socialist Civil Code of 1964. And finally the possibility of defending the public interest in private litigation by way of an unlimited standing of prosecutors in virtually all types of civil proceedings has been in place in Poland since 1950. Most of these legal institutions (save for the preliminary reference procedure) were legal transplants from the Soviet Union, i.e. legal solutions derived from the socialist legal tradition. Nevertheless, following, if necessary, some adaptations of the legal framework, they proved to be capable of also being applied after 1989. This mere fact undermines the dominant 'blackout' narrative and sheds more light on the positive developments in Polish legal culture during the period of actually existing socialism. Therefore, legal survivals of the period of actually existing socialism can be more aptly described as useful legal institutions than as 'demons of the past.' This is because they have passed the only valid test in the life of the law—that of practical utility.

5

Feminist Legal Education in Croatia: A Question of Fundamentalism or a Fundamental Question?

Ivana Radačić

5.1 Introduction

Like other types of education, legal education is a 'socially facilitated process of cultural transmission.'[1] Despite its trade school mentality and the focus on conveying formal knowledge, law school is a place of ideological training,[2] as it also upholds a system of values. As a professional socialization process, legal education moulds students' consciousness as future lawyers and legal system officials.[3] Hence, the legal, political, and cultural messages sent by the structure and content of the law curriculum and the pedagogy utilized are profoundly important. Choices of pedagogy and the content of curriculum shape the profession and the law itself. Law is a powerful tool which can be used either to maintain the status quo or to challenge different forms of domination and oppression. Legal education very much influences the way it will be used.

In this chapter, I critically examine Croatian legal education, focusing in particular on the marginalization of feminist perspectives from core curriculum content and from legal scholarship, questioning the causes and consequences of such a marginalization.[4] I start with defining what I mean by feminist legal theorizing and feminist approaches to (legal) education.

---

[1] Philip W. Jackson, *What is Education* (Chicago: The University of Chicago Press, 2012), 10 (emphasis removed).

[2] Duncan Kennedy, 'Legal Education and the Reproduction of Hierarchy,' *Duncan Journal of Legal Education* 32 (1982), 591–615.

[3] Isabel Marcus, 'The "Woman Question" in Post-Socialist Legal Education,' *Human Rights Quarterly* 36 (2014), 507–68.

[4] While I am concerned with the exclusion of critical perspectives from Croatian legal academia in general, and while I believe that an inclusive feminist approach has to engage with other critical theories of law (such as critical race theory, postmodern, and queer theories), the focus of this article is on the exclusion of feminist perspectives. However, much of what I state here concerning causes and consequences of the exclusion of feminist perspectives is applicable to the exclusion of other critical legal approaches in Croatian legal academia as well.

I then analyze the situation in Croatia. I first describe the wider social context and academic structures within which law schools are placed, as well as the organization of law schools and the dominant pedagogy employed in them. I then look into the law schools' curricula for the inclusion of feminist topics, as well as legal scholarship. After examining legal education in Croatia, I probe into the causes and consequences of the marginalization of feminist thinking in legal academia and propose ways of addressing the problems identified.

5.2 Feminist Approaches to Law and Legal Education

As there is no common definition of feminism, there is also no common definition of feminist jurisprudence and of what constitutes a feminist approach to (legal) education. Barlett defines feminist jurisprudence as 'a family of different perspectives or frameworks used to analyze the actual and the desirable relationship between law and gender.'[5] These perspectives differ both in their view of the relevance of gender difference (and accordingly in the manner they conceptualize gender equality), and their political orientation.[6] There are, however, some common characteristics of feminist jurisprudence. As Rhode noted, at the substantive level different feminist perspectives share their commitment to equality between the sexes and the broader issues of social justice, and at the methodological level a commitment to gender as a focus of concern and to analytic approaches that reflect women's concrete experiences.[7] Moreover, feminist jurisprudence is characterized by an interdisciplinary approach and by its practice oriented nature; it is 'a combination of theory and practice, constructed through the development of a methodology which ensures that the insights of theory are reflected in the politics of action, and that the insights of practice are reflected in theory construction.'[8] The goal of feminism is to change both theory and practice to insure equality and freedom for all 'sexed beings.'[9]

---

[5] Katherine T. Barlett, 'Perspectives in Feminist Jurisprudence,' in *Feminist Jurisprudence, Women and the Law: Critical Essays, Research Agenda and Bibliography*, ed. Betty Taylor et al. (Littleton: Rothman & Co, 1999), 3.

[6] While so-called sameness (liberal) feminism focuses on the irrelevance of difference, the so-called difference feminisms emphasize not only the differences between women and men but also among women. Difference feminisms include cultural and radical feminism as well as the so-called diversity feminisms (lesbian feminists, feminists of colour, and post-colonial perspectives), and postmodern feminism. Martha Chamallas, *Introduction to Feminist Legal Theory* (New York: Aspen Publishers, 2003).

[7] Deborah L. Rhode, 'The "No Problem" Problem: Challenges and Cultural Change,' 100 *Yale Law Journal* (1991), 1731–43.

[8] Carol Smart, *Feminism and the Power of Law* (London: Routledge, 1989), 69.

[9] Drucilla Cornell, *At the Heart of Freedom: Feminism, Sex and Equality* (New Jersey:

These characteristics of feminist jurisprudence—its explicit political goal, interdisciplinary character and engagement with practice—present a challenge to the predominant positivist conceptualization of law as an objective system of regulation and dispute resolution, separated from politics and morality, and a corresponding idea of legal education as a process of imparting technical knowledge in an objective fashion. Feminist legal theorists argue that the legal concepts of impartiality, objectivity and neutrality are just the viewpoints of dominant groups, which are culturally enabled to deny their positionality.[10] They show how law exercises power by its claim to 'truth,' the main vehicle for this claim being an objective legal method.[11]

Interested in examining how the myth of law's objectivity is justified, feminist theorists also analyze legal education, challenging the dominant norms of knowledge production for its male (and other) biases.[12] Torthon has, for example, shown how the technical way of teaching enables law to present itself as neutral, apolitical and innocent.[13] Exposing legal education's political nature, she focused in particular on how the recent trends of vocationalism and academic capitalism in Australian legal education facilitates neoliberal global capitalism.[14] Critical legal scholars have similarly shown how despite—or because of—the trade school mentality, law schools are highly political places where the dominant ideology is being thought, which supports different forms of hierarchy and domination.[15]

The focus of the critique of legal education for the feminist scholars has not only been the content and method of teaching but the broader issues of the organization and structure of legal academia, as well as the relationships within law schools (primarily between professors and students). Feminists have criticized not only the insufficient attention paid to feminist and broader social justice issues in the law school curricula, but have

Princeton University Press, 1998).

[10] Margaret Davies, *Asking the Law Question* (Law Book Co of Australia, 2008, 3rd ed); Katherine A. MacKinnon, 'Method and Politics,' in *Toward a Feminist Theory of the State* (Cambridge, MA: Harvard University Press, 1989), 114.

[11] Carol Smart, *Feminism and the Power of Law* (New York: Routledge, 1989), 10–11.

[12] Carrie Menkel Medow, 'Feminist Legal Theory, Critical Legal Studies, and Legal Education or "The Fem-Crits Go to Law School",' *Journal of Legal Education* 38 (1988), 61–85.

[13] Margaret Thornton, 'The Demise of Diversity in Legal Education: Globalisation and the New Knowledge Economy,' *International Journal of the Legal Profession* 8 (2001), 37–56.

[14] 'Academic capitalism,' a phrase coined by Sheila Slaughter and Larry L. Leslie captures the idea of the encroachment of the profit motive onto the academy, see Sheila Slaughter and Larry L. Leslie *Academic Capitalism: Politics, Policies, and the Entrepreneurial University* (Baltimore, John Hopkins, 1997), 9 and 43.

[15] Kennedy, 'Legal Education and the Reproduction of Hierarchy' (1983), accessed 16 February 2016, http://duncankennedy.net/documents/Photo%20articles/Legal%20Education%20and%20the%20Reproduction%20of%20Hierarchy_J.%20Leg.%20Ed.pdf.

also argued against the authoritarian one-way transmission of knowledge through lectures, showing how this contributes to the dehumanization and objectification of law.[16] Moreover, they have argued against the hierarchical manner of teaching and the overemphasis of the cognitive to the exclusion or the marginalization of emotional and personal experience in the learning process, pointing out the need to include experiential learning.[17] Often drawing on the experiences of women's studies and their challenge to the dominant mode of knowledge production, feminist law professors have proposed a number of changes in legal education and the organization of law schools. Starting from the idea that the goal of education is not simply knowledge transmission but 'emotional and intellectual empowerment' of their students,[18] different feminist and critical law professors have proposed changes to legal education, ranging from shared leadership and collaboration between teachers and students, revaluation of the ethics of care in the classroom, using the personal as a source of knowledge and the integration of the affective within intellectual learning.[19] Particular proposals include the use of the methods of consciousness raising and storytelling, small group teaching, collaborative teaching, and clinical teaching.[20]

In the next part of this chapter I shall examine to what extent feminist critiques are applicable to Croatian legal education. Before analyzing the curriculum of the law schools, I shall first outline the approach to law and legal education in Croatia, situating it briefly within wider socio-political developments in Croatia in its recent history.

5.3 Approach to Law and Legal Education in Croatia

Like in many other post-socialist states,[21] the dominant approach to

---

[16] See generally, Thornton, 'The Demise of Diversity;' Margaret Thornton, 'Among the Ruins: Law in the Neo-liberal Academy,' *Windsor Yearbook of Access to Justice* 20 (2000), 3–23.

[17] Menkel Medow, 'Feminist Legal Theory, Critical Legal Studies, and Legal Education or "The Fem-Crits Go to Law School".' Shauna Van Praagh, 'Stories in Law School: An Essay on Language, Participation, and the Power of Legal Education,' *Columbia Journal of Gender and Law* 2 (1992), 111–44.

[18] Morrison Torrey, Jackie Casey and Karin Olson, 'Teaching Law in a Feminist Manner,' *Harvard Women's Law Journal* 13 (1990), 109.

[19] See, for example: Toni Pickard, 'Experience as Teacher: Discovering the Politics of Law Teaching,' *University of Toronto Law Journal* 33 (1983), 279–314; Medow, 'Feminist Legal Theory;' Praagh, 'Stories in Law School;' Kennedy, 'Legal Education;' Jaff, 'Frame Shifting: An Empowering Methodology for Teaching and Learning Legal Reasoning,' *Journal of Legal Education* 36 (1988), 249–67; Torrey et al. 'Teaching Law in a Feminist Manner.'

[20] Praagh, 'Stories in Law School.'

[21] Zdenek Kuhn, 'Worlds Apart: Western and Central European Judicial Culture at the Onset of the European Enlargement,' *The American Journal of Comparative Law* 52/3

law in Croatia is still the 19th century type of positivism, according to which law is understood as a closed system of internally coherent written norms. In line with this, legal education is predominantly seen as a simple transmission of technical knowledge in a non-critical manner.[22] While after the Second World War countries of Western Europe disposed of the most problematic features of legal formalism and adopted more open, substantive, policy-oriented approaches to law, the socialist states adopted a textual approach to law, paradoxically eliminating sociological elements from legal science.[23] When socialism failed, post-socialist states largely returned to nineteenth century liberal theories of law, missing out on critical legal approaches, such as feminism, critical race theory, post-modernism, and queer theory that started flourishing in the last decades of the last centuries in 'Western countries,' particularly those of common law jurisdictions. The two opposing trends of the post-war rise of nationalism, the return of traditionalism and Catholicism on the one hand, and attempts at modernization and democratization within the supranational and international (neoliberal) political and economic orders on the other, also had an influence on the law and legal scholarship in Croatia. While law and legal education were reformed in the process of EU accession with the aim, inter alia, of making them more open and susceptible to social development, the reform was largely cosmetic, as it was not (fully) in line with social values.[24] Law remains a deeply conservative discipline in Croatia.

There are four law schools in Croatia, all of which are public. Since Croatia adopted the Bologna Declaration in 2001, all law schools offer a five year integrated undergraduate and graduate university programme, completion of which entitles the students to the title of 'Master of Laws,' which is however not comparable to LLM programmes abroad, being programmes of the second cycle.[25] Indeed, the reform has been criticized for simply prolonging the previous four year LLB programme.[26] While two

(2004), 531–67.

[22] Kuhn, 'Worlds Apart'; Siniša Rodin, 'Discourse and Authority in European and Post-Communist Legal Culture,' *Croatian Yearbook of European Law and Policy* 1 (2005), 1–22.

[23] Rodin, 'Discourse,' 1–22.

[24] I will deal with question of the potential of the EU reforms for radical reordering of the society, envisaged by feminist and other critical theorists, in the part in which legal scholarship is discussed.

[25] Siniša Rodin, 'Razmišljanja o provedbi bolonjskog procesa u Hrvatskoj' [Thinking about the Implementaiton of the Bologna Process in Croatia], *Revija za socijalnu politiku* 16 (2008), 175–208.

[26] The second cycle is in practice eliminated in Croatia, studies offering a *de facto* 5+0 programme, rather than 3+2 or 4+1 programmes. Zoran Kurelić, 'Antibolonja i društvo znanja' [Anti-Bologna and the Society of Knowledge], in *Društvene pretpostavke društva znanja*, ed. Darko Polšek (Zagreb: FF Press, 2011). Zoran Kurelić and Siniša Rodin, 'Failure of the Croatian Higher Education Reform,' *CEPS Journal* 2 (2012), 29–52.

law schools (Zagreb and Osijek) offer specialization in the last year of studies, last year students at Rijeka and Split law schools can choose from a (wider or narrower) range of optional subjects. In addition to the integrated programme, the schools also offer specialist post-graduate specialist courses and all three save Split Law School offer doctoral programmes.[27]

The law schools are organized in a very structured and hierarchical manner. They are compartmentalized into departments corresponding to the (already) recognized fields of law, with small variations in the names and structures of the departments. The academics do research predominantly in the department's area of expertise, while research into areas of other departments is not encouraged and there is little inter-departmental co-operation. Such structure is not conducive to the development of different perspectives on the established fields of law or interdisciplinary approaches to law, as the heads of the departments largely determine the content and the boundaries of any given field of law.

The departments are not only autonomous in how they define a particular field of law but also have a great autonomy in hiring, with the head of the department usually having the most powerful role in the hiring process. New academics are hired usually immediately after they finish the LLM (previously LLB) for a fixed term period in which they have to finish their PhD. The senior staff in the department usually have an influence in choosing the research topic of the junior member who very often becomes an assistant of the head or other senior member. This procedure ensures that knowledge remains within the confined boundaries of a certain field of law.

The process of promotion also presents an obstacle for the development of new, critical approaches to law.[28] Titles are issued by the National Committee for Law, a body of senior legal scholars nominated by the National Committee for Science, Higher Education, and Technological Development. First a commission of experts is set up within one of the law schools (usually where the candidate works) to assess whether the candidate fulfils the criteria in terms of the number and the categorization of publications (though it is not clear whether this is a formal or a substantive review process).[29] Their opinion is then forwarded to the

---

[27] Kurelić and Rodin are both critical of the specialist postgraduate courses, defining them as anomalies in the sytem, see Kurelić and Rodin, 'Failure of the Croatian Higher Education Reform,' 29–52; see also Zoran Kurelić, 'How Not to Defend Your Tradition of Higher Education,' *Politička misao* 46 (2009), 9–20.

[28] Tenure and promotion levels are generally disciplinary sites, see Margaret Thornton, 'Discord in the Legal Academia: The Case of the Feminist Scholar,' *Australian Feminist Law Journal* 3 (1994), 66.

[29] Under the new proposal of the 'Rules on Promotion,' a candidate for promotion in the fields of social sciences and humanities has to have at least two publications in Croatian for each promotion. This not only has a negative impact on persons publishing in international

National Committee for Law for confirmation or rejection (in specified circumstances). While the idea behind the national level assessment was to secure uniform, objective standards for all legal academics, the process allows for a lot of arbitrariness and can be used to sanction those whose research does not fit within the established structures of legal fields or whose relationships with senior colleagues are (perceived as) problematic.[30] Further, as positions are usually opened for a particular person in a particular department after he/she has been promoted, though formally opened, they are in most cases closed to anyone who is outside the system or who has studied or worked as an academic abroad. This minimizes competition and ensures that the people hired as PhD students remain throughout their career in one institution, while those who started their career elsewhere will very rarely be let in, which is yet another obstacle for any new perspectives and methodologies to enter the law school.

Similarly to the organization of law schools and the relationships between the academics, teaching is done in a hierarchical manner. Despite a certain modernization of teaching methods and the introduction of a quality insurance system in the law schools within the Bologna process, the dominant method of transmitting knowledge is still *ex cathedra* lecturing to a large number of students. Relevant knowledge is still predominantly understood to consist exclusively of the legal rules found in written texts, which students have to know by heart, while the critical questioning of the rules is not generally encouraged. There is rarely any discussion of policy considerations behind the norms or their application in practice, and case law analysis is still rarely used.[31] Available textbooks summarize codes and mostly avoid issues of interpretation and construction. Examinations are usually oral, whereby the simple reproduction of knowledge is evaluated.

However, compared to the time when I studied law at the Zagreb Law School (1996–2001) there seems to be an improvement in pedagogy, at least in new departments such as the Department of Public EU Law at

---

publications, it gives the editors of domestic articles, which are few in each discipline, great power. Nacrt Pravilnika o izboru u znanstvena zvanja, accessed 1 May 2016, http://www.nvzvotr.hr/images/stories/dokumenti_novi/Nacrt%20Pravilnika%20o%20uvjetima%20za%20izbor%20u%20znanstvena%20zvanja%20Javna%20rasprava.pdf.

[30] Uniformity and objectivity, the desirability of which could be questioned, cannot be achieved under the current system as candidates are subjected to different treatment depending on whether they work in or outside the institution which is entitled to set up a commission. While procedures for the candidates working in the law school finish normally within a year of requesting the evaluation, mine ended five years later after I instituted legal proceedings against the National Committee for Law, as I was originally denied a title in law, on account of my scholarship not fitting under any recognized area of law. Joseph Weiler, 'Editorial: The strange case of Dr. Ivana Radačić,' *European Journal of International Law* 24 (2013), 1–11.

[31] The case law is still not available on the Internet. The Supreme Court publishes only selected cases of the lower courts.

Zagreb Law School, which uses smaller group interactive teaching, and which relies heavily on analysis of case law. Also, there is now clinical and moot court education available at each law school, which was not the case ten years ago. However, it is only at Zagreb Law Clinic where students actually work with the clients, though supervision is provided almost exclusively by junior faculty. Other so-called clinics are different fora for acquiring practical experience, such as internships with the law firms or courts, or practical courses utilizing hypothetical cases. In addition, adoption of the credit system has opened up opportunities for students to study abroad, though a five-year integrated law education presents an obstacle for mobility of students at the masters level.[32]

Finally, there has been a proliferation of subjects. The rise in the courses concerning social justice issues has been slower in comparison to other areas, though in the last two years there has been significant expansion of human rights courses. Still, out of 15 specialist post-graduate degrees available at the four law schools in the academic year 2015/2016, only one is human rights masters programme, and there is no PhD programme in human rights. In the integrated programme one human rights class at Osijek Law School, two at Split and Rijeka Law Schools, and three at Zagreb Law School are offered, but there is no specific course on women's rights or gender and human rights.[33] There is only one course on women's rights (Women, Sex/Gender and Human Rights) at the postgraduate specialist studies on human rights at Osijek Law School.[34] There is no specific course on feminist theory/feminist jurisprudence, or gender and law,[35] though there is a course entitled 'Legal History of Women' in the integrated programme and 'The Specificities of Delinquency of Women' in the PhD programme at Zagreb Law School and Rijeka Law School.

The marginalization of feminist perspectives from the core curricula of the integrated programme of the law schools is analyzed in the next section.

---

[32] Kurelić, 'Antibolonja i društvo znanja;' Kurelić and Rodin, 'Failure of the Croatian Higher Education Reform;' Rodin, 'Razmišljanja o provedbi bolonjskog procesa u Hrvatskoj.'

[33] These are: Human Rights and Administrative Law; Human Rights and Criminal Justice; International Protection of Human Rights at Zagreb Law School; European Convention on Human Rights; and International Human Rights Law at Rijeka Law School; International Protection of Human Rights; Protection of Human Rights in the European and Comparative Perspective at Split Law School; and International Protection of Human Rights at Osijek Law School.

[34] This is feminist interdisciplinary course taught by a prominent feminist scholar Biljana Kašić (sociologist) and myself, neither of whom are employees of the Law School.

[35] Feminist theory/feminist jurisprudence, women's human rights, and gender are all different concepts. Gender equality and feminist projects might be very different. See, e.g. Biljana Kašić, 'Feminist Cross-Mainstreaming Within "East-West" Mapping: A Post-Colonial Perspective,' *European Journal of Women Studies* 11 (2004), 473–85.

5.4 Marginalization of Feminist Perspectives in Croatian Legal Academia

While all law school curricula could be examined for the inclusion of feminist perspectives and gender inquiry as an important critical tool of analysis (and would need to be examined for a more comprehensive understanding), I chose the categories of courses particularly relevant for feminism, and where one would expect feminist approaches to be included. There are: 1) introductory subjects to law and society—theory of law and state; sociology; 2) courses explaining the political and legal systems of which Croatia is a part—EU law, international law, constitutional law; 3) courses concerning areas of law and life where women are found to be at a particular disadvantage—family law, labour and social law, criminal law.

I examined the teaching plans for the integrated five year graduate studies available at Zagreb and Osijek Law Schools,[36] course syllabi at Split Law School and course syllabi of Rijeka Law School and, where available, other materials for the academic year 2015/2016, such as power point presentations.[37] In addition, I sent questionnaires concerning the inclusion of feminist topics to lecturers by e-mail where needed for clarification, but not all responded.[38] Hence, the information gained is not comprehensive and the level of detail varies for different courses, which complicates comparisons of different schools' programmes. Further, while this material can indicate what topics are included, it does not tell us what is *actually* thought and how. However, the data presented here are sufficient for some preliminary conclusions concerning the topic of this article.

5.5 First Year Introductory Subjects

The Theory of the Law and State is an introductory subject to legal studies (both to legal concepts and methods), which deals with the issues such as the types of social regulation and political governance, state

---

[36] University of Zagreb Law School, Integrated Undergraduate and Graduate University Studies, Informational Pack for the Academic Year 2015/2016 (Teaching Plans), accessed 1 May 2016, http://www.pravo.unizg.hr/_news/17221/4_Integrirani_preddiplomski_i_diplomski_pravni_studij%202015%202016%20-%207%202015.pdf; University J.J. Strossmayer Law School in Osijek, Integrated Undergraduate and Graduate University Studies, Teaching Plan for the Academic Year 2015/2016, accessed 1 May 2016, file:///C:/Users/hp/Downloads/integrirani-2015-2016-izvedbeni%20(4).pdf.

[37] Course syllabi for Split Law school are available at the webpage of each course at www.pravst.hr. Course syllabi for Rijeka Law School are not publicly available.

[38] The emails were sent in September 2013. Originally, teaching plans for the academic year 2013/2014 were analyzed, but as the publication process took time, the analysis was updated. I would like to express my gratitude to my teaching assistant, Marija Antić, for helping me with this.

(organization, elements, types), legal and social norms, legal relationships, legal systematization, application of law and techniques of interpretation, and legal theories. The following theories are included: natural law, positivism, pure theory of law, integral theories, natural law, historical legal approaches, theories of interests and theories of solidarity, normative theories.[39] Feminist theory is not included in any of the teaching plans. Only one of the theory of law professors stated that he includes feminist theories in his lectures, and he does so under the rubric of fundamentalist social movements![40]

The sociology course introduces basic sociological concepts and aims to develop critical thinking by revealing the social structures and processes that shape diverse forms of human life.[41] The teaching plans include the topics such as: methods; different sociological perspectives and theorists (such as Comte and positivism; biologism; psychoanalysis; Marxism; Durkheim; theories of elites; Weber; functionalists; sociology of law), and basic concepts are research areas (such as social stratification; social mobility; socialization; family; deviancy and crime; power; state; democracy, parties and movements; globalization; nation and nationality; political culture; religion). Only Rijeka Law syllabus includes gender and sexuality as one of the key topics of the course, and gender issues are also included under other topics, such as class, stratification; religion and society; family. The Osijek Law School sociology seminar plan mentions status of women in society as one of the topics, and Zagreb Law School sociology seminar plan includes gender and gender equality. There are power point presentations for lectures in sociology available at Zagreb Law School: two professors' presentations do not have any mention of feminism, while one professor's presentations refer to feminism/feminist jurisprudence (under modern theories; sociology of law—other perspectives; ideologies of the 21st century) sex/gender (under social stratification), feminist perspective (under family; and socialization), family violence (under family), and sex and voting (under under democracy).[42] Sociology hence seems to be more

---

[39] Osijek Law School teaching plan includes realism, and sociology and anthropology of law.

[40] One senior professor at Zagreb Law School (no longer working in 2016) denies its status as a theory, while junior professors are more sympathetic but say that the limited amount of time does not allow them to include it. The head of the Department for Theory of Law and State, Philosophy of Law, Human Rights and Public Policy at the Rijeka Law School did not respond to my repeated e-mails.

[41] University of Zagreb Law School, Integrated Undergraduate and Graduate University Studies, Information Pack (Teaching Plans) for the Academic Year 2015/2016, Sociology, 768.

[42] Powerpoint presentations of the lectures of Professor Ravlić, accessed March 2016 http://www.pravo.unizg.hr/SOC/predmet/soc_b/prezentacije_s_predavanja/prof._dr._sc._s._ravlic

inclusive of feminist topics in comparison to the theory of law and state (particularly by some professors), but there is still room for improvement, plans of the three law schools not including gender explicitly as one of its topics.

5.6 Subjects Introducing Legal and Political Orders

Constitutional Law, International Law and European Union law are all important subjects, which give an overview of the constitutional, international and supranational orders in which Croatia is situated, all of which have gender implications.[43] However, there is no mention of feminism, gender equality or women's rights in the Constitutional Law and International Law teaching plans of any law school (for example, under the unit concerning human rights). However, in e-mail correspondence with the law professors I learnt that most professors of international law and constitutional law do include the topic of women's rights and gender equality either through teaching or by offering it as a seminar topic for students. Syllabi for EU Law do not have reference to gender equality (they include the topic of fundamental rights), but the lecturers I contacted confirmed that the topic of gender discrimination is included. However, explicitly including gender equality as a key topic in the teaching plans would send a clearer message about its importance for all three areas of law.

5.7 Courses with a Subject Area of a Specific Relevance to Women

Discrimination is mentioned in the Labour and Social Law teaching plans of all save Split Law School, and the social protection of motherhood is mentioned in Osijek and Rijeka Law Schools teaching plans. Zagreb Law School's teaching plan also includes maternity and parental leave as one of the topics, and Rijeka Law School includes special protection of women (and minors and persons with diminished work capacity) as its topic. The Split Law school teaching plan, which is not very detailed, does not mention any of these issues. Hence, generally, in Croatian law schools, the teaching plans for this course do not seem to sufficiently reflect women's disadvantaged position on the labour market.

There is no mention of feminist scholarship in Family Law and Criminal Law teaching plans, even though these areas of law are obviously gendered

---

[43] I looked only at the basic subjects: European Public Law at Zagreb Law School and Osijek law School, EU law at Rijeka Law School and Basics of EU Law at Split Law School.

and include topics such as gender-based violence and reproduction. The topic of domestic violence is included only in the Family Law syllabus at Osijek Law School and Zagreb Law School.[44] However, the weekly teaching plans for Family Law course at Zagreb University do not mention this topic. Zagreb Law School teaching plans further includes the topic of medically assisted reproduction. However, the Head of the Department at Zagreb Law School is known for her conservative stand with respect to this topic and reproductive rights in general, as well as women's rights and LGBT rights more broadly.[45]

Sexual violence is included as a topic in the teaching plans of Criminal Law under the 'special part of criminal law' unit, but there is no mention of feminist scholarship on the issues of gender-based crimes, neither in the content of the plans nor the reading lists. The teaching plans for both of these courses exclude feminist scholarship.

From this brief discussion we can conclude that women's experiences are marginalized from the core curriculum content. Feminism is only covered in sociology courses (but not by all lecturers, and not explicitly, except at Rijeka Law School), while there is no mention of feminist jurisprudence in legal theory courses. Women's rights and gender equality are mentioned in some of the courses on constitutional, international, and EU law but are not treated as a separate teaching unit. Women's disadvantageous position in the workplace is not a specific topic of Labour and Social Law courses though certain professors include it, while gender-based violence is not analyzed from a feminist perspective in either Family Law or Criminal Law courses. The next section will analyze to what extent feminist perspectives are present in scholarly production.

---

[44] I did not get the syllabus for Family Law at Rijeka Law School, as the Head of the Department did not respond to my e-mails.

[45] She was the head of the Expert Committee which drafted the 2009 Act on Medically Assisted Reproduction, which was one of the most conservative in the world (replaced in 2012). She was one of the key legal experts for the initiative 'In the Name of the Family' which successfully called for a referendum that resulted in amending the Constitution to include a provision defining marriage as a union between a man and a woman. She also claimed that the new Partnership Act, regulating homosexual unions, is unconstitutional. See Jutarnji list, 24 January 2015, *Tko je konzervativna profesorica koja je strušila novi Obiteljski zakon* [Who is a Conservative Professor who Overturned New Family Law], accessed 1 May 2016, http://www.tportal.hr/vijesti/hrvatska/366956/Tko-je-konzervativna-profesorica-ko-ja-je-srusila-novi-Obiteljski-zakon.html. Most recently, she wrote an article on abortion in which she claimed that Croatian liberal abortion law is unconstitutional and contrary to the practice of the European Court of Human Rights. Dubravka Hrabar, 'Pravo na pobačaj—pravne i nepravne dvojbe' [The Right to Abortion—Legal and Non-legal Dillemas], *Zagreb University Law Review* (2015) 65, 791–831. She was also the head of the Commission in my promotion procedure, which concluded that my scholarship on feminism and human rights did not fall under any recognized branch of law.

5.8 Exclusion of Feminist Perspectives from Scholarly Production

A similar exclusion of feminist perspectives and women's experiences exists in relation to scholarly production. There is very little feminist legal literature in Croatia.[46] There is, however, a growing scholarship on anti-discrimination law. Of particular scholarly interest, primarily to EU law and labour law professors, are the various aspects of EU gender equality law. However, this work is mostly not informed by feminist scholarship. Most of the academics dealing with gender equality do not have a feminist (activist) background, which is anyhow strongly discouraged in light of the dominant dogma in respect of the objectivity of law and neutrality of academics.

While the rise of scholarship on gender equality and anti-discrimination legitimatizes gender as a subject of legal studies and gives it a visibility that was previously non-existent, the non-critical endorsement of the EU gender equality project may result not only in the depolarization of gender (before it has even became politicized as a critical tool of investigation), but also in legitimizing a dominant political and socio-economic framework based on hierarchies of gender, race, class, etc. Indeed, as noted by Kašić, the endorsement of the strategy of gender mainstreaming by the legal establishment in Croatia pushed by the EU accession project has resulted in hyper-normativity and hyper-institutionalization without a change in social attitudes and social and political structures.[47] As Rodin has noted, the transposition of the EU directives does not secure the change of legal culture necessary for its effective implementation.[48] Further, the EU gender equality project is itself limited by its primary economic occupation of creating a free market and protecting women as workers.[49] The EU accession project has done little to challenge the socio-legal norms of sexuality responsible for widespread violence against women.[50] This situation cannot

---

[46] I have written extensively on feminist theory and women's rights and have developed the only reader in Croatia (Ivana Radačić, *Women and Law: Feminist Legal Theory* [Zagreb: Centre for Women's Studies, 2009]), but this literature is to my knowledge not used in the law schools. Further, I have had problems publishing in certain law journals in Croatia due to the action I had taken against Zagreb Law School in 2002 for not recognizing my degree from the University of Cambridge.

[47] Biljana Kašić, 'Feminist Cross-Mainstreaming Within "East-West" Mapping: A Post-Colonial Perspecitve,' *European Journal of Women Studies* 11 (2004), 473–85; see also Ivana Radačić, 'Human Rights of Women and the Mechanisms of their Implementation in Croatia with the Focus on Regulation of Violence against Women,' in *Young Women in Post-Yugoslav Societies: Research, Practice and Politics*, ed. Mirjana Adamović et al. (Zagreb: IDIS, 2014), 237–57.

[48] Siniša Rodin, 'Closing the Gap? Impact of EU Accession on Transformation of Croatian Judiciary,' *Advocate* (2013), 2–6.

[49] Ivana Radačić, 'Human Rights of Women.'

[50] Indeed, as my research of the judicial practice in rape cases show, the Croatian judicial

be remedied simply by a top down approach of incorporating the EU *acquis*. Non-critical transmission of the EU gender equality rules through writings and teaching will not, therefore, alone be able to produce the radical change of legal education necessary for changing social norms on gender relations.[51]

But critical legal scholarship, based on feminist legal theory is rejected. I was thus initially denied the title of a 'research associate in law,' because my field of research—feminism and human rights—allegedly does not fall under any recognized branch of law. The Commission of the Zagreb Law School were of the opinion that I should be placed in gender studies, despite having obtained a PhD in law from UCL. While gender studies have in 2009 been recognized as an 'interdisciplinary scientific field,'[52] there is no gender studies programme at any university, while the first academic centre for women's studies was inaugurated in March 2016 at the Faculty of Arts, University of Rijeka.

Feminism and women's gender studies have been comprehensively taught only at the NGO Centre for Women Studies. Unlike the law schools, this one year non-degree programme has from its beginning in 1995 incorporated feminist legal theory and women's rights as its subjects of inquiry. It is this organization that has published the *Reader on Feminist Legal Theory* and produced much of the Croatian and regional feminist scholarship. However, despite its role in producing feminist scholarship (or because of it), it has not yet been integrated into the academic system, which might be one of the reasons that it remains an open critical space.[53]

5.9 Conclusion: The Way Forward

Legal education in Croatia is gendered both in its conceptualization of legal education as the transmission of technical apolitical knowledge

---

system endorses the patriarchal norms of sexual and gender relations. See Ivana Radačić, 'Rape Myths and Gender Stereotypes in Croatian Laws and Judicial Practice,' *Feminist Legal Studies* 22 (2014), 67–87; Ivana Radačić, *Seksualno nasilje: mitovi, stereotipi i pravi sustav* [*Sexual Violence: Myths, Stereotypes and the Legal System*] (Zagreb: TimPress, 2014).

[51] Of course, legal education alone cannot change social norms, but the reform of the law schools is one of the crucial steps due to the power of law.

[52] Pravilnik o znanstvenim i umjetničkim područjima, poljima i granama (Rules on scientific and artistic areas, disciplines and fields), Official Gazette 118/2009.

[53] On the dilemma of integration see: Biljana Kašić, 'Towards a Critical Knowledge: Gender Sensitive Education in the Abyss or an Illusion?' in *Young Women in Post-Yugoslav Societies: Research, Practice and Politics*, ed. Mirjana Adamović et al. (Zagreb: IDIS, 2014). For the risk of disciplination of women's/gender studies see Claire Hemming, 'Ready for Bologna? The Impact of the Declaration on Women's and Gender Studies Programme in the UK,' *European Journal of Women's Studies* (2006) 13, 315–23.

and its exclusion or insufficient attention to feminist (or even gender) issues in the curriculum and legal scholarship. The exclusion of feminist (and other critical) perspectives in legal education has significant negative impact on the legal profession and the development of law, as it maintains and perpetuates the patriarchal nature of law and the legal profession in Croatia.

There are many obstacles to incorporating feminist perspectives and creating feminist legal scholarship in Croatia, as discussed above. Some of them are of institutional nature and relate to the structure and the organization of the law schools, as well as the entry and promotion procedures in (legal) academia. Feminism is defined by inter/trans-disciplinarity and as such it cannot easily be placed within a single field of law and categorized within corresponding departments. The compartmentalization of legal academia is not only an obstacle for the inclusion of feminist perspectives but also other critical perspectives and for the development of law in general. Hence, the departmental organization should be abolished.

Further, the system of entry and promotion within legal academia discourages new research and alternative interdisciplinary theoretical and methodological perspectives and acts as a barrier for truly open employment procedures. Hence, it might be best to leave the promotions procedure to the institution where a person is employed. To secure a more open entry into legal academia as well as a motivating environment for interdisciplinary and new perspectives, titles should not be given in a specific field of law (at least not exclusively). A positive step in this direction is the instruction given to the National Committee of Law by the former National Committee on Science that titles should not be given in a specific field of a discipline.[54] Further steps should be taken to transform the statist system of promotions.[55]

Other obstacles for the inclusion of feminist perspectives are found in the organization of studies, the content of curricula, and the pedagogy

---

[54] This was a result of my correspondence with the National Commission for Science with respect to my case. The procedure for promotion started in November 2009. After the Commission of the Law School stated that I satisfied criteria to gain the title of a research associate but proposed that I get a title in gender studies, I was left in an abyss without a legal remedy. Hence, in January 2013 I started the procedure again, this time before the Osijek Law School Commission. This Commission issued an opinion that I should be given the title in international law, as I mostly publish on international human rights law. However, the National Committee of Law rejected this opinion without giving any reasons. I appealed to the Administrative Court who annulled the decision. After that, the National Committee of Law issued a title in law, without specifying the field.

[55] Siniša Rodin, 'Kao brodovi u noći: hrvatsko visoko obrazovanje i slobode unutarnjeg tržišta Europske unije' [Like ships in the night: Croatian high education and the freedoms of internal market of the EU], accessed 1 March 2016, https://www.pravo.unizg.hr/_download/repository/Rodin_market.pdf.

used. As seen above, there are no courses that deal with feminism or gender issues in the integrated programme and there is a very limited coverage of feminist topics in other subjects, while there is limited provision for law students to attend non-legal courses. To remedy this exclusion, new courses on feminism should be developed and feminist scholarship should be incorporated in different courses, including feminist and other critical legal theories' insights on legal methodology and pedagogy. This would require interested professors to familiarize themselves with feminist jurisprudence and to support younger interested scholars in undertaking feminist and other critical legal research, as well as to cooperate with legal and non-legal academics and activists who are not employed at the law school. The Centre for Women Studies has unique knowledge and resources and could be a great partner in incorporating feminist perspectives into the law schools, but legal academia is still suspicious of NGOs and generally of non-legal experts. A positive development in this respect is the cooperation of certain law schools with NGOs on clinical education, but there is no clinic on women's rights yet. Clinics, small seminar groups, and other different forms of experimental learning which would allow for the non-hierarchical collaboration of students, academics (including from different disciplines), activists, and practicing lawyers are particularly suitable for the development of feminist praxis in Croatia. My hope is that this chapter contributes to this endeavour.

6

The Social Construction of Femininity in the Discourse of the Polish Constitutional Court

Hanna Dębska & Tomasz Warczok

6.1 Introduction

While considered banal in contemporary social sciences, the fact of recognizing the social world as construction should be considered a major breakthrough. It was strictly critical in nature as it stood against (and still does) a common sense understanding of the world as a settled reality that is given to us just the way it seems. It does not need mentioning that the social sciences, guided by positivistic reason, shared a similar vision for a long time. The change came with the anti-positivistic revolution and acceptance of an assumption that what is perceived as reality is an effect of interpretation and an endless process of giving meaning, as performed by people. The area of gender studies saw the introduction of a fundamental distinction between the cultural and biological sexes. With continuing investigations the constructionist position became increasingly radical until the view emerged that only interpretation exists. Postmodernist scholars veered towards extreme relativism, claiming that there could be no objective reality (including truth). In gender research this resulted in questioning the very distinction between the biological and the cultural—the biological sex was also considered to be a social construction.[1]

While this chapter does not directly consider the validity of other radical and/or mild constructivism, some assumptions still need to be made in this regard. We agree with the view that reality is socially constructed, and as such, what we are interested in investigating is the way this process works and what social conditions enable it. We are particularly interested in how femininity is socially created and sustained through the judgments of the Polish constitutional court (*Trybunał Konstytucyjny*, hereinafter 'TK'). The TK, which is as a legal institution hidden behind purported universal and impartial structures, can use its structural position to impose

[1] Judith Butler, *Gender Trouble: Feminism and the Subversion of Identity* (New York: Routledge, 1999).

several ideological visions of the world on the society.[2] Critical discourse analysis (examination of vocabulary, grammar, and text structures) and Pierre Bourdieu's social theory (especially his field theory) are very useful in explaining this phenomenon. They both complement each other.[3] While Bourdieu's theory is our basis, critical discourse analysis allows us to reconstruct the TK's discursive strategies, ideological patterns and, consequently, hidden political content. Our inquiry is focused on a TK judgment concerning abortion. This case is a good illustration for the argument we would like to put forward. There is no doubt that the law enforces basic classifications (for instance, by deciding what constitutes normal and deviant behaviour) and the relative autonomy of the legal field makes this possible. The effect of these actions is a naturalized social order, with misrecognized arbitrariness and universalized particularisms.

This chapter is divided into two parts. Theoretical assumptions are presented in the first part, while in the second, empirical data are analyzed according to these theoretical approaches.

6.2 The Social Construction of Reality—Towards Material Anthropology

When considering the social conditions of gender construction, it seems appropriate to start by revisiting the determinations of Berger and Luckmann's 'social creation of reality,' a key work for mild constructivism.[4] According to these authors, a subject, through constant interpretation, creates reality by emphasizing subjectively important aspects of the world. Through contact with others one reconciles different visions of the world. This knowledge, in the context of broader interactions between individuals, acquires a quality of being objective—determining the way actors perceive and experience the world, and organizing their actions. Such an objectivized symbolic world is subjectively experienced daily as natural and, is not doubted or questioned.

Socially constructed reality requires legitimizations—specific procedures designed to sustain it. There are two basic types of legitimizations: 'the self-legitimizing facticities'[5] and multilevel discursive legitimizations. In

---

[2] Hanna Dębska, *Władza, symbol, prawo. Społeczne tworzenie Trybunału Konstytucyjnego* (Warszawa: Wydawnictwo Sejmowe, 2015).

[3] Tomasz Warczok, 'Dyskurs Ucieleśniony—dyskurs skontekstualizowany' [Discourse embedded, discourse contextualized. An approach inspired by Pierre Bourdieu's theory] *Qualitative Sociology Review* 9.1 (2013), 32–47.

[4] Peter L. Berger and Thomas Lukmann, *The Social Construction of Reality* (London: Penguin University Books, 1966).

[5] Peter Berger, *Sacred Canopy. Elements of a Sociological Theory of Religion* (New York: Anchor Books, 1967).

the gender context, a self-legitimizing facticity would be an unwritten and unspoken (directly) assumption that the gender division is essential in nature, based on non-reductive biological differences. Discursive legitimizations are both pragmatic sentences and sayings, aphorisms and moral maxims (i.e. a woman should care for the household) as well as, on a higher conceptual level, the outlines of theories (i.e. a woman should not choose her career over her child, as it may adversely affect the child's development). At the highest level one encounters theories removed from everyday reality, i.e. sociological functional theories stating that women perform an expressive function and men perform an instrumental one—both are complementary, and allegedly indispensable for maintaining the operations of the entire social system.[6]

While explaining a number of mechanisms of the social creation of reality, Berger and Luckmann's theory has some deficits. First of all, it seems to stop at the level of 'self-legitimizing facticity.' At this point, the theory should continue to explain how this level of experience is socially created. It is particularly important as this 'basic reality,' described by Bourdieu as 'doxa,' is analytically basic in meaning—determining peoples' behaviour in an unspoken and covert way. Doxa is commonly referred to as 'common sense, but its actual meaning is not what it is usually taken to be. According to Bourdieu:

> Common sense is a stock of self-evidences shared by all, which, within the limits of a social universe, ensures a primordial consensus on the meaning of the world, a set of tacitly accepted commonplaces which make confrontation, dialogue, competition and even conflict possible, and among which a special place must be reserved for the principles of classification, such as the major oppositions structuring the perception of the world. ... Being, as a consequence, common to all the agents participating in that order, they are what makes possible the agreement in disagreement of agents who are situated in opposite positions (high/low, visible/obscure, rare/common, rich/poor, etc.) and who are characterized by distinctive properties, themselves different or opposite in social space. In other words, they are what makes it possible for all agents to refer to the same oppositions (such as high/low, up/down, rare/common, light/heavy, rich/poor, etc.) to think the world and their position in the world, while sometimes giving opposite signs and values to the terms they counterpose.[7]

Therefore, a classificatory schemata of reality, deposited at the level of individuals in the form of dispositions are not, as proponents of social phenomenology (such as the aforementioned Bergman and Luckmann) believe,

---

[6] Talcott Parsons, *Essays in Sociological Theory* (New York: The Free Press, 1964).
[7] Pierre Bourdieu, *Pascalian Meditations* [1997] (Stanford: Stanford University Press, 2006), 98.

already given, but are an effect of particular actions—more specifically of social struggles:

> The representation of the social world is not a given, or (which amounts to the same thing) a recording or a reflection, but product of the countless acts of *construction*, always ready made and always to be remade. It is deposited in common words and phrases, performative terms that make the meaning of the social world as much as they record, watchwords (*mots d'ordre*) which help to produce the social order by informing thought about that world and producing the groups they designate and mobilize.[8]

Therefore, doxa is a result of a struggle—what is known as symbolic violence—based on the imperceptible shaping of specific visions of the world.[9] Symbolic violence is actualized through imposed categories of perception and valuation. Its functioning is hard for individuals to detect, because it is effectively a universalization of a determined particularism whose arbitrariness is misrecognized due to specific social processes.

It should be remembered that symbolic violence, or doxa, understood as a neutral 'common sense,' is not an ideology (in the Marxist sense).[10] While ideology constituting the body of an idea belongs to the realm of what is conscious (i.e. false consciousness), doxa is a practical knowledge intrinsic to particular actions.[11] It is thus not strictly discursive in nature. It is rather the grounds for all discourse—its framework and a structuring structure. Allowing for simplification, one might say that just as (in structural linguistics) *langue* is a form or ground on which *parole* is constructed as actual expressions, so doxa is for discourse.[12] As already mentioned, usually doxa takes a dichotomous form, arising around oppositional semantic schemata. This is not an accident. Bourdieu states that all symbolic structures (doxa) are grounded in social structures. An experience of a world as natural, devoid of problems and self-evident is called 'doxic.'[13] Such experience arises because the social structures in which one acts (i.e. the social class one belongs to) appears in one's experience as a dichotomous mental structure. Since the social world is usually divided into 'the dominant' and 'the dominated' (higher and lower classes), the aforementioned mental categories will determine one's perception of the world (i.e. elite vs masses,

---

[8] Pierre Bourdieu, *The Bachelors' Ball: The Crisis of Peasant Society in Béarn* [2002] (Chicago: University of Chicago Press, 2008), 193–4.
[9] On the concept of 'symbolic violence,' see generally Pierre Bourdieu, *Language and Symbolic Power* [1982] (Cambridge: Polity Press, 1991).
[10] Karl Marx and Friedrich Engels, *The German Ideology* (1845) accessed 1 May 2014, http://www.marxists.org/archive/marx/works/1845/german-ideology/ch01a.htm.
[11] Pierre Bourdieu, *Pascalian Meditations* (Stanford: Stanford University Press, 2006).
[12] Ferdinand de Saussure, *Cours de linguistique générale* (Paris: Payot, 1995).
[13] Bourdieu, *Pascalian Meditations*, 152.

superior vs inferior, educated vs uneducated, cultured vs uncultured).

Nevertheless, the mental categories correlated with social structures do not arise spontaneously. All meanings, dominant representations of the social world that individuals use like 'cognitive glasses' in their everyday experiences are being created in specific social contexts that Bourdieu dubbed fields. This observation is particularly valid for the so called *fields of cultural production* (academic field, artistic field, media field, religious field, etc.).[14]

6.3 Fields and the Production of Meaning

Fields are slices of social reality. They are sets of positions occupied by agents who *play against* one another. Each field (social universe) has a unique 'capital'—a supply doubling as a tool to be used in such a game. In the academic field capital is the prestige one enjoys among one's peers, and the goal of the game is to make one's theory or vision of science the dominant, most adequate, obvious, and accepted one. This of course is done by convincing others of one's way of thinking (theory, methodology, etc.). The game works similarly regardless of the field. In the field of religion, the goal is the domination of one religion or creed. In the artistic field the dominant is the one whose artistic current is most highly valued, most recognizable and considered right. In the political field, one strives to make one's political ideology dominant.

Each field creates its own schemata—vision of the world imposed by agents enjoying hegemony within the field.[15] These schemata directly correspond to the structure of the fields, which, like social class, also adopt the dominating v. dominated form (the classics v. the avant-garde, the ruling party v. the opposition, the dominant religion v. heresy, etc.). While autonomous to a varying degree, in many instances the fields are also interconnected. Because of this, we are able to conduct a precise analysis of the phenomenon known in discourse analysis as intertextuality—the ways in which given texts are transferred from one field to another, maintaining their basic and ideological meaning while changing their form.[16] This is particularly important because it is in these transfers that the transformation of a text occurs—more specifically, the political sense of the text is being hidden.

---

[14] Pierre Bourdieu, *The Field of Cultural Production: Essays on Art and Literature* (New York: Columbia University Press, 1993).

[15] Pierre Bourdieu, *The Rules of Art, Genesis and Structure of the Literary Field* (Stanford: Stanford University Press, 1996).

[16] Norman Fairclough, *Analyzing Discourse: Textual analysis for social research* (London: Routledge, 2003), 39–62.

All currently operating fields (academic, artistic, philosophical, etc.) are historically conditioned, being the effects of prior struggles from which arose not only the structurizations of these fields, but also their field-specific rules. A specific historically worked out 'space of possibilities' may be found in each field. This space of possibilities consists of available subjects and a language used for interaction and forming relations between acting individuals, etc.[17] A space of possibilities is time-relative, meaning that, for example, the same philosophical problem will be analyzed differently today than it was one hundred years ago. This is not a result of knowledge acquisition but of a change in the space of possibilities. Thus, it may be said that each field has its own specific way of creating texts. However, there are two important assumptions. Firstly, each field is an area of struggle, generally not different from struggle in the field of politics. It should be noted, however, that symbolic struggles need to adhere to field-specific rules, which entails that every field has a specific 'censorship' which sublimates the struggle into a mode coherent with the nature of said field (for example, in the field of science *libido dominandi* is sublimated into *libido sciendi,* whereby what is political hides in a form of scientific knowledge).[18] Secondly, fields interact with one other in specific ways, which is particularly important for relations involving the field of politics. To put it differently, in accordance with the legal field's censorship, that which is the political may be expressed solely in legal terms.

Therefore, while the form may undergo constant change, the political meanings hidden behind the varying language rules of each field remain the same. This is particularly important because the transfer of texts from one field to another, executed in the manner described above, may gradually disguise the relations of power contained within the basic classificatory schemata of reality, which will seem perfectly neutral on the level of, for example, legal discourse. According to the above-mentioned thesis, what persist in such a 'wandering' text are basic, naturalized, binary categories.

The particular power of each field to 'censor' by hiding political content and transforming it into more 'neutral' and thus symbolically effective communications is not dependent so much on the communication itself, but on the character of a given field.[19] However, this character (i.e. philosophical and legal fields seems to be more ideologically neutral than political fields) does not result from the fields' immanent qualities, but from the relations between the fields. More specifically, it results from the total configuration of fields. Such a holistic system of fields, or rather of

---

[17] Pierre Bourdieu, *Political Ontology of Martin Heidegger* [1988] (Stanford: Stanford University Press, 1991).
[18] Bourdieu, *Pascalian Meditations*, 111.
[19] Bourdieu, *Political Ontology*, ch. 4.

their dominant parts, creates a meta-field described by Bourdieu as the 'field of power.'[20] It spans (to mention only the most important) from the superordinate economic field (through the fields of politics, media, law, administration, academia) to the subordinate, yet most autonomous, field of art. Therefore, when a communication or an idea is 'transferred' from a political field (where legitimizations mentioned by Berger and Luckmann, like ideas and visions of the world, are created in the most open manner) towards the autonomic pole of power, it gradually 'loses' its openly ideological character and is 'transformed' into a more 'neutral' legitimization. And so, the issue of gender, while present in the field of politics in the form of openly feminist or anti-feminist communications, once transferred to the academic (i.e. sociological) field is transformed, through field censorship, into a descriptive and explanatory discourse, seemingly neutral when stated in scientific terminology.

The administrative (bureaucratic) field, located in the centre of the field of power will be of prime importance to our inquiry. It is the field of the state to which other fields are necessarily related. Additionally, not only does a state have a monopoly of physical violence,[21] it also has a monopoly of symbolic violence.[22] It is the institutions of the state's administrative field that are the final authority and which imperceptibly imposes the basic categories of perception and valuation upon which the legitimizations of other fields are built.[23] Due to an unparalleled access to tools used for constructing the social world (categories and classifications), the state has the ability to create identities and even entire groups. Among others, it separates adults from children (an arbitrary boundary of 18 years of age), it creates categories of sick and handicapped persons (through physicians delegated by the state), it separates the 'able' and 'gifted' from the 'inept' and 'lazy' (through the system of education—schools). It even constructs the temporal order perceived by individuals as 'natural' (the division of time into holidays and a school year reinforces other divisions, like the specific sectioning of television programmes). In similar vein, the state establishes what constitutes a legitimate family (by providing various direct and indirect forms of assistance to families of a certain structure), and through this, it also indirectly establishes the legitimate role of a man and a woman.

Although all these endeavours (and many others) are arbitrary and

[20] Pierre Bourdieu, *The State Nobility. Elite Schools in the Field of Power* (Stanford: Stanford University Press, 1996).
[21] Max Weber, *Economy and Society. An Outline of Interpretive Sociology* (Berkeley, Los Angeles: University of California Press, 1987).
[22] Bourdieu, *The State Nobility*, 117.
[23] Pierre Bourdieu, *Sur l'État: Cours au Collège de France (1989–1992)* (Paris: Seuil, 2012), passim.

particular in nature, through the neutrality of the administrative field they become universalized and naturalized. This is so because the administrative field lies in the middle of the field of power—in a neutral space—which, in theory, balances external forces.[24] It is supposed to be guided by the republican virtue of the 'common good.' The bureaucrats of the administrative field internalize such rules and follow them at least formally. Therefore, the farther the administrative field is removed from the political field, the greater its neutrality and the better its ability to universalize the particular. At the same time, the administrative field is not unitary and homogeneous, but is in itself a field of struggle. Its structure, much like the structure of the field of power can be bisected into economic (also political) and cultural poles. What is more important, this bisection is reflected in 'gender' association and corresponds to social hierarchy— the dominant 'masculine,' like the ministry of finance and the ministry of defence (perceived as 'hard,' 'aggressive,' 'tough'); and the dominated 'feminine,' like the ministry of labour and social policy, or the ministry of culture (perceived as 'soft,' 'delicate,' 'cooperative').[25]

It would seem then that the practically most neutral, and thus symbolically most efficient, space is that of the administrative field that borders or even overlaps with the academic field, as it hides the ideological within doxa. This one space provides the best way for 'officialization' of a given communication—its universalization through making it public;[26] the other provides a 'neutral' and 'objective' (scientific) language.[27] Because of this, institutions delegated by the state but manned by individuals from the scientific field will be key in constructing the symbolic order of the social world. In the Polish context, among such institutions will be the Monetary Policy Committee (*Rada Polityki Pieniężnej*, for economic matters) and the TK (with regards to a broad array of matters relating to social life). The latter is fundamentally important because it is a legal institution. What is more, law itself serves a fundamental function in the creation of basic divisions of social life, which include particular identities (adult/child, healthy/ill, etc.). However, contrary to other institutions involved in the creation of law, like the Ministry of Justice or Parliament, the TK, as removed from the political field and associated with the academic field, is characterized by a particular symbolic effectiveness—the ability to create

---

[24] Pierre Bourdieu and Luc Boltanski, *La production de l'idéologie dominante* (Paris: Raisons d'agir/Demopolis, 2008).

[25] Pierre Bourdieu, 'The Abdication of the State,' in *The Weight of the World: Social Suffering of Contemporary Society*, ed. Pierre Bourdieu et al. [1993] (Stanford: Stanford University Press, 1999), 181–8.

[26] Bourdieu, *Sur l'État*, passim.

[27] Frédéric Lebaron, 'The Space of Economic Neutrality. Trajectories and Types of Legitimacy of Central Bank Managers,' *European Societies* 3/1 (2001), 91–110.

'neutral' communications. These, as will be shown below, carry with them specific political contents hidden within the schemata of political doxa, which while 'wandering' from the political, through the administrative, to the academic field 'lose' their explicitly expressed ideological layer.

6.4 Social Changes after Political Transformation in 1989

For our purpose, we will be focusing on the TK's judgments regarding the situation of women, particularly those pertaining to abortion (the one issued soon after the beginning of the second decade of the TK's functioning and the most recent one).[28] As it turns out, the issue of abortion focuses and even objectivizes the key dichotomous classifications that determine dispositions of individuals in the mode of social perceiving. While we will be focusing on analyzing the ways in which the TK's judgments construct a certain vision of femininity, how the relation between sexes is reproduced and what implications it carries with it, first we will need to look at the background of social changes that took place in Poland.

In her research, Małgorzata Fidelis stresses that during the Polish socialist period (1945–89), women were encouraged to pursue professional careers—a stark contrast to the west. This tendency was strongest during the Stalinist period (1948–55), not just because of the low level of income received by men, but mostly for ideological reasons (i.e. access to social services was restricted to individuals who were in active employment). This encouragement period did not last long, and was halted in the middle of the 1950s. The gender hierarchy based on male superiority was sustained in Polish society with the help of different rules. Equality was not promoted by appealing to men to take up household chores. Gender inequality was maintained as women were rarely promoted to better posts, particularly in 'masculine' occupations to which women had little or no access (the tractor driver woman myth was quickly abolished). Additionally, women were often doubly or even triply burdened. Not only did they perform household chores, they had also social and professional responsibilities. These experiences fuelled a certain dislike for feminism in the 1990s.

Contrary to common belief, there was also no equality within the sphere of sexuality. Although certain reproductive rights were strongly enforced (the right to terminate was guaranteed by the law), there was a dominant double standard when it came to the male and female sexuality. There were attempts at proving that women have a natural tendency towards

---

[28] TK judgment of 15 July 2010 Case K 63/07; TK resolution of 15 July 2010, Case S 2/10; TK Judgment of 29 September 1997, Case K 15/97; TK judgment of 28 May 1997, Case K.26/96; TK Judgment of 22 July 2008, Case K 24/07.

a family life while simultaneously stressing the male inability to control their urges.[29]

Together with the transformation of the political system and the democratization process came a partial reversal of the emancipatory tendencies connected with the permissible termination of pregnancy. While abortion was legal in socialist Poland under the Act of 1956 regarding the conditions of termination of pregnancy,[30] after 1989 there was a characteristic backlash much like the one in Kansas described by Thomas Frank.[31] In a manner similar to the US state, the socially aggrieved lower classes of Poland (particularly women of these classes), who in the new capitalism were losing social status and the ability to support a family the fastest, were offered a higher moral status in place of the foregone economic one.[32] As often happens in similar situations, 'positively ban[ning] women from holding any of the better paying jobs' soon created a moral elite siding with an outright ban on abortion.[33]

The Catholic Church in Poland played an important role in this process. Due to the special role the Catholic Church played in both the *Solidarność* movement and later in the period preceding the transformation, it was seen as the only space for expression of freedom. In other words, the position of the Church was not only maintained throughout the socialist period, but was also strengthened. Therefore, after 1989 the Catholic Church could

---

[29] Małgorzata Fidelis, *Women, Communism and Industrialization in Postwar Poland* (Cambridge: CUP, 2010).

[30] *Ustawa z dnia 27 kwietnia 1956 r. o warunkach dopuszczalności przerywania ciąży* [Act of 27 April 1956 on the Conditions of Permissibility of Pregnancy Termination] (Dz. U. no. 12, item 61). According to Art. 1 (1), the Act allowed termination of pregnancy, if performed by an authorized physician, in the following three instances: *1)* when the pregnancy threatens the health and life of the mother or the foetus; *2)* if there is a justified suspicion that the pregnancy is a result of a crime; *3)* due to the difficult life situation of the pregnant woman.

[31] Thomas Frank, *What's the Matter with Kansas? How Conservatives Won the Heart of America* (New York: Metropolitan/Owl Books, 2005).

[32] Research conducted by the Centre for Public Opinion show that in the 1990s there was a conservative turn in people's opinion regarding abortion. There was a marked decrease in public acceptance of termination in cases when the child would be born suffering from mental retardation or where the so-called social premises (the personal or material situation of the woman) applied. Research shows that supporters of the introduced anti-abortion solutions predominantly come from the lower classes. The report states that 'the support for an outright ban on abortion is most common among individuals with basic education, persons dissatisfied with their own living standards (27%), people over the age of 64 (26%), welfare clients (24%), farmers (21%) and people living in villages (20%).' Religion also plays an important part in holding an antiabortion view—in this group most people are over the age of 55. See 'Opinie na temat dopuszczalności aborcji' [Opinions on abortion], BS/100/2010, Centrum Badania Opinii Społecznej, Warszawa 2010, accessed April 4, 2014, http://www.cbos.pl/SPISKOM.POL/2010/K_100_10.PDF.

[33] Randall Collins, *Sociological Insight. An Introduction to Non-obvious Sociology* (New York, Oxford: OUP, 1992), 152–3.

take a significant position in the field of power. Topics, which in public discourse were omitted (i.e. women's reproductive rights) could become, with the church taking this position of power, doubly present. Moreover, conservative ideas and institutions needed to be strengthened due to the danger of secularization, which could come together with democratization of the system.

This conservative turn is also confirmed by researchers studying feminism in Central and Eastern Europe. It appears that in the early democratic years of the former post-communist states the first problem the authorities tried to tackle using legal acts was abortion.[34] In other words, the abortion law became a calling card of the new authorities of the region.[35] In Poland, the conflict started in March 1989 when a group of seventy members of parliament tabled a proposal for a Protection of the Unborn Life Act, prepared mainly by experts of the Polish Episcopate.[36] Although this matter divided society—some wanted a referendum, while others demanded an immediate adoption of the Act—at that time

> very few would have guessed that this was the starting point of one of the longest and most vicious legalisative struggles in post-war Poland. A struggle which would fire up social emotions, start mass support and protest actions and divide the society into supporters and opponents of planned solutions.[37]

In January 1993 the Family Planning, Protection of Human Foetus and Conditions for Termination Act was passed (Hereinafter: 'Family Planning Act 1993').[38]

---

[34] Peggy Watson, 'Anti-Feminism After Communism,' in *Who is afraid of Feminism. Seeing Through the Backlash*, ed. Ann Oakley and Juliet Mitchel (London: Hamish Hamilton 1997), 144–62.

[35] Agnieszka Graff, *Świat bez kobiet* [The world without women] (Warszawa: W.A.B., 2011), 31.

[36] Robert Alberski, *Trybunał Konstytucyjny w polskich systemach politycznych* [The Constitutional Court in the Polish Political Systems] (Wrocław: Wyd. Uniwersytetu Wrocławskiego, 2010), 263–6.

[37] Wojciech Pawlik, 'Spór o aborcję, czyli sztuka parlamentarnej erystyki' [The Controversy Surrounding Abortion, or The Art of Parliamentary Eristic], in *Cudze problemy. O ważności tego co nieważne. Analiza dyskursu publicznego w Polsce* [The Problems of Others. On the Importance of the Unimportant. An Analysis of the Polish Public Discourse], ed. Marek Czyżewski, Kinga Dunin and Andrzej Piotrowski (Warszawa: Wyd. Akademickie i Profesjonalne, 2010), 159.

[38] *Ustawa z dnia 7 stycznia 1993 r. o planowaniu rodziny, ochronie płodu ludzkiego i warunkach dopuszczalności przerywania ciąży* [Act of 7 January 1993 on Family Planning, the Protection of Human Foetus and Conditions for Termination of Pregnancy (hereianfter: 'Family Planning Act 1993')] (Dz. U. no. 17, item 78). According to Art. 4a, the procedure for terminating a pregnancy may only be performed by a physician in the following three instances: 1) when the pregnancy poses a threat to the health or life of the pregnant woman; 2) prenatal examination or other medical facts point to a high probability of severe and irreversible retardation of the foetus, or an incurable life threatening disease; 3) there is a

The second term Parliament (1993–97) tried twice (1994 and 1996),[39] unsuccessfully, to liberalize the provisions of the Family Planning Act 1993 . When on 30 August 1996, after an amendment to the Family Planning Act 1993 was adopted,[40] the Act was contested and brought before the TK,[41] it issued one of the judgments that will be discussed in this part of the chapter.[42] Partly due to the judgments issued by the TK, the debate regarding abortion was transferred from the political and media fields into the field of law. The shape the debate took was partly determined by the involvement of the TK, as both sides brought actions before it, considering it to be a defender of the status quo.[43]

As already mentioned, the 'transfer' of contents between fields must abide by specific rules of discourse. In Bourdieu's words, every relatively independent field has its own logic—its 'conditions of exchange'—which are inscribed in both its structure and in the dispositions of its agents. For these reasons, contexts from outside the field need to acquire a 'claim to validity' if they wish to be introduced into a given field.[44] The same applies to political contents. This process needs to be properly executed, as the incorporating field—the legal universe—needs to appear as professional, absolutely impartial, and removed from valuations since it safeguards the universal affairs of the entire society. Therefore, only authorized social parties (like constitutional judges) obliged to use only the tools permitted in the legal field (like legal language) may introduce political contents. The TK is thus responsible for the apparent neutralization of political conflicts. Much like the process of codification of law, which hides its social (constructed and imposed) genesis and thus protects its neutrality and universality,[45] the formalized legal language of the TK's judgments objectivizes phenomena and the processes and parties occurring in them. The

---

justified suspicion that the pregnancy is a result of a prohibited act.

[39] As regards 1994, see Parliament Print 157, II term; as regards 1996, see Parliament Print 1502, II term. In 1996, Art. 4a(4) was inserted into the Family Planning Act 1993 which permits termination in the event of the woman being in a difficult financial or personal situation. (Dz. U. no. 139, item 646).

[40] *Ustawa z dnia 7 stycznia 1993 r. o planowaniu rodziny, ochronie płodu ludzkiego i warunkach dopuszczalności przerywania ciąży* [Act of ... amending the Family Planning Act 1993] (Dz. U. no. 139, item 646).

[41] TK judgment of 28 May 1997 r., Case 26/96. The decision was handed down by all twelve judges then sitting on the TK with three dissenting opinions. The provisions of Article 4a(4) of the Family Planning Act 1993 lost legal force as from 23 December 1997.

[42] Before 1993 the TK issued two rulings with regards to this topic. The first ruling, from 15 January 1991 (Case U 8/90) concerned the decree of the Ministry of Health and Social Services of the 30 April 1990 (DZ. U. no. 29, poz. 178). The second ruling from the 7 October 1992 (Case U 1/92) concerned the Doctor's Ethics Code.

[43] Alberski, *Trybunał Konstytucyjny*, 269.

[44] Bourdieu, *Pascalian Meditations*, 111–14.

[45] Bourdieu, *Language and Symbolic Power*, 137–59.

TK adopts one point of view, which is a particular ideological view, and presents it to the legal field as objective and universal.[46] In this way, when a particular chosen view becomes universal, symbolic power—imposing mental schemata on actors of social life[47]—is being realized. Femininity discourse is an example of such a social construction. Its recognition reveals the symbolic power of legal institutions like the TK.

6.5 Femininity as Constructed Judgment in the Case Law of the TK

Bourdieu points out that in the modern world one can discern a private and a public realm. The former is concerned with the household and family—what is 'inside.' The latter concerns authority, economics, (the market) and politics—what is 'outside.' While women are mostly kept to the private realm (primarily due to their role in motherhood and the raising of offspring), the public realm is male-dominated. If the feminine is described in the judgments of the TK as weak, emotional, sentimental, needing protection (because of motherhood)—then, by virtue of an unspoken opposition, the masculine is understood as strong, rational, and self-sufficient. This division, universal for a conservative world view, connotes further elements. We thus have an opposition: strong (rational, public) versus weak (emotional, private). This kind of world order: private—feminine, public—masculine, is strictly hierarchical. The private is perceived as less important, socially inferior, and less prestigious, which is confirmed by the lack of salary for doing household chores and by women's very attitude to them.[48]

Sherry B. Ortner puts forward similar conclusions by pointing out that in all known cultures the roles, products, and the social environment of women enjoy less social prestige and a lower status than those of men. This results in an exclusion of women from participation in structures of power, regardless of whether it is a sacral ritual or a political debate.[49] The

---

[46] Hanna Dębska, 'Legal Doxa as a Form of Neutralization of Values in the Law. The Case of Constitutional Court Judgments,' in *Neutralization of Values in Law*, ed. Krzysztof Pałecki (Warszawa: Wolters Kluwer, 2013), 303–51. In order to secure its socially important position, the field of law needs to separate itself from the political field, which is often seen as a subjective, particularist universe, serving only itself and the ruling party.

[47] See generally Bourdieu, *Language and Symbolic Power*. Put simply, 'Every power to exert symbolic violence, i.e. every power which manages to impose meanings and to impose them as legitimate by concealing the power relations which are the basis of its force, adds its own specifically symbolic force to those power relations' (Pierre Bourdieu and Jean-Claude Passeron, *Reproduction in Education. Society and Culture* [London: SAGE, 1990], 4).

[48] Pierre Bourdieu, *Masculine Domination* [1998] (Stanford: Stanford University Press, 2001).

[49] Sharry B. Ortner, 'Is female to male as nature is to culture?,' in *Woman, Culture, and*

number of female judges sitting on the TK is a prime example of this. This institution is highly authoritative, enjoying great prestige and is the epitome for any legal career. Historically, the majority of judges sitting on the TK were male. Even though with each term the proportions shift slightly in women's favour,[50] from the inception of its operations in 1986, 81% of the TK judges were male.[51] This could have had an impact on the ruling of cases concerning women's matters, like abortion.

Now let us take a closer look at some fragments of judgments issued by the TK, which should help us identify the discursive strategies used to construct femininity:

> Because in a social world, a woman generally occupies a weaker position (which is, among others, an effect of a special role of a woman in the field of motherhood and upbringing of children), there is a constitutional justification for an introduction of regulations which give a woman some privileges in comparison with a man, because it is an instrument of providing women with a factual equality of rights. In other words, the so called affirmative action is constitutionally permissible, i.e. legal privileges aimed at reduction of real inequalities occurring between males and females in the social life context … In certain situations however, when biological and social differences between men and women are particularly apparent (like, for instance, in mining) establishing such affirmative action becomes a constitutional obligation of the lawmakers. In case this difference persists within 'affirmative action' framework, hence, if sufficient social arguments support it, particularly the consideration of providing a woman with a real employment equality, then this difference may be deemed justified by such constitutional values like the general rule of justice, particularly the rule of equality.[52]

> Such rights take into account the *biological and familial conditions*. … Therefore they constitute a form of extending and strengthening the status of a woman.[53]

The Court's judgment in Case K 6/89 states that 'the biological and social differences between men and women' are important when looked at from the perspective of the 'process of exhaustion by work,' and therefore constitutes a

---

Society, ed. M. Z. Rosaldo and L. Lamphere (Stanford: Stanford University Press, 1974), 68–87.

[50] In comparison to the first composition, the number of women sitting on the TK has changed in their favour (there was only one woman, Natalia Gajl, who was chosen to sit on the TK in the first term). The current composition consists of eleven men and four women, which gives 73% and 26.7% respectively. Databased accessed 15 May December 2015, www.trybunal.gov.pl.

[51] Hanna Dębska, Płeć i władza. Kobiety w Trybunale Konstytucyjnym' [Gender and Power: Women on the Constitutional Court], *Studia Podlaskie* 22 (2014), 87–107.

[52] TK judgment of 29 September 1997 r., Case K 15/97.

[53] TK judgment of 29 September 1997 r., Case K 15/97.

criterion for differentiation of retirement entitlements which favours women.[54] Different treatment is permissible due to *objective biological* or social *considerations*.[55]

Presently a decrease in social (functional) differences can be observed. *Biological differences between persons of different sex* however *are objective in nature* and thus will always be present. Nevertheless, since in many occupations these differences have no bearing, or little influence on the health, safety, and the quality of work, therefore in the future they will justify legal decisions regarding retirement age differentiation pertaining to the general population to a lesser degree.[56]

The above quoted judgments reveal a dichotomous vision of the world, divided, like Durkheim's *sacrum* and *profanum*,[57] into 'the male' and 'the female' together with an entire system of characteristics connoting this opposition. One should be reminded that these codes dividing the social world into homogenous pairs of oppositions (i.e. tall/short, good/evil, left/right) serve to order the social world and actions of its agents. This is key for symbolic power, as these categories are adjusted to the contemporary existing social order. They therefore seemingly remain objectively necessary for social parties, while in reality they are arbitrary and imposed.

Reading passages from the judgments of the TK allows us to observe what Bourdieu calls 'double speech'—contents hidden behind the censure of the field of law.[58] On the so called 'surface' level we find a rational argumentation—a model representation of legal interpretation. On the deeper layer of text however, one can find the dichotomous ideological structure creeping underneath the obviousness of common sense. Woman's social position, described as 'weaker,' requiring protection and resulting in the necessary introduction of additional entitlements stems from her role as a mother. Such tying together of woman and motherhood shows that in judicial discourse, a woman is, to a substantial degree, defined by being identified with her biological sex (ability to procreate). The phrase 'biological and familial determinations' used by the TK, points to just this fact.[59] Also, the claim that biological differences between men and women are 'objective,'[60] *ipso facto* objectivizes and absolutizes the sex. Taken in this way, sex appears to be strictly natural and thus objective and

---

[54] TK judgment of 29 September 1997 r., Case K 15/97.
[55] TK judgment of 15 July 2010, Case K 63/07.
[56] TK resolution of 15 July 2010 r., Case S 2/10. All quotes from judgments translated by the authors. All emphases in the judgments added by the authors.
[57] Émile Durkheim, *The Elementary Forms of Religious Life* (Oxford: OUP, 2011).
[58] Bourdieu, *Language*, ch. 6.
[59] TK judgment of 29 September 1997 r., Case K 15/97.
[60] TK resolution of 15 July 2010 r., Case S 2/10.

unavoidable. In other words, the social perception of a woman is limited to her body, which is, to a large degree, socially shaped. As a consequence, subsequent classifications responsible for ordering our thinking about the world overlap.

The TK's seemingly rational arguments aimed at 'protecting' subjects that are weaker, more prone to 'exhaustion' by work, and requiring positive discrimination in the form of 'affirmative action' hide a mechanism reproducing relations between sexes.[61] The above quoted fragments of judgments show how a specific conservative vision of masculinity/femininity, devoid of the particularities of the political field, becomes binding in the field of law. It is being smuggled in by the ideology hidden behind doxic structures. These are both the objective and thus neutral and obvious biological differences between men and women, and the hidden codes associating womanhood with motherhood, weakness, as well as emotionality, sensitivity, and intuitiveness. By ascribing women with particular qualities, the TK, acting in the name of the state, creates them as a category and 'calls them up to social life.'

By associating women with motherhood the TK imposes on them a specific social role—the role of a mother—as the basic and most natural, when in reality it is historically and culturally specific. Research conducted by Élisabeth Badinter proves that today's idea of 'motherhood' as well as the concept of 'motherly instinct' were born of religious ideology, appearing as late as the Victorian era and since then reinforced as correct and desirable.[62] Moreover, the arbitrary way in which the TK establishes and then legitimizes a woman's place in social discourse excludes ones that are childless by chance or by choice.

Taking into consideration this context, it is worthwhile looking closely at a fragment of Case K 26/96 which investigates the constitutionality of the so-called social premise permitting abortion.

> In light of this Act [The Family Planning, Protection of Human Foetus and Conditions for Termination Act of 7 January 1993], the subjective opinion of a woman regarding the possible threat to her material standing, personal relations, or possibilities of realizing her own needs, rights, and freedoms becomes a legal good. *The premises* specified in Art. 4 (a) (1) (4) [Family Planning Act 1993] *do not pertain to borderline situations*, which could simultaneously be considered contrary to the rule of protecting human dignity. Moreover, from the preamble to the Act one can infer that the premise for the establishment of these regulations was, among others, the recognition of a universal right of each person to make a decision regarding having children. From the standpoint

---

[61] TK judgment of 29 September 1997 r., Case K 15/97.
[62] Élisabeth Badinter, *L'amour en plus. Histoire de l'amour maternel (XVIIe-XXe siècle)* (Paris: Flammarion, 1980).

of constitutional standards, a comparison of thus specified goods, which remain in conflict, disqualifies the regulation delineated in Art. 4 (a) (1) (4) [Family Planning Act 1993]. *Human life, as stressed by the preamble itself, is a fundamental human good.*[63]

The use of the phrase 'the premises do not pertain to borderline situations' suggests (provided one consequently reads this TK ruling in its entirety in light of motherhood) that a woman ought to 'sacrifice' her rights and freedoms for the benefit of the foetus, which is consequently referred to by the TK as a 'child.' It should be highlighted, both for the motherhood discourse and the 'motherly instinct' associated with it, as well as for this case, that the idea of mother's 'self-sacrifice' (so-called total motherhood) is historically fairly recent—again created in Victorian times. While it would seem that feminism (particularly the liberal kind) has changed this attitude, the researchers studying this part of social reality prove that the contemporary discourse associated with childcare is—even in the Western, seemingly less discriminating societies—strongly grounded, even among women themselves.[64] Harriet Bradley adds that although the motherhood discourse took different forms in different times, it always had a common core which may be summed up in the phrase 'motherhood is destiny.' This means that a woman is created for motherhood; ones that do not become mothers regret their decision later on in life; they are unhappy and unfulfilled; ones that do become mothers have the motherly instinct which allows them to put the needs of the child before their own. Mothers that lack this instinct will be forced, by moral pressure, to adopt such a 'sacrificial' approach.[65]

This relation between a woman and motherhood consequently stressed by the TK and supporting the idea of 'motherhood as a calling' impacts the understanding of 'family.' Bourdieu points out that the family model we presently recognize as natural is a result of fairly recent historical conditions. Moreover, the model, treated as a standard (the nuclear family) in most modern societies is rather an exception than the rule. He proves that every social reality, taken to be natural and obvious, is nothing more than a social fiction, a well-grounded illusion.[66] The Court in Case K 26/96

---

[63] TK judgment of 28 May 1997, Case K 26/96.
[64] Harriet Bradley, *Gender* (Cambridge: Polity Press, 2013).
[65] Bradley, Gender, 151.
[66] Pierre Bourdieu, *Practical Reason* [1994] (Stanford: Stanford University Press, 1998), 66. 'In other words, they are what makes it possible for all agents to refer to the same oppositions (such as high/low, up/down, rare/ common, light/heavy, rich/poor, etc.), to think the world and their position in the world, while sometimes giving opposite signs and values to the terms they counterpoise: thus the same freedom of manners may be seen by some as 'shameless,' impolite, rude, and by others as 'unaffected,' simple, unpretentious, natural.' (Bourdieu, *Pascalian*, 98). This refers even to such basic (and seemingly natural) concepts as a mother, job, relationship, or love.

states that:

> *The fundamental procreation function of a family* requires an assumption that the life of a conceived child needs to benefit from a protection, which is provided for the family by the constitution, thus becoming a constitutional value.[67]

In this way the TK legally determines the basic role of a family, while completely omitting families consisting of spouses only. The fact of having a child or children becomes a measure of the value of a family and its constitutionally warranted protection, rather than the legally warranted freedom to shape one's private life, including making decisions regarding the shape of the household. The TK lays down a legal definition of what a family is, and warrants it with its own authority as a state institution. In Bourdieu's words:

> Every time we use a classificatory concept like 'family,' we are making both a description and a prescription, which is not perceived as such because it is (more or less) universally accepted and goes without saying. ... In short, the family in its legitimate definition is a privilege instituted into a universal norm: a *de facto* privilege that impose symbolic privilege of being *comme il faut*, conforming to the norm, and therefore enjoying a symbolic profit of normality.[68]

This however is not the only consequence of the TK's discourse. In further sections of the ruling, the TK only introduces a positive restriction on the right to decide regarding having offspring. It states that the freedom to shape one's family applies exclusively to having children, because:

> One cannot make a decision regarding having a child when a child is already in the prenatal stages of development, and in this sense, the parents already have it. Therefore, the right to have a child may only be interpreted in its positive aspect and not as the right to terminate a developing human foetus.[69]

What can be read from the above fragment? A person creating a text always, even unconsciously, makes certain assumptions regarding the way she views social reality. The favoured standpoint is most commonly presented as the only one, which results in representing the world and its phenomena as consistent and homogenous, which in turn makes the preferred vision appear as obvious, the only one possible, and thus true.[70] This leads to different views being excluded from the discourse because

---

[67] TK judgment of 28 May 1997 r., Case K 26/96.
[68] Bourdieu, *Practical Reason*, 66, 69.
[69] TK judgment of 28 May 1997 r., Case K 26/96
[70] Norman Fairclough, *Language and Power* (London: Longman, 1990), passim.

due to these procedures anything different seems false. In its argumentation, the TK omits contradictory positions, ones representing pro-choice organizations, supporting 'freedom of procreation,' woman's right to choose, and her right to her own body.

In the above quote, the TK explicitly refers to a developing 'foetus' as a 'child.' The same can be observed in the fragment regarding self-sacrifice, where a woman's freedom and her right to choose are confronted not with the rights of a 'foetus,' but with the 'dignity of a human being.'[71] This directly indicates that here, according to the TK, we are dealing with a person who is independent from the woman. The same goes for the fragments regarding family: the protection of a family stems from the protection of an unborn child. As a consequence, should a foetus be considered a 'child already had by the parents,' all laws pertaining to parental duties will automatically apply, even though Polish law states that the institution of 'motherhood' arises with the birth of a child. Article 61⁹ of the Family and Guardianship Code states that 'a mother of a child is a woman who gave birth to it.'[72] Therefore, according to the Polish law, the motherhood relationship arises at the moment of childbirth. If, however, the term 'child' is interpreted in this particular (chosen and arbitrary, not neutral and obvious) way, i.e. when it is co-extensive with the term 'foetus,' then the TK makes it so that a pregnancy is not a physiological state describing a woman. Pregnancy 'becomes independent' of a woman. The 'foetus' becomes an autonomous being (a human). As such, a pregnant woman is not a mother to be, but a mother per se, one that already bares the responsibilities of motherhood. Other expressions when viewed against this background, reinforce this ideology.

> The concept of motherhood expresses the necessary relation between a mother and a child—this relation is multi-layered: biological, emotional, social and legal.[73]

Although the moment when new life is created is not a legal issue, but rather a medical or a philosophical issue, by supporting the pro-life arguments the TK takes it upon itself to specify this exact moment. This is seen in the phrase like 'a child is already in the prenatal stages of development, and in this sense, it is already had,' as well as in the following statements:

> In this situation, *due to a life created*, the right to decide regarding having a

---

[71] TK judgment of 28 May 1997 r., Case K 26/96.
[72] *Ustawa z dnia 25 lutego 1964 r.—Kodeks rodzinny i opiekuńczy* [Act of 25 February 1964—Family and Guardianship Code] (Dz. U. 2012, item 788).
[73] TK judgment of 28 May 1997 r., Case K 26/96.

child would have to be reduced to the right to not give birth to the child.[74]

> Acknowledging that *a human being, from the moment of conception, is entitled to have its life protected* appears also in the ordinary legislation ... The only reason for prohibiting the termination of pregnancy, pertaining in general ... to the pregnant woman herself, *has to be the acknowledgement of the value of a conceived human being's life*.[75]

Equally important is the fact that in 2004 the European Court of Human Rights refrained from issuing a pan-European interpretation of whether and until what moment abortion is permissible, saying that it was unable to determine the moment when a foetus becomes a human being.[76] In this respect, the TK forgot not only about its systemic limitations in this regard (acting as a 'court of law,' not a 'court of facts'),[77] but also about the declarations it made in these matters.[78] The TK is able to specify the moment life is created due to its symbolic power, which enables it to impose legally and socially legitimate meanings. Employing this legal discourse, together with its seemingly neutral and objective terminology, allows the ideological vision to be perceived as a description of reality. The decision to call a foetus a 'human being' is in fact a value statement which mimics a description.[79] The political discourse is objectivized through transfer to the field of law. Moreover, equating 'a conceived human being' with 'a child' strengthens this vision making it universal.

The TK argues that a human life (including, as will be shown below, the 'unborn child') may not be differentiated regardless of the stage it is in. It supports its argument by appealing to the Convention on the Rights of the Child, even though the Convention does not specify the exact moment a

---

[74] TK judgment of 28 May 1997 r., Case K 26/96.
[75] TK judgment of 28 May 1997 r., Case K 26/96.
[76] ECHR ruling from the 8th of July 2004, Vo v France, Center for Reproductive Rights (intervening) and Family Planning Association (intervening), Judgment, Merits, App No 53924/00, ECHR 2004–VIII [2004] ECHR 326, (2005) 40 EHRR 12.
[77] Marek Safjan, 'Ewolucja funkcji i zadań Trybunału Konstytucyjnego—próba spojrzenia w przeszłość' [Evolution of the Functions and Tasks of the Constitutional Court: An Attempt at Looking into the Past] in *Księga XXV—lecia Trybunału Konstytucyjnego. Ewolucja funkcji i zadań Trybunału Konstytucyjnego—założenia a ich praktyczna realizacja* [Studies to Celebrate the 25th Anniversary of the Constitutional Court: Evolution of the Functions and Tasks of the Consitutional Court—The Assumptions and the Practice], ed. Krzysztof Budziło (Warszawa: Wyd. Trybunału Konstytucyjnego, 2010), 26. As the 'court of the law,' the TK performs only an abstract control of normative acts and not the correctness of application of law in individual cases (in contrast, for instance, with the Czech constitutional court which enjoys such a power).
[78] Bohdan Zdziennicki, 'Trybunał nie chce być trzecią instancją sądową' [The Court does not want to be a court of third instance], Dziennik Gazeta Prawna (2008), accessed 4 April 2014, http://edgp.gazetaprawna.pl/index.php?act=mprasa&sub=article&id=209672.
[79] Graff, *Świat bez kobiet*, 129.

life begins. In Article 1 it merely states that:

> a 'child' means every human being below the age of eighteen years unless under the law applicable to the child, majority is attained earlier.[80]

Nevertheless, the Court infers much more from the Convention:

> The inclusion of [the prenatal] life stage within the scope of constitutional protection finds confirmation in the Convention on the Rights of the Child, ratified by the Republic of Poland on the 30th of September 1991, which declares in paragraph 10 of its preamble ... that *a child, due to its lack of maturity, both physical and mental, requires special protection and care, particularly legal protection both before and after birth*. The inclusion of this rule in the preamble necessarily leads to a conclusion that warranties contained in the Convention also refer to the prenatal stage of human life. ... [T]herefore, *regardless of the wording of paragraph 10 of the Convention's preamble, in light of which the concept of a child used in the Convention should also include a child before birth*, [its] Article 24 contains a direct indication that the right to the best possible health includes a child from the moment of conception. This is the only way to justify the obligation to provide mothers with prenatal care resulting from paragraph 2 [of that Article]. This obligation was not introduced with regard to the interests of a pregnant woman alone, but, as it is clearly stated in Article 24 (2), *in principio* to provide a full realisation of this right (prescribed by paragraph 1). *It is clear that consideration here is for a conceived child* to benefit from the best possible health. The grounds for constitutional protection of the health of a conceived child may also be found in Article 79 (1) which acknowledges the constitutional value of both motherhood and family.[81]

Therefore, the most important result of the discourse conducted by the TK is not just the derivation of the protection of a subject of a particular category from the function of the family, but primarily the creation of a new subject—'a conceived child.' At the same time, this turns the attention away from the pregnant woman and her rights. Art. 24 (2) Convention on the Rights of Child states that participating states will strive to 'provide mothers with proper healthcare, both before and after childbirth.'[82] By

---

[80] Office of the United Nations High Commissioner for Human Rights, *Convention on the Rights of the Child*, accessed 1 March 2016, http://www.ohchr.org/EN/ProfessionalInterest/Pages/CRC.aspx.

[81] TK judgment of 28 May 1997 r., Case K 26/96.

[82] In the Art. 21, the Convention on the Rights of the Child states that: 'States Parties that recognize and/or permit the system of adoption shall ensure that the best interests of the child shall be the paramount consideration and they shall: (a) Ensure that the adoption of a child is authorized only by competent authorities who determine, in accordance with applicable law and procedures and on the basis of all pertinent and reliable information, that the adoption is permissible in view of the child's status concerning parents, relatives and legal guardians and that, if required, the persons concerned have given their informed

stating that 'this obligation was not introduced with regard to the interests of a pregnant woman alone' but with regards to 'consideration for a conceived child' the TK controls the discourse. In this way, partly due to the actions of the TK, public attention is diverted form the rights of a woman to those of a foetus that is innocent, defenceless, but most importantly, possessing its own subjectivity.[83]

In other words, under the guise of seemingly neutral and objective legal language, as well as the competencies granted to it by the state, the TK first introduces and then legitimizes a particular vision of the social and biological reality which it chooses arbitrarily. In ruling K 26/96 presented above this process is gradual and seamless. At the beginning of the justification the TK states that the goal of the conducted action is to 'determine the extent to which the life and health of a foetus falls under the protection of constitutional regulations.'

However, in the following sections the 'foetus' slowly stops being a foetus. It is given a new identity. It becomes a 'conceived human being' and a 'conceived child,' therefore a 'human being,' a 'child which [the parents] have,' until finally it becomes fully 'human.' Discourse analysis literature postulates that one of the reasons behind the conflict regarding abortion was the change in the language of the debate. A problem, which was formerly situated between the fields of medicine and populist politics, was transferred to the fields of politics and law. Because of this, the formerly 'marginalized' and 'domesticated' issue of terminating pregnancy, which had nothing to do with 'killing unborn people,' suddenly became a pressing matter.[84] We encounter this phenomenon of 'circling discourse'—the transfer of the political and media language onto the field of law—in the TK ruling where the issue of 'terminating pregnancy' becomes the issue of 'deprivation of life.' This is further confirmed by another fragment of the grounds in which the TK points out that the lawmaker permits the termination of pregnancy, which means a removal of a developing foetus

---

consent to the adoption on the basis of such counselling as may be necessary; (b) Recognize that inter-country adoption may be considered as an alternative means of child's care, if the child cannot be placed in a foster or an adoptive family or cannot in any suitable manner be cared for in the child's country of origin; (c) Ensure that the child concerned by inter-country adoption enjoys safeguards and standards equivalent to those existing in the case of national adoption; (d) Take all appropriate measures to ensure that, in inter-country adoption, the placement does not result in improper financial gain for those involved in it; (e) Promote, where appropriate, the objectives of the present article by concluding bilateral or multilateral arrangements or agreements, and endeavour, within this framework, to ensure that the placement of the child in another country is carried out by competent authorities or organs.' Office of the United Nations High Commissioner for Human Rights, *Convention on the Rights of the Child*, accessed 1 March 2016, http://www.ohchr.org/EN/Professional-Interest/Pages/CRC.aspx.

[83] Graff, *Świat bez kobiet*, 130.
[84] Pawlik, *Spór o aborcję*, 159.

from the mother's organism, and which is *'equal to causing its death* [and so] necessarily connected with deprivation of life.'[85]

Therefore termination (a medical term) is equated to 'causing death' and 'necessarily to deprivation of life.' Were the TK's argumentation applied consistently, one would be forced to claim that terminating a pregnancy is always a taking of a life, and thus a killing of a human being. It would then be necessary to equate the punitive measures for abortion with ones for murder or to admit that in Poland people are being lawfully killed.

By arguing in this way the TK reinforces a particular position in the public discourse, according to which:

> Those who recognise a woman's moral right to decide if she wants to carry an unwanted pregnancy to term are relegated to the position of 'enemies of life' or simply murderers, while those objecting to this right to choose become 'defenders of life.' They do not need to explain their reasons to anyone, they stand for the right.[86]

Kristin Lucker is right in saying that in reality, the abortion debate is all about the definition and the role of a woman. What is more, this debate shows the sacred value of motherhood held by those fighting for the foetus and hence the moral high ground of those who are against abortion.[87] Values like 'freedom,' 'choice,' 'informed decision,' and 'responsibility' lose their power to convince when juxtaposed against an absolute value such as 'life.'[88]

6.6 Conclusions

These discursive procedures aimed at using particular terms and meanings (strongly valuating and non-neutral) are a display of the TK executing its symbolic power. Through these procedures, the discourses (pro-life and pro-choice), normally competing with one another in the social space, are neutralized (presented in neutral, objective, and obvious categories) and the vision chosen by the TK becomes mandatory. This is possible because the TK functions in the relatively autonomous administrative and legal field (and within the legal field it predominately occupies its academic pole, because most of judges are scholars); to put it precisely, the TK occupies the position where these two fields overlap. Because of this, strictly ideological content coming from the political field is neutralized and presented as a

---

[85] TK judgment of 28 May 1997, Case K 26/96.
[86] Pawlik, *Spór o aborcję*, 131.
[87] Kristin Lucker, *Abortion and the Politics of Motherhood* (California: University of California Press, 1984).
[88] Graff, *Świat bez kobiet*, 132.

purely objective and legal statement. As such, the legally enforced and naturalized dichotomy of masculine (rational, public, socially important, superior) and feminine (emotional, homely, socially less important, inferior) is transferred to other areas of life. As already mentioned, the overlapping classification schemata have a tendency to present as given and natural the structures that underlie them. In this way the symbolic power of the TK is achieved. Added to it, imperceptibly as usual, is the choice between the 'foetus' and the 'conceived child.' In this particular case, it is the choice of a strongly emotional term, which is directly connected to the vision of femininity. The earlier postulated remark regarding the 'calling to life' of a social category is fully adequate with regards to 'women' (presented in relation to roles traditionally ascribed to women), 'family' (the traditional, catholic vision), and 'foetus' (as a child).[89] The identity of these subjects, created in this particular way, constitutes a substantial encroachment on the way we perceive, divide, and classify the world while being a stark example of the existence of symbolic power, a real display of which may be observed in a dissenting opinion to the TK's ruling in Case K 24/07 written by Judge Teresa Liszcz some ten years later. Accepting the discourse present in Case K 26/96 she states that

> the benefit of the mother is treated by the legislator as particularly important. They [viz. the legal acts] are concerned with the health, or more broadly—the well-being of the pregnant woman, but *most importantly with the life and health of her unborn child*. ... Primarily though, these protective rules are concerned with the *correct development of the child*. ... What particularly needs stressing is that which is special in the state of pregnancy—and that is the fact that it is not only the mother's health and life that is at stake when the mother is suspected or accused of committing a crime, but also the life and health of the *unborn child—a person who undoubtedly is innocent and having the right to full protection*.[90]

As seen in the above quote, Judge Liszcz does not use the term 'foetus.' She consequently uses terms like 'child' or 'an unborn child,' which clearly shows her adoption of specific classification schemata. Legal discourse legitimizes the situation in which a foetus is treated as an autonomous individual, to which one ascribes such qualities as innocence,

---

[89] Judge Zbigniew Czeszejko-Sochacki in an extensive dissenting opinion also notices that the constitutional court 'has given a particular meaning to both 'motherhood' and 'family,' one which diverges form the previous understanding of these terms in the doctrine, as well as from the provisions of the new constitution' (Judge Czeszejko-Sochacki's dissenting opinion of 28 May 1997 in Case K 26/96). Supplementing his argument with symbolic explanation may constitute an important element in considerations regarding the symbolic dimension of legal institutions.

[90] Judge Teresa Liszcz's dissenting opinion of 28 July 2008, Case K 24/07.

defencelessness, purity etc. This in turn strengthens the symbolic process which brands a woman who decided to terminate. Agnieszka Graff confirms this observation and points out that in the last couple of years words like 'foetus' and 'pregnancy' have practically disappeared from the public sphere in Poland. They were replaced with 'an unborn child' and 'protecting the unborn.' The same goes for 'abortion' and 'pregnant woman.' They were substituted for 'murder' and 'mother.'[91] Bourdieu pertinently describes the effects of this kind of discourse. He notices that

> because the social principle of vision constructs anatomical difference and because this socially constructed difference becomes the basis and apparently natural justification of the social vision which founds it, there is thus a relationship of circular causality which confines though within the self-evidence of relations of domination inscribed both in objectivity, in a form of objective divisions, and subjectivity, in a form of cognitive schemes which, being organized in accordance with these divisions, organize the perception of these objective divisions.[92]

The under-representation of women in the TK is not surprising in this context. The social order is organized in accordance with anatomical differences which become the justification of the very same social order. In other words, the arbitrary dichotomy which is imposed by the TK becomes naturalized and is perceived as taken for granted and objective. Taking into consideration the fact that social visions and division are inscribed in the dispositions of individuals, women are not only structurally excluded but they also exclude themselves from positions of power. Thus the socially produced vision of femininity is maintained in the minds of men and women, strengthening the patriarchal status quo.

---

[91] Graff, *Świat bez kobiet*, 124.
[92] Bourdieu, *Masculine Domination*, 11–12.

7

Structural Violence and its Gender Dimension in Polish Law

Lidia Rodak

7.1 Introduction

The central issue I intend to address in this chapter is that of structural violence perpetrated in the realm of law. This phenomenon has no obvious or unambiguous character, not only because it is by definition hidden but also because the nature of law is necessarily linked with violence.[1] In this chapter, I shall investigate the central forms of structural violence perpetrated within law against women in the Polish socio-legal context.

The Polish legal and socio-political space, analyzed in terms of gender relations is not only peculiar among European countries, but also among post-communist countries.[2] At a first glance, legal provisions guarantee full equality of rights of men and women, on the level of both domestic and international law. However, in spite of all the legislation introduced to combat discrimination and provide equal opportunities, gender inequality still persists in nearly all institutions and areas of social life. There exist several formal legal regulations devised to prevent gender inequality, yet the statistics and reports by non-governmental organizations show that the introduction of equality law has not resulted in gender justice in the full sense (see below). This is mainly caused by the persistence of social and cultural norms characteristic of patriarchal societies as well as by the fact that most of equality law was 'imported' from European legislation. After the country's transformation, throughout the nineties, social life was dominated by so-called 'Christian democratic values.' This dynamics has helped to maintain traditional views on gender roles and family values in

---

[1] Jacques Derrida, 'Force of Law: The "Mystical Foundation of Authority",' *Cardozo Law Review* 11 (1990), 919. On law's inner violence, see Walter Benjamin 'Critique of Violence,' in *Selected Writings*, vol. 1, ed. Marcus Bullock and Michael W. Jennings (Cambridge: Harvard University Press, 1996 [1921]).

[2] Olga Avdeyeva, 'When Do States Comply With International Treaties? Policies on Violence Against Women in Post-Communist Countries,' *International Studies Quarterly* 51 (2007), 877–900.

society.³ Interestingly, the first legal act of the democratic government in 1989 was an anti-abortion law.

The feminist movement has always been a marginalized social force and never had any significant influence on social life. Recent years have only witnessed cosmetic changes in public life, such as the formation of a political organization known as 'Women's Congress' and the hottest public debate to date addressing equality and women's rights, during which Polish society became familiar with the hitherto unknown term 'gender.' All of this could substantiate the claim that the position of a woman in the public sphere is rather weak. In principle, the situation should be different in the private sphere, e.g. in the family, where the place of a woman should be more prominent due in particular to the status assigned to her by the Catholic church, which stresses the importance of women to the stability of the family. However, this can also be questioned. In fact, the 'central' position of women is defined by patriarchal standards, which typically regard women as 'happy slaves.'⁴

These aspects provide the background against which structural violence should be read. I am interested in unearthing this form of violence embedded in the definition of equality accepted by the Polish community as well as the way it is represented by Polish law. To support my argument, I will discuss the category of objectivity of/in law as a form of gender oppression, in other words, as an example of structural violence. Second, I shall analyze the relations between the legal regulation of gender issues and the idea of violence of different types from the perspective of official and non-official law.

The aim of this chapter is to show that both official law and non-official law are systems of structural violence. The power of all structural inequality derives mostly from an informal context that in fact dominates official law. Due to the very diverse character of these two systems, structural violence may be hidden in different ways. If in official law the main instrument of masking violence is objectivity, within unofficial law it may be attributable to freedom. In the first part, I shall introduce the concept of structural violence and its gender dimension, examining the characteristics of law as objective and objectivity in law. In the second part, I shall explore the relation between formal and informal rules regulating gender justice in order to show how formal regulations are influenced by informal rules, which represent a social order based on structural violence. In my

---

³ Steven Saxonber, 'Polish Women in the mid-1990s. Christian Democrats in a Country without a Christian Democratic Party,' *Czech Sociological Review* 8 (2000), 233–53.

⁴ Henryk Domański, *Zadowolony niewolnik idzie do pracy. Postawy wobec aktywności zawodowej kobiet w 23 krajach* [The Happy Slave Goes to Work: Attitudes Towards Women's Occupational Activity in 23 countries] (Warszawa: Wydawnictwo IFIS PAN, 1999).

investigation, I shall draw on the sociological approach to law developed by Adam Podgórecki.

7.2 Structural violence in law and its gender dimension

The problem of violence has been extensively analyses by many philosophers, who either criticized it or advocated it.[5] As a result, different types of violence have been identified: psychological, symbolic, structural, epistemic, hermeneutical, as well as aesthetic violence.[6]

The concept of structural violence has been debated by structural theorists from Johan Galtung and James Gilligan to Paul Farmer.[7] The term 'structural violence' is commonly ascribed to Johan Galtung,[8] who defines three types of violence: personal (direct), structural (indirect, e.g. poverty) and cultural (e.g. media glorification of violence). As Galtung explains, structural violence takes place when some social structure or social institution may harm people by preventing them from meeting their basic needs. Structural violence is not a direct act of any decision or action made by a particular person but a result of an unequal distribution of resources.[9] This means that the distribution of rights or goods exclude some groups. As Galtung writes, 'sinful social structures' are characterized by poverty and steep inequality, including racism and gender inequality.

For Paul Farmer, its core feature is that violence is exerted systematically,[10] which results in structural violence as a form of oppression. However, oppression can be the result of manifold conditions that are not always conscious. That is why, except for 'sinful' conditions, he also indicates 'nobody's fault' forms of desocialization as other possible forms

---

[5] Benjamin 'Critique of Violence, 277–300; cf. Friedrich Nietzsche, *On the Genealogy of Morals. A Polemic. By way of clarification and supplement to my last book Beyond Good and Evil* (Oxford: OUP, 2008).

[6] Beatrice Hanssen, *Critique of Violence: Between Poststructuralism and Critical Theory*, (London: Routledge, 2000), 9.

[7] The concepts of structural and institutional violence are often used interchangeably. However, sometimes, some differentiations are made. For example, institutional violence is explained as more properly restricted to legally sanctioned violence. It is also said that institutional violence refers to violence committed by certain institutions, not the law itself. See also 'Structural Violence' in *The Blackwell Dictionary of Western Philosophy*, ed. Nicholas Bunnin and Jiyuan Yu, accessed 19 July 2016, DOI: 10.1111/b.9781405106795.2004.x.

[8] Johan Galtung, 'Violence, Peace, and Peace Research,' *Journal of Peace Research* 6 (1969).

[9] 'Structural Violence,' accessed 15 July 2016, http://peacejustice.msu.edu/exhibits/show/structuralviolence/meaning.

[10] Paul Farmer, 'Anthropology of Structural Violence,' *Current Anthropology* 45 (2004), 307.

of exclusion.[11] Finally, James Gilligan defines structural violence as 'the increased rates of death and disability suffered by those who occupy the bottom rungs of society, as contrasted with the relatively lower death rates experienced by those who are above them.'[12]

Structural violence with reference to gender is defined as being patriarchal structure violence,[13] where patriarchy is defined as a system or structure of exploitation that normalizes socially constructed gender differences in ways that reproduce and legitimize male domination.[14] Understanding patriarchal structural violence means locating and analyzing the socio-cultural, economic, and political systems that perpetuate or condone physical, sexual, and psychological violence against women.[15] Gender as a social construct organizes social life in hierarchical, mutually exclusive categories, which are in a relationship of sub/super-ordination to one another. It follows that the construction of gender relations owes much to violent hierarchical subordination, where the superior status of violence owes much to gender relations.[16] Violence is a process through which social relations are built, legitimized, reproduced, and naturalized. By understanding gender as a social construct that embodies relations of power, feminism shows that violence is made possible by the existence of power/gender relations.[17]

According to feminist theory, the constructions of social relations are built upon male domination, which means that structural violence is embedded in the definition of equality that is accepted by the community. In other words, what is considered equal in patriarchal society in fact prioritizes male interests that are fully recognized and protected. On the contrary, women are either directly discriminated against and overlooked or not considered to be essentially different from men. It seems that this state of things demands a special mechanism of recognition in order to prevent violent exclusion. The issue has frequently been analyzed and deconstructed by critical feminist theory, including feminist jurisprudence, and its manifestations have been identified by feminist political movements in all areas of social life.[18] What is common to all types of feminisms, both intellectual

---

[11] Farmer, 'Anthropology,' 307.

[12] James Gilligan, *Violence: Reflections on a National Epidemic* (New York: Vintage Books, 1997), 45.

[13] Birgit Brock-Utne, *Feminist Perspectives on Peace and Peace Education* (New York: Pergamon Press, 1989), 73–172.

[14] Teresa L. Ebert, *Ludic Feminism and After: Postmodernism, Desire, and Labor in Late Capitalism* (Ann Arbor: University of Michigan Press, 1996), 70.

[15] Catia C. Confortini, 'Galtung, Violence and Gender: The Case for a Peace Studies/Feminism Alliance,' *Peace & Change* 31 (2006), 336.

[16] Confortini, 'Galtung,' 336.

[17] Confortini, 'Galtung,' 336.

[18] There is no one feminism. Feminist theory has undergone such a dynamic development

and political movements, is an anti-essentialist and anti-fundamentalist approach, questioning 'one right' source of legitimization of power within a community. By challenging rigid social structures, the feminist approach indicates that the generalization and universalization of male standards invisibly excludes other-than-male participants from the social organization. In addition, some liberal forms of feminism and Marxist feminism have pointed out that sexual and economic forms of discrimination are crucial to the hierarchical subordination of women. The overall result is the suppression of women in the private sphere. Other approaches like the feminism of difference have indicated invisible forms of exclusion in the sphere of culture,[19] language and psychology,[20] and so on.

In my analysis, I seek to investigate structural violence both on the level of social relations (informal rules) and official regulations of the legal system (formal rules). Following the approach of the feminism of difference, on the level of informal rules I assume that patriarchal domination is a form of structural violence embedded in the construction of social community. On the level of formal rules, gender inequality is more difficult to identify since it is concealed behind the veils of legal objectivity and neutrality. In this analysis I am following feminist institutionalism,[21] which provides a conceptual framework for further investigation. Feminist institutionalism, with its central focus on 'informal rules and norms as institutions,'[22] investigates the process of continuity and change in institutions,

in recent years that nowadays it is no longer possible to enumerate all the orientations and approaches to which the label of feminism is attached. It is however possible to single out three main stages of the development of the feminist movement: 'the old wave' (1840–1920), mostly concerned with the struggle for the equality of political and legal rights by bringing them to the same level as those of male members of society; 'the second wave' (1960–1970s), usually identified with the liberation movement; and 'the third wave,' called also 'post-feminist' and lasting from 1970s until now, which has yielded difference or cultural feminism and deconstruction. Such critical theory, including feminist jurisprudence, has developed in step with political movements. For more, see Catherine Villanueva Gardner, *Historical Dictionary of Feminist Philosophy* (Lanham: The Scarecrow Press, 2006), XXV and XXIX.

[19] Nancy Chodorov, *The Reproduction of Mothering: Psychoanalysis and the Sociology of Gender*, (Berkeley: University of California Press, 1978), 1–221; Carol Gilligan, *In a Different Voice: Psychological Theory and Womens' Development* (Cambridge: Harvard University Press, 1993) 1–177; Julia Kristeva, 'The Meaning of Equality,' in *Contemporary French Feminism: Oxford Readings in Feminism*, ed. Kelly Olivier and Lisa Walsh (Oxford: OUP, 2004), 91.

[20] Luce Irigaray, 'Equal or Different,' in *The Irigaray Reader*, ed. Margaret Whitford (Oxford: Blackwell Publishers, 1991), 32. See also Hilaire Barnett, *Introduction to Feminist Jurisprudence*, (London: Cavendish, 1998), 151.

[21] Mona Lena Krook and Fiona Mackay, 'Introduction: Gender, Politics and Institutions,' in *Gender, Politics and Institutions: Toward a Feminist Institutionalism*, ed. Mona Lena Krook and Fiona Mackay (Basingstoke: Palgrave Macmillan, 2011), 1–20.

[22] Gretchen Helmke and Steven Levitsky, 'Informal Institutions and Comparative Politics: A Research Agenda,' *Perspectives on Politics* 2 (2004) 725–74. I treat informal institutions and norms synonymously. See more Fiona Mackay 'New Institutionalism Through

looking at the interplay between formal and informal institutions.[23] In feminist institutionalist studies, shared cultural values and expectations and organizational context are all included in the concept of informal institutions.[24]

7.3 Official/Unofficial Law

To explain the roots of structural violence and how it operates, it is crucial to invoke Adam Podgórecki's conceptualization of the legal system. His broad conception of law, understood as both official and unofficial law, helps to explain the problem of structural violence in law or, more precisely, in official law. As he claims, law should be perceived as not only formal rules, which 'are communicated and enforced through channels widely accepted as official' (official law), but also as informal rules, 'socially shared rules, usually unwritten, that are created, communicated and enforced outside of officially sanctioned channels.'[25] We might find the justification for such an approach in his sociology of law,[26] in which he developed this conceptual framework, originally construed by L. Petrazycki and Eugen

---

a Gender Lens: Towards a Feminist Institutionalism?' *International Political Science Review* 31 (2010), 581.

[23] Informal mechanisms within institutional processes have been studied in differing informal parliamentary conventions and norms in Latin America (Susan Franceschet, 'Gendered Institutions and Women's Substantive Representation: Female Legislators in Argentina and Chile,' in Krook and Mackay, *Gender, Politics and Institutions*, 58–78); instances of powerful actors forgetting innovations in new institutions in post-devolution Britain (Fiona Mackay, 'Institutionalizing 'new politics' in post devolution Scotland: 'nested newness' and the gendered limits of change' [Paper presented at the European Conference on Politics and Gender, Queen's University Belfast, 21–23 January 2009]); strategies of partial or non-compliance by country signatories and the reluctance of key personnel to utilize powers granted to the International Criminal Court (Chappell Louis, 'Nested Newness and Institutional Innovations. Expanding Gender Justice in the International Criminal Court,' in Krook and Mackay, *Gender, Politics and Institutions*, 163–80.

[24] An example of such legal scholarship concerning the study of informal institutions is the analysis of judicial interpretations of the International Criminal Court, which has found that women's rights were treated as less significant than others. See also, Chappell Louis, 'Nested Newness,' 163–80.

[25] This definition is used by authors such as Gretchen Helmke and Steven Levitsky, see Helmke and Levitsky 'Informal Institutions,' 725–74. However, for the original, see Daniel Brinks, 'Informal institutions and the rule of law: the judicial response to state killings in Buenos Aires and Sao Paulo in the 1990s' *Comparative Politics* 36 (2003), 1–19; and is consistent with Douglass C. North, *Institutions, Institutional Change and Economic Performance* (Cambridge: CUP, 1990); Guillermo O'Donnell, 'Illusions About Consolidation,' *Journal of Democracy* 7 (1996), 34–51; Iohn M. Carey, 'Parchment, equilibria, and institutions,' *Comparative Political Studies* 33 (2000), 735–61; Hans-Joachim Lauth, 'Informal institutions and democracy,' *Democratization* 7 (2000), 21–50.

[26] Adam Podgórecki, *A Sociological Theory of Law* (Milano: Giuffrè, 1991), 100.

Ehrlich.[27] This concept has gone by several names: 'unwritten law,' 'living law,' 'informal law,' and 'folk law.' The essence of intuitive law is that it operates in social reality on the basis of informal attitudinal compulsions.[28] Mutually related sets of duties and claims have an obligatory force for the parties involved in a given social situation, irrespective of written norms or norms applied, supported, or sanctioned by a governing authority.[29] Behaviours influenced by informal rules must thus be viewed as solely a product of internal compulsions.

The law of democratic countries is based on constitutional tenets that all people are equal by virtue of their humanity. As the Constitution of the Republic of Poland holds, 'The inherent and inalienable dignity of the person shall constitute a source of freedoms and rights of persons and citizens. It shall be inviolable. The respect and protection thereof shall be the obligation of public authorities.'[30] In addition, in the possession of rights, all citizens are equal before the law and all persons shall have the right to equal treatment before public authorities. Furthermore, 'no one shall be discriminated against in political, social, or economic life for any reason whatsoever.'[31] These legal provisions specific to democratic legal systems have the regulatory function of, inter alia, equalizing social relations. However, the hierarchical structure of social community is automatically reflected in law since social relations are reconstructed and repeated in legal relations.[32] The law, as a cultural phenomenon, shows a direct link between culture or the broader social structure and the legal procedures and types of crime and conflicts that are regulated by the law

---

[27] Adam Podgórecki, 'Intuitive Law versus Folk Law' in *People's Law and State Law*, ed. Anthony Allott and Gordon R. Woodman (Berlin, Boston: De Gruyter Mouton, 2011), 71–2.

[28] Adam Podgórecki, 'Intuitive Law versus Folk Law,' *Zeitschrift fur Rechtssoziologie* 1 (1982), 74–81.

[29] Podgórecki, *A Sociological Theory of Law*, 100 n. 27.

[30] Art. 30 The Constitution of the Republic of Poland of 2 April 1997, *Dziennik Ustaw* no. 78, item 483.

[31] Art. 32 Constitution of the Republic of Poland.

[32] According to Podgórecki, the effectiveness of a legal system directly depends on the relation between formal rules (official law) and informal rules (unofficial law). If there is no reciprocal and supporting relation between them, the integrative function of law gets weaker and, consequently, social life takes on the characteristics of anomia (the breakdown of social bonds resulting in the fragmentation of social life). An ideal legal system of high effectiveness, capable of integrating social life, is based on the reciprocal relation between these two orders. If official and unofficial law are opposed to each other, the legal system becomes perverse and is not able to work properly. For more, see Podgórecki, *Sociological Theory of Law*, 100. There must be a minimum coherence between formal and informal rules to make the legal system work effectively, yet the level of integration may not be equal in all the areas of social life. In my analysis I strive to indicate that despite the apparent integration of official and unofficial rules in Polish law, informal rules affect the way formal rules are applied.

and recognized by the courts.³³ Considering gender issues, the family code will reflect the social roles of family members. This process of transmitting values conveys patterns of domination and exclusions that are not always visible at first sight.

Accepting Podgórecki's model, which involves both official law (formal rules) and unofficial law (informal rules), one can say that a patriarchal structure (based on structural violence) dominates unofficial law, which is mainly based on informal rules. However, looking more closely at the official law, we can see examples of structural violence that are deeply hidden in its structure. Since law is a phenomenon that embraces both top-down and bottom-up regulations, it cannot avoid violence that is well established in social relations.

To discover structural violence that is mostly hidden, one must study the relations between formal and informal rules. This is because gender violence is a phenomenon that occurs in both the private and public sphere. Its complex nature is connected with the intermingling of the private and public spheres (see below).

7.4 Informal Rules and Gender Violence

Informal rules that, inter alia, legitimize violence—in other worlds, socially shared rules, usually unwritten, that 'are created, communicated, and enforced outside of officially sanctioned channels'³⁴—have made it normal rather than disruptive. Very often, it is difficult to identify what informal rules are; however, breaking the formal rule might be a signal or a strategy to identify them. This is surely the case with informal rules with regard to gender relations.

The most common characteristic of informal rules in the gender context is the fact that they are paternalistic and follow 'traditional norms,' according to which women are 'private,' that is, ordained to the private sphere. Cross-cultural studies have found that cultural norms favouring male dominance, female economic dependency, patterns of conflict resolution emphasizing violence, toughness and honour, and male authority in the family lead to higher levels of domestic violence and rape.³⁵

---

³³ In perverse types of legal systems, where formal and informal rules do not cooperate, there is no continuity between socially shared rules and rules imposed by the legal system from the top.

³⁴ Helmke and Levitsky 'Informal Institutions,' 725–40.

³⁵ Leigh Raymond et al.,'Making Change: Norms and Informal Institutions as Solutions to "Intractable" Global Problems,' *Political Research Quarterly* 20 (2003), 10–11; see also Elisabeth J. Friedman, 'Women's Human Rights: The Emergence of a Movement,' in *Women's Rights, Human Rights: International Feminist Perspectives*, ed. Julie S. Peters and

In addition to this, the most troubling feature of informal rules from the point of view of gender violence is that they are based on a shame and honour system, which makes women and men think that problems should be solved within the family. In addition, what complicates the identification of problems is the close relationship between victims and perpetrators and the dependency of feelings and values. This makes victims unwilling to punish their abusers. This is the cause of major difficulties in dealing with the problem of violence in the private sphere since it is one of the most under-reported crimes in police statistics. It is estimated that, in Poland, a million women a year experience sexual and physical violence.[36] According to Feminoteka Foundation, there could be as many as 250,000 rapes every year. Meanwhile, official police statistics recorded only 2,000.[37] By comparison, in Scandinavian countries, where the mechanisms of equality have developed in the best way among European countries, the level of reported violence as measured is approximately 50%,[38] while in Poland it reaches no more than 19%. As the report on domestic violence makes clear, this difference can be explained by different levels of awareness and sensitivity to the problem of violence. In particular, in the rural areas of Poland these levels appear especially low and are strongly affected by traditional beliefs and stereotypes.[39] Last but not least, the problem of

---

Andrea Wolper (New York: Routledge, 1995)18–35; Lee Lakeman, *Obsession, with Intent: Violence against Women* (New York: Black Rose Books, 2005); Weldon, S. Laurel, *Protest, Policy and the Problem of Violence against Women: A Cross-National Comparison* (Pittsburgh: University of Pittsburgh Press, 2005).

[36] Joanna Piotrowska and Alina Synakiewicz, ed., *Dość milczenia. Przemoc seksualna wobec kobiet i problem gwałtu w Polsce* [Enough of Silence: Sexual Violence Against Women and the Problem of Rape in Poland] (Warszawa: Feminoteka Foundation 2011), available online at: http://feminoteka.pl/wp-content/uploads/2016/04/dosc_milczenia.pdf [last accessed: 25/7/2016]. It is estimated that in 2004 around 800,000 women experienced violence in Poland, see Joanna Piotrowska, 'Przemoc wobec kobiet,' in Anna Dzierzgowska and Joanna Piotrowska (eds) *Białe plamy na mapie (nie)równości* (Warszawa: Feminoteka Foundation, 2001), 117–140, 119, accessed 25 July 2016, http://www.wmaa.fika.pl/download.php?path=downloads&file=07012015100234bialeplamy.pdf.

[37] Joanna Piotrowska, 'O przemocy wobec kobiet' (interviewed by Przemysław Prekiel), *Przegląd Socjalistyczny* internet portal, 24 February 2012, accessed 25 July 2016, http://www.przeglad-socjalistyczny.pl/wywiad-tygodnia/756-prekiel.html.

[38] Denmark 52%, Finland 47%, Sweden 46%, Poland 19%, see Joanny Banasiuk (ed.), *Czy Polska powinna ratyfikować Konwencje Rady Europy o zapobieganiu i przeciwdziałaniu przemocy wobec kobiet i przemocy domowej?* [Should Poland Ratify the Council of Europe Convention on Preventing Violence Against Women and Domestic Violence?] (Warszawa: Fundacja Instytut na rzecz Kultury Prawnej Ordo Iuris, 2014), 5–6, accessed 25 July 2016, http://www.ordoiuris.pl/public/pliki/dokumenty/Raport_przemoc_OI.pdf.

[39] Jowita Radzińska and Małgorzata Radziszewska-Manikowska, *Zjawisko przemocy w rodzinie wobec kobiet i mężczyzn. Jakościowa część badania* [The Phenomenon of Violence within the Family Directed Against Women and Men: The Qualitative Part of the Research], accessed 25 July 2016, https://www.mpips.gov.pl/gfx/mpips/userfiles/_public/3_2010_Raport%20z%20badania%20jakosciowego_01-03-11.pdf.

domestic violence is framed by family bonds and dependency of feelings and values. The solution proposed by formal rules, such as the isolation and imprisonment of the perpetrator, are often ineffective, since the victim does not want to pursue legal action against relatives.[40]

As we can see, the problem of gender violence is well hidden even when it comes to its direct form. The hierarchical social relations that dominate structures in the family and the legitimization provided by structural violence can offer an important insight into explaining this phenomenon. The private sphere is mainly based on informal rules, unwritten law that is simply practised in social relations. Domestic violence is typical, for the private sphere is protected by the rights of privacy. However, this does not mean that the private sphere is untouchable. As we can observe, the development of formal rules protecting women's rights strengthens and increases women's awareness of the possibility to exercise their rights.[41] Women demand respect for their rights and pursue their own interests. As is shown by police statistics, the number of reported cases of the violation of women's rights systematically decreased between 2005 and 2012 but subsequently increased.[42] However, these figures do not exactly capture the scale of the phenomenon as the police statistics for such crimes suffer from the problem of under-reporting. The violation of formal rights and rules reported by the police could be interpreted as proof of existing informal rules that clash with formal regulations. This, however, can be a sign of the power of informal rules that override formal mechanisms.

Formal institutions are 'rules and procedures that are created, communicated and enforced through channels widely accepted as official.'[43] They aim to provide or guarantee equal rights and the protection of women's special rights. Taking into account a number of legal regulations

---

[40] Radzińska and Radziszewska-Manikowska, *Zjawisko przemocy*.

[41] Re the development of formal rules protecting women's rights in Poland since 2011, see Regulation of the Council of Ministers of 13 September 2011 on the 'Blue Card' procedure (*Dziennik Ustaw* no. 209, item 1245). In accordance with Art. 9 (d) of the Act of 29 July 2005 on combating domestic violence (*Dziennik Ustaw* no. 180, item 1493), the intervention in the environment of the family affected by the violence takes place in accordance with the procedure 'Blue Card' and does not require the consent of a person affected by domestic violence. Mistreatment of a family member is a crime under Art. 207 Polish Criminal Code (1997). This offence is prosecuted ex officio, which means that the police and the prosecutor owe a duty to institute criminal proceedings against the perpetrators of violence if they have information (no matter from whom and how acquired) that in a given family, mistreatment has taken place. See further, Radzińska and Radziszewska-Manikowska, *Zjawisko przemocy*.

[42] From around 90,000 in 2005 to around 50,000 in 2012. However, between 2012 and 2015 the number has been growing reaching approximately 69,000 in 2015. See also Policja [Police], 'Przemoc w rodzinie,' accessed 25 July 2015, http://www.statystyka.policja.pl/st/wybrane-statystyki/przemoc-w-rodzinie/50863,dok.html.

[43] Helmke and Levitsky, 'Informal Institutions,' 726–27.

focused on gender justice, one may conclude that there is nothing to do in equalizing gender status or preventing violence. However, as the statistics indicate, the problems have not been solved. There is a full package of legal norms (coming from international, European, and Polish law) available to the Polish courts that seek to provide or guarantee gender equality.[44] When it comes to legal norms specifically preventing violence against women in Poland, there is only a general legal statute against family violence[45] and a signed and recently ratified convention on preventing and combating violence against women and domestic violence (Istanbul, 11 May 2011). What is particularly noteworthy about the convention is that it recognizes the problem of structural violence against women. The preamble reads: 'Recognizing the structural nature of violence against women as gender-based violence, and that violence against women is one of the crucial social mechanisms by which women are forced into a subordinate position compared with men.'[46] However, in spite of all the legislation introduced to combat discrimination and to provide equal opportunities, gender inequality persists in nearly all institutions in the public and private spheres. It seems that the problem is that formal rules alone are generally not sufficient to promote change because they interact with informal rules.

7.5 Structural Violence in Polish Law

The law, as a male-dominated practice, structurally excludes women at the levels of both legislation and enforcement. In the first case, which could be called substantial, legal regulations either do not protect the rights enjoyed by women specifically (an absence of the law regulating abortion), or when such regulations standardize some issues, they disregard

---

[44] The Convention on the Elimination of all Forms of Discrimination against Women (CEDAW); Act of implementation of certain provisions of the EU on equal treatment: Council Directive 86/613/EEC of 11 December 1986 on the application of the principle of equal treatment between men and women engaged in an activity, including agriculture, in a self-employed capacity, and on the protection of self-employed women during pregnancy and motherhood; Council Directive 2000/43/EC of 29 June 2000 implementing the principle of equal treatment between persons irrespective of racial or ethnic origin; Council Directive 2000/78/EC of 27 November 2000 establishing a general framework for equal treatment in employment and occupation; Council Directive 2004/113/EC of 13 December 2004 implementing the principle of equal treatment between men and women in the access to and supply of goods and services; Directive 2006/54/EC of the European Parliament and of the Council of 5 July 2006 on the implementation of the principle of equal opportunities and equal treatment of men and women in matters of employment and occupation (recast).
[45] Act of 29 July 2005.
[46] Preamble to The Council of Europe Convention on preventing and combating violence against women and domestic violence (Istanbul Convention 11 May 2011)1249 U.N.T.S. 13.

and trivialize women's issues (e.g. sexual harassment). Secondly, through the way law is interpreted by the courts, the use of objective yet 'male' categories applied to different types of subjects, results in the unequal distribution of resources.[47] Overall, this does not mean that law is not objective in the sense that it explicitly excludes some of the subjects, resulting in oppression. With specific reference to structural violence, one is excluded in a hidden way, using objective narratives as a cover for masculine discourse. In order to approach this issue, I shall provide a deeper analysis of the phenomenon of objectivity of/in law and introduce some examples further substantiating my argument.

Objectivity is fundamental to official law, both to the creation of law and to its application. While its role in law creation is generally considered both necessary and crucial,[48] the use of objectivity in the application of law is commonly the subject of criticism and strong attacks. In this section, I shall focus on objectivity in a practical legal discourse to demonstrate that it can be used as a tool to exercise structural violence. As objectivity functions on the level of official law, the source of structural inequality comes from an informal context.[49]

Before proceeding with this analysis, it is important to provide clarification of some aspects of the use of the concept of objectivity in this context. First, a distinction must be drawn between 'objectivity *of* law' and 'objectivity *in* law.'[50] The first concerns the conceptualization of law and the second practical legal discourse. The two are interrelated in that the objectivity of law influences objectivity in law, and objectivity in law reshapes and influences the objectivity of law. The character of this relation shows how the objectivity of law influences objectivity in

---

[47] Małgorzata Fuszara, 'Feministyczna socjologia prawa,' 2 *Prace Instytutu Stosowanych Nauk Społecznych Uniwersytetu Warszawskiego* (1999), 383.

[48] Ronald Dworkin, *Freedom's law: the moral reading of the American Constituition* (Harvard University Press, USA, 1996) 397-99.

[49] The aspect of objectivity in law as a mask of inequality on the level of formal rules is discussed in literature: Jules L. Coleman and Brian Leiter, 'Determinancy, Objectivity, and Authority' in Andrei Marmor (ed), *Law and Interpretations: Essays in Legal Philosophy* (Oxford: OUP, 1995), 331-49, who helpfully discuss this literature in detail. See also Martha Minow, 'Rights For the Next Generation: A Feminist Approach to Children's Rights,' *Harvard Women's Law Journal* 9 (1986), 1-24; Ann C. Scales, 'The Emergence of Feminist Jurisprudence: An Essay,' *Yale Law Journal* 95 (1986), 1373-403; Duncan Kennedy, 'Form and Substance in Private Law Adjudication,' *Harvard Law Review* 89 (1976), 1685-778; Kimberlé Williams Crenshaw, 'Race, Reform, and Retrenchment: Transformation and Legitimation in Antidiscrimination Law,' *Harvard Law Review* 101 (1988), 1331-87; and Richard Delgado, 'On Telling Stories in School: A Reply to Farber and Sherry,' *Vanderbilt Law Review* 46 (1993), 665-76.

[50] The 'objectivity of law ... in the first place means that it is a normative order which is the same to everyone, independently of anyone's subjective attitudes.' Jerzy Wróblewski, *Wartości a decyzja sądowa* [Values and the Judicial Decision] (Wrocław: Zakład Narodowy im. Ossolińskich, 1973), 150.

legal argumentation. The hierarchical structure of the legal system imposes the concept of objectivity from a top-down perspective. The self-created authority of law makes this ascription possible and enables legal decisions to be institutionalized. The accepted legal narrative thus requires objectivity as a tool to express and justify its decisions.

As a consequence, there are different aspects of how objectivity is used in legal discourse. On one hand, objectivity allows the closure of the discourse and does not give recognition to subjectivity and particularisms. On the other hand, 'objectivity of law' is necessary because it enables the process of taking decisions by providing coherent justifications.[51] By 'objectivity in law,' I refer to a practical perspective of applying law in a specific judicial context. The process of legal interpretation and argumentation due to its specific character comprises elements that are both objective and subjective. Legal interpretation adopts an essential feature of the legal discourse that must be objective, while also referring to the feature of an interpretation that is 'subject dependent.' The character of an interpretation (including legal interpretation) emphasizes individual or subjective influences of the person of an interpreter on the interpretative decision. As it is construed by legal hermeneutics, legal language is only one amongst many elements comprising law, the others being legal culture and the interpretative community.[52] A practical legal perspective is not only necessarily linked to subjects' actions but also to their motivations and feelings and, consequently, it is necessarily subjective. Yet the law objectifies individual stories into its fixed categories, constructing coherent judicial narratives, which according to its inner standards should be objective. Accordingly, it ensures that this process very often results in inequality.

The objectified legal narrative is strongly connected with the organization of the legal world itself and especially with the general rules of legal justifications. When a court considers arguments, it gives priority to those that can be recognized publicly, have reasons that are confirmed and justified, and match the criteria used by a reasonable person, rather than personalized criteria. By definition, the impartial court mainly takes into account objective facts, not the subjective motives of the parties.[53] Subjective motives must be objectively justified from the point of view of a reasonable person. Parties must deliver evidence for their behaviour

---

[51] Lidia Rodak, 'Objectivity as Coherence in Practical Discourse,' in *The Rule of Law and the Challenges to Jurisprudence*, ed. Péter Cserne (Frankfurt am Main: Peter Lang, 2014).

[52] Gregory Leyh, 'Introduction' in *Legal Hermeneutics: History, Theory and Practice*, ed. Gregor Leyh (Berkeley: University of California Press, 1992), XII.

[53] This is the most common perspective, especially in public law, but it should be stressed that, in private law, the situation is different in some situations: subjective mistakes can be excuses in criminal or private law. Subjective meaning matters in interpreting wills, etc.

to make their arguments convincing and credible. Thus, parties in a trial should introduce their stories in objective, not subjective terms. Through changing the narrative, a particular individual becomes a legal subject and must change the empirical facts of the case into legal institutional facts. The legal subject needs arguments confirming his credibility in the legal world, in the same way as, to give a very basic example, being visited by a doctor requires issuing a certificate.[54]

Let me produce some examples illustrating mainly the aspect of the organization of the legal world. In a 2013 case,[55] the court claimed that what is introduced by the party is merely a subjective conviction that cannot be confirmed by an objective justification. 'The plaintiffs claim that placing the monument in the square led to the breakdown of their relationship with the art work, which is at most only their subjective belief, and objective justification cannot be found.'[56] From a decision of the Polish Supreme Court,[57] we learn that 'feelings of the plaintiff do not have any objective justification and are not included in the accurate evaluation of the Court of Appeals. It is not sufficient to conclude that personal safety has been compromised or threatened by the publication of the disputed texts.'[58]

As the aforementioned examples indicate, objective categories do not consider subjective individual feelings, unless they find objective justification in the reasoning of the court. Another example from Polish jurisprudence provides a clear further illustration of how objective standards may represent a male perspective in a particular case concerning women.[59] The Foundation 'Gender Center' sued an Internet provider for violating the personal rights of a woman pictured lying down in a poster accompanied by the slogan: 'Starting from September we will be giving it to you for free,' implicitly suggesting that the subject of this donation was the woman represented. The judgment states that, 'the form and the content of the advertising message does not violate the personal rights of the plaintiff.'[60] The court justified the decision on the basis of 'objective reasons' and the 'principle of equality,' that is, objective legal and social standards. As the court explains, 'to evaluate if the personal rights have been violated, one should refer to the social norms. In order to do this, one

---

[54] Kent Greenawalt, *Law and Objectivity* (Oxford: OUP, 1992), 93–120.

[55] Court of Appeal in Krakow judgement of 12 March 2013, Case I ACa 510/03, TPP 2004/1-2/143.

[56] Voivodeship Administrative Court judgement of 30 December 2005, Case III SA/Wa 2680/05, Lex no.881853.

[57] Supreme Court judgement of 16 September 1999, Case II CKN 465/98, LEX no. 512047.

[58] Supreme Court judgement of 16 September 1999.

[59] Court of Appeal in Warsaw judgement of 12 March 2013, Case I ACa 1034/12 Lex no. 1298984.

[60] Court of Appeal in Warsaw judgement of 12 March 2013.

should use objective criteria, taking the perspective of a reasonable man, and not the perspective of the violated person.'[61]

In this case the court can evaluate the situation exercising judicial discretion. However, in evaluating the case, the court introduces it as being based on the objective criterion of the perspective of a 'reasonable man.' Still, the objective standards seem to be male standards, however objectified and universalized they may be. Such a perspective is applied to all possible types of legal subjects participating in the legal discourse. Identifying a reasonable man's point of view with the perspective of an 'average citizen' amounts to the position excluding the protection of women's rights. Thus the values of Polish society according to an impartial judge are defined as follows: 'Personal goods are defined as values derived from a social evaluation, which are recognized by society and created by it. These values, which are commonly socially recognized, are accepted by a given legal system.'[62] This illustrates how the social order composed of a given set of values structurally excludes women's rights from the general protection. Women's rights are out of the protection by both legal regulations and social norms, that is, both formal and informal rules. Despite the declaration of equality between men and women, the court only respects the equity of the rules, not the equity of the results. As the court argues, 'the catalogue of personal rights attributed to all men and women is the same. Obviously, there are biological or mental differences between sexes. However, they cannot sufficiently justify differential treatment, which means creating separate categories of rights for men and women.'[63]

One of the most telling examples of how law excludes women from the legal discourse, using its power of objectivity, is the neutral narrative of its language. The law is mostly worded neutrally in terms of gender, but it can be noted that where gender appears it is mostly with reference to the female kind. That is, the female form is used to emphasize that there might be exceptions for women, which undoubtedly implies that the law was originally addressed to men. In her analysis of Polish law, Malgorzata Fuszara finds that it is generally written in the male gender, while the exceptions are formulated with respect to female issues.[64] This gives the impression that the law creates objective standards that are the

---

[61] Court of Appeal in Warsaw judgement of 12 March 2013.
[62] Adam Szpunar, *Ochrona dóbr osobistych*, (Warszawa: Państwowe Wydawnictwo Naukowe, 1979); in Judgment of the Court of Appeal in Warsaw of 12 March 2013 I ACa 1034/12, Portal Orzeczeń Sądu Apelacyjnego w Warszawie, accessed 25 July 2016, http://orzeczenia.waw.sa.gov.pl/content/$N/154500000000503_I_ACa_001034_2012_Uz_2013-03-12_001.
[63] Judgment of the Court of Appeal in Warsaw of 12 March 2013.
[64] Małgorzata Fuszara, *Feministyczna socjologia prawa* [A Feminist Sociology of Law] (Warszawa: Prace ISNS nr 2,1999), 383–411.

same for everyone. The law seems objective and neutral but it is essentially masculine. The objective law introduces universal rules to be applicable to all, with the masculine standards, while, of course, not all its subjects are men. Thus values informing the criteria whilst created by and for men have been called objective and valid for everyone.[65]

When we limit our comparison to formal legal regulations or values that constitute the main objective of the legal system, the domination of a male perspective is not visible at all. As Fuszara indicates, male domination becomes visible only when through the deconstruction of legal practice.[66] Despite the neutral way in which Polish law is formulated in terms of gender, it results in discrimination and exclusion of women. Moreover, as Ewa Letowska stresses, the mechanisms of equalization of rights on the scale of the whole legal system are adjusted to male standards.[67] This is especially true in the case of structural violence, where violence is deeply hidden and inscribed in the structure of the law. Even if discrimination and exclusion are revealed, the mechanisms of reparation are still not able to equalize rights.

At this particular juncture it would be helpful to introduce an example of the case in which formally neutral objective rules result in inequality in the process of their applications by the courts. The Polish Family Code states that 'spouses have equal rights and responsibilities in marriage.'[68] The obligations of a man, as they are interpreted by the court, lead us to believe that they are described negatively, i.e. as a range of behaviours that a husband should not perform: he should not drink excessively, hit his wife and children, cause fights (especially involving verbal abuse), or cheat on his wife.[69] This particular example demonstrates how the application of a neutral and objective legal provision is influenced by informal rules that are patriarchal. The process of interpretation of legal provisions as strongly influenced by both the cultural context and subjective evaluation of a decision maker is highly dependent on informal rules. Fuszara's report indicates that there are many examples when women judges, especially in divorce cases, tended to sustain stereotypes of male and female roles in the family. As one can see, in patriarchal societies, the same traditional patterns of gender are passed on to both sexes and then applied by them in professional life, including work. In addition, family courts are mainly

---

[65] Catharine A. MacKinnon, *Feminism Unmodified: Discourses on Life and Law* (Cambridge: Harvard University Press, 1987).
[66] Małgorzata Fuszara, *Rodzina w sądzie*, (Warszawa: ISNS UW, 1994), 210.
[67] Ewa Łętowska, 'Czy polskie prawo ma płeć?' [Does Polish Law Have a Gender], lecture given at the *Krytyka Polityczna* on 14 November 2014, accessed 25 July 2016, http://www.krytykapolityczna.pl/wydarzenia/debata-czy-polskie-prawo-ma-plec
[68] Art. 23 Polish Family and Guardianship Code.
[69] Fuszara, *Feministyczna socjologia prawa*, 383–411.

dominated by women because they are considered specialists in family issues.

This phenomenon can be explained by the concept of substantially gendered Polish courts. Institutions have mostly a formally neutral appearance, but gender is always hidden within them. Feminist scholars have demonstrated how gender is deeply implicated in institutions.[70] It is claimed that institutions are gendered in two ways: nominally, men traditionally continue to hold positions of power in greater numbers than women and,[71] substantially, male mechanisms dominate in institutions because an increasing number of women does not necessarily make a significant difference.

The statistics report and analysis demonstrate that the phenomenon of gendered institutionalism takes place in Polish courts.[72] In 2000, there were 4,594 women judges in the Polish courts, giving them a majority over men at 63.6%. Compared to 1968, when women judges represented 33.2% of the total, this is a very significant increase in numbers. However, women judges mostly occupy lower positions in the lower courts: in 2007, there were 66% of women in regional courts, 58% in districts courts, 53% in courts of appeal, 26% in the Supreme Courts, and 21% in the Constitutional Tribunal.[73]

7.6 (In)formal Rules and Structural Gender Violence

In this part of the chapter, my intention is to discuss the relation between formal and informal rules regulating gender justice to show how formal regulations are influenced by informal rules. The explanation provided will mostly concern the public and private sphere.

Before the feminist revolution, there was a clear separation between men and women as actors playing their respective roles in the public and private spheres. The division into the public and the private was also the border between the sphere of personal freedom and the zone of state interference. Once granted their social and legal rights, women entered the public sphere. However, the equalization of rights was mainly effective in the public sphere while in the private sphere the situation of

---

[70] Louise Chappell and Georgina Waylen, 'Gender and the Hidden Life of Institutions' (paper presented at the MPSA, Chicago, April 2012).

[71] Anne Witz and Michael Savage, 'Theoretical Introduction: Gender in Organizations,' in *Gender and Bureaucracy*, ed. Mike Savage and Anne Witz (Oxford: Blackwell, 1992).

[72] Małgorzata Fuszara, 'Women Lawyers in Poland under the Impact of Post 1989 Transformation,' in *Women In the Worlds Legal Profession*, ed. Ulrike Schulz and Gisela Shaw (Oxford: Hart Publishing, 2003), 375.

[73] Bożena Chołuj, ed., *Polityka równości płci. Polska 2007* [Gender Equality Policy: Poland 2007] (Warszawa: Fundacja Fundusz Współpracy, 2007), accessed 25 July 2016, http://www.bezuprzedzen.org/doc/polityka_rownosci_plci_raport.pdf.

women remained untouched. This is the reason why legal instruments which secure equality may only be applied to the public sphere. However, a vast majority of discriminatory practices take place in the private sphere. Due to the protection of a personal right to freedom, which is considered sacrosanct, the state is supposed to be kept 'out of the bedroom.' The public sphere, as stressed by feminist theory, was originally organized and dominated by male standards. Thus women as recent actors in the public sphere must play according to male rules. The dominance over women and their discrimination has no obvious character but is rather hidden in the deep structures of discourse. Structural violence is hence embedded in the way private and public spheres are organized and the differences between them have a purely formal character. But from the pragmatic point of view, it does not make much difference if the law does not reach the private sphere and regulates equity in the public sphere only formally. The former sphere is manifestly dominated by patriarchal rules and standards, while the latter is colonized by the informal rules of patriarchy in a covert way. Providing full equity to social relations would probably call for the structural remodelling of social architecture, its basic concept and social roles based on traditional patterns defined by patriarchy. Some authors even suggest that to reach equality we need to create public and private spheres anew or at least to work out some mechanisms capable of reaching informal institutions.[74]

Concerning gender issues, formal rules aim to provide or guarantee equal rights, but when applied within the context of informal social rules they very often result in different forms of exclusion and/or oppression, in other words in structural violence. This is determined by the fact that informal rules can play a major role in changing the intended effect of formal rules. As stated in the literature, this can be negative but also positive or seemingly neutral.[75] In the case of gender issues, we can observe the clash between two orders: the formal, which equalizes rights, and the informal which is based on hierarchical domination. However, the dynamic can have different negative forms depending on whether it relates to the public or private sphere. That is why it seems worthwhile to investigate the factors that influence the phenomenon of gender violence in both official law and non-official law, taking into account the dynamics between formal

---

[74] Jean L. Coen, *Regulating Intimacy: A New Legal Paradigm* (Princeton: Princeton University Press, 2002). The idea of regulating the private sphere is developed on the basis of the notion of formal institutions built in an informal context. Intimacy can involve gendered power relations, so 'privatizing intimacy' could be a way to regulate, e.g. sexual expression in the workplace, to undo gender hierarchy and to prevent various forms of oppression.

[75] See Steve Leach and Vivien Lowndes, 'Of Roles and Rules Analysing the Changing Relationship between Political Leaders and Chief Executives in Local Government,' *Public Policy and Administration* 22 (2007), 183–200.

and informal rules in private and public spheres respectively.

The specific context of a private sphere is founded on the domination of informal rules. They are mostly based on traditional patterns representing hierarchical social structures. Here, the violation of formal rights and rules is reported by police statistics. However, to repeat a point constantly stressed by non-governmental organizations, the scale of violations of formal rights is under-reported, especially in the cases of violence in the family.[76] It is related to the idea that a private sphere represents the sphere of people's freedom, which is untouchable without their permission. The violation of formal rules, which could be interpreted as proof of existing informal rules, indicates the clash with formal regulations. Thus, in the private sphere, the prevailing equilibrium based on informal rules results in the violation of new formal rules. That is, breaking the formal rules is a kind of confirmation of the informal order and its power. A new set of formal rules, which is in opposition to informal rules, results in the disturbance of the existing equilibrium.

The public sphere is regulated by equality and anti-discrimination law which protects and equalizes the situation of men and women. At first glance we might think that violence is not a problem present in the public sphere. However, the analysis of the problem of the objectivity of law as a mechanism of oppression leads to the conclusion that the public sphere can be threatened by violence to a similar extent as the private sphere. Furthermore, violence in the public sphere is very difficult to identify as it is concealed through forms of formality, generality, or objectivity. That is why, examining the relation between formal and informal rules in the public sphere, it is possible to point out three ways in which informal rules influence the effectiveness of formal rules:

---

[76] Throughout a year, the police carry out more than 90,000 family violence interventions. However, only part of the domestic interventions are classified as family violence. In 2006, the police reported 620,662 cases of domestic interventions and 96,099 interventions related to family violence. Only 15% of the interventions were started according to the procedure of the 'Blue Card.' Ultimately, it was stated that only 24 offences referred to Art. 207 Polish Criminal Code. The Police sometimes do not respond to calls in such cases (Wojciechowska, 2007). Women represent almost 90% of adult victims of domestic violence. About 40% of all victims are children of both sexes. On the other hand, the offender is in the 95% of cases male. See further: Agata Teutsch and Eleonora Zielińska, 'Sprawiedliwość i Prawa Człowieka,' in Chołuj, *Polityka równości*, 85. In 2013 there have already been 61,047 cases reported according to the procedure of the Blue Card, so we can observe a growing tendency in cases of family violence. Still, a vast majority of cases are underreported. 18% of surveyed women (University of Oxford survey) revealed that there was an instance of direct violence in their lives. Among surveyed married women 41% said that they personally know or have met a woman beaten by her husband in their immediate surroundings. See futher: Jolanta Szymańczyk, 'Przemoc w rodzinie. Zarys problematyki' [Violence within the Family: An Outline of the Problem] Biuro Studiów i Ekspertyz Sejmu RP—*Raport* no. 181 (2000), 13, accessed 25 July 2016, http://biurose.sejm.gov.pl/teksty_pdf_00/r-181.pdf.

1. *'Dead rules'*—Formal rules are not implemented and women's rights are ignored and not exercised as if they have never existed in a legal system. 'Dead formal rules' protecting women's rights are very often not enforced because informal rules influence the interpretation of existing formal rules, making people look at the situation through gender lenses. The same applies to the interpretation of actual facts of individual cases that are very often dismissed as irrelevant. Formal rules protecting women's rights exist, but due to the force of informal patriarchal rules they are not exercised in practice. This type of relation between formal and informal rules in the public sphere is represented by cases that were not recognized by the court/public body as deserving legal protection for at least two types of reasons:

a. Lack of recognition that a given case deserves legal protection; e.g. it is common to discontinue proceedings of mistreatment of family members (80% of cases are discontinued by the prosecutor's office) due to the negligible social harm of the act or a lack of justification that a criminal offense has taken place.[77] Another example is when law enforcement authorities neglect the reports of victims intimidated by perpetrators or do not recognize sexual violence as a crime to which women are particularly vulnerable.[78]

b. Lack of recognition caused by a narrow/literal interpretation of protecting rules. It is evidenced in the courts, due to the narrow positivist approach to the interpretation of the rules of anti-discrimination law, which, according to the judges, is always associated with the presence of a protected right.[79] When there is no specific protecting rule, the case might be rejected by the court for the lack of a formal rule protecting the right. The criteria established by formal rules are far more significant than the actual facts of individual cases. On rare occasions, courts do embark on an interpretation process to broaden the scope of the protecting rules, or, alternatively, to apply directly the principle of general Constitutional equity.

2. *Lesser effectiveness*—Formal rules are formally respected, but

---

[77] A common practice is to divide a case of domestic violence into several separate cases by extracting an individual allegation; the next thing to do is to discontinue the proceedings under Art. 207 Polish Criminal Code, indicating that it can be brought as a private prosecution. See Dzierzgowska and Piotrowska, *Białe plamy*; Chołuj, *Polityka równości*.

[78] A judicial order to leave the house by the perpetrator, without contacting their victims or detention, is rarely used (for example, out of the examined 121 criminal cases under Art. 207 Penal Code, there were only two cases of detention and one of a restraining order). In recent years, a tendency to punish mildly the perpetrators of domestic violence has been maintained; a majority of convicts received lower sentences, while in the 90% of cases, the execution of the imposition of imprisonment was suspended. See Dzierzgowska and Piotrowska, *Białe plamy*; Chołuj, *Polityka równości*.

[79] Monika Wieczorek and Katarzyna Bogatko, ed., *Monitoring report on the antidiscrimination law in Polish courts of general jurisdiction 2012–2013* (Warszawa: Polskie Twarzystwo Prawa Antydyskryminacyjnego, 2012).

interpreted through gender lenses, which results in indirect discrimination or discrimination by association (e.g. the regulation concerning maternity leave becomes an exception to the general rule regulating leave for men and women[80]).

This phenomenon has also been illustrated by the example of substantially gendered institutions (see section 3 above), when Polish female judges apply the law as if they were believers in paternalistic ideology. Judges' attitudes toward the problems of discrimination and equality are the reasons why the rules are not exercised in practice: the judges themselves are burdened with stereotypes and rely on them. Some judges believe that the source of discrimination is inherent in the attitudes and actions of the same people who are discriminated against.[81] This type of influence of informal rules on the way formal rules are applied certainly lower their effectiveness.

3. Lack of development—Formal rules do not develop because they are in stark contrast to informal rules. An example is abortion law or in vitro reproduction in Poland, which are not permitted. Simultaneously, we may conclude formal rules are against women's rights (e.g. anti-abortion laws), when contrasted with another type of informal rules that support a traditional patriarchal model. In this case, a very strong Catholic tradition with its pro-life orientation puts a great deal of pressure on the current shape of formal legislation.

3.1. Blocking and delaying development of formal rules—An example illustrating this point is the Polish public discussion on the ratification of The Council of Europe Convention on preventing and combating violence against women and domestic violence, the so-called Istanbul Convention of 11 May 2011. On the 6 February 2015 the Istanbul Convention was ratified by the Polish Sejm.[82] The arguments presented in the public debate on the ratification of the convention had a mere ideological and political character and were exchanged by right-wing parties on the one hand and liberal circles and left-wing parties on the other. The main arguments presented

---

[80] Re indirect discrimination, see ECJ's interpretation in Danfoss, C-109/88 [1989] ECR 3199.

[81] Wieczorek and Bogatko, *Monitoring report*. Similar findings are shown in Feminoteka's report on gender violence, '*The politics of gender equality: Poland 2007.*' Judges surveyed typically held the view that alcohol is a major cause of domestic violence, that guilt often lies on both sides, and that victims provoke violence upon themselves. Almost 73% of the judges questioned felt that the victims contribute to the violence they suffer, and that violence is most common in families with low social status, low education, and low income.

[82] Among 437 deputies, 254 voted for and 175 against. The votes against the Istanbul Convention came mainly from right-wing parties (Law and Justice and Fair Poland). The support was voiced by left-wing parties (Democratic Left Alliance) and the center-left (Your Movement), while liberal-conservative deputies (Civic Platform) and agrarian, Christian-democratic deputies (The Polish People's Party) failed to reach a common position.

by right-wing circles indicated that the Istanbul Convention 'stands against a Polish family,' that it 'is directed against Polish religion, tradition, and culture' and that it is aimed at remodeling the ideology of Polish society.[83] The Polish Episcopate called the Istanbul Convention 'a neo-Marxist document,' which in the Polish context is particularly pejorative. As one can see, the core of the discussion did not focus directly on the central problem, which is violence against women and the protection of women's rights. Instead, it was an arena for the ideological battle between two competing schemes, traditional and liberal. The political opposition, including the Polish Catholic Church, expressed fear that the dominating position of a traditional patriarchal culture with its fixed gender roles in the family and society was threatened. The supporters of the Istanbul Convention, focusing on the equality of rights, expressed a liberal vision of the social order. Moreover, the ratification took place in the period marked by the general weakening of the position of the Polish Catholic Church in political life, also caused by its cold relations with the Vatican, and the event was close to the time of presidential elections. In other words, the ratifying of the Istanbul Convention by President Bronislaw Komorowski on 13 April 2015, that is, one month before the election, was probably a decision influenced by the context of the political campaign. Immediately afterwards, the right wing contested the decision as incompatible with the Polish constitutional legal order and announced it would attempt to challenge the Istanbul Convention before the Constitutional Tribunal. The case illustrates how informal patriarchal rules may significantly delay and possibly block the exercise of basic human rights of people affected by violence, just for the sake of maintaining the status quo.

Figure 1: Forms of Structural Violence in Law

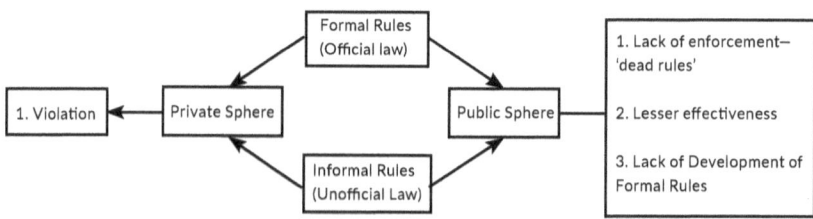

---

[83] Adam Leszczynski, Gazeta Wyborcza, 2 May 2015, accessed 25 July 2016, http://wyborcza.pl/1,75968,17362790,Okreslenie__neomarksistowska_ideologia_gender__nie.html.

7.7 Conclusions

The relations of formal and informal rules seem to be different in the public and private spheres. However, they do not differ that much. Despite the fact that official and non-official law represent different types of orders, protecting different kinds of values, it can be observed that the domination of informal rules in gender issues is, in both types of law, very similar. It seems that patriarchal types of rules operate overtly in the private sphere, but are covert in the public sphere protected by the formal rules of official law. As can be seen in the case of gender justice, both official and non-official law are dominated by informal rules. What really makes a difference is the way patriarchal rules function in both of these spheres. In official law, which protects equality, structural violence is deeply hidden. Gender, as one of the most important elements of the social structure, and, consequently, also of the legal structure, basically shapes these relations. As a result, gender not only differentiates but also discriminates, dominates, and excludes.[84] This perspective reveals a hierarchical submission of women in both official and non-official law. What is called objectivity of/in law represents only a 'masculine narrative' which works to preserve the mechanisms of structural violence. Objectivity not only plays the role of masking power relations in official law as a 'hypocritical notion,'[85] but is also an excellent foundation for maintaining structural violence.

The case of gender violence investigated through the analysis of formal and informal rules indicates that what seems to be at the beginning of the collision of two different orders is in fact, as a whole, similarly dominated by the power of informality from the non-official social sphere. These two types of orders resonate very well with each other, which results in lessening the effectiveness and power of formal rules. The dynamic of formal and informal rules in the public sphere shows first the naïve worshipping of the formality of law that never becomes exclusively formal; second, that the public character of law is never only public, but also colonized by private power. This all means that the system of control in micro-power relations between people remains so strong that granting wide rights will not ensure their performance. Hence, there is no probability of their realistic exercise.

---

[84] Nicola Lacey, 'Feminism and the Tenets of Conventional Legal Theory' 11 Humboldt ForumRechts (1996), accessed 25 July 2016, http://www.humboldt-forum-recht.de/english/11-1996/index.html.

[85] See Sandra Harding, 'Rethinking standpoint epistemologies: what is "strong objectivity"?' in *Feminist Epistemologies*, ed. Linda Alcoff and E. Potter (New York: Routledge, 1993); M. C. Nussbaum, 'Women's capabilities and social justice,' in *Gender, Justice, Developments and Rights*, ed. E. Molyneux and S. Ravazi (Oxford: OUP, 2002); Carol Gilligan, *In a Different Voice: Psychological Theory and Women's Development* (Cambridge, Mass: Harvard University Press, 1993); Martha Minow, 'Rights For the Next Generation;' and Ann C. Scales, 'The Emergence of Feminist Jurisprudence.'

8

A Technicist Perspective and the Contemporary Perception of the Role of Lawyers in Polish Society

Jacek Srokosz

8.1 Introduction

After the collapse of communist rule in Poland in 1989 a new order was introduced which led to many spheres of social life being touched by the process of marketization.[1] The resulting changes had a great influence on the legal professions, their practices and the perception of the role of lawyers in society. The term 'lawyer' in this chapter is used in a context similar to the meaning of the Polish word *prawnik*, which has a broad meaning covering not only the Polish equivalents of solicitors and barristers, but also judges, public notaries, prosecutors, and sometimes bailiffs. Therefore, the word 'lawyer' is used to refer to any of the legal professions. This chapter aims to show how these changes altered the perception of the role of lawyers in contemporary Poland, and the connections between the current perception and the technicization process. The chapter is divided into two parts. In the first, the technicist approach's meaning and significance in social science and the factors reinforcing this approach will be discussed. The second part is concerned with the technicist approach in law in Poland, including legal education and visions of law which support the technicist approach, as well as its use in legal practice.

8.2 The Technicist Approach in Social Sciences

8.2.1 *The Meaning and Genesis of Technicism*

It is necessary to clarify the meaning of 'technicist' and 'technicism' as

---

[1] The meanings and range of the marketization process are discussed in: Uwe Schimank, Ute Volkmann, Economising and Marketisation in a Functionally Differentiated Capitalist Society—A Theoretical Conceptualisation, in *The Marketisation of Society: Economising the Non-Economic*, ed. Uwe Schimank and Ute Volkmann (Bremen: University of Bremen, 2012), 47–56.

used within this chapter. The notion of technicism should be distinguished from 'technocracy' despite the fact that these terms are very often used interchangeably. 'Technicism' represents a specific way of thinking which is based upon the assumption that every social problem can be easily solved with technology or scientific methods.[2] In short, technicism emphasizes the use of scientific methods. Despite some similarity, the word 'technocratic' has a different meaning which refers to the idea of technocracy, which means that society should be governed by technicians using a method of management based upon the knowledge and application of social science, for instance in factories.[3] This kind of idea was put forward in the first half of the 19th century by, among others, the French utopian socialist Henri Saint-Simon in his concept of industrial society and the rule of professionals.[4] Put simply, 'technocratic' means that the greatest emphasis is put on the person who applies scientific methods to solving problems in the social sphere. For the purposes of this chapter it is more important to show the action than the person who acts, therefore the notion of technicism is adopted.

The concept of technicism emerged in the late 19th and early 20th century and was closely associated with the rapid development of science at that time. Scientific progress as well as a flood of new inventions during this period led people to believe that science could solve every human problem.[5] Of course, that conviction was based upon substantial over-reliance and excessive confidence in the technical advances of science which in some way was justified by the visible outcomes of that progress, which in turn led to the belief that, once broadly understood, science would discover solutions in areas of human life which at the time were out of its reach.[6] Therefore,

---

[2] Egbert Schuurman, 'A Confrontation with Technicism as the Spiritual Climate of the West,' *Westminster Theological Journal* 58 (1996), 70.

[3] Tadeusz Klemantowicz, Krzysztof Pieliński, *Politycy i technokraci. Kierowanie w państwie i w systemie światowym: między teorią a ideologią* [Politicians and Technocrats. Management in the State and World System: Between Theor and Practice] (Białystok: Oficyna Wydawnicza Politechnika Białostocka, 2011), 71–115; See also Krzysztof Pieliński, 'O ewolucji doktryny technokratycznej' [On Evolution of Technocratic Doctrine], *Państwo i Prawo* 8 (1980); Krzysztof Pieliński, 'Koniec historii—utopia technokratyczna' [The End of History—Technocratic Utopia], *Economy and Management* 2 (2011), 19; Jean Meynaud, *Technocracy* (London: Faber & Faber, 1968).

[4] On the concepts of Saint-Simon, see generally Arthur John Booth, *Saint-Simon and Saint-Simonism: A Chapter in the History of Socialism in France* (London: Longmans, Green, Reader, and Dyer, 1871); Frank Manuel, *The New World of Henri Saint-Simon* (Cambridge: Harvard University Press, 1956); Ghita Ionescu, The Political Thought of Saint-Simon (London: OUP, 1976).

[5] Leo Marx, 'The Idea of "Technology" and Postmodern Pessimism,' in *Technology, Pessimism, and Postmodernism*, ed. Yaron Ezrahi et al. (Dordrecht: Springer, 1994), 12.

[6] On the technicistic approach in US, see Irving Louis Horowitz, *Veblen's Century: A Collective Portrait* (New Brunswick, New Jersey, 2002); Howard P. Segal, *Technology and Utopia* (Washington: American Historical Association, 2006); Alex Hall, '"A Way of

proponents of this way of thinking claimed they could apply science to many social processes, such as government, education, healthcare, etc. This kind of idea of managing social life by using methods based on scientific knowledge might be termed 'the technicist perspective.'

The essence of the technicist perspective in relation to social processes is based upon the assumption that most of society's problems and conflicts can be solved by applying the methods of science and technology, and that it is science's job to deliver the required tools or to steer social processes in the right direction.[7] These tools can be discovered and delivered only by conducting thorough research on social processes and drawing conclusions based upon the obtained results. The process of implementing research results into governing processes runs on three successive levels.[8] On the first level the relevant research is conducted, and on the basis of the results the objectively proven regularities within society can be described. This level could be called a descriptive level as its purpose is to collect and analyze the aggregated information in order to formulate general assumptions concerning any given segments of social life. On the next level these assumptions are transformed into teleological directives which indicate what should be done in order to achieve a designated outcome. This level could be called normative because concrete rules of conduct can be formulated on the basis of the gathered information. The last level has a practical character as it concerns enforcing the formulated directives in order to achieve the desired results.[9]

This technicist approach to solving social problems can be regarded as a simple transfer of methods from the realm of science to social science. Advocates of this approach argue that science—understood as the usage of scientific tools in governing society—offers the best chance of achieving social harmony and guaranteeing the welfare and peaceful life of citizens. The significance of this idea is currently growing and is visible in many segments of contemporary social life.[10] This technicist formula clearly

Revealing": Technology and Utopianism in Contemporary Culture,' *Journal of Technology Studies* 31 (2009) 58–66.

[7] Egbert Schurmann, *The Technological World Picture and an Ethics of Responsibility. Struggles of Ethic in Technology* (Sioux Centre: Dordrecht Collage Press, 2005), 19–20.

[8] Jerzy Wróblewski, 'Prawoznawstwo: Perspektywa technicystyczna i humanistyczna (Z problemów III Kongresu Nauki)' [Jurisprudence: Technicistic and Humanistic Perspective (From Problems of III Congress of Science)], *Państwo i Prawo* 4 (1986), 4–5.

[9] Wróblewski, 'Prawoznawstwo,' 4–5.

[10] A great example of that kind procedure in Poland might be indicated by the most popular research grant proceeding where the applicant is required to prepare a project as well as to describe what kind of results can be achieved. The formula of evaluating the entries is quite simple. The applicant has to be able to substantiate that his research brings specific results important for science or society. Then the evaluation of the realization of the research grant is made in respect of his estimation of whether the designated scientific targets were achieved and the scheme of research was fulfilled. Use of these kinds of procedures

derives from typically utilitarian approaches as it attempts to find the easiest and most efficient way to solve social problems.[11] One might say this is the most reasonable, natural, and logical way to solve a problem, therefore it should be implemented without any doubt about its usefulness. This assumption would probably be found to be effective in scientific terms, however it could completely fail in the real world. The technicist approach considers social relations to be very similar to the orderly systems of proper science. This attitude could be a danger to the harmonious running of social life because it underrates the difference between the short-term and long-term effects of social processes and actions. Short-term effects are predictable, thus making a technicist approach very profitable as it is enough to identify the desired outcome and choose and implement the most proper methods. However, long-term effects are not so predictable due to fluctuations in social relations and circumstance. Moreover, the eventual long-term outcome could be affected by many complex factors, so it would be almost impossible to choose the precise actions which would lead to the intended outcomes. Another problem would be the potential conflict between short-term and long-term effects as realization of the first can be harmful to the latter.

8.2.2 *Factors Reinforcing the Technicist Approach*

The application of the technicist approach in the social sciences and processes of governing of society is based upon a few assumptions: *1)* the beneficial effects of technical progress, *2)* the belief that this assumption can be applied in social life, *3)* the objective and ideologically uncommitted character of science, and *4)* the conviction of an existing post-political era in contemporary society. Each of these assertions will be discussed below.

The first assertion assumes that there is steady progress in science and technology which is very profitable for humanity. This development is regarded as being inevitable and beneficial to standards of living, while its negative impact on human life is neglected or underestimated. Proponents

---

are somewhat justified due to the desire not to waste money, especially taxpayers' money, but this could generate problems within the branches of science where the outcomes of experience are hardly predictable. Additionally, this way of financing research favours those branches of science where the results seem to be profitable and do not include a possibility of failure, and at the same time neglects research where the outcomes are uncertain or unpredictable. See further Jan Kozłowski, 'Doskonałość w nauce' [Perfection in Science], *Forum Akademickie* (2012) 7–8; accessed: 30 April 2015: https://forumakademickie.pl/fa/2012/07-08/doskonalosc-w-nauce/ Piotr Szejnach, 'Przyśpieszona nauka konkurencji. Przewodnik dla zabłąkanych w gąszczu reform' [The Rapid Training of Rivalry: Guidance for Lost in the Jungle of Reforms], *Studia Litteraria Historica* 1 (2012), 1–2.

[11] Victor Ferkiss, 'Daniel Bell's Concept of Post-Industrial Society: Theory, Myth, and Ideology,' *Political Science Reviewer* 9 (1979), 94.

of this stance believe that development is beneficial for humanity and that its benefits outweigh its shortcomings. This optimistic view corresponds with the second assumption that technical progress would eventually provide solutions to all the problems that have plagued humanity since the dawn of history.[12] In other words, almost all mankind's problems can be solved simply by the proper usage of scientific tools.[13] This assertion is supported by history and the long list of problems from the past which were finally overcome by the development of science and technology, such as high infant mortality rates or many contagious diseases such as chickenpox, the plague, or measles. From this point of view, the current problems of humanity should be treated as transitional as one day science will find solutions for each of them.

Although no reasonable person can deny that human life has been improved by science and technology, it is not always beneficial and has many limitations and dangers.[14] Therefore, the problems with assuming that social life has an unambiguous nature must be mentioned. Technicists believe that the social dimensions of human life can easily be ordered into discrete transparent schemes according to the outcomes of scientific research. It could be said that this approach, with all its assertions of the possibility of embracing whole segments of social life, should be placed within a philosophy of sociological naturalism.[15]

The consequence of sociological naturalism is that culture and the spiritual dimensions of human life are treated as a product of human

---

[12] For a broad discussion on the human attitude to technology, see Robert C. Scharff and Val Dusek, *Philosophy of Technology: The Technological Condition: An Anthology* (Oxford: Willey Blackwell, 2014).

[13] This assumption was related to a 'technicistic spirit' of progress in the modern age, see Leo Marx, 'The Idea of 'Technology' and Postmodern Pessimism,' in *Does technology drives The History? The dilemma of technological determinism*, ed. Roe Merrit Smith and Leo Marx (Massachusetts: MIT Cambridge Press, 1994), 251.

[14] Although some researchers emphasize the dominance of the pessimistic view of science and technology, which was the basis for the origin of postmodernism, see Leo Marx, 'The Idea of "Technology",' 238–57. Disappointment in technology is also stressed by Ellul, but in his opinion the disillusion of technology was covered by a bluff, see Jacques Ellul, *The Technological Bluff* (Grand Rapids, Mich.: W. B. Eerdmans Publishing, 1990).

[15] See Brian Leiter, *Naturalising Jurisprudence: Essays on American Legal Realism and Naturalism in Legal Philosophy* (Oxford: OUP, 2007). On naturalism and its argument with antinaturlism, see generally Lech Morawski, 'Naturalizm i antynaturalizm—dwie opcje nauk prawnych' [Naturalism and Anti-positivism—Two Options of Legal Science], in *Teoria prawa. Filozofia prawa. Współczesne prawo i prawoznawstwo* [Theory of Law. Philosophy of Law. Contemporary Law and Jurisprudence], ed. Mirosław Kocoł and Wiesław Lang (Toruń: Wydawnictwo Uniwersytetu Mikołaja Kopernika, 1998), 187–88; Jerzy Stelmach, 'Naturalistyczny i antynaturalistyczny model teorii prawa' [Naturalistic and Anti-positivistic Model of Theory of Law], *Studia Prawnicze* (1984) 3–4; Inga Gołowska, 'Naturalizm-antynaturalizm jako spór o charakterze metodologicznym. Wprowadzenie historyczne' [Naturalism—Anti-positivism as a Dispute on Methodological Character. Historical Introduction], *Ruch Prawniczy, Socjologiczny i Ekonomiczny* LXV/1 (2003), 5–12.

mutual relations and are therefore just another part of mankind's natural environment. In this case it is enough to discover the objective rules which drive human behaviour and, more broadly, social life in order to find the objective general order in each human community. Humanity's problems can then be solved through the application of this knowledge. Of course, the problem is that social relations are not similar to the objective rules of physics or chemistry. Firstly, the decision to use a concrete tool to achieve some goal cannot be treated like a simple scientific test in the laboratory as there are too many factors which can impact the final outcome. For this reason, it is very difficult to clearly and unambiguously predict all of the effects of any one tool. The technicist approach disregards these problems and at the same time overrates the ability of science to solve all social problems, as scientific methods are considered to be the key to understanding and managing all of society's problems.

The next assumption concerns the character of science and technology. Technicists assert that both science and technology are objective and therefore completely removed from ideological or political discourse.[16] The objectivity of science and scientific method makes it absolutely ideologically neutral and completely politically uncommitted.[17] Of course, social life is a common arena for ideological and political fights, and social tensions can lead to more severe social problems, but technicists believe they can all be solved through the application of scientific methods. Every conflict, irrespective of its origin and intensity, can easily be solved with the use of appropriate tools by the authorities, who can be considered to be social technicians. The position of social technicians allows them to remain separate from the solution process as they are expected to act like scientists who have just delivered the best solution for a given situation based upon hard science, without moral or political doubts.[18]

The term 'post-political' means that mutual relations in society are no longer based on nor driven by ideological, moral, racial, or religious differences as they were in the past.[19] All these differences have lost significance

---

[16] Yaron Ezrahi, 'Technology and the Illusion of the Escape from Politics,' in *Technology, Pessimism, and Postmodernism*, 29–37; Leo Marx, 'The Idea of "Technology",' 246–7.

[17] Jaques Ellul, *The Technological System* (New York: Continuum, 1980), 362. That assumption was also widely criticized by Heidegger, see Martin Heidegger, *The Question Concerning Technology and Other Essays* (New York: Harper and Row, 1977), 182.

[18] Daniel Bell, *The Coming of Post-industrial Society: A Venture In Social Forecasting* (New York: Basic Books, 1973) 343–5.

[19] Of course there are other definitions of that term, see Paweł Kusiak, 'Postpolityka. W poszukiwaniu istoty zjawiska' [Postpolitic. Searching for the Essence of the Phenomenon], *Colloquium Wydziału Nauk Humanistycznych i Społecznych* 3 (2011) 157–180. The term 'post-politic' is often used to mean the tendency to confine public life to the consensus orientated and technocratic rather than traditional understanding of policy. Beniamin Knutsson, 'Swedish environmental and sustainability education research in the era of post-politics?'

in contemporary society and so have ceased to cause social problems. Historically, social conflicts were based on one or more of the aforementioned differences, and the governing process boiled down to an attempt to implement visions created by religion or the ideology of political groups. Nowadays, we have reached such a level of social development that the political, religious, racial, or historical roots of these conflicts have disappeared due to the high quality of social life and the fact that many values are accepted by everyone without exception.[20] In modern societies there is and never will be conflict or tension based upon these differences from the past, leading to the need for new modes of government. Foremost, the process of governing society should be treated like rational management, rather than the traditionally understood and politically involved governing of the past.[21] The latter was always based upon rivalry between religious, moral, or ideological groups which focused on fighting and forcing others to accept their point of view, very often leading to irrational and apparently random outcomes. The new method of managing is based on rational action derived from scientific research of human behaviour, thus having an objective character which allows the fulfilment of all human needs without resorting to violence and force. In this kind of society there are no groups of winners and defeated opponents, but instead a fully functioning harmonious community preferring rational discourse over ideological rivalry.[22]

The assumption outlined above is supported and reinforced by consumerism, which prevails in many societies, especially in Europe and the US. The term 'consumerism' in this chapter refers to the kind of social order and ideology that encourages the acquisition of goods and services, and treats

---

Utbildning & Demokrati 2 (2013), 107. See also Chantal Mouffe, *On the Political* (London: Routledge, 2005); Jacques Rancière, *Disagreement: Politics and Philosophy* (Minneapolis: University of Minnesota Press, 1999); Slavoj Žižek, *The Ticklish Subject: The Absent Centre of Political Ontology* (London: Verso, 1999).

[20] This is of course democracy, liberalism, and free market; see Francis Fukuyama, *The End of History* (New York, 1989), 3 and n. For critical approaches to this stance, see Samuel Huntington, 'No Exit. The Errors of Endism,' *The National Interest* (1989), 3; Stephen Holmes, 'The Scowl of Minerva,' *New Republic*, March 23 (1992), 27; Jonathan R. Macey and Geoffrey P. Miller, 'The End of History and the New World Order: The Triumph of Capitalism and the Competition between Liberalism and Democracy,' *Cornell International Law Journal* 25 (1992), 277; David Held, 'Liberalism, Marxism and democracy,' *Theory and Society* 22 (1993), 249; David Held, 'Anything but dog's life? Further comments on Fukuyama, Callinicos and Giddens' *Theory and Society* 22 (1993), 293.

[21] Zdzisław Dobrowolski, 'Koncepcja społeczeństwa informacyjnego Daniela Bella' [Daniel Bell's Concept of Information Society], in Od informacji naukowej do technologii społeczeństwa wiedzy [From Scientific Information to Technology of Society of Knowledge], ed. Barbara Sosińska-Kalata, Maria. Przastek-Samokowa, and Andrzej Skrzypczak (Warszawa: Wydawnictwo SPB, 2005), 102; Kevin Robins and Frank Webster, 'Information as capital: A critique of Daniel Bell,' in *The Ideology of the Information Age*, ed. Jennifer Daryl Slack and Fred Fejes (Norwood, NJ: Ablex, 1987), 95–117.

[22] Knutsson, 'Swedish environmental,' 107–9.

the consumption of them as the meaning of life.²³ Generally, many scholars and philosophers researching consumerism associate it with capitalism and a free market economy, but it should not always be associated as such. Doubtlessly, in some ways the principles of liberalism and the free market economy favour consumerist attitudes, but this phenomenon should be treated in a broader sense. The essence of consumerism is human activity, which leads people to fulfil their selfish needs and obtain ever greater amounts of goods.²⁴ Obviously, mere fulfilment of needs is a natural part of human life, but this can become harmful when most human activity is limited only to the consumption of goods and services.²⁵ Of course, the consumerist attitude is not new and has been described and analyzed previously, but all researchers have emphasized its increasing importance in contemporary social life. The consumerist point of view now covers new areas of social life which were previously driven by other values, such as education, culture, or health protection.²⁶

8.2.3 The Technicization of University Studies in Poland

Now it is appropriate to consider the significance of the relationship between the roles of lawyers in society and the technicist method, especially on the basis of the analysis of the situation in Poland after 1989. This date marks the end of the communist regime in Poland and denotes a great breakthrough in the perception of the role of lawyers in society. Firstly, the education of lawyers should be discussed as it is a good example of the processes of consumerism within higher education, which quite naturally results in the application of a technicist approach.

After the transformation of 1989 most Polish people were astonished by the pace of change and the move from an inefficient social economy towards a free market economy.²⁷ This process was closely connected with changes in attitudes towards consumption and the job market. After over

---

[23] Jean Baudrillard, *The Consumer Society: Myths and Structures* (London: Sage, 1998); Zygmunt Bauman, *Work, Consumerism and the New Poor* (Cambridge, Polity Press, 1998); George Kantona, *The Mass Consumption Society* (New York: Mc Graw Book Comp., 1964).
[24] Czesław Bywalec, *Konsumpcja a rozwój społeczny i ekonomiczny* [Consumption and Social and Economical Development] (Warszawa: C.H. Beck, 2010), 8.
[25] Maria Miczyńska-Kowalska, 'Społeczeństwo konsumenckie jako rys kultury ponowoczesnej w ujęciu Zygmunta Baumana' [Society of Consumers as a Sketch of Postmodern Culture in Zygmunt Bauman's Thought], in *Kultura a rynek* [Culture and Market], ed. Sławomir Partycki (Lublin: Wydawnictwo KUL, 2008), 65.
[26] Regarding consumer society, see Alan Aldridge, *Konsumpcja* [Consumption] (Warszawa: Wydawnictwo Sic!, 2006), 69 and n.; Zygmunt Bauman, *Konsumowanie życia* [The Consumption of Life] (Kraków: Wydawnictwo Uniwersytetu Jagiellońskiego, 2009), 14 and n.
[27] Bywalec, *Konsumpcja*, 239 and n.

forty years of limited access to basic goods in communist times, Poles were finally able to meet their needs, and they rapidly became interested in a consumer lifestyle. Of course, consumption requires income, which is dependent on the job market. In the 1990s and the first decade of the twenty-first century, Poles were stunned by the free market economy and unquestioningly accepted its demands along with its pros and cons. For this reason many areas of social life, which had traditionally been driven by completely different values, were suddenly embraced by the need for efficiency, cost minimization and profit maximization.

One of these fields was higher education. For the purposes of this chapter it is only necessary to depict the situation concerning legal education, but of course similar processes took place in all areas of study.[28] Generally, for many years higher education in Poland was considered to be more than just professional training, it also contributed to the development of students' character, the acquisition of social competence, and the ability to think creatively. Put simply, it was a time for shaping character and personality.[29] This type of education should be called humanistic because it emphasizes and values the shaping and development of personality and character as well as the building of knowledge from many domains of social life.[30] A well-educated person should first and foremost be in some way a Renaissance man or woman who has interests which are not solely concentrated on one single field, and who is conscious of the complexity of social life. Moreover, the social position which a well-educated person occupies demands that he or she actively engages in social life and accepts this responsibility as being inextricably linked with the ethos of the intellectual class.[31] Education and the role of the intellectual class (which of course

---

[28] John L. Davis, 'A Revolution in Teaching and Learning in Higher Education: The Challenges and Implications for the Relatively Traditional University,' *Higher Education in Europe* 4 (2001), 501–14. On the new social role of the university, see Marek Kwiek, 'The University and the State in Golden Age: renegotiating the traditional social contract,' *European Education Research Journal* 4 (2005) 324–41; Marek Kwiek, *The University and the State. A Study into Global Transformations* (Frankfurt am Main: Peter Lang Pub Inc, 2006); Anthony Smith and Frank Webster, *The postmodern university? Contested visions of higher education in society*, Buckingham: Society for Research into Higher Education (Bristol: Open University Press, 1997).

[29] Wiel Veugelers, 'A humanist perspective on moral development and citisenship education,' in *Education and humanism. Linking autonomy and humanity*, ed. Wiel Veugeler (Rotterdam: Sense Publishers, 2011), 9 and n.

[30] Jacek Srokosz, 'Między humanizmem a technicyzmem. Spór o model nauczania prawa w polskim dyskursie prawniczym' [Between Humanism and Technicism. The dispute on the Legal Teaching Model in Polish Legal Discoursee], in *Integracja zewnętrzna i wewnętrzna nauk prawnych* [Inner and Outer Integration of Legal Science], ed. Adam Bartczak, Monika Król, and Monika Zalewska (Łódź: Wydawnictwo Uniwersytetu Łódzkiego 2014), 47–61. See also Anna Turska, ed., *Humanizacja zawodów prawniczych a nauczanie akademickie* [Humanization of Legal Professions and University Teaching] (Warszawa: Liber, 2002).

[31] Borys Łapicki, 'O humanistycznym wychowaniu prawnika' [On the Humanistic

also includes all legal professions) will not always be in harmony with the demands of the free market economy and job market. The marketization process of many spheres of social life in Poland had to clash with this traditional vision of university teaching and the social roles of graduates. In the following section, attention will be focused on legal education and the role of lawyers in society.

8.3 Technicism in Law

8.3.1 *Technicist Law Teaching*

The contemporary discussion on Polish legal education is influenced by the free market economy, which rapidly changed the character of legal teaching. The first and probably most important claim of reform advocates was the need for a direct correlation between university teaching and the needs of the job market.[32] The role of universities should not be to provide theoretical legal education, but to prepare graduates to easily enter the job market.[33] The fulfilment of this goal required the restructuring of legal education to make it more practically oriented as the main goal of law faculties was no longer the shaping of the character, mind, and moral backbone of future lawyers, but instead the provision of practical knowledge and skills which would be necessary in legal practice.[34] To facilitate their employment law graduates should be equipped with up-to-date legal knowledge as well as the practical argumentation skills which are appropriate to the job market.[35] A great example of this approach can be seen in the US, which is considered by many to currently have the best legal education in the world.[36]

Upbringing of a Lawyer], *Państwo i Prawo* 5–6 (1948), 95.

[32] Krzysztof Bondera, Marcin Kołodziejczyk, 'System edukacyjny w Polsce wobec potrzeb rynku pracy' [The Educational System in Poland and Work Market Needs], *Ruch Prawniczy, Socjologiczny i Ekonomiczny* 3 (2009), 163–74; Andrzej Jajszczyk, 'Polskie uczelnie—czas na jakość' [Polish Universities—The Time for Quality], in *Misja i służebność uniwersytetu w XXI wieku* [The Mission and Duties of University in 21th Century], ed. Jerzy Woźnicki (Warszawa: Oficyna Wydawnicza Politechniki Warszawskiej, 2013), 219–22.

[33] Anna Marszałek, 'Znaczenie uniwersytetów w gospodarce opartej na wiedzy' [Significance of Universities in Economy Based on Knowledge], *Przegląd Organizacji* 7–8 (2007) 3–6.

[34] Fryderyk Zoll, *Jaka szkoła prawa? Czy amerykańskie metody nauczania prawa mogą być przydatne w Polsce?* [What Kind of School of Law? Can American Methods of Law Teaching be Useful in Poland?] (Warszawa: Dom Wydawniczy ABC, 2004), 102 and n.

[35] Adam Makosz, 'Skostniałe uczelnie nie zreformują programów' [Rigid Universities will not Reform Curricula], *Dziennik Gazeta Prawna* 12 (2012), 4–5.

[36] Arkadiusz Radwan, 'Uniwersytecka edukacja prawnicza w dobie globalizacji' [Universities' Teaching in the Age of Globalisation], *Państwo i Prawo* 11 (2004) 90–102.

This tendency to demand practical knowledge and skills from law faculties is also reinforced by the fact that the relationship between the universities and their students is increasingly akin to that between a service provider and client.[37] This trend is confirmed by the 2012 teaching reform implemented by the minister of Science and Higher Education,[38] which requires completely new syllabuses from all universities.[39] According to these syllabuses lecturers should precisely determine not only the exam requirements but also, more importantly, the knowledge, skills, and social competence that should be obtained by the student during the course. The intention of this reform was to guarantee that students receive a certain quality of education. Most universities criticized the essence of this reform, accusing it of reducing the teaching process to a merely technical matter. Furthermore, this reform implies the very optimistic but unjustified assertion that it is enough to precisely specify what students should know and what kind of skills and social competences they should acquire in order to guarantee that upon completion of their education they will achieve the required level of competence.

Relationships solely based upon commercial principles are especially visible with part-time studies which must be paid for, leading students to expect to obtain practical knowledge and skills which will guarantee their earnings and prosperity on the free market directly after finishing their studies. Not many of these students are interested in deepening their knowledge about the social, philosophical, or moral problems of law and its application, which of course might be very beneficial for them in the long term even though nobody can guarantee this. Most students prefer short-term results which can be confidently predicted on the basis of economic

---

[37] Seweryn Cichoń, 'Szkoła wyższa na rynku usług edukacyjnych' [Universities on Market of Educational Services], *Edukacja Ekonomistów i Menedżerów* 3 (2012), 11–27; Ryszard Skarzyński, 'Ewolucja znaczenia historii doktryn politycznych i prawnych w warunkach przekształcenia uniwersytetu w zakład usługowy' [The Evolution of Meaning of the Political and Legal Thought in Circumstances of Transformation of Universities into Service Providers], in *Tendencje rozwojowe w polskiej myśli politycznej i prawnej* [Tendencies in Polish Political and Legal Thought], ed. Marek Maciejewski, Maciej Marszał, and Mirosław Sadowski (Wrocław: e-Wydawnictwo, 2014), 135–50.

[38] *Rozporządzenie Ministra Nauki i Szkolnictwa Wyższego z dnia 2 listopada 2011 r. w sprawie Krajowych Ram Kwalifikacji dla Szkolnictwa Wyższego* (Dz.U. 2011 nr 253 poz. 1520) [Regulation of the Minister of Science and Higher Education of 2 November 2011 establishing a Framework for Higher Education Qualifications (Journal of Laws [Dz. U.] no. 253/2010, Item 1520)].

[39] The description of methods of preparing those syllabuses are included in Andrzej Kraśnikowski, *Jak przygotowywać programy kształcenia zgodnie z wymaganiami Krajowych Ram Kwalifikacji dla Szkolnictwa Wyższego?* [How to Prepare a Curriculum According to the Requirements of the Framework for Higher Education Qualifications] (Warszawa: Ministerstwo Nauki i Szkolnictwa Wyższego, 2011), accessed 30 April 2010, http://www.nauka.gov.pl/g2/oryginal/2013_05/66ac97d0be9ed5cec5e62b50fbd41d21.pdf.

calculations, thus leading to a typical technicist attitude to education.[40] Of course, this attitude is not only limited to part-time students, but it is more visible amongst them.[41] Legal education is closely connected with common perceptions of the role of law and lawyers in society.

8.3.2 *Legal Policy and the Technicist Approach*

In the context of this chapter, law is the most important area of social life influenced by technicism, which regards it as another sphere of social life in which scientific tools can be easily applied. Furthermore, law could be considered to be one of the best technicist tools as it is created by the state in order to achieve certain outcomes, therefore having some role and function in social life. The sociological vision of law appeared and progressed in parallel to the great scientific developments at the turn of the twentieth century, especially in France.[42] This vision could be found in many types of legal precept, all of which can be included in the broadly defined realistic concepts of law because the basis for distinguishing them is the treatment of law as a social fact or a part of social life created for assuring social order. One of the consequences of treating law as a social factor necessary for maintaining social harmony was the appearance of the concept of legal policy, which was based on the assumption that legal norms were excellent tools for applying proper and well-intended social policy.[43]

It can be claimed that there is no visible difference between social policy and the technicist approach as both have very similar schemes and use devices to achieve their intended goals. However, the technicist approach is

---

[40] The model of legal education in Poland in reference to the policy of the state was depicted in *Polityka prawa a model edukacji prawniczej* [Legal Policy and Law Teaching Model], ed. Tadeusz Biernat (Kraków: Oficyna Wydawnicza AF, 2007).

[41] The occurrence of disregarding long-term results, regarded by them as precarious, and the favouring of short-term certain outcomes also appears in many others fields in social life in Poland, for instance most companies do not have research departments because to do so seems too expensive in the short term and the possible benefits seem too distant and uncertain to justify incurring such expenditure. Marcin Ratajczyk and Magdalena Mądra, 'Źródła i bariery finasowania innowacji w sektorze MŚP' [The Sources and Barriers of Financing of Investments in the Sector of Small and Medium-sized Enterprises], *Zeszyty Naukowe SGGW w Warszawie. Ekonomika i Organizacja Gospodarki Żywnościowej* 69 (2008), 43–53.

[42] Mostly it was associated with A. Comte and L. Durkheim, see Mathew Deflem, *Sociology of Law: Vision of a Scholar Tradition* (Cambridge: CUP, 2008), 56–75. See also Jerzy Szacki, *Durkheim* (Warszawa: Wiedza Powszechna, 1964).

[43] Broadly on the issue of legal policy see: Tadeusz Biernat and Marek Zirk-Sadowski, ed., *Politics of Law and Legal Policy. Between Modern and Post-modern Jurisprudence* (Warszawa: Wolters Kluwer, 2008).

shallower as its basis is the use of the simplest and most unequivocal tools, combined with the belief that it is possible to solve even very complicated problems in this way. As was mentioned previously, it is a method very similar to a laboratory test in which a certain action leads to a clear outcome, and the likelihood of side effects or, more importantly, external factors which could impact the outcome are underrated. In contrast, legal policy involves much more complex and profound consideration of a given situation, and usually takes into account many different factors which impact this situation. For these reasons it is hard to recommend a technicist approach to legal policy because a true policy of law should include many factors beyond the scientific perspective of social life, especially factors deriving from culture (for instance, cultural differences inside communities), moral systems, customs, etc. As previously stated, the technicist approach ordinarily disregards these elements of social life, preferring instead simple solutions similar to the results of mathematic equations.

8.3.3 Legal Positivism and the Technicist Approach

Despite the aforementioned issues, the law is being increasingly treated in a technicist manner, and this tendency could be reinforced by other factors and concepts of law. Primarily, the technicist approach is reinforced by legal positivism and its treatment of the law as the clearly written and validated orders of the authorities.[44] From this point of view, the priority is to follow the legal norms included in codes or acts, and the only role of the lawyer is to check if a rule should be enforced according to whether or not a given situation can be subsumed to a concrete norm. The goal of the person applying the law is to act according to the law in force. Firstly, the meaning of a rule should be determined on the basis of canons of statutory interpretation. Secondly, the rule should be appropriate for the situation. Thirdly, rules should be applied if they turn out to be adequate to the situation.[45] This can be called a technicist approach because it avoids every social, moral, and religious requirement of rational behaviour and simply applies the law according to the situation. Of course, this is typical 'hard

---

[44] Broadly on legal positivism, see Jules L. Coleman and Brian Leiter, 'Legal Positivism,' in *A Companion to Philosophy of Law and Legal Theory*, ed. D. Petterson (Chichester West Sussex: Blackwell Publishing Ltd., 2010), 228–49; Jules L. Coleman, 'Negative and Positive Positivism,' *Journal of Legal Studies* 11 (1982), 139–64; Jules L. Coleman, 'Reason and Authority,' in *The Autonomy of Law: Essays on Legal Positivism*, ed. R. George (Oxford: OUP, 1995).

[45] On this matter the technicistic approach is very similar to formalism, see Marcin Matczak, *Summa iniuria: o błędzie formalizmu w stosowaniu prawa* [Summa Iniuria: On the Mistake of Formalism in Applying Law] (Warszawa: Scholar, 2007).

positivism' which would not be applied so rigidly in normal circumstances, nevertheless it is very often used by the state and judges due to their desire for safety and effortless law enforcement with a sure and easily justified outcome.[46]

In Polish legal proceedings it is easy to see that lawyers are reluctant to reinterpret laws because they are constrained by the literal meaning of legal norms. This attitude is justified to some extent by the communists' historical instrumental usage of the law as a means to hold onto their power.[47] During the period of the Polish People's Republic many judges and prosecutors used the law as a tool to support the authorities and fight real or potential enemies of the legal system with a total disregard for the principles of justice and the rule of law. Under these conditions the law did not have a certain and clear meaning but was instead interpreted according to concrete situations in a way that almost always favoured the authorities.[48] The Communist Party, in accordance with the Marxist concept of the law, used it as an instrument for supporting the power of the dominant working class and oppressing the subordinated classes. The communists treated the law as part of their political reality, which of course meant that everybody who applied the law was supposed to do that from the point of view of the socialistic ideology. Therefore, applying the law simultaneously applied the policies of the Communist Party, so it is not surprising that the law was regarded as uncertain and that its meaning depended more on circumstance and the socialistic 'spirit' than the 'letter' of the law.[49]

After 1989 lawyers in Poland saw the strict and clear understanding of the law as a remedy for the lawlessness of communist legal practice.[50]

---

[46] On the basis of conducted research under ruling set by judges of Main Administrative Court of Poland from 2004 to 2007, M. Matczak, claimed that in most case sentence was very strictly connected with the literally meaning of act, and that was base for assumption of high level of formalism in polish courts. Matczak, *Summa iniuria*, 202. See more: Krzysztof Pałecki, 'Społecznie oczekiwany wzorzec orzekania sądowego' [Socially Expected Model of Judiciary], in *Sądy w opinii społeczeństwa polskiego* [Courts in Opinion of Polish Society], ed. Maria Borucka-Arctowa and Krzysztof Pałecki (Kraków: Polpress, 2003), 151.

[47] Broadly about Polish 'hyperpositivism' see Rafał Mańko, 'Weeds in the Gardens of Justice? The Survival of Hyperpositivism in Polish Legal Culture as a Symptom/Sinthome,' *Pólemos—Journal of Law, Literature and Culture* (2013), 214–26, see also Rafał Mańko, Survival of the Socialist Legal Tradition? A Polish Perspective, *Comparative Law Review* 4/2 (2013).

[48] Tomasz Stawecki, 'Niezależność zawodów prawniczych i rządy prawa w społeczeństwie postkomunistycznym' [Indepencence of Legal Professions and the Rules of Law in Postcommunist Society], in *Niezależność sądownictwa i zawodów prawniczych jako fundamenty państwa prawa. Wyzwania współczesności* [Independence of the Judiciary and Legal Professions as Foundations of the Rule of Law. Contemporary Challenges], ed. Tomasz Wardyński, and Magdalena Niziołek (Warszawa: Lexis Nexis, 2009), 53.

[49] Stawecki, 'Niezależność,' 54.

[50] The problem of the rule of law in post-communist societies was discussed in *Rethink-*

This attitude led to the positivist vision of law which required the judiciary to strictly enforce legal rules.[51] Of course the positivist vision of the law not only favours safety and certainty, but also undermines the significance of adjusting the law to social processes and the changeable perception of justice and equity.[52] This positivist approach led to the tendency for the application of the law to become more technicist as it consisted mostly of enforcing the law according to its literal meaning. This technicist method came to be of value in itself as it seemed to be a guarantee of legal certainty and the only way to protect the community against the political application of the law, as the communists had previously. The legal professions in Poland could be accused of being reluctant to be politically involved as they are afraid of being accused of applying the law as the communists did. Furthermore, they see themselves as the primary stronghold protecting society from the political application of the law.[53]

It is not only the positivistic approach that is very susceptible to the technicist method.[54] Technicism can also embrace other approaches to law, including the realistic approach, which treats law as the result of the activity of judges and administrative organizations. In this context, the application of law consists of choosing types of arguments or techniques of behaviour in the courtroom which would persuade the judge and deliver the desired outcome. Therefore, the technicist method, like the positivistic approach, separates the application of law not only from morality, but

---

ing the Rule of Law after Communism, ed. Adam Czarnota, Marcin Krygier, and Wojciech Sadurski (Budapest and New York: Central European University Press, 2005); Csongor Kuti, Post-communist Restitution and Rule of Law (Budapest and New York: Central European University Press, 2009).

[51] Ewa Łojko, Role i zadania prawników w zmieniającym się społeczeństwie [The Role and the Tasks of Lawyers in a Changing Society] (Warszawa: Wydawnictwo Uniwersytetu Warszawskiego, 2005), 200–1.

[52] Artur Kozak, Granice prawniczej władzy dyskrecjonalnej [The Limits of Lawyers' Discretional Power] (Wrocław: Kolonia Limited, 2002), 79 and n.

[53] The problem of isolating courts and judges from society, and this treatment of every criticism as an assault on judicial independence, caused a 'besieged stronghold effect' amongst the judiciary, see Jacek Ignaczewski, Wymiar sprawiedliwości—teraźniejszość i przyszłość [Judiciary—Present and Future] (Warszawa: C.H. Beck, 2008), 57 and n. On the will of the Polish legal community to isolate adjudication from politics, based on Pierre Bourdieu's methodology, see Dębska and Warczok, 'The Social Construction of Feminity,' ch. 6 of the present volume, and Hanna Dębska, 'Iluzje prawniczego rozumu. O społecznych warunkach praktyck (bez)refleksyjnych' [Illusions of the legal mind. On the social conditions of (non) reflexive practices], Studia Prawno-Ekonomiczne 92 (2014) 11–25.

[54] For a demonstration of this connection between legal positivism and the technicist approach, see Margaret Thornton, 'The Law School, the Market and the New Knowledge Economy,' Legal Education Review 17 (2008), 10 and Tamara Walsh, 'Putting Justice Back into Legal Education,' Legal Education Review 17 (2008) 126. That stance was criticized by John R. Morss, 'Part of the Problem or Part of the Solution? Legal Positivism and Legal Education,' Legal Education Review 18 (2008), 55.

also from a social sense of justice or social circumstances,[55] by simply finding and applying all measures or arguments necessary to achieve the desired outcome. This leads to an approach which favours effectiveness and considers the law to be a set of tools or techniques of argumentation which would allow the mechanical achievement of the goal, without profound reflection on the implications of actions.

8.3.4 The Technicist Approach in Polish Legal Practice

Of course, using the law as an instrument to achieve some objectives, sometimes very cynically, meets the requirements of a limitless free market in which a lawyer should be primarily an expert who best represents the interests of clients. In other words, a lawyer should primarily be successful at winning clients' cases, thereby gaining a reputation as a 'good lawyer' who is effective and represents the client well.[56] From this point of view there is no difference between a lawyer and any other service provider acting in the free market. This perspective generally concerns only some of the legal professions, which in Poland includes advocates (*adwokat*), legal counsellors (*radca prawny*) and in some matters, public notaries. The first two of these professions have a rather free market character, while the last has a mixed character which combines both free market and public elements. Of course other legal professions such as judges, prosecutors, and in some way bailiffs have only a public character, but their situation is different and will be discussed later.

As was previously stated, the market-oriented legal professions are often expected to be driven mostly by the principles of the free market economy and the requirements of efficiency.[57] Nevertheless, the legal professions cannot be treated like typical free market professions such as hairdressers, grocers, or plumbers because of their special status in society. Moreover,

---

[55] From that point of view, Langdel's method of law teaching—most popular in US law schools—was criticized for leading students to moral relativism see Ruta K. Stropus, 'Mend It, Bend It, and Extend It The Fate of Traditional Law School Methodology in the 21st Century,' *Loyola University Chicago Law Journal* 27 (1996), 458; William J. Heffernan, 'Not Socrates but Protagoras: The Sophistic Basis of Legal Education,' *Buffalo Law Review* 29 (1980), 339–402; Andrew Moore, 'Conversion and the Socratic Method in Legal Education: Some Advice for Prospective Law Students,' *University of Detroit Mercy Law Review* 80 (2003), 505–7.

[56] On the term 'good lawyer,' see generally 'What does it mean be a good lawyer? Zealous Advocacy and Problem-Solving Courts, An edited transcript of a discussion among a judge, attorneys, a court administrator, and academics. Edited by John Feinblatt and Derek Denckla,' *Judicature* 4 (2001) 206–14.

[57] For a discussion on the future and the tendency of changes in the legal services market, see Richard Susskind, *Tomorrow's Lawyers: Introduction to your future* (Oxford: OUP, 2013) and Richard Susskind, *The End of Lawyers? Rethinking the nature of legal service* (Oxford: OUP, 2008).

to practice law it is necessary to meet many stringent requirements which limit accessibility.[58] Members of the legal industry have some privileges compared to other free market professions, but their standing is strictly related to some social duties which are not imposed on other professions. This is primarily a result of tradition as the legal professions were not historically treated as simple service providers, but more as a complex service for the public good, justice, and the rule of law; and secondly a result of the significance to the community of the practicing of the legal profession.[59] The duties imposed upon all legal professions by legislators have a strong significance in social life. For instance, Art. 1 Advocates' Profession Act 1982 lists advocates' duties and tasks as follows: providing legal assistance, cooperation in the protection of rights and freedoms of citizens and taking part in the processes of formulating and applying the law. As can be seen, this range of responsibilities far exceeds typical service provision that occurs within a free market economy.[60]

In terms of public legal professions, the technicist approach has a different effect. One of the biggest problems of the Polish justice system is the excessive length of judicial proceedings, which causes many complaints about the protraction of judicial proceedings to be put forward by Polish citizens against Poland before the European Court of Human Rights in Strasbourg.[61] The reason for this protraction is systemic, for example the lack of adjustment of the Polish judiciary to the number of cases, a lack of judges, and the excessive formalism of proceedings,[62] all of which make the court system ineffective and chronic.[63] To overcome these problems some

---

[58] Grażyna Skąpska, 'Zawód prawnika czy rola społeczna' [The Profession or the Social Role of Lawyer], in *Społeczne role prawników (sędziów, prokuratorów, adwokatów)* [The Social Roles of Lawyers (Judges, Prosecutors Attorneys)], ed. Grażyna Skąpska, Janina Czapska, and Maria Kozłowska (Wrocław: Ossolineum, 1989), 6 and n. See also Zygmunt Ziembiński, *Socjologia prawa jako nauka prawna* [Sociology of Law as Legal Science] (Warszawa: Państwowe Wydawnictwo Naukowe, 1975).

[59] Łojko, *Rola i zadania*, 114–57, 179–222.

[60] *Ustawa z dnia 26 maja 1982 r. Prawo o adwokaturze (Dz. U. 1982 nr 16 poz. 124.)* [Advocates' Profession Act 1982 (Journal of Laws [Dz. U.] no. 16/1982, Item 124)].

[61] Marcin Górski, 'Najnowsze wyroki ETPCz stwierdzające naruszenie Konwencji przez Polskę,' *Europejski Przegląd Sądowy* 5 (2012), 31–40. The implementation of sentences of the European Court of Human Rights in Strasbourg by Poland was discussed in Ireneusz C. Kamiński, Robert Kownacki, and Karolina Wierczyńska, 'Wykonanie orzeczeń Europejskiego Trybunału Praw Człowieka w polskim systemie prawnym' [Implementations the Rulings of the European Court of Human Rights in Polish Legal System], in *Zapewnienie efektywności orzeczeń sądów międzynarodowych w polskim porządku prawnym* [The Assertion of Effectiveness of the Rulings of International Courts in Polish Legal System], ed. Andrzej Wróbel (Warszawa: Wolters Kluwer, 2011), 89–227.

[62] See Mańko, 'Weeds in The Garden of Justice,' 225.

[63] The problems of the Polish Judiciary was described in *Niedostatki wymiaru sprawiedliwości* [Shortcomings of Judiciary], ed. Marek Zubik (Warszawa: Instytut Spraw Publicznych, 2001).

improvements to the system have been implemented, but the essence of most of these reforms was of a technicist nature in order to make judicial proceedings more efficient and faster.

A good example of these reforms was the introduction of electronic monition proceedings in civil cases,[64] meaning only advocates or legal counsellors could file a lawsuit which includes only a list of pieces of evidence needed to prove claims, and the assertion that the plaintiff has them.[65] These court proceedings are very fast and formal as the judge, without hearing the defendant, issues an order for payment if all of the formal requirements are met. The defendant has one week to submit an objection before the order for payment becomes enforceable.[66] Therefore, the judge's decision is made without either hearing the defendants or thoroughly considering the case, which of course is enough in simple cases, although it creates great opportunities for abuse.[67]

[64] Electornic monition proceeding which was implemented into Polish law in 2009 and is regulated in articles 50528 to 50538of Polish Code of Civil Procedure. Also in Polish legal system there are injunction proceeding and monition proceeding. See: Rafal Mańko, *Order for payment in the EU*, accessed 20 April 2016, http://www.europarl.europa.eu/eplibrary/Orders-for-payment-in-the-EU.pdf.

[65] Jarosław Ciesielski, 'Czynności adwokata w elektronicznym postępowaniu upominawczym' [Attorney's Actions in a Writ Proceeding], *Palestra* 3–4 (2013), 311–12. See also Michał Sadowski, 'Co oznacza zakaz dołączania dowodów oraz obowiązek ich wskazania w treści pozwu wniesionego w elektronicznym postępowaniu upominawczym' (art. 50532 § 1 k.p.c.)' [The Meaning of the Prohibition on Attachment of Proofs and the Obligation to Indicate them in Suit during Writ Proceedings (Art. 50532 § 1 of the Code of Civil Procedure], *Polski Proces Cywilny* 2/2 (2011) 122–28.

[66] The implemented solution was controversial and caused great debate within the legal environment in Poland. See the literature devoted to this proceeding: Anna Kościółek, *Elektroniczne czynności procesowe w sądowym postępowaniu cywilnym* [Electronic Procedural Acts in Judicial Civil Proceedings] (Warszawa: Wolters Kluwer, 2012); Sławomir Cieślak, '*Elektroniczne postępowanie upominawcze*' [Writ Proceeding], *Monitor Prawniczy* 7 (2010) 359–69; Katarzyna Franczak, '*Elektroniczne postępowanie upominawcze. Zalety i wady dla stron postępowania*' [Writ Proceeding. Advantages and Disadvantages for Parties], *Przegląd Prawa Handlowego* 7 (2011) 48–55; Jacek Gołaczyński, ed., *Informatyzacja postępowania sądowego i administracji publicznej* [Informatization of Court Proceeding and Public Administration] (Warszawa: C.H. Beck, 2010); Jacek Gołaczyński, ed., *Elektroniczne postępowanie upominawcze. Komentarz* [Writ Proceeding. Commentary] (Warszawa: Wolters Kluwer, 2010); Bogdan Pękalski, *Elektroniczne postępowanie upominawcze. Ogólna charakterystyka* [Electronic Monition Proceedings. General Characteristic] (Warszawa: Ministerstwo Sprawiedliwości, 2008); Patrycja Potejko, '*Elektroniczne postępowanie upominawcze—fikcja wymiaru sprawiedliwości*' [Electronic Writ Proceedings—The Fiction of Justice], *Monitor Prawniczy* 7 (2010) 16–23; Jacek Widło, *Elektroniczne postępowanie upominawcze* [Electronic Monition Proceedings] (Warszawa: Lexis Nexis, 2010).

[67] The evaluation of the social effect of that proceeding includes a report of the Helsinki Foundation for Human Rights: Jakub Pawliczak, 'Elektorniczne postępowanie upominawcze—założone cele a praktyka funkcjonowania' [Electronic Monition Proceedings—Intended Targets and Practice of Functioning], accessed 10 April 2014, http://www.hfhr.pl/wp-content/uploads/2011/09/J_pawliczak_elektroniczne-postepowanie-upominawcze-zalozone-cele-a-praktyka-funkcjonowania.pdf; Anna Brenk-Czapska, 'Elektroniczne

Not only judges but also prosecutors are pressured by their superiors to terminate judicial proceedings on the basis of an agreement with the accused to submit voluntarily to the penalty.[68] Of course, the aforementioned process is swift and therefore regarded as efficient, but in many cases the victim is left with a sense of injustice.[69] Obviously, cases need to be completed within a reasonable time frame, therefore it was necessary to explore ideas that could expedite proceedings. However, this necessity should have been balanced with the social impact of the process.

8.3.5 Advantages and Disadvantges of the Technicist Approach in Legal Practice

After this exploration of the essence of technicism and its significance within the law, it is now appropriate to assess its influence on the application of the law and the advantages and disadvantages of this approach. Firstly, the dangers should be disclosed. Primarily, technicism can make the law and its implementation very technical and sterile as the social impact and broader dimensions are disregarded. This narrow and shallow treatment of the implications of applied law can easily make it mechanical, which could be very detrimental to social life and justice.[70] Technicism can work very well only in simple cases without any complex entanglement of social circumstances, and its outcomes can easily be foreseen only in the short term. Indeed, if the objective is short term then this method will work, but it will fail for complex situations in which profound knowledge and thorough consideration are necessary.[71] This method is also better suited to

---

postępowanie upominawcze—uwagi na temat rzeczywistego funkcjonowania e-sądu' [Electronic Monition Proceeding—Remarks on the Actual Functioning of the e-Court], *Prawo Mediów Elektronicznych* 2 (2012), 5–8.

[68] Ewa Ivanowa, 'Sermet ratuje statystyki Polecił podwładnym: kończcie sprawy byle szybko' [Sermet Rescues the Statistics. He ordered his subordinates: Finish your Cases—Immediately], *Gazeta Prawna* (2013), accessed 10 April 2014, http://prawo.gazetaprawna.pl/artykuly/766421,prokurator-generalny-polecil-podwladnym-konczcie-sprawy-byle-szybko.html.

[69] The problem of the victims in a plea bargaining proceeding in the Polish legal system was depicted in *Maria Zbrojewska, Dobrowolne poddanie się karze w kodeksie postępowania karnego* [Plea Bargaining under the Code of Criminal Procedure] (Białystok: Temida 2, 2002); Sławomir Steinborn, *Porozumienia w polskim procesie karnym. Skazanie bez rozprawy i dobrowolne poddanie się odpowiedzialności karne* [Agreements in Polish Criminal Proceedings, Sentencing without Trial and Plea Bargaining] (Kraków: Zakamycze, 2005); Katarzyna Kurowska, 'Konsensualne sposoby zakończenia postępowania karnego a sytuacja procesowa pokrzywdzonego' [Consensual Ways for Finishing Criminal Proceedings, and the Situation of Victims of Crime], *Prokuratura i Prawo* 8/4 (2002) 12–29.

[70] Marek Safjan, *Rola prawnika we współczesnym świecie* [The Role of a Lawyer in the Contemporary World] (Lublin: Towarzystwo Naukowe KUL, 2004), 24.

[71] In such cases the application of law should be more responsive, i.e. being adequate to social needs and perceptions. For more about responsive law, see Philippe Nonet and Philip

simple and unequivocal situations for which outcomes can confidently be predicted, but problems will arise when the broader context of a situation is taken into consideration.

Technicism is hardly appropriate for the proper practice of the legal profession and the fulfilment of the role of lawyers in society. The legal professions are not typical service providers, nor simple problem-solving occupations, even if they sometimes seem to be very similar. The behaviour not only of judges and prosecutors, but also of lawyers has a great impact on the social perception of justice and the rule of law with which the confidence of the state and its administration is closely connected.[72] If the application of law is treated as the strict fulfilment of even the most inadequate nonsensical rules, but inscribed within an act of parliament or code, or if the law's meaning is dependent upon the arguments and persuasive skills of lawyers and can be understood to be changeable due to particular needs, then a lack of social trust in the state and its justice could arise.[73] The situation in post-communist societies is especially dangerous as they are accustomed to the law being treated as a simple instrument to realize the aims of rulers, usually at the expense of society. Admittedly, the solution for this situation in societies with very weak awareness and confidence in the law would be similar to what currently happens in Poland, this being the strict enforcement of the law according to legal norms in order to strengthen the social perception of legal certainty. However, this is also the easiest way to make the law overly formal and clear but completely unjust.[74] The technicist application of law can easily cause a complete lack of identification with the law as it appears to be something hostile to citizens. Of course, in countries like Poland it is easier for judges to act strictly and in accordance with the literal meaning of the law than to find alternative outcomes because this behaviour does not need effort for its justification.[75]

In Europe, there is also the problem that law is used as a remedy for all

---

Selznick, *Towards Responsive Law. Law and Society in Transition* (New Brunswick and London: Transactions Publishers, 2001).

[72] W. Komarnicki, 'Rola prawnika w wyzwolonej Polsce, wykład wygłoszony 23 marca 1942 roku na Uniwersytecie St. Andrew' [The Role of a Lawyer in Independent Poland—Lecture from 23 of March 1942 on St. Andrew University] as cited in Safjan, *Rola prawnika*, 33.

[73] *Raport badań CBOS. O przestrzeganiu prawa i funkcjonowaniu wymiaru sprawiedliwości w Polsce* [The Report of CBOS on Observing the Law and Functioning of Justice in Poland], BS/5/2013, accessed 15 April 2014, http://cbos.pl/SPISKOM.POL/2013/K_005_13.PDF.

[74] Marek Zirk-Sadowski, 'Uczestniczenie prawników w kulturze' [Lawyers' Participation in Culture], *Państwo i Prawo* 9 (2002) 3–6.

[75] Mańko, 'Weeds,' 226; Stawecki, *Niezależność zawodów*, 58–9; Anna Machnikowska, 'Niezależność sądów we współczesnej myśli politycznej' [Judicial Independence in Contemporary Political Thought], in Maciejewski et al., *Tendencje rozwojowe*, 268.

social problems, which leads to a flood of legislation.[76] This scheme is very simple: if a problem appears, the first reaction of most politicians is to put forward new parliamentary acts regulating the given situation.[77] Of course this is also a typical technicist approach to law, which is also proof of the immaturity of the political class of Poland when it comes to solving social problems.[78] In these situations it is hard to change society's attitudes which regard the state as well as the law as institutions which are hostile to mere citizens, and which in turn serve only the interests of the ruling class.[79]

This chapter has presented a very critical approach to technicism and its methods, especially within the contemporary circumstances of Polish society, but this is not to say that the author is not able to perceive any of the positive aspects of this approach. The technicist method can be very useful and beneficial for society in situations which enforce and foster the professional behaviour of lawyers. Also, it can be useful in uncomplicated legal situations, such as invoice payment proceedings, for which there is no need for thorough consideration. However, problems arise when this method—and indications are that this happens often in Poland—is overrated and considered without any critical insight to be the only right way of acting. Of course it would make the work of judges and lawyers easier, but this would not always be the most valuable and desired effect.

8.4 Conclusions

The technicist approach to law in Poland, which in the author's opinion is increasingly commonplace, has a couple of origins and supporting trends.

Firstly, it is a result of lawyers' desire to clearly separate the spheres of law, politics, and morality. Law is perceived as being clear, strict, precise, predictable, and easily justifiable in contrast to policies or morality, which

---

[76] This problem is tightly connected with the process of juridification, see broadly Gunter Teubner, 'Juridification—Concepts, Aspects, Limits, Solutions,' in *Juridification of Social Spheres. A comparative Analysis in the Areas of Labour, Corporate Antitrust and Social Welfare State*, ed. Gunter Teubner (Walter de Guyter: New York, Berlin 1987); Lars Christian Blichner and Andreas Molander, 'Mapping Juridification,' *European Law Journal* 14/1 (2007) 36-54.

[77] Sławomira Wronkowska, 'Polski proces prawotwórczy—miedzy autonomią a polityką' [Polish Legislative Procedure—Between Autonomy and Politics], *Ius et Lex* 3 (2005), 199.

[78] Regarding problems of the Polish legislature generally see Robert Borkowski, 'Normatywna erozja—uwagi o patologii procesu legislacyjnego w systemie III RP' [Normative Erosion—Remarks on the Pathology of the Legislature in the System of the Third Republic of Poland], *Studia Humanistyczne* 3 (2005), 87-8.

[79] Adam Zieliński, 'Przyszłość polskiego wymiaru sprawiedliwości' [The Future of the Polish Justice System], in *Przyszłość Polskiego wymiaru sprawiedliwości* [The Future of the Polish Justice System], ed. Adam Zieliński and Marek Zubik (Warszawa: Wydawnictwo Instytutu Spraw Publicznych, 2002), 14.

are full of ambiguity and subjective meaning, making them hard to justify without reference to a concrete moral system. The lawyers' quest for assurance and clarity, which for them is justified within the conditions of pluralism and morality and the values of contemporary community, causes the lawyers' technicist perspective to become the only universally accepted normative system. Therefore, lawyers are limited by the meaning of the words used by legislators. They do not have to interpret the law and can justify their choices *ex post facto* by referring to social needs and morality.

Secondly, the technicist approach is reinforced by free market demands which treat the application of the law as a kind of activity very similar to service provision. This concerns not only the work of the legal professions typically associated with the free market, but also the public legal professions, whose activities and administration of justice is evaluated in terms of typical economic values, such as efficiency or effectiveness. Regardless of the factors leading to a technicist approach, it constitutes a threat to the proper functioning of law in society because it makes it narrow, shallow, schematic, and overly mechanical.

9

From Sublimation to Naturalization: Constructing Ideological Hegemony on the Shoulders of Roman Jurists

Paulina Święcicka

[Roman law] has indelibly impressed its character on European legal and political thought.[1]

—Peter Stein

9.1 Introduction

At the *Musei Vaticani* in the *Stanza della Segnatura* one can see the fresco 'Justinian Receiving *Digesta*—the Pandects (civil laws) from Tribonian,' painted in 1511 by Lorenzo Lotto, but based on Raphael's drawing. It shows the contemporaneity of ancient legal thought at the time of the Renaissance, its practical usefulness and its continuous relevance. Justinian—as he appeared according to the understanding of the fresco creator—is a Romano-Christian emperor dressed in Renaissance clothes and the founder of contemporary civil law. Of course, this is not the only example of such a 'foundational' vision of Justinian who, in the first part of the sixth century, ordered the compilation of the legal remnants of the ancient Romans. Almost every depiction, however, turns Justinian into a sort of legendary or mythical founder of the legal order.[2]

Justinian may or may not be considered the founder of contemporary civil law, but almost every textbook on Roman law and legal history, as well as every more complex study concerning contemporary legal institutions and concepts understands Roman law to be highly sophisticated, technically

---

[1] Peter Stein, *Roman Law in European Legal History* (Cambridge: CUP, 1999), 1–2.

[2] For such an example see the fresco by Andrea da Bonaiuto, painted between 1365 and 1367 entitled 'The triumph of St. Thomas Aquinas' with a similar depiction of Justinian, i.e. as a founder of the whole order, including the legal order, but this time the Emperor is holding his Codex. This fresco from Firenze (from the Capella degli Spagnioli of the Santa Maria Novella) was mentioned by Kaius Tuori, *Ancient Roman Lawyers and Modern Legal Ideals. Studies on the impact of the contemporary concerns in the interpretations of ancient Roman legal history* (Frankfurt am Main: Vittorio Klostermann, 2007), 1.

superior to every other legal order, and to have played a fundamental role in the creation of the idea of the common European culture. As Andrew Borkowski and Paul du Plessis put it:

> Roman law provides an invaluable introduction to the understanding of legal concepts and a passport to the appreciation of Continental legal systems. It would nevertheless ... be eminently worthy of study for its own sake. For it is the product of the genius for good order and organised common sense of a remarkable ancient civilization, and it constitutes a legacy that has had profound influence in subsequent ages.[3]

Such a narrative practice may be observed in almost every European country, including Poland which has claimed, ever since the fundamental changes during the 1990s, that it belongs to the Western European cultural circle. An example of this narrative from Polish studies on Roman law and the common legal tradition is the following by Antoni Dębiński:

> Indeed, the 'posthumous life of Roman law' ..., i.e. its functioning after the fall of the Roman state ... is a legal and historical phenomenon. ... [No ancient legal system became, as Roman law, the 'source of everlasting inspiration.' ... The presence of the Roman legal thought in the contemporary law is noticeable in numerous terms, expressions and maxims defining the essential principles or legal solutions. ... They express universal and ageless ideas, thus comprising a crucial element of the axiology of law. They are used in judicial decisions, in legal motions and opinions and belong to the legal rhetoric. ... They are referred to when drawing up codifications and establishing legal institutions. ... The significance of Roman law may also be seen from the viewpoint of its 'spirit,' that is 'ethical values.' If so, it appears as a universal and unchanging idea, the embodiment of good and just law and the general principle of social culture.[4]

The same narrative can be found in a book devoted to the Roman law of succession written by another Polish scholar, Franciszek Longchamps de Bérier:

> Roman law is, above all, the legacy of legal thought. ... The study of experience of Roman law enables us to see which legal principles work, what actually is constant, and what, regardless of the changing circumstances, can

---

[3] See, e.g. Andrew Borkowski and Paul du Plessis, *Textbook on Roman Law*, 3rd ed. (Oxford: OUP, 2005), x–xi. Spelling and grammar maintained from the original and likewise for all future quotations. For other examples, see also Tuori, *Ancient Roman Lawyers*, 1–2 nn. 2–3.

[4] Antoni Dębiński, 'Introduction to the Subject of the Conference: The Role and Significance of Roman Law in the Legal History of Europe,' in *Roman Law and European Legal Culture: Cooperation of Universities supporting the development of the Lublin and Lviv regions*, ed. Antoni Dębiński and Maciej Jońca (Lublin: Publishing House of Catholic University of Lublin, 2008), 12–14.

always be brought back. ... The phenomenon of decodification is conducive to redefinitions. For those who are aware of this evolutionary path of contemporary law, Roman law—understood as a tradition that is characterized by its reasonableness—can serve as a guide.[5]

The use of Roman law as presented in these and many other studies,[6] both by Polish and non-Polish authors, allows one to speak of a dominant narrative concerning Roman law and the place of this law in the modern world which can be distilled into three distinct ideas, akin to programmatic postulates of contemporary scholars of Roman law: *1)* Roman law institutions have scientific value for contemporary jurists, *2)* there exists a continuity in legal thought from Roman times as well as from the later Roman law tradition, and *3)* Roman law has an inherent value in itself as a legal order.

The aim of the present chapter is, however, to carry out a critical analysis of such references to 'Roman law' in just such a dominant narrative in respect of the European legal tradition—mostly civilian, but not only[7]—and which are particularly reflected in Polish writings produced in the second half of the twentieth century and the first decade of the twenty-first. In addition, there is an attempt to look at the theoretical and practical legal discourse of Polish lawyers, particularly judges,[8] in which the *argumentum ex iure romano* appears. For this purpose I will resort to the category of 'sublimation,' (Eng. the sublime; Ger. *Sublimierung*), i.e. the category of philosophical reflection concerning the possibility of encountering (feeling directly) the world, which, in my opinion, can be used as a tool to analyze the narrative of legal historians, legal theorists, philosophers, or even the narrative of representatives of various legal dogmatics who, in most cases, are also practitioners. Historical and modern legal scholarship is undoubtedly not free from such non-epistemological ways of understanding the legal past, present, or even future. As long as historical narratives

---

[5] Franciszek Longchamps de Bérier, *Law of Succession: Roman Legal Framework and Comparative Law Perspective* (Warsaw: Wolters Kluwer, 2011), 10–11.
[6] For more titles from the literature in Polish, see Maria Zabłocka, *Romanistyka polska po II wojnie światowej* [Polish Roman Law Scholarship After World War II] (Warszawa: Liber, 2002), 161–5; Maria Zabłocka, *Romanistyka polska w pierwszym dziesięcioleciu XXI wieku* [Polish Roman Law Scholarship in the First Decade of the 21st Century] (Warszawa: Liber, 2013), 135–53; some of these studies will be quoted in this chapter.
[7] See, e.g. remarks on the dominant narrative concerning constitutional institutions as shaped by the ancient tradition: Moses I. Finley, *Democracy Ancient and Modern*, 2nd ed. (London: Rutgers University Press, 1985); Peter J. Rhodes, *Ancient Democracy and Modern Ideology* (London: Gerald Duckworth & Co. Ltd, 2003).
[8] By practical legal discourse I understand, generally speaking, final judgments and interlocutory decisions or orders passed in cases decided by various courts. References to Roman law, Roman institutions, or elements of the common legal tradition, such as Latin maxims, sometimes appear in theses judgments and more often in formal justifications of such solutions, decisions, and judgments.

are not free from such an understanding, one may assume, as Hayden White once stated, that legal practice will not be also free from it.⁹

It is also worth explaining that the notion of 'the sublime' is an element of a set of concepts used to characterize the non-epistemological (non-intellectual) experience of the world. The idea of experience in the sense of a direct perception (i.e. not based on the process of logical reasoning, but has to be described as an experience, i.e. 'feeling the sublime') of reality has, in such an understanding, a fundamental position. Such way of constructing the image of reality came with Postmodernism, and was a reaction to deficiencies of Modernism, which failed to reach the optimistically founded aim, i.e. the total intelligibility of the reality and the one and only truth. Richard Rorty, one of the main representatives of the Postmodern stream, claimed that something that represented reality was not necessarily its reflection, and, therefore, the model of interpretation of scientific knowledge should consist of constructing the image of reality (also, the past reality) in the form of its narrative representations (models, theories etc.), independently of the concept of the truth.¹⁰

The chapter is divided into several parts. In the next part I shall provide

---

⁹ Hayden White, 'The Politics of Historical Interpretation: Discipline and De-Sublimation,' *Critical Inquiry* 9/1 (1982), 113–37, republished in Hayden White, *The Content of the Form. Narrative Discourse and Historical Representation* (Baltimore-London: The John Hopkins University, 1987), 18–82; see also Franklin R. Ankersmit, *Sublime Historical Experience* (Stanford: Stanford University Press, 2005). Compare some examples of sublimated historical events and facts in the Polish historical narrative mentioned by Topolski in Jerzy Topolski, 'Wzniosłość jako kategoria refleksji filozoficznej nad narracją historyczną. Wzniosłość a mitologizacja narracji' [The Sublime as a Category of Philosophical Reflection on the Historical Narrative. The Sublime and Mythologization of the Narrative], in *Historia, idee, polityka. Księga dedykowana profesorowi Janowi Baszkiewiczowi* [History, Ideas, Politics. Studies Dedicated to Professor Jan Baszkiewicz], ed. Franciszek Ryszka (Warszawa: Wydawnictwo Naukowe Scholar, 1995), 178–91, republished in Jerzy Topolski, *Jak się pisze i rozumie historię. Tajemnice narracji historycznej* [How to Write and Understand History. The Secrets of the Historical Narrative], 2ⁿᵈ ed. (Warszawa: Oficyna Wydawnicza Rytm, 1998), 234–52; see also studies in *The Most Sublime Act. Essays on the Sublime*, ed. Tadeusz Rachwał and Tadeusz Sławek (Katowice: Wydawnictwo UŚ, 1994). Compare Michał Rusinek, *Między retoryką a retorycznością* [Between Rhetoric and The Rhetorical] (Kraków: Universitas, 2003), 43–4, about a certain sublimation of the narrative on rhetoric and its history.

¹⁰ Richard Rorty, *Philosophy and the Mirror of Nature* (London: Blackwell, 1980); Richard Rorty, *Contingence, Irony and Solidarity* (Cambridge, New York, Melbourne, Sydney: CUP, 1988). Compare, however, a critique by Peter Munz, 'Philosophy and the Mirror of Rorty,' *Philosophy of the Social Sciences* 14/2 (1984), 195–238; see also Franklin R. Ankersmit, 'Modernistyczna prawda, postmodernistyczne przedstawienie i po-postmodernistyczne doświadczenie' [Modernist Truth, Postmodernist Representation, Post-postmodernist Experience], in *Historia: o jeden świat za daleko?* [History: One World Too Far?], ed. and trans. Ewa Domańska (Poznań: Wydawnictwo Naukowe IH UAM, 1997), 1–35; Franklin R. Ankersmit, 'Historical Representation,' History and Theory 27/3 (1988), 205–29; Franklin R. Ankersmit, 'Representation as the Representation of Experience,' *Metaphilosophy* 31/1–2 (2000), 148–69.

an introduction to the theme and then, in part three, I shall explain the mechanisms leading to the fact that owing to the sublimation of a certain element of reality (here: a historical source sacralized as a particular remnant of the past) a certain ideology enters the scene. Then, in part four, I shall discuss the presence of the notion of the sublime in the dominant historical narrative in order to lay bare the mechanisms of formation of the myth of Roman law and the ideology that the formative reality of European legal tradition, past and future, is based on Roman law. Finally, in part five, I shall try to answer the question of whether the sublimation of a certain item from the past can impact on the nature of *argumenta* present in contemporary Polish legal discourse; or if such sublimation can even be decisive in describing law in general.

9.2 Monumental Roman Law and the Ideology of Continuity

For the purpose of some preliminary elucidations on the topic, it is worth remarking that Roman law—especially that part of private law created and developed by Roman jurists which was later collected in Justinian's Digest and considered the most important part of his compilation—was for centuries, and may still be, the object of a certain monumentalization or sublimation, understood in the sense attributed to it by 'postmodern' philosophers, such as Jacques Derrida and Jean-François Lyotard (following on the heels of Burke,[11] Kant,[12] Scheler,[13] etc.).[14] In general, the sublimation of the past (heroes, events, etc.) means, aside from a sense of nostalgia,[15]

---

[11] Edmund Burke, *A Philosophical Enquiry into the Origin of Our Ideas of the Sublime and Beautiful* (London: Printed for R. and J. Dodsley, 1757; repr. Oxford-New York: OUP, 1990).

[12] Immanuel Kant, *Beobachtungen über das Gefühl des Schönen und Erhabenen* (Königsberg: J.J. Kanter, 1764); the English edition: *Observations on the Feeling of the Beautiful and the Sublime*, trans. John T. Goldwait (Berkeley: The University of California Press, 1960). In particular, see also Paul Crowther, *The Kantian Sublime. From Morality to Art* (Oxford: Clarendon Press, 1989), 11–6.

[13] Max Scheler, 'Der Mensch im Weltalter des Ausgleichs (1927),' in *Gesammelte Werke*, Hrsg. Maria Scheler, seither von M.S. Frings (Bern-München: Francke Verlag /Bonn: Bouvier Verlag, 1986–1969).

[14] Jacques Derrida, 'Parergon,' in *La Vérité en peinture* (Paris: Éditions Flammarion, 1978), the English edition: 'Parergon,' in *The Truth in Painting*, trans. Geoffrey Bennington and Ian McLeod (Chicago-London: The University of Chicago Press, 1987); Jean-François Lyotard, *La condition postmoderne. Rapport sur le savoir* (Paris: Seuil, 1979), the English edition: *The Postmodern Condition: A Report on Knowledge*, trans. Geoffrey Bennington and Brian Massumi, Foreword by Fredric Jameson (Manchester: Manchester University Press, 1984).

[15] Malcolm Chase, Christopher Shaw, 'The Dimension of Nostalgia,' in *Imagined Past: History and Nostalgia. Conference Proceedings*, ed. Malcolm Chase and Christopher Shaw (Manchester-New York: Manchester University Press, 1989), 1–17.

giving to particular elements from the past an unreal dimension—a sort of mythologization—in order to describe both the past and the present world.[16] Through such sublimation—from the Middle Ages and the medieval Bologna renaissance, across epochs traditionally distinguished in legal history,[17] namely legal humanism, Dutch elegant jurisprudence, the historical school of Savigny and the Pandectists, and, finally, the so-called Neopandectists of the twentieth century—legal historians and lawyers, via their narratives,[18] found themselves engaging in monumentalizing Roman law. As a result, today this law is considered to be the embodiment of eternal legal wisdom, the ideal of equitable law,[19] the cornerstone of the European legal tradition, and/or the remedy for a weak European legal order insofar as it is seen as the basis for the creation of a *ius commune*

---

[16] The links between sublimation and mythologization of a certain item of reality were underlined already by Nietzsche: Friedrich Wilhelm Nietzsche, 'Vom Nutzen und Nachteil der Historie für das Leben,' in Friedrich Wilhelm Nietzsche, *Unzeitgemässe Betrachtungen. Sämtliche Werke* (Kritische Studienausgabe in 15 Bänden, 1873–1876), cit. after the Polish edition: Friedrich Nietzsche, 'O pożytkach i szkodliwości historii dla życia' [On the Advantage and Disadvantage of History for Life], in Friedrich Nietzsche, *Niewczesne rozważania* [Untimely Meditation], trans. by Małgorzata Łukasiewicz (Kraków: Znak, 1996), 95–102, 104–5.

[17] See, e.g. Olivia F. Robinson, T. David Fergus, and William M. Gordon, *European Legal History*, 3rd ed. (Oxford: OUP, 2000).

[18] For an explanation of ways of the presence in and influence of Justinian's compilation on the medieval and modern legal world, see especially Franz Wieacker, *A History of the Private Law in Europe, with particular reference to Germany*, trans. Tony Weir (Oxford: OUP, 1995); Mario Talamanca, 'Il *Corpus Iuris* Giustinianeo fra il diritto romano e il diritto vigente,' in vol. 2 of *Studi in onore di M. Mazziotti di Celso* (Padova: CEDAM, 1995), 771–807; Stein, *Roman Law*, passim; Manlio Bellomo, *The Common Legal Past of Europe 1000–1800*, trans. Lydia G. Cochrane (Washington: The Catholic University of America Press, 1995); Antonio Padoa Schioppa, *Storia del diritto in Europa. Dal medioevo all'età contemporanea* (Bologna: Il Mulino, 2007); Lauretta Maganzani, *Formazione e vicende di un'opera illustre. Il Corpus Iuris nella cultura del giurista europeo* (Torino: Giappichelli, 2002). For an indication of problems appearing in the course of research on the process of formation of a common legal tradition, see Ricardo Orestano, *Introduzione allo studio storico del diritto romano* (Torino: Giappichelli, 1961); and more recently Mario Bretone, *Diritto e tempo nella tradizione europea* (Roma-Bari: Laterza, 1994).

[19] E.g. a Polish Romanist and legal historian, Marek Kuryłowicz, entitled his book on Roman law and its place in the twentieth century: *Symbol prawa ludzkiego. Szkice o prawie rzymskim w utworach Louisa Aragona i Mieczysława Jastruna* [The Symbol of Human Law. Sketches on Roman Law in Works by Louis Aragon and Mieczysław Jastrun] (Lublin: UMCS, 2008). The author explains references to Roman Law in French and Polish literature as references to the metaphor of a universal ethic, a basis for Latin and European legal culture, and finally as a universal symbol of 'human law' (143). See also Marek Kuryłowicz, 'Roman law as a Universal Ethical Metaphor,' in Dębiński and Jońca, *Roman Law and European Legal Culture*, 107–15.

europaeum,[20] a new common legal pan-European system.[21]

> The phenomenon that is known as decodification, and the related Europeanization of particular national legal systems, has triggered mechanisms for discussing the process of creating the law which resemble the way in which Roman jurisprudence as 'ius commune' lawyers functioned. Framing the legal order within a deductive system has not been entirely successful. Roman law is the legacy of legal thought, and it allows us to illustrate how law reflects values and what those values might be. ... [I]ncluding the Roman and civil law tradition in the discussion about new order of private law in Europe provides more flexibility for legal regulations.[22]

Derrida, following mostly Kant, but also Burke, stated that the feeling of the sublime came not so much from the nature of the object, but flowed more from the man and his mind. The feeling of the sublime is therefore a particular 'emotion of the mind,' a sensation, and a sensitivity. One of the most characteristic aspects of the sublime is its secretiveness and irregularity, and sublimation of a particular object makes it sublime and awakens respect towards it.[23] Therefore, one may say that such an exemplarily chosen vision of the Roman law as the one quoted above, is the outcome of a peculiar historical process, i.e. the sacralization via the sublimation of Roman law over the centuries which translated this law into its great and everlasting Romanist tradition thus provoking the formation of a certain ideology as an effect of such a Romanist tradition constantly influencing

---

[20] Reinhard Zimmermann, 'Savigny's Legacy: Legal History, Comparative Law and the Emergence of a European Legal Science,' *The Law Quarterly Review* 112 (1996), 576–605, republished in *The Europeanisation of Law*], ed. Thomas G. Watkin (Oxford: Alden Press, 1998), 1–38. Compare some skeptical remarks on such an approach by Lord Rodger of Earlsferry, '"Say not the Struggle Naught Availeth": The Costs and Benefits of Mixed Legal Systems,' *Tulane Law Review* 78 (2003), 419–34; and ironic comments by Douglas J. Osler, 'The Fantasy Men,' *Rechtsgeschichte* 10 (2007), 190–2.

[21] See, e.g. Philip J. Thomas, 'The eternal value(s) of Roman law,' in vol. 2 of *Roman Law as Formative of Modern Legal Systems. Studies in Honour of Wiesław Litewski*, ed. Janusz Sondel et al. (Cracow: Jagiellonian University Press, 2003), 173: 'It should, however, be kept in mind that Roman law has been responsible for some of the most important changes in the history of law.'; or Gianni Santucci, 'Alterità e identità ('apparenti,' 'tralatizie,' 'vere') fra diritto romano e diritti moderni,' in *Roman Law and Legal Knowledge. Studies in Memory of Henryk Kupiszewski*, ed. Tomasz Giaro (Warsaw: Stowarzyszenie Absolwentów WPiA UW, 2011), 107: 'In recent decades, the scientific and cultural debate over the idea of a common European private law, whose formation has been repeatedly stressed by the European Parliament since 1989, did regard Roman law and, above all, the Roman tradition as a natural unifying element for the future private law common to the Member States of the European Union' [trans. from Italian by Paulina Święcicka].

[22] Wojciech Dajczak and Franciszek Longchamps de Bérier, 'Prawo rzymskie w czasach dekodyfikacji' [Roman Law and the Process of Decodification], *Forum Prawnicze* 2/10 (2012), 8.

[23] Derrida, 'Parergon,' 122–3. See also Emanuel Prower, 'The Sublime and C.S. Peirce's Category of Firstness,' in Rachwał and Sławek, *The Most Sublime Act*, 59–67.

the dominant narrative on Roman law and a common legal past. Put simply, it is the 'ideology of continuity' from antiquity to the present day.[24] Thus for centuries lawyers have sought in Roman law solutions or the confirmation of the accuracy (rationality or equity) of their own decisions (*argumentum ex auctoritate iuris romani*) by building, sometimes unconsciously and sometimes almost forcibly, genetic or functional links between legal institutions formed by Roman jurists and similar legal institutions of modern law.[25] The same can be said about the predominant belief in both past and present legal scholarship based on one fragment from the Digest (D. 1.2.2.41, Pomponius *libro singularis enchiridii*: *Post hos Quintus Mucius Publii filius pontifex maximus ius civile primus constituit generatim in libros decem et octo redigendo*. = 'Quintus Mucius, son of Publius and a *pontifex maximus*, became the first man to produce a general compendium of the civil law by arranging it into eighteen books.')[26] and related comments and interpretations started by a Spanish polymath, Gregorio Mayáns y Siscar (1697–1781), who first raised the issue of science in his biography of Quintus Mucius,[27] and brought to completion with representatives of the German Pandectistics who used the Maiansus' interpretation for their own needs while interpreting the law of Roman jurists as a kind of precedent for professorial law-making, regarding it as a substitute for

---

[24] Cf. Pier Giuseppe Monateri, 'Black Gaius: A Quest for the Multicultural Origins of the "Western Legal Tradition",' *Hastings Law Journal* 51 (2000), 479–555.

[25] Numerous instances of the continuous application and influence of the principles of Roman law in modern legal systems are stressed in scientific literature. A typical example is Reinhard Zimmermann, *The Law of Obligations. Roman Foundation of Civilian Tradition* (Oxford: OUP, 1996), which 'presents all institutions of the law of obligations as being products of an organic evolution from the Law of the Twelve Tables until the BGB,' as remarked by Rafał Mańko, 'Is the Socialist Legal Tradition "Dead and Buried"? The Continuity of Certain Elements of Socialist Legal Culture in Polish Civil Procedure,' in *Private Law and the Many Cultures of Europe*, ed. Thomas Wilhelmsson et al. (Alphen aan den Rijn: Kluwer, 2007), 85.

[26] Translation of vol. 1 of *The Digest of Justinian*, ed. Alan Watson (Philadelphia: University of Pennsylvania Press, 1985), 9. On this passage see, e.g. Fritz Schulz, *History of Roman Legal Science*, 2nd ed. (Oxford: The Clarendon Press, 1953), 94: 'The most considerable work of our period [i.e. the Late Republic] was beyond doubt Q. Mucius Scaevola *Ius civile*. ... [T]he book which laid the foundations not merely of Roman, but of European jurisprudence;' or Bruce W. Frier, *The Rise of Roman Jurists: Studies in Cicero's pro Caecina* (Princeton: PUP, 1985), 163, 168, 171: 'Q. Mucius is the father of Roman legal science and of the Western legal tradition.'

[27] See Gregorius Maiansius, *Ad triginta jurisconsultorum omnia fragmenta quae exstant in juris civilis corpore commentarii* (Geneve: Apud fratres de Tournes, 1764), 178–9, 183: *Q. autem Mucius Jus Civile construxit. ... Hic Juris argumenta distribuisse, singola tractans generatim, hoc est, definitionibus, sive regulis: qua ratione scientia tradi debet*. = Q. Mucius built the *ius civile*. ... [H]e systematized the arguments and collected definitions and rules of law under the influence of scientific reason [trans. Paulina Święcicka].

codification.[28] According to this understanding (contemporarily adopted[29]), Roman jurisprudence is the origin of Western legal science, which served and continues to serve the construction of lawyers' identity.[30]

Therefore, 'Monumental Roman Law' during the centuries became a sort of treasury, where, to quote Hermann Kantorowicz, 'everybody could enter and find what he needed to solve a legal problem.'[31] One can also observe such practices even today; and such awareness is of vital importance especially because almost the same narrative that was used to promote Roman law for centuries, in particular in the nineteenth century by representatives of the German Historical School and the Pandectists, is now re-used to advocate its revival in the new European civil law.[32] Generally, such narrative does not even entail any attempt at gaining an historical understanding of Roman law, nor of clarifying the genetic links between ancient and modern legal institutions or concepts (*nota bene*, such clarification can be extremely difficult or even impossible to demonstrate). Instead, it signifies treating Roman law as a 'brainwave'—a sort of inspiration, i.e. something from the domain of aesthetics, but not law, as it was explained by Lyotard, according to whom the sublime as a category of experience of the world, allows one to percieve the object which is not able to self-show itself, i.e. the subject cannot see what would be really seen in the object in accordance with the Modernists' presumptions. In other words, the category of the sublime makes it possible to perceive the inner-tear in the object, what may be named as the capture of the unattainable.[33] Therefore, to say it differently, in the dominant narrative and in contemporary legal discourse, monumental Roman law—still the law from a particular past, created in a certain way, in a specific historical moment for a particularly organized society—is a dimension of the 'unreal,'

---

[28] See especially Georg F. Puchta, 'Geschichte des Rechts bei dem römischen Volk,' in Bd. 1 of Georg F. Puchta, *Cursus der Institutionen nach dem Tode des Verfassers besorgt von Paul Krüger*, 8 Aufl. (Leipzig: Breitkopf und Härtel, 1875), 174–5, 244–9.

[29] During the next century the 'foundational narrative' was elaborated in detail by numerous authors, e.g. Moritz Voigt, Paul Jörs, and Fritz Schulz. Paul Krüger gave Q. Mucius the title of the *Gründer der Rechtswissenschaft*—'the founder of legal science.' For a detailed and critical analysis of this topic see Tuori, *Ancient Roman Lawyers*, 21–69; Kaius Tuori, 'The myth of Quintus Mucius Scaevola: Founding father of legal science,' *Tijdschrift voor Rechtsgeschiedenis / Revue d'histoire du droit* 72 (2004), 243–62. See also critical remarks of such attempts at describing Roman jurisprudence with objective and modern criteria: Tomasz Giaro, 'Die Illusion der Wissenschaftlichkeit,' *Index* 22 (1994), 118–28.

[30] Cf. Francisco Javier Andrés Santos, 'Roma y los Juristas en modelo romano en la jurisprudencia europea del siglo XIX,' *Minerva. Revista de Filología clásica* 15 (2001), 281–301.

[31] Hermann Kantorowicz, *Bractonian Problems* (Glasgow: Jackson, 1941), 126.

[32] See, e.g. James Q. Witman, *The Legacy of Roman Law in the German Romantic Era: Historical Vision and Legal Change* (Princeton: PUP, 1990).

[33] Cf. Lyotard, *The Postmodern Condition*, 77–8.

which raises law to the category of a legal myth present in the minds of historians and jurists for centuries.[34]

Even if some concrete solutions of Roman law are today no longer accepted for a variety of reasons, they are marginalized because Roman law as a whole is seen as monumental and, as such, becomes a form of ideology in itself, captivating the minds of legal historians and lawyers.

Derrida emphasized the role of a proper distance between subject and object (hence the objects from the past are perfectly susceptible to sublimation).[35] The object which provokes the sensation of the sublime has to be located at such a distance as to appear 'colossal' and to provoke astonishment. At the same time, it cannot be located too far from the subject because it could render impossible seeing the object in its impressive colossal integrated totality:

> What is the colossal? ... The *colossal*, which is not the prodigious, nor the monstrous, qualifies the 'mere presentation' (*blosse Darstellung*) of a concept. But not just any concept: the mere presentation of a concept which is 'almost

---

[34] On 'legal myths' see especially: Paolo Grossi, *Mitologie giuridiche della modernità*, 3rd ed. (Milano: Giuffrè, 2007); Jerzy Stelmach, 'Mity prawnicze' [Legal Myths], in *Świat, Europa, Mała Ojczyzna. Studia ofiarowane Profesorowi Stanisławowi Grodziskiemu w 80-lecie urodzin* [World, Europe, Little Motherland. Studies Dedicated to Professor Stanisław Grodziski], ed. Marian Małecki (Bielsko-Biała: WSA, 2009), 1145–55; for the historical and meta-historical perspective see Peter Heehs, 'Myth, History and Theory,' *History and Theory* 1 (1994), 1–20; see also studies by Topolski collected in Jerzy Topolski, *Jak się pisze*, 205–18; 219–31, 269–76, 278–93; for the analysis of the process of invention of some myths in the past, see Douglas J. Osler, 'The Myth of European Legal History,' *Rechtshistorisches Journal* 16 (1997), 393–410; Osler, 'The Fantasy Men,' 169–192; Tuori, *Ancient Roman Lawyers*, 21–69; and also my studies: Paulina Święcicka, 'Sinusoid of Legal History. Learning from Roman Law—A Fascinating Challenge for our (Post) Modernity,' in *Turning Points and Break Lines. Jahrbuch Junge Rechtsgeschichte* 4 (München: Peter Lang, 2009), 454–88; Paulina Święcicka, '*Communis opinio doctorum* comme *ius commune universale*? Réflections autour de l'idée de la culture juridique commune dans l'Europe médiévale et moderne,' *Krakowskie Studia z Historii Państwa i Prawa* 3 (2010), 237–53; Paulina Święcicka, '... *connectiones inter iura variorum observamus...* En recherchant l'explication de la notion d' «acculturation juridique»,' in *Modernisme, tradition et acculturation juridique*, ed. Bart Coppein et al. (Brussel: KVAPBWK, 2011), 7–32; Paulina Święcicka, 'Some Aspects of the Myth of *Communis Opinio Doctorum* as *Ius Commune Universale*,' in *European Traditions: Integration or Disintegrations*, ed. Janwillem Oosterhuis et al. (Nijmegen: Wolf, 2012), 63–84; Paulina Święcicka, '"Przewroty Kopernikańskie" w dziejach europejskiej kultury prawnej—refleksja romanistyczna' ["Copernican Revolutions" in the History of the European Legal Culture—A Reflection of a Romanist], in *Regnare Gubernare Administrare. Prawo i władza na przestrzeni wieków. Prace dedykowane profesorowi Jerzemu Malcowi z okazji 40-lecia pracy naukowej* [*Regnare Gubernare Administrare*. Law and Power over the Centuries. Studies Dedicated to Professor Jerzy Malec], ed. Stanisław Grodziski and Andrzej Dziadzio (Kraków: Oficyna Wydawnicza AFM, 2012), 207–19; for the inventions present in the contemporary narrative on European common law, see Cosmin Sebastian Cercel, 'European Legal Integration as Phantasmagoria: On Jus Commune and Political Theology,' *Journal of Contemporary European Studies* 18/2 (2010), 241–52.

[35] Derrida, 'Parergon,' 141–2.

too large for any presentation' (*der für alle Darstellung beinahe zu gross ist*). A concept can be too big, *almost too big* for presentation. *Colossal* (*kolossalisch*) thus qualifies the presentation, the putting on stage or into presence, the catching-sight, rather, of something, but of something which is not a thing, since it is a concept. And the presentation of this concept inasmuch as it is not presentable. Nor simply unpresentable: *almost unpresentable*. And by reason of its size: it is 'almost too large.' This concept is announced and then eludes presentation on the stage. One would say, by reason of its almost excessive size.[36]

Only emotions deprived of burdens are able to produce the sublime and such emotions may be produced by objects from the past, as not quite clear (so, somehow obscure) and lacking accurate contours. A historian is, in fact, always an externally positioned narrator who does not have handles to the psyche of the people of the past, so the distance that falls between the subject and the object somehow naturally produces fascination and the sublime. The past, because of its irretrievable doom, appears as something categorically different from the present, and this combating of points of view of the presence of the object is one of the cornerstones of Derrida's philosophy.

It follows that in the dominant narrative concerning Roman law and the common legal tradition, the sublime has different faces. First of all, it is the ontological sublime as a certain emotional sensation provoked by Roman law that is felt by a legal historian or a legal practitioner educated in the continental legal culture (where Roman law is continuously taught). But the sensation of the sublime can be triggered also by the narrative itself, which is the rhetorical sublime. These two kinds of sublime can interact and the ontological sublime can lead to the rhetorical sublime, but the rhetorical sublime does not necessarily have to occur, i.e. an admiration for Roman law does not necessarily lead to its evocation in legal discourse. Yet, whenever it occurs, a narrative constructed in such way is usually used as a tool of manipulation, i.e. the text (the narrative)[37] is used to provoke a certain effect—here the effect of sublimation. It is therefore important to clarify that the sublime evoked by the past or by a certain item from it, the feeling of astonishment (Burke) or surprise, the infiltration of respect (Kant), the feeling of the colossal (Derrida), the searching for the unreachable (Lyotard), when mixed with ideology, i.e. approval or disapproval of the source of the sublime, translates itself within the narrative and practical legal discourse into various metaphorical narrations and argumentations. The latter, however, cannot express the sublime itself (because

---

[36] Derrida, 'Parergon,' 124–5.
[37] After Umberto Eco, *I limiti dell'interpretazione* (Milano: Bompiani, 1990), 32–3: '*uso del testo*' as something different from '*interpretazione del testo.*'

it is inexpressible),[38] but can become its substitute. In other words, a legal historian and a practising lawyer may want to convey in the narrative or in an opinion on law their proper feeling of the sublime. They may do so unconsciously (the ontological sublime) or consciously if they want to evoke in the audience the feeling of the sublime (the rhetorical sublime). In this last case the aim is to produce in the *auditorium* a certain mood predetermined by the author of the historical narrative or a particular argument referring to the past, and, at the same time, to submit the audience to a certain form of ideology or to strengthen its acceptance.[39] Such is the predominant historical narrative on Roman law and its impact on legal discourse operated by contemporary lawyers and legal scholars obsessively caught up in the ideology of legal continuity.

9.3 The Dominant Historical Narrative about Roman Law and Roman Legal Tradition: The Sacralization of the Legal Source and the Narrative Concerning the Roman Roots of Institutions of Contemporary Law

Contemporary relevance is always a vital part of writing about history and the progress of scholarship.[40] Writings on legal history have always been influenced by its ideological and cultural context; and historical interpretations served distinct functions of their time, having a clear contemporary purpose. This hypothesis also applies to present studies in law and legal history. We can find good examples of this in studies on the ideological connotations of the supposed continuity between Roman law and modern law, where there is a particular sacralization of historical

---

[38] Derrida, 'Parergon,' 123.

[39] On the problem of impact of certain ideologies on the historical narrative and its objectivity and neutrality, see Peter Novick, *That Noble Dream. The 'Objectivity Question' and the American Historical Profession* (Cambridge: CUP, 1988); Thomas L. Haskell, 'Objectivity is not Neutrality: Rhetoric vs. Practice in Peter Novick's That Noble Dream,' *History and Theory* 29/2 (1990), 129–37; Mark Bevir, 'Objectivity in History,' *History and Theory* 33/3 (1994), 328–44; see also Jerzy Topolski, 'Problemy ideologii, obiektywizmu i neutralności w konstruowaniu narracji historycznej' [Problems of Ideology, Objectivity and Neutrality in the Historical Narrative], in Topolski, *Jak się pisze*, 368–76.

[40] See, e.g. a book by Herbert F. Jolowicz, *Roman Foundations of Modern Law* (Oxford: Clarendon Press, 1957); or those published recently by a Polish Romanist: Wojciech Dajczak, *Dobra wiara jako symbol europejskiej tożsamości prawa* [Good Faith as a Symbol of European Legal Identity] (Poznań: Księgarnia św. Wojciecha, 2006); Wojciech Dajczak, *Rzymska 'res incorporalis' a kształtowanie się pojęć 'rzeczy' i 'przedmiotu praw rzeczowych' w europejskiej nauce prawa prywatnego* [The Roman *res incorporalis* and the Formation of Concepts of 'Thing' and 'Object of Property' in the European Theory of Private Law] (Poznań: UAM, 2007).

sources, especially Justinian's Digest.[41] As Alan Watson put it, 'the Corpus Iuris is so central in history for understanding how law develops, and is so important today.'[42] One can also find examples of this in the narrative on European legal unity, which stresses a common legal past and common legal tradition,[43] even for those countries where the legionary's foot has never stood:

> The influence of Roman law in the modern world has been immense: it constitutes the historical and conceptual basis of many legal systems throughout the world. Its impact has not been confined to those countries in Western Europe that historically formed part of the Roman Empire. Wherever Europeans settled, they normally took their law (usually based to some extent on the principles of Roman law) with them. And some countries, although not witnesses to European settlement, adopted legal codes that were largely based on Roman-law principles. As for those countries with systems derived from the English common law, they too have not been untouched by the influence of Roman law.[44]

The myth of the historical source created via its sacralization, i.e. where the sublimation of the source incarnates remnants of the past regardless of criticisms of the source, ascribes to it a status than is not normal ('normal' here means an ordinary item from the past). Instead, the sublime ascribes to the historical source the status of a 'certificate,' a depository of truth, through the term *fons iuris* (a historical source) itself. This is done in the form of a metaphor (though today a clichéd metaphor, or a conventional one),[45] suggesting that just as pure water flows from its source, the truth flows from a historical source too.

However, in addition to the informational substructure, the recognition of the historical source in myth imposes additional substructures on the historical narrative, namely a persuasive substructure and, more importantly, an ideological substructure which steers the whole narrative.[46] The

---

[41] Watson, *Roman Law and Comparative Law* (Athens GA: University of Georgia Press, 1991), passim.

[42] Watson, *Roman Law*, 79.

[43] See, e.g. Gianni Santucci, 'Introduzione,' in *Fondamenti del diritto europeo. Seminari trentini*, a cura di Gianni Santucci (Napoli: Giuffrè, 2012), 2; Zimmermann, *The Law of Obligations*, passim; Reinhard Zimmerman, *Roman Law, Contemporary Law, European Law. The Civilian Tradition Today* (Oxford: OUP, 2001), 109–10.

[44] Borkowski and du Plessis, *Textbook*, 354.

[45] For more, see George Lakoff and Mark Johnson, *Metaphors We Live By* (Chicago & London: University of Chicago Press, 2003).

[46] On the layers of historical narrative, see especially Hayden White, 'Storytelling: Historical and Ideological,' in *Centuries' Ends, Narrative Means*, ed. Robert Newman (Stanford: Stanford University Press, 1996), 58–78; Jerzy Topolski, 'A Non-Postmodernist Analysis of Historical Narratives,' in *Historiography Between Modernism and Postmodernism. Contributions to the Methodology of the Historical Research. Poznań Studies in the*

selection of the information constitutes the starting point of the narrative and afterwards determines their place in the narrative; prioritizing particular information in the course of the creation of the narrative depends on the aforementioned two additional layers of narrative.

Justinian's Digest, a historical source per se, has been for centuries placed in the sphere of *sacrum*, and such a sacralization was, in fact, somehow presupposed in the narratives of the Romans themselves (D. 50.13.1.5: *est quidem res sanctissima civilis sapientia... ingressus sacramenti* [the knowledge of private law is, indeed, a most hallowed thing]; C. 1.17.15: *{Digesta sunt} ... sanctissimum templum iustitiae dedicatum* [The Digests ... are dedicated to the most sacred temple of justice]).[47] In fact, before the sixteenth century the access to the manuscript of Justinian's Digest called *littera Florentina* regarded as *codex pervetustus*—an archetype, was almost impossible, because it was kept, as an extremely valuable specimen, under lock and key in a special *tabernaculum* named *sancta sanctorum* in the sala delle Udienze of the Medici's Palazzo Vecchio in Firenze. Since the Middle Ages the Digest has embodied and represented the idea of 'true' Roman law as the best developed and the most sophisticated legal system in the ancient world. It has also embodied the idea of Roman law as a system of vigorous capacity, able to renew itself in its subsequent lives,[48] and which even today can serve as a basis for actual governance; and as the idea of Roman law as a particular ethical genius of legal affairs and legal scholarship, and, finally, as the idea of Roman law as the root of the Western legal tradition. In the contemporary dominant narrative, this belief is present particularly in scholarly efforts—inspired by the scientific veracity of a source that legitimized it as a global role model—to establish links, especially genetic

---

Philosophy of the Sciences and the Humanities, ed. Jerzy Topolski (Amsterdam: Rodopi, 1994), 9–85; Topolski, *Jak się pisze*, 101–15, 243.

[47] E.g. Maganzani, *Formazione*; about the manuscript of the Digest and its 'real sacralization,' see in particular *Le Pandette di Giustiniano. Storia e fortuna della « Littera Florentina »*, ed. Enrico Spagnesi (Firenze: Olschki, 1983), passim, 51–60.

[48] After the expression invented in 1909 by Paul Vinogradoff, *Roman Law in Mediaeval Europe* (repr. New Jersey: The Lawbook Exchange, 2001), 4. Following this scholar, many authors developed the idea of 'successive incarnations of Roman Law.' See, e.g. Joseph A. C. Thomas, *Textbook of Roman Law* (Amsterdam et al: North-Holland Publishing Company, 1976), 3: 'the resurrection of Roman law'; or Watson, *Roman Law*, 86–8: 'Roman law reappeared in so many ways at so many times in so many places that one would properly have to speak of "lives".' In Polish legal history, the first to use this concept of 'posthumous life of Roman law' was Stefan Grzybowski, *Dzieje prawa. Opowieść, refleksje, rozważania* [History of Law: Story, Reflection, Deliberation] (Wrocław et al: Ossolineum, 1981), 82–92; also Ewa Borkowska-Bagieńska, 'Prawo rzymskie we współczesnej kulturze prawnej Europy' [Roman Law in the Contemporary Legal Culture of Europe], in *'Honeste vivere'... Księga pamiątkowa ku czci Profesora Władysława Bojarskiego* [Honeste vivere... Liber Amicorum Professor Władysław Bojarski], ed. Ewa Gajda and Andrzej Sokala (Toruń: UMK, 2001), 22; and also—using all these ideas—more recently: Tomasz Giaro, 'Roman Law always dies with a codification,' in Dębiński and Jońca, *Roman Law and European Legal Culture*, 15–26.

ones, of continuity between ancient and modern legal institutions and concepts. Such a belief can also lead to an unconscious use of anachronistic terms to describe any ancient institution (modernization of the notion as a way to sublimate the past).[49] So, an author may state, for example, that the ancient Romans were already aware of notions concerning the protection of the environment or banking transactions.[50] This explains why Tony Honoré added a new subtitle to the second edition of his biography of Ulpianus: 'Pioneer of Human Rights,'[51] probably seeing Ulpian—a late classical jurist—as a champion of equality, dignity, and freedom. This also explains why Franciszek Longchamps de Bérier found the origins of the concept of abuse of right precisely in classical Roman law.[52]

The paradigm of legal continuity has a strong tradition in the history of Roman law: the continued use of writings of classical Roman jurists by Justinian's compilers, the so-called revival of Roman law as a learned law in the eleventh and twelfth centuries, the continued use of Roman law as a learned law (*communis opinio doctorum*), the reception of Roman law in Germany and the *usus modernus Pandectarum*—the practical use of Roman law, and the similarly named Roman-Dutch law. As Myron P. Gilmore asserted, 'the appeal to an unchanging text creates the illusion of

---

[49] See, in particular Hans R. Hoetink, 'Les notions anachroniques dans l'historiographie du droit,' *Tijdschrift voor Rechtsgeschiedenis / Revue d'histoire du droit* 23 (1955), 1–20.

[50] Witold Wołodkiewicz, 'Protection de l'environnement naturel et gestion de l'eau d'hier et d'aujourd'hui,' in *Concepts, pratique et enjeux environnementaux dans l'Empire Romain*, ed. Robert Bedon (Limoges: Pulim, 2005), 53–75; Aniela Talecka and Piotr Niczyporuk, 'Czynności bankowe w starożytnym Rzymie a współczesne polskie prawo bankowe' [Banking in Ancient Rome and in Contemporary Polish Law], in *Pieniądz i banki (tezauryzacja, obieg pieniężny, bankowość)—wspólnota dziejów* [Money and Banks (Thesaurisation, Money Circulation, Banking)—a Common History], ed. Krzysztof Filipow (Warszawa: PTN, 2002), 17–26; Aniela Talecka and Piotr Niczyporuk, 'Rzymska antyczna bankowość wspólnym dziedzictwem Europy' [Ancient Roman Banking as a Common Heritage of Europe], in *Pieniądz-symbol-władza-wojna-wspólne dziedzictwo Europy: studia i materiały* [Money-Symbol-Power-War-Common Heritage of Europe: Studies and Materials], ed. Krzysztof Filipow and Barbara Kuklik (Warszawa: PTN, 2010), 268–82; Aniela Talecka and Piotr Niczyporuk, 'Początki instytucji współczesnego prawa bankowego w starożytności' [The Origins of Modern Banking Law in Antiquity], in *Podstawy materialne państwa. Zagadnienia prawno-historyczne* [The Material Basis of the State. Legal and Historical Issues], ed. Daniel Bogacz and Marek Tkaczuk (Szczecin: WNUS, 2006), 337–52.

[51] Tony Honoré, *Ulpian: Pioneer of Human Rights*, 2nd ed. (Oxford: OUP, 2002).

[52] Franciszek Longchamps de Bérier, *Nadużycie prawa w świetle rzymskiego prawa prywatnego* [The Abuse of Rights in the Light of Roman Private Law] 1st ed. (Wrocław: Fundacja na Recz Nauki Polskiej, 2004), 2nd ed. (Wrocław: Wydawnictwo Uniwersytetu Wrocławskiego, 2007); the Italian edition: *L'abuso del diritto nell'esperienza del diritto privato romano* (Torino: Giappichelli, 2013). The book lead to controversies between Aleksander Stępkowski [*Zeszyty Prawnicze* [UKSW] ('ZP') 5/1 (2005), 255–74; 6/2 (2006), 189–219] and Tomasz Giaro [*ZP* 6/1 (2006), 279–300; 7/1 (2007), 273–91], who discussed precisely the methodological problems of researching Roman law and legal history.

continuity.'⁵³ This effect is even stronger if one regards this historical text as monumental, as a part of the *sacrum*. This enduring idea of continuity and its narrative foundation is perfectly demonstrated in the words of Rudolf von Jhering, who in his introduction to *Geist des römischen Rechts* (1907), wrote:

> Three times had Rome dictated laws to the world, three times bound nations to unity, the first time when the people of Rome were at the height of their power, to the unity of the state, the second time when already fallen into ruin, to the unity of the church, the third time through the reception of Roman law, in the Middle Ages, to the unity of law; the first time with external coercion through the forces of arms, both following times with the might of the spirit.⁵⁴

The aim is to evoke in the audience the same belief as the author had, *i.e.* the belief in legal continuity. However, this impression of a continuum, which an audience is supposed to feel via a particularly shaped narrative of varying degrees of rational and analytical analysis, quite often demonstrates discrepancies between Roman sources and the reconstruction of events in legal historiography. As early as 1955 Hans R. Hoetink warned of the use of anachronistic models and concepts. However, he also admitted that Roman legal historians should employ in their narratives some concepts of modern law, but he cautioned against the influence of particular traditions in interpretation.⁵⁵

The use of Roman law as a precedent is also popular in contemporary legal debates concerning currently binding law and its possible supranational shape. Such an attitude, however, was assumed almost a century ago by the Pandectists. The aforementioned Jhering was one of the first to claim that the Pandectists wished to project their own complicated views on the Romans, and, at the very end of the nineteenth century, he accused his contemporaries (i.e. the Pandectists) of planting the thoughts of modern scholars in the minds of the Romans.⁵⁶

It is, however, quite often clearly obvious that Roman legal history is

---

⁵³ Myron P. Gilmore *Argument from Roman Law in Political Thought 1200–1600* (Cambridge: Harvard University Press, 1941), 3.

⁵⁴ Rudolf von Jhering, *Geist des römischen Rechts* (1907, ed. cit. Aalen 1993), Bd. 1, 1 [trans. Paulina Święcicka].

⁵⁵ Hoetink, *Les notions anachroniques*, 1–20; see also Paulina Święcicka, '*Libertas scribendi—libertas philosophandi*. Some Remarks on the Method of Research in the Field of Legal History in Relation to a Book by Jerzy Kolarzowski, The Idea of Individual Rights in the Writings of the Polish Brethren. Birth of the Concept of Human Rights,' (Warsaw University Press, Warsaw 2009, pp. 241), *Krakowskie Studia z Historii Państwa i Prawa* 5/1 (2012) [publ. 2013], 79–84, published also in Polish in *Czasopismo Prawno-Historyczne* ['CPH'] 64/2 (2012), 223–39.

⁵⁶ Jhering, *Geist*, Bd. 3, 323.

irrelevant to the value of Roman law as contemporary material. As Polish Romanist and legal historian Tomasz Giaro has pointed out, if current law is traced from the past then the distinction between a legal normative discourse and a contemplative historical discourse is rendered impossible. The historical legal dogmatics of the nineteenth century had to preserve, manipulate, and legitimize Roman law.[57] And today, such a narrative also provides legitimacy, firstly, to the Romanists themselves and the continuing relevance of Roman law as a source of legal solutions; secondly, as a particular *tertium comparationis* in comparative studies where the so-called *praesumptio similitudinis* between ancient and modern institutions is often applied;[58] and, finally, as a subject in the university curriculum.[59]

In a strictly historical sense, then, the following constitute false beliefs: 1. Justinian's Digest is the sacred sourcebook reflecting both the ancient and modern image of the world; 2. Roman law was the best developed and most sophisticated legal system in the ancient world; 3. Roman law is at the root of the Western legal tradition, making it particularly Western.[60] But

---

[57] Tomasz Giaro, 'Geltung und Fortgeltung der römischen Juristenrecht,' *Zeitschrift der Savigny-Stiftung für Rechtsgeschichte. Romanistische Abteilung* 111 (1994), 70, 89–91; Tuori, *Ancient Roman Lawyers*, 10–9, 46–9, 61–69, 90–4, 104, 112–20, 124–7, 131–4.

[58] Konrad Zweigert, 'Die "praesumptio similitudinis" als Grundsatzvermutung rechtsvergleichender Methode,' in vol. 2 of *Inchieste di diritto comparato. Scopi e metodi*, ed. Mario Rotondi (Padova-New York: CEDAM, 1973), 735–58; for a critical view, see, inter alia, Roderick Munday, 'Accounting for an encounter,' in *Comparative Legal Studies: Traditions and Transitions*, ed. Pierre Legrand, Roderick Munday (Cambridge: CUP, 2005), 12–4. Cf. also André Aymard, 'L'évolution des methodés de la recherché historique,' in *L'Encyclopédie française* (Paris 1959), vol. 20, 4–20; Juliusz Bardach, 'Metoda porównawcza w zastosowaniu do powszechnej historii państwa i prawa' [A Comparative Method in Use of the History of Law and State], in idem, *Themis a Clio czyli Prawo a Historia* [Themis and Clio, Means Law and History] (Warsaw: Liber, 2001), 99–146.

[59] See, e.g. Wojciech Dajczak, 'Kazusy rzymskich jurystów jako element dzisiejszej edukacji prawniczej' [Cases of Roman Jurists as an Element of Modern Legal Education], in *Wybrane problemy nauki i nauczania prawa* [Selected Problems of Legal Science and the Teaching of Law], ed. Ewa Kozerska et al. (Opole: Wyd. Uniw. Opolskiego, 2010), 93–102; Maria Zabłocka, 'Kształcenie jurysty XXI wieku a prawo rzymskie' [Teaching a Jurist in the 21st Century and Roman Law], *Przegląd Prawniczy Uniwersytetu Warszawskiego* [The Legal Review of the University of Warsaw] 6/2 (2007), 124–34; Jan Zabłocki, 'Il giurista del dopo Duemila. Appunti polacchi,' *Diritto@Storia* 1 (2002), accessed 1 June 2016, http://www.dirittoestoria.it/memorie/Testi%20delle%20Comunicazioni/Jan%20Zablocki.htm; cf. Tomasz Giaro, 'Cywilizacja prawa rzymskiego a problemy współczesnej romanistyki' [The Civilisation of Roman Law and Problems of the Contemporary Romanistics], *Acta Universitatis Wratislaviensis* 305 (2008), 69–78.

[60] Cf. the critique of the idea of the central role of Roman law in European legal history and present unification of Europe, as ideologically founded, by Monateri, *Black Gaius*, 472, 479–555. The author, however, did not reach the core of the continuity argument. Monateri only claimed that Roman law was the spurious root of the Western legal tradition and called for a re-examination of Roman law in the Mediterranean context, especially with regard to its Afro-Semitic roots. So, it is just a critique of a certain tradition of continuity via the foundation of another one.

despite being false, they are still the beliefs that help to form the identity of modern lawyers and as such it is the ideology of continuity that becomes relevant to the scene.

9.4 Impacts of the Ideology of Continuity of the Common Legal Tradition on Legal Practice—the Polish Example

The change of the political system—the transformation—in the countries of 'real socialism' increased and even resurrected interest in Roman law. Poland was no exception.

It has to be explained, however, that even if the attitude to Roman law in the twentieth century in the Soviet Union and countries of real socialism changed over time,[61] in general this law was regarded as the law of the slave-type state, contrary to the vision of the new communist order which was supposed to arise as a result of the global revolution. Roman law as a manifestation of bourgeois law was contrary to the principles of socialist law, where there was no room for such concepts as private property or freedom of contract.[62] There was even an attempt to separate totally the civil law of the socialist countries from the legal doctrine of countries of the still pre-socialist order because the latter based their principles on concepts derived from Roman law.[63] Furthermore, the teaching of Roman law in countries with 'people's democracy' was regarded with hostility. Roman law was considered a subject of mere historical relevance, i.e. irrelevant to laws of the socialist bloc. Its only use was to provide socialist lawyers with some knowledge of the bourgeois law of the enemy, as preparation

---

[61] Compare e.g. the views of the nineteenth century classics of Marxism, such as Marx or Engels, who recognized Roman law as an important factor in the formation of the subsequent socio-economic systems other than the one that created this law. See further Witold Wołodkiewicz, 'Reżimy autorytarne a prawo rzymskie' [Authoritarian Regimes and Roman Law], *CPH* 45/1–2 (1993), 441; Adam Bosiacki, 'Roman Law in Totalitarian Systems. Soviet Union, Italy and Germany—Case Study,' in vol. 1 of *Au-delà des frontières. Mélanges de droit romain offerts à Witold Wołodkiewicz*, ed. Maria Zabłocka et al. (Varsovie: Liber, 2000), 131–8.

[62] Witold Wołodkiewicz, 'Łacińskie paremie prawne w orzecznictwie sądów polskich' [Latin Legal Maxims in the Jurisprudence of Polish Courts], in *Łacińskie paremie w europejskiej kulturze prawnej i orzecznictwie sądów polskich* [Latin Maxims in European Legal Culture and in the Jurisprudence of Polish Courts], ed. Witold Wołodkiewicz and Jerzy Krzynówek (Warszawa: Liber, 2001), 8, where some ideas expressed by Lenin or Stalin concerning Roman law and the Latin language are presented; see also Bosiacki, 'Roman Law in Totalitarian Systems,' 133–4.

[63] René David, *Les grands systèmes de droit contemporains*, 6th ed. (Paris: Dalloz, 1974), 22–8, about four main law families; Wołodkiewicz, 'Reżimy,' 437–44; Witold Wołodkiewicz, 'Il diritto romano quale fattore d'integrazione dei diversi sistemi giuridici europei (Oservazione sulla classificazione delle famiglie del diritto proposta da René David,' in *Europa e le sue regioni*, ed. Enzo Sciacca (Palermo: Arnaldo Lombardi, 1993), 305–11.

to combat them effectively or to conduct business with them for the good of the Soviet Union.[64]

In the Polish People's Republic, despite the reforms in the system of education effected in 1946, lectures on Roman law were not abolished.[65] In 1949 Jan Wasilkowski, one of Polish specialists in civil law and, later, one of the main authors of the Polish Civil Code of 1964, emphasized that the importance of teaching Roman law stemmed from the fact that it achieved an extremely high degree of progression and was even the most developed law in general, and that it provided an ideal *tertium comparationis* for modern lawyers and a treasury of information about the evolution of legal concepts and legal institutions.[66] Other great representatives of Polish legal science, representing the disciplines of positive law and theory of the state and law, such as Witold Czachórski,[67] Alfred Ohanowicz,[68] Jan Gwiazdomorski,[69] and Adam Szpunar,[70] propounded similar ideas, although there were some opponents among the representatives of Polish legal dogmatics. Despite the skeptical voices, Roman law survived in Poland as a subject in the university curriculum. In those times it was mainly considered as a propaedeutic to civil law and civil procedure or a starting point for comparative studies,[71] although Polish Romanists of those times stressed its importance for the process of the general training

---

[64] See more deep analyzis see Elemér Polay, 'L'insegnamento del diritto romano nei paesi socialisti,' *Index* 1 (1970), 131–43; cf. Witold Wołodkiewicz, 'L'insegnamento e lo studio di diritto romano nei paesi ex socialisti'—a paper presented at VII Colloquio dei romanisti dell'Europa centro-orientale e d'Italia, Rome 3–5 December 1998 (photocopy).

[65] For more details see: Witold Wołodkiewicz, 'L'insegnamento del diritto romano in Polonia,' *Index* 6 (1976), 383–94; Witold Wołodkiewicz, 'Il diritto romano nella cultura giuridica polacca,' in vol. 7 of *Sodalitas. Scritti in onore di Antonio Guarino*, ed. Vincenzo Giuffrè (Napoli: Jovene, 1984), 3389–409; Witold Wołodkiewicz, 'Il diritto romano e la cultura giuridica d'oggi,' *Drevnee pravo* 13 (1998), 159–68.

[66] Jan Wasilkowski, 'Reforma studiów prawniczych' [The Reform of Legal Education], *Życie i Myśl* 6–7 (1949), 329–30. See also Borys Łapicki, 'O humanistycznym wychowaniu prawnika' [About a Humanistic Education of a Lawyer], *Państwo i Prawo* ['PiP'] 3/5–6 (1948), 90–7. Compare Rafał Taubenschlag, 'Nauka i nauczanie prawa rzymskiego i antycznego w Polsce' [Science and the Teaching of Roman law and Ancient Law in Poland], *Życie Nauki* 5/3–8 (1950), 647–55. See also a survey on teaching of legal history subjects at the faculties of law carried out in countries of real socialism, announced in the Polish Journal: CPH 9/1 (1957), 393–420; CPH 9/2 (1957), 391–434; see also a detailed analysis by Wołodkiewicz, 'Łacińskie paremie,' 10–3.

[67] CPH 21/2 (1969), 169.
[68] CPH 21/2 (1969), 176.
[69] CPH 22/1 (1970), 198.
[70] CPH 21/2 (1969), 181–2.
[71] E.g. Adam Wiliński, 'Das Problem einer didaktischen Zusammenarbeit von Romanisten und Zivilisten,' in *Einzelne Probleme der Rechtsgeschichte und des römischen Recht. Acta Universitatis Szegediensis de Attila József Nominatae. Acta Juridica et Politica* 17/27 (1970), 343–6; Kazimierz Kolańczyk, 'Über den Bildungswert der römischen Ziviprozesslehre für den sozialistischen Juristen,' in *Einzelne Probleme*, 279–99.

of a lawyer.⁷²
The collapse of real socialism caused many new social and legal problems. In the process of the transformation of European post-communist states the principles of the market economy coincided (and still coincide) with remnants of the socialist system.⁷³ The aspirations of the former Soviet bloc countries to join the European structures brought about another fundamental transformation. Amendments and new codifications of civil and commercial law meant that the representatives of civil law doctrine felt the need for knowledge of Roman law in their search for the Roman roots of the institutions of contemporary Polish law.⁷⁴ In the face of a particular ideological vacuum, which appeared after the removal of socialist ideology, there was a need to fill the void. Old but still colossal Roman law served (and constantly serves) this purpose perfectly. And, as it seems, in post-transformation Polish legal scholarship and legal practice Roman law has worked not only as a foundation of Polish legal solutions, but also as a symbol (the so-called myth of Riccardo Orestano's *romanesimo*, i.e.

---

⁷² Marek Kuryłowicz, 'Wokół zagadnień nauczania prawa rzymskiego' [Issues Concerning the Teaching of Roman Law], *Życie Szkoły Wyższej* 22/3–4 (1974), 57–63; see also Wacław Osuchowski, Program studiów uniwersyteckich w zakresie prawa rzymskiego' [The University Programme of the Teaching of Roman Law], *CPH* 18/1 (1966), 279–84; Jan Baszkiewicz, O modernizacji studiów prawniczych i administracyjnych' [About Modernisation of Education in Law and Administration], *PiP* 4 (1975), 30–3; Henryk Kupiszewski, 'Znaczenie prawa rzymskiego dla współczesności' [The Importance of Roman Law for Contemporaneity], *PiP* 8 (1981), 69–80; Janusz Sondel, 'O współczesnych wartościach prawa rzymskiego' [On the Contemporary Values of Roman Law], *Przegląd Humanistyczny* 20/8 (1983), 85–93; Mieczysław Żołnierczuk, 'Rola prawa rzymskiego w kształtowaniu polskiego prawnika' [The Role of Roman Law in Formation of a Polish Lawyer], *Rzeszowskie Zeszyty Naukowe „Prawo-Ekonomia-Rolnictwo"* 1 (1983), 7–20.

⁷³ See, in particular Rafał Mańko 'The Unification of Private Law in Europe from the Perspective of Polish Legal Culture,' *Yearbook of Polish European Studies* 11 (2007–8), 117–24; Rafał Mańko, 'Unifikacja europejskiego prawa prywatnego z perspektywy społeczeństwa polskiego—przyczynek do dyskusji' [Unification of Private Law in Europe and the Polish Society], *Nowa Europa. Przegląd Natoliński* 2 (2008), 47–51; Rafał Mańko, 'Is the Socialist Legal Tradition…,' 86–8, and for some examples in civil procedure: 88–102; Rafał Mańko, 'Survivals of the Socialist Legal Tradition? A Polish Perspective,' *Comparative Law Review* 4/2 (2013), 1–28; Rafał Mańko, Weeds in the Gardens of Justice? The Survivals of Hyperpositivism in Polish Legal Culture as a Symptom / Sinthome,' *Pólemos: Journal of Law, Literature and Culture* 7/2 (2013), 207–33.

⁷⁴ See, some general remarks by Witold Wołodkiewicz, 'Il diritto romano nei paesi del "socialismo reale" ed il cambiamento delle opinioni dopo il crollo del sistema totalitario,' in *Diritto romano e regimi totalitari nel '900 europeo. Atti del seminario internazionale. Trento, 20–21 ottobre 2006*, ed. Massimo Miglietta (Trento: Università degli Studi di Trento, 2009), 143–73. And for more detailed analysis see especially Mańko, 'Survival,' 1–2; Mańko, 'Is the Socialist Legal Tradition…,' 86–8, who, e.g. pointed out that in the 'Commentary on the Polish Code of Civil Procedure,' published in 1996 and designated properly for legal practitioners, a cassation was linked directly with the French Revolution; and the history of appeal was presented from Roman law until the Polish Pre-War Code of Civil Procedure 1930, with a rupture in 1950 and its resurrection in 1996.

the idea always referred to Roman law) of just law, a hypostasis of several various aspirations for justice or for the rationality of the legal solution—law written in capital letters.[75] Roman law was and still is considered to be a factor that shapes modern legal culture in Poland as belonging to a common Europe founded on Roman law,[76] or as a sign of the return of the *aetas aurea* of the market economy.[77] Hence the title of a study written by one Polish Romanist, Bronisław Sitek, sounds symptomatic: '*Roma communis nostra patria est* (D. 50.1.33) or perhaps *Europa communis nostra patria est?*' [Rome is our common homeland (D. 50.1.33) or perhaps Europe is our common homeland?].[78] At the same time the ideological obsession with Roman law as the basis of any European (thus Polish) legal order is accompanied by the tendency to cut Poland off, even by force, from the legal remnants of communism.[79] Putting Roman law on a pedestal is a way to search for a new Polish identity and to justify the presence of a new Poland in Europe—a new Poland as a country with the same elements of legal tradition as the longed-for West, no matter which elements the Polish legal system has actually built.[80]

---

[75] Orestano, *Introduzione*, 457. The concept of *romanesimo* was and still is very popular in the Polish literature on Roman law and many Polish Romanists recall it repeatedly.

[76] To quote only a few Polish authors: Marek Kuryłowicz, 'Prawo rzymskie jako fundament europejskiej kultury prawnej' [Roman Law as a Cornerstone of European Legal Culture], ZP 1 (2001), 9–25; Marek Kuryłowicz, 'The Importance of Roman Law in Shaping European Legal Culture,' in *European Integration through Education. Traditions the Present and the Future,* ed. Ryszard Kucha (Lublin: UMCS, 2004), 25–35; Antoni Dębiński, 'Rola i znaczenie prawa rzymskiego w dziejach prawa Europy' [The Role and Importance of Roman Law in the History of European Law], in *'Gaudium et Litteris.' Księga Jubileuszowa ku czci Księdza Arcybiskupa Profesora Stanisława Wielgusa* ['Gaudium et Litteris.' A Jubilee Book of Archibishop Professor Stanisław Wielgus] (Lublin: Wydawnictwo KUL, 2009), 501–10; Antoni Dębiński, 'Prawo rzymskie jako fundament europejskiej kultury prawnej' [Roman Law as a Fundament of the European Legal Culture], *Przegląd Uniwersytecki KUL* 5–6 (2009), 22–5, also published in *'Amicus hominis et defensor iustitiae.' Księga Jubileuszowa w 70. Rocznicę urodzin Sędziego Ferdynanda Rymarza* ['Amicus hominis et defensor iustitiae.' A Jubilee Book of Judge Ferdynand Rymarz], Lublin 2010, 133–9; Witold Sobczak, 'Prawo rzymskie źródłem europejskiej kultury prawnej' [Roman Law as a Source of the European Legal Culture], *Fundamenta Europaea* 2/2–3 (2003), 41–5; Borkowska-Bagieńska, 'Prawo rzymskie,' 21–7; Karolina Wyrwińska, 'Prawo rzymskie kluczem do zrozumienia dziedzictwa prawnego Europy. Uwagi na marginesie europejskich tendencji do harmonizacji prawa prywatnego' [Roman Law as Key to Understanding European Legal Heritage. Some Remarks on European Tendencies of Harmonisation in Private Law], in *'Leges Sapere.' Studia i prace dedykowane Profesorowi Januszowi Sondlowi w 50-tą rocznicę pracy naukowej* ['Leges Sapere.' Studies Dedicated to Professor Janusz Sondel], ed. Wacław Uruszczak et al. (Kraków: WUJ, 2008), 697–706.

[77] Wołodkiewicz, 'Łacińskie paremie,' 15.

[78] Bronisław Sitek, '*Roma communis nostra patria est* (D. 50.1.33) czy może *Europa communis nostra patria est?*,' *Studia Prawnoustrojowe* 12 (2010), 219–29.

[79] Mańko, 'Survival,' 1–2; Mańko, 'Is the Socialist Legal Tradition...,' 86–8.

[80] E.g. it is very popular these days to start any topic concerning a particular Polish legal institution with the statement that: 'There were ancient Romans who had already known,

A peculiar manifestation of this sublimation of Roman law in contemporary Poland, in addition to the aforementioned longing for the common European roots of certain institutions of contemporary Polish law (though, as it was emphasized, without paying attention to the fact that contemporary Polish legal solutions may differ from Roman ones),[81] is the frequent reference to Roman law and quotation of Latin legal maxims, i.e. maxims coined in ancient times or later in connection with the preserved sources of Roman law. In legal practice this can be observed not only in various courts,[82] but also in the declarations of other authorities involved in public life.[83] This Polish reality is, of course, not an isolated phenomenon

applied, invented etc. something.' See Zabłocka, *Romanistyka polska po II wojnie światowej*, 161–5; Zabłocka, *Romanistyka polska w pierwszym dziesięcioleciu XXI wieku*, 135–53. Such an approach is not totally without sense, but seems to be justifiably allowed only when the author is able to show every subsequent step of transfer of the particular legal idea from ancient times up to the present. See a criticism of such an a-historical attitude, described as 'omnia in Corpore Iuris inveniantur' by Tomasz Giaro in Pier Giuseppe Monateri, Tomasz Giaro, and Alessandro Somma, *Le radici comuni del diritto europeo. Un cambiamento della perspectiva* (Roma: Carocci, 2005), 110–4. Compare several studies by Rafał Mańko, n. 73, who dedicated himself to the search for remnants of the socialist legal tradition in Polish law and also in Polish legal culture understood as a culture of legal professionals. The author termed these legal remnants—legal survivals of the past fifty years—symptoms: see Mańko, 'Weeds,' 210, 225–33. Cf. also Mańko, 'Demons of the Past?' ch. 4 of the present volume.

[81] E.g. Witold Wołodkiewicz, 'Tradycja prawa rzymskiego we współczesnym prawie cywilnym' [The Roman Law Tradition in Contemporary Civil Law], *Palestra* 10–11 (1987), 66–85; Witold Wołodkiewicz, 'I cambiamenti del codice civile polacco dopo 1989 possono essere trattati come segno del ritorno alla tradizione romanistica?,' in *The Roman Law Tradition in Societies in Transition. Proceeding of the International Conference held in Prague 14–16 May 2002*, ed. Petr Belovský and Michal Skřejpek (Praha: Vodnář, 2003), 129–42; Władysław Rozwadowski, 'Tradycje rzymskie w polskim prawie cywilnym' [Roman Traditions in Polish Civil Law], in *System Prawa Prywatnego. Prawo cywilne—część ogólna* [System of Private Law. Civil Law—A General Part], ed. Marek Safjan (Warszawa: CH Beck, 2007), 1–28; Antoni Dębiński, 'Roman Law and Polish Legal Culture,' *Review of Comparative Law* 10–11 (2005–6), 10–21; Antoni Dębiński, 'Roman Law and the Legal Culture of Poland,' in *A Synthesis of Polish Law*, ed. Tadeusz Guz et al. (Frankfurt am Main: Peter Lang, 2009), 41–58, published also in Polish in *Prawo polskie. Próba syntezy*, ed. Tadeusz Guz et al. (Warszawa: CH Beck, 2009), 39–54.

[82] See Witold Wołodkiewicz, 'I brocardi latini nella pratica giudiziaria polacca. A proposto delle iscrizioni latine sul nuovo Palazzo di Giustizia di Varsavia,' *IURA. Rivista Internazionale di Studi Romanistici* 47 (1996), 27–41; Witold Wołodkiewicz, 'Łacińskie paremie prawnicze w polskiej praktyce prawniczej' [Latin Legal Maxims in Polish Legal Practice], *Meander* 55/4 (2000), 279–99; Witold Wołodkiewicz, 'Łacińskie paremie,' 7–30; Piotr Pogonowski, 'Znaczenie paremii rzymskich dla współczesnej procedury cywilnej' [The Importance of the Roman Maxims for Modern Civil Procedure], in *Starożytne kodyfikacje prawa* [Ancient Codifications of Law], ed. Antoni Debiński (Lublin: KUL, 2000), 187–98; Marek Sobczyk, 'Łacińskie paremie prawnicze w polskim postępowaniu cywilnym' [Latin Legal Maxims in Polish Civil Procedure], *Zeszyty Naukowe Wyższej Szkoły Suwalsko-Mazurskiej* 10 (2005), 80–102; Andrzej Sokala, 'Del significato delle regole del diritto romano per attuale diritto reale polacco,' in *Leges Sapere*, 527–36.

[83] Magdalena Marquez, 'Paremie łacińskie w wystąpieniach Rzecznika Praw Obywatelskich' [Latin Maxims in exposés of the Polish Ombudsman], in *Łacińskie paremie*,

as it is the practice in many European countries as well as at pan-European level.[84] Here again we can find decisions of courts or of other authorities using old maxims (sometimes even with a proper explanation of their ancient provenance), quoted in the original Latin, which is still regarded as *lingua franca* of lawyers across Europe.[85]

> The Latin juridical rules derived from our common legal history have caused, for the moment, a larger consensus in the Board of Appeal of the European Patent Office than provisions of national laws. ... The Enlarged Board of Appeal read the Digest too. ... Whoever wishes to succeed before this Board should forget the national codifications of the last three centuries and turn to the ancient common law of Europe as it was produced—in a still comprehensible form—in Latin language.[86]

The following are examples from Polish legal practice.[87] In 1922 the Supreme Court,[88] in a case concerning the crime of abandoning an infant according to Art. 490 of the then binding Penal Code of Tagancev (1903), referred to the Roman construction of a crime known as '*expositio*

227–44. See also Witold Wołodkiewicz, 'Prawo rzymskie w wypowiedziach polskich parlamentarzystów' [Roman Law in Statements of Polish Deputies], Palestra 52/9–10 (2007), 184–98; Witold Wołodkiewicz, 'La nozione "diritto romano" nelle polemiche del Parlamento polacco dopo la trasformazione del sistema politico,' in vol. 8 of *Fides Humanitas Ius. Studi in onore di Luigi Labruna*, ed. Carla Masi Doria and Cosimo Cascione (Napoli: Editoriale Scientifica, 2007), 5959–73.

[84] See, e.g. Karol Rebro, *Latinské právnické výrazy a výroky* (Bratislava: Vydatelstvo Obzor, 1986); Rolf Lieberwirth, *Lateinische Fachausdrücke im Recht* (Heidelberg: C.F. Müller, 1986); Aleksander Stępkowski, 'Maksymy prawne na Wyspach Brytyjskich' [Legal Maxims in Great Britain], in *Łacińskie paremie*, 71–107; Heikki E.S. Mattila, 'Locuzioni e brocardi latini nei linguaggi giuridici moderni,' *Diritto@Storia* 6 (2007); Rolf Knütel, '*Ius commune* und Römisches Recht vor Gerichten der Europäischen Union,' *Juristische Schulung* 36 (1996), 768–78, published also in Italian: 'Diritto romano e *ius commune* davanti a corti dell'Unione Europea,' in vol. 3 of *Nozione formazione e interpretazione del diritto dall'età romana alle esperienze moderne. Ricerche dedicate al professor Filippo Gallo*, a cura di Silvio Romano et al. (Napoli: Jovene, 1997), 521–57; David A.O. Edward, 'The Role and Relevance of the Civil Law Tradition in the Work of the European Court of Justice,' in *The Civilian Tradition and Scots Law: Aberdeen Quincentenary Essays*, ed. David L. Carey Miller, Reinhard Zimmermann (Berlin: Duncker & Humblot, 1997), 309–20; Jean Michael Rainer, 'Il diritto romano nelle sentenze delle Corti europee,' in *L'anima 'europea' dell'Europa*, ed. Danilo Castellano (Napoli: Edizioni Scientifiche Italiane, 2002), 45–50; Francisco Javier Andrés Santos, 'Epistemological Value of Roman Legal Rules in European and Comparative Law,' *European Review of Private* 3 (2004), 347–57; Marek Sobczyk, 'Prawo rzymskie przed sądami Wspólnot Europejskich' [Roman Law at the Courts of the European Communities], *Studia Prawnoustrojowe* 7 (2007), 279–94.

[85] Cf. Marike Ristikivi, 'Latin: The Common Legal Language of Europe?,' *Juridica International* 10 (2005),199–202.

[86] Knütel, '*Ius commune*,' 777 [trans. Paulina Święcicka].

[87] Examples are taken from the Polish database: System Informacji Prawnej 'LEX Omega' [Trans. Paulina Święcicka].

[88] SN 30.05.1922, OSN(K) 1922/1/335; LEX no. 948644.

infantium' (exposition of infants) and explained that

> in ancient Rome abandoning infants was somewhat widespread, which, in the third century after Christ, grew to an intimidating size, and therefore the Roman Empire from the time of Christians started the fight back, enforced in the Decree of Constantine the Great issued in 318 and in the Novel 153 passed by Justinian in 331. Roman law differentiated between two types of abandoning infants: a) the abandonment in hazardous, difficult conditions (in deserted places, in woods, in baskets thrown into a river etc.), which was punished as a murder, and b) the abandonment in non-dangerous circumstances (*expositio publicis locis vel sanctis*), which was not penalized. This classification was introduced into the canon law and the Germanic laws and remained in force throughout the Middle Ages and onwards.

In a decision in 1923,[89] the Supreme Court resorted to Roman law in order to justify the need to penalize the 'humiliation of the state and the nation,' by pointing out that 'already at the time of the Caesars of Rome, verbal insults affecting the dignity of the State were regarded as crimes,' and even citing a fragment from *Pauli Sententiae*, '*Quod crimen non solum facto, sed et verbis impiis ac maledictis maxime exacerbatur* (Paul Sent. lib. V lit. XXIX § 1).'

In a 1934 decision,[90] the Supreme Court referred to Roman law in order to interpret Art. 231-2 Penal Code (1932) regarding abortion. The Court rejected the literal interpretation in favour of one based on Roman law, pointing out that although 'the wording of Art. 231 and 232 of the Polish Penal Code suggests that the crime penalized by Art. 231 is considered *delictum proprium* of a pregnant woman,' nevertheless:

> Under influence of Roman law, according to which the foetus (*nasciturus*) was a part of the mother's body, and for this reason the abortion was not regarded as an attempt on life of an independent human being, or that due to a particular mental state of the pregnant woman the pregnant woman deserves less severe treatment than others who commit an attempt on the foetus' life in the womb.

Turning to more recent examples of references to Roman law in the Polish Supreme Court case law, a case from 1992[91] in which the Roman maxim *nemo plus iuris ad alium transferre potest quam ipse habet* was found to be binding in Polish private law as 'an unwritten rule' that constitutes a general principle and that individual articles of the Code (like Art. 169) are only exceptions from it.

---

[89] SN 12.06.1923, OSN(K) 1923/1/153; LEX no. 919903.
[90] SN 17.05.1934, III K 412/34; LEX no. 75742.
[91] SN 30.03.1992, III CZP 18/92; LEX no. 3758.

Interpreting the scope and effects of the abuse of right doctrine (Art. 5 Civil Code 1964), the Supreme Court in a 1995 case referred to the Roman notion of '*ultimum remedium*,'[92] pointing out that:

> Already in Roman law the *ultimum remedium* institution was introduced, that is the institution of final measure according to which persons wrongfully affected by negative effects of the application of the law, may receive help. Transmission of the principle into modern law is undoubtedly seen in the general clause of Art. 5 Polish Civil Code which can be used in such cases.

In a 2000 case,[93] the Supreme Court found that the rules on calculating time in the Civil Code are actually an application of 'the *computatio civilis* principle, elaborated in the Roman tradition, which regarded a calendar day as the smallest unit of time in calculation.'

Three years later, in a 2003 decision,[94] the Supreme Court found that 'the Roman principle *nemo potest commodum capere de iniuria sua propria* is still valid, so no one can benefit from an injustice that he has committed,' and therefore a 'perpetual crime in omission does not change over time into a licit action.'

In 2010,[95] the Supreme Court declared that despite the imprecise definition of a term in Art. 492 Polish Civil Code (1964), the clause *lex commissoria* mentioned therein belongs to regulations already known to Roman law, so 'in the case of the preliminary contract it is permissible to claim a contractual right of withdrawal.'

There are several judgments concerning the liability for damage caused by water pouring from one apartment to another, such as the following 2012 case in which the Supreme Court linked the contemporary binding rule of liability (Art. 433 Polish Civil Code) with Art. 150 Code of Obligation (1933) stating that such a rule has a long pedigree in European legal traditions,[96] i.e. 'it derives from the Roman *actio de effusis vel deiectis*, introduced in pretorian law during the period of the Republic and then adopted by Justinian's legislation.' The Court also gave a proper historical justification for the introduction of such a rule by a Roman magistrate, declaring, inter alia, that:

> The main aim of this remedy was to protect traffic, therefore its introduction was justified both by a need to ensure the safety of people and things in the streets (the protection of the public interest), as well as a need to ensure the victim a real ability to repair the damage when the indication of the real

---

[92] SN 21.07.1995, WZ 143/95; LEX no. 24572.
[93] SN 22.08.2000, IV CZ 60/00; LEX no. 530647.
[94] SN 29.10.2003, IV KK 250/02; LEX no. 152075.
[95] SN 24.06.2010, IV CSK 67/10; LEX no. 621351.
[96] SN 18.07.2012, III CZP 41/12; LEX no. 1289172.

perpetrator of this tort was in many cases impossible or, at least, very difficult (the protection of private interests).

A similar rationalization was repeated in the resolution of the Supreme Court of 19 February 2013,[97] where the court revealed that:

> From Roman times to the introduction of water supply and sewage systems in cities, liability for *effusum vel deiectum* was primarily useful for redressing damages caused by rubbish being thrown out into the streets. Therefore, this aim supports the idea of maintaining its traditional function by the current provision.

Finally, in a 2014 case dealing with the problem of a delay in filing a motion by a complainant,[98] the Court of Appeal in Wrocław a justified a negative decision with the reference to the principle *ignorantia iuris nocet* as 'known for over two thousand years, and derived from Roman law.'

In this way the Polish judicial authorities continue a kind of tradition of using Roman law arguments (*argumentum ex iure romano*) as if they were universal, a tradition formed in the interwar period of the Second Republic of Poland,[99] when knowledge of Roman law was considered a *condicio sine qua non* of being a properly educated and trained lawyer.[100]

What is more, reaching for Roman law is undoubtedly attested to by the conviction of those who apply the law that when they arrive at the supposed roots of contemporary universal legal knowledge, they consider law so applied as the manifestation of the wisdom of a legal culture created under the influence of Roman law and 'ancient legal truth.' While this can be the result of the application of the unconscious remains of ancient Roman law and *ius commune* in the minds of judges, it also serves as a way to strengthen the authority of Polish law in its link with this admired and monumental tradition.

> Law requires authority. This need frequently bends law out shape. Law is wanted, say needed, by a judge. But there is no authority. The judge cannot say: 'This is my judgment because I like it!' So the judge borrows from an approved system such as Roman law.[101]

But is there nothing more to it? Perhaps it is rather a search for the

---

[97] SN 19.02.2013, III CZP 63/12; LEX no. 1271658.
[98] SA Wrocł. 14.05.2014, II AKa 118/14; LEX no. 1466730.
[99] Cf. e.g. Wojciech Dajczak, 'Łacińskie terminy i paremie w polskim orzecznictwie do prawa rzeczowego BGB z lat 1920–1939' [Latin Terms and Phrases in Polish Judgements in Law of Property in Relation to BGB in 1920–1939], *CPH* 55/2 (2003), 265–72.
[100] For more details see Witold Wołodkiewicz, 'Nauczanie prawa w II Rzeczypospolitej' [The Teaching of Law in the Second Republic of Poland], *Życie Szkoły Wyższej* 21/6 (1973), 103–20.
[101] Watson, *Comparative Law*, 101.

'opium' of Roman law as a remedy for the aforementioned emptiness that arose (because it always arises) as a result of the revolution in the legal system subsequent to the 1990s systemic transformation. One can even say that for the last two centuries lawyers in Poland have lived continuous legal revolutions,[102] resulting in a lack of continuity.[103] In the light of such discontinuity, the Polish legal community needs and seeks out something that can give a sense of security and a cultural and historical identity etc., and the ideology of legal continuity from ancient to modern times provides the answer. Therefore, due to the break of legal continuity in 1795, Polish lawyers find their national identity in Roman law, just as the nineteenth century German Pandectists found theirs in Roman law as opposed to the Germanists.[104] In fact, as Rafał Mańko has pointed out, the interwar period (1918–39) was too short to form the 'Polish' basis of continuity for modern Polish lawyers, hence, the popularity of having recourse to Rome following the transformation from actually existing socialism to capitalism in 1989.[105] It thus seems that this particular 'iusromano-gigantomania' is part of a broader ideological post-transformational policy pursued by lawyers for lawyers as well as for the rest of the society.

In Poland such iusromano-gigantomania is also clearly evidenced by the presence of eighty-six inscriptions of Latin legal maxims on the new building of the Supreme Court in Warsaw,[106] a huge number of studies on the presence of Latin maxims in Polish legal practice,[107] and several compendia of maxims useful for a courtroom or legal practice in general.[108]

[102] See Mańko, 'Unifikacja,' 55.
[103] See, in general Henryk Kupiszewski, 'Continuità nel diritto,' *Studia Iuridica* 12 (1985), 181–4; but regarding the notions of continuity and discontinuity and a particular dialectical tension between them: Mańko, 'Weeds,' 212–4; Mańko, 'Is the Socialist Legal Tradition...,' 84–5.
[104] See, in particular, Tuori, *Ancient Roman Lawyers*, 124–134; see also Giaro, 'Geltung,' 69–71.
[105] Mańko, 'Unifikacja,' 50.
[106] See Wołodkiewicz, 'Łacińskie paremie,' 24–30; Witold Wołodkiewicz, 'Le iscrizioni latine sull'edificio nuovo della Corte Suprema a Varsavia come segno d'interesse in Polonia per la tradizione del diritto Romano,' *Ius antiquum* 9 (2002), 225–34; Witold Wołodkiewicz, 'Introduction' in Agnieszka Kacprzak, Jerzy Krzynówek, and Witold Wołodkiewicz, *Łacińskie inskrypcje na kolumnach Sądu Najwyższego Rzeczypospolitej Polskiej* [*Regulae iuris. The Latin inscriptions on the columns of the Building of the Supreme Court of the Republic of Poland*], ed. Witold Wołodkiewicz, 3rd ed. (Warszawa: CH Beck, 2006), 13–5; see also Rafał Mańko, 'The Culture of Private Law in Central Europe after Enlargement: A Polish Perspective,' *European Law Journal* 11/5 (2005), 544–7.
[107] See studies mentioned in nn. 82 and 83.
[108] See, e.g. Jerzy Pieńkos, '*Praecepta iuris.' Łacina dla prawników. Terminy, paremie, wyrażenia w porządku systematycznym* ['Praecepta iuris.' Latin for Lawyers. Terms, Maxims, Expressions in the Systematic Order] (Warszawa: Oficyna Prawnicza Muza SA, 1999); *Łacińska terminologia prawnicza* [Latin Legal Terminology], ed. Jerzy Zajadło (Warszawa: Wolters Kluwer Polska, 2005); Krzysztof Burczak and Antoni Dębiński, and Maciej Jońca, *Łacińskie sentencje i powiedzenia prawnicze* [Latin Legal Maxims and Dicta]

Sometimes these rules are combined directly with Roman law or the Roman legal tradition,[109] and sometimes they are even linked with other ethical commandments that are considered universal.[110]

Lech Gardocki, the former first president (chief judge) of the Polish Supreme Court, declared:

> With the passing of time, the more we move away from the completion of the construction of the new building of the Supreme Court, the more the Latin inscriptions placed on the columns appear to us as a natural and obvious component of the building. I am convinced that it was a good idea. ... The edifice was created in a way to give it the appearance of being coated with the 'patina of time.' Latin inscriptions placed on it are also a kind of 'intellectual patina.' Whilst reading the inscriptions we feel a sense of continuity of civilization, we remind ourselves of our relationships with Roman civilization, with Roman law, as well as with subsequent sources, largely inspired by Roman models.[111]

It would appear that in the post-communist era, lawyers from the countries of 'new democracy' need Roman law as a myth and a symbol much more desperately than lawyers from the West. Iusromanogigantomania is a specific component in the Polish post-transformational mentality of lawyers. Perhaps it is even an element of the 'transformation syndrome.'[112]

9.5 Conclusions

Bernard Lewis claimed that there are two social purposes for remembering the past: one is to explain and justify the present; the other is to control the future. For both of these purposes, there is a rich tradition of invention

---

(Warszawa: CH Beck, 2007); Wojciech Bojarski and Wojciech Dajczak, and Andrzej Sokala, *Verba iuris. Reguły i kazusy prawa rzymskiego* ['Verba iuris.' Maxims and Cases of Roman Law], 3rd ed. enlarged (Toruń: Wydawnictwo Dom Organizatora, 2007); Marek Kuryłowicz, *Słownik terminów, zwrotów i sentencji prawniczych łacińskich oraz pochodzenia łacińskiego* [A Dictionnary of Latin Terms, Frases and Legal Maxims and Derived from Latin], 4th ed. (Warszawa: Wolters Kluwer Polska, 2012).

[109] See, e.g. Maria Zabłocka, 'Ustawa XII Tablic źródłem zasad współczesnego prawa' [The Law of the Twelve Tables as a Source of the Principles of Modern Law], in *Honeste vivere*, 287–302; Maria Zabłocka, 'Le XII Tavole—fonte dei principi del diritto contemporaneo,' *IURA. Rivista Internazionale di Studi Romanistici* 53 (2002), 1–16.

[110] E.g. Maria Zabłocka, 'Reguły prawa rzymskiego do dziesięciu przykazań Bożych' [The Principles of Roman Law in Relation to the Ten Divine Commandments], ZP 1 (2001), 71–8; Maria Zabłocka, 'Regulae iuris Romani ad «Leges divinarum tabularum decem»,' *Łacińskie paremie*, 31–43.

[111] Lech Gardocki, 'Przedmowa' (*Preface*), in *Regulae iuris*, xi. [trans. Paulina Święcicka].

[112] Cf. Mańko, 'Weeds,' 210, 225–33.

to embellish, correct, and censor the image of the past in both popular and academic history.[113]

The fact that the dominant narrative concerning Roman law, Roman legal tradition and jurisprudential law has been used to create a sense of unity between the legal past and the legal present is an example of the creation of the ideology of continuity. The shared values and ideals of today are founded in the presentation of the past via its sublimation. Therefore, the notions of shared past and the continuity from the ancients to the present are fundamental constants in the modern history of Roman law and European legal tradition. This concept of legal continuity has its direct roots in the Historical School and its way of presenting itself in the role of a direct descendant of Roman legal tradition. Also today such a concept consists in the belief in the Roman foundations of contemporary law and contemporary legal science. Just as all creative narratives are assumed to be based on historical sources, so the one here referred to as the dominant narrative (of legal continuity) is based on a particular way of presenting the past as perceived and believed to be colossal and astonishing in its greatness and influence.

Hayden White asserted not long ago that while writing about history one almost necessarily makes a leap into fiction because the explanatory power of history is based on the creative, not simply chronical, narratives. Therefore, an author of such a narrative, following his own beliefs or presupposed aims, weaves the isolated facts of a chronicle into a sequence, resulting in kind of a plot which is fictitious by its nature. In fact, even according to its own self-image, history is a mixture of facts and their interpretations.[114] Legal scholars, ignoring the desire of legal discourse for rationality, are tempted to declare:

> Polish law belongs to the Western legal tradition, its laws for historical and cultural reasons belonging to the Germanic and Romanistic legal families. This influence survives strongly to this day, notwithstanding a fifty-year period of submission to the so-called 'socialist family.'[115]

What is, however, the outcome of such sublimation of Roman law and common legal tradition, a sublimation that has and continues to be

---

[113] Bernard Lewis, *History: Remembered, Recovered, Invented* (Princeton: PUP, 1975), 54–9.

[114] Hayden White, *Tropics of discourse: Essays in cultural criticism* (Baltimore: Johns Hopkins University Press, 1978), 83, 98–9; Hayden White, *Metahistory: The Historical Imagination in Nineteenth-Century Europe* (Baltimore: Johns Hopkins University Press, 1990), 5–7.

[115] Rafał Stroiński, 'Report from Poland,' *European Company Law* 3/1 (2006), 39. See also more exemplary quotations and a critical comment on this statement by Mańko, 'The Unification,' 124–5; Mańko, 'Socialist Legal Culture,' 86–7, 103; Mańko ,'Weeds,' 212 and n. 26.

formative for contemporary Polish legal tradition and present in the theoretical and practical legal discourse of Polish Romanists, legal historians, and lawyers/practitioners? It is certainly not the proper understanding of Roman sources!

Such practice is evidence for the role played by legal tradition (founded on Roman law) and the ideology of continuity in the modern development of Polish law. This practice can also be considered as evidence of the psychological need of judges to emphasize the impact of the European legal tradition long regarded as colossal. It shows that there are those who believe that ancient Roman law and the old *ius commune* are the grounds to reconstruct European legal unity, with Poland included. Consequently, ancient remnants appear as a deep structure of Polish private law. However, in reality this practice also produces another outcome: it makes Polish law more Western thanks to the adaption of the same legal roots for its institutions. Polish law has thus started to belong to the same legal tradition as the laws of other European countries, basing itself on the same European legal thought, and using the same legal lingua franca, i.e. legal Latin.[116]

> Roman law is the story about law, which persists in today's legal solutions and provides the identity of our legal culture.[117]

In many cases, however, the very nature of the story of the common legal tradition involves a measure of delusion about the possibility of historical continuity. But as the fundaments or roots are always located in the dawn of a history, what is 'real' later disappears and what is invented becomes ideologically legitimized by calling upon the continuing authority of the Romans. The great sublimated past established the continuity of the present and the future, and as such it is marketed to the consumers.[118] Thus, the Derridian colossal appears.

---

[116] Paul Koschaker dreamed of this almost 50 years ago. See Paul Koschaker, *Europa und das römische Recht*, 2 Aufl. (München-Berlin: Beck, 1953), 124.

[117] Franciszek Longchamps de Bérier, 'Rachunek sumienia dla historii prawa. (Recenzja "The Oxford International Encyclopedia of Legal History", S. Katz (wyd.), t. 1–6, OUP 2009)' [Self-examination for Legal History. A Review of 'The Oxford International Encyclopedia of Legal History,' ed. S. Katz, vol. 1–6, OUP 2009], *Forum Prawnicze* 2/2 (2010), 95. [trans. Paulina Święcicka].

[118] Eric Hobsbawm, 'Introduction: Inventing Traditions,' in *The Invention of Tradition*, ed. Eric Hobsbawm and Terence Ranger (Cambridge: CUP, 1983), 1–7.

10

The Role of Václav Havel in Czech Critical Legal Thought

Markéta Klusoňová

10.1 Introduction

The past has left its significant traces over the evolution of Czech legal culture. Inasmuch as the critique of law both scrutinizes and mirrors the legal life of a community, an engagement with its past seems essential to a thorough understanding of law's intricate status in society. This chapter claims that the critique of law is not necessarily a lawyers' monopoly. Indeed, under actually existing socialism, critique was ushered in against establishment legal discourse by dissidents developing a culture of resistance outside the state's legal apparatus.

Perhaps the most important figure of the dissident movement was Václav Havel, who later became president of the Czech Republic. His work had a crucial influence over civic legal consciousness during the era of actually existing socialism. Although not stemming from a purely legal standpoint, his critique of the law proved to be highly influential in Central and Eastern Europe. Under the form of drama or of literary essays, his criticism of the law subverted the communist ban on any form of resistance to the law. More importantly, even after the demise of actually existing socialism, Havel stood as an important critical figure exposing the failures of the Czech state, society, and its law.

In this chapter I shall focus on Havel's texts dealing with law in artistic form. My aim is to investigate how Havel as an important European and international critical figure influenced legal discourse in Central and Eastern European countries.

This chapter is divided into four parts. The first deals with the relationship between critical legal thought in Czechoslovakia and the Critical Legal Studies ('CLS') movement. The second is focused on Havel as the main figure of Czech dissent. Then Havel's texts are analyzed. In the fourth part, the role of dissidents in the Czech critical legal thinking is emphasized.

10.2 Legal Critique in the Czech Republic

Critical thought in post-communist countries is a controversial issue due to its presumed non-existence during the era of actually existing socialism. It is becoming increasingly difficult to ignore the persisting differences between Western and Eastern countries in many fields, including economy, politics, and of course critical thought. In recent years, there has been an increasing interest in non-Western authors of contemporary critical thought such as Slavoj Žižek.[1] So far, however, there has been little discussion about critical legal thought in Central and Eastern Europe during the communist period.

The aim of this chapter is to answer the question of whether it is even possible to use the ideas of CLS as a whole in the discourse of Central and Eastern Europe.[2] As we shall see, my central thesis is that critical legal thought was already present in former Czechoslovakia. While we should acknowledge that Czech critical thought at the time differed from critical thought in democratic countries in many ways, with most of these differences a result of the daily socio-economic basis of the post-communist regime and living in lies.[3] However, many analogies to the CLS movement can still be found. Havel in Czech critical thought is the most significant example of such an analogy. A further aim of this chapter is not to judge the value of CLS or for that matter Marxist theory, but to answer whether a theoretical concept (abstract and theoretically universal) that is nonetheless based on a specific historical and political experience is transferable to a different cultural and legal environment.

For the purposes of this chapter, the term 'critical legal thought' is understood in a broader sense than is usual in the CLS movement.[4] It is focused more on the 'critical' part than on its explicitly legal characteristic and uses a Law and Literature approach more than the original CLS movement.[5] It looks for arguments for the existence of a critical approach to legal and political questions in Czechoslovakia during the era of real socialism but cannot provide any analysis of the similarities and differences between the legal and political situation in Western countries and Czechoslovakia in the 1960s and 70s.

From this further questions arise. Firstly, we can ask whether there is at least a similar tradition of critical legal thought in the Czech Republic

---

[1] Jodi Dean, 'Why Žižek for Political Theory,' *International journal of Žižek studies* 1/18 (2007), accessed 1 March 2014, http://zizekstudies.org/index.php/IJZS/article/view/7.
[2] See also Martin Škop, 'The Importance of Being a Linguist,' ch. 2 of the present volume.
[3] Václav Havel, 'The Power of the Powerless,' accessed 12 December 2014 http://vaclavhavel.cz/showtrans.php?cat=eseje&val=2_aj_eseje.html&typ=HTML.
[4] Jiří Přibáň, 'Kritická právní věda a sociologie práva,' *Právník* 12 (2001), 1211.
[5] James Boyle, *Critical Legal Studies* (New York: New York University Press, 1992).

or whether it was something quite new when it appeared after the Velvet Revolution, or if it actually continued in an already established tradition. If so, the second question is if this tradition of post-communist countries is in any way compatible with the CLS movement. In expectation of some positive answers to these questions, a way to achieve synthesis shall be proposed in the conclusion.

The argument I advance here is supported by an analysis of select artistic writings, including essays written by Havel during the era of actually existing socialism. Trensky claims that Havel highlighted the critical approach to the official system of actually existing socialism:

> The work of Havel epitomizes the state of Czech literature in the middle 1960s, which is characterized by two main features: first, an orientation toward the West in general philosophical questions and literary techniques, and, secondly, an outspokenly critical attitude toward Stalinism and its contemporary vestiges.[6]

Two major works dealing with issues of law, critical thought, and justice (*Czech Lot?* and 'Power of the Powerless') and two artistic (*The Garden Party* and *The Memorandum*) will be examined. They were all written by Havel between 1968 and 1989.

10.3 Critical Legal Thought and the CLS movement

Central to the entire discipline of CLS is a critical approach to law and politics. There have been numerous works dealing with the CLS movement, such as those of Unger, Hutchinson, Boyle, and Přibáň (in Czech discourse). While a variety of definitions of the term CLS have been suggested, this paper will use the definition first suggested by Přibáň who defines it as a radical critique of modern law and modern legal science which was founded in the 1970s and 1980s in Anglo-American legal culture.[7] Its method is based on a strong critique of modern law's 'pseudo' neutrality usually connected with the liberal states of Western Europe. Přibáň argues that critical legal thought is a necessary consequence of the legal realist movement which argues for the necessary consideration of social context in the application of law. In one programmatic text of CLS, Unger argues that it is necessary to permanently reconstruct a political democracy to avoid its degeneration and to achieve a post-liberal society.[8] Nowadays,

---

[6] Paul Trensky, 'Václav Havel and the Language of the Absurd' *The Slavic and East European Journal* 13 (1969) 42.
[7] Přibáň, 'Kritická,' 1211.
[8] Roberto Mangabeira Unger, 'The Critical Legal Studies Movement,' *Harvard Law Review* (1983), 561.

the content of CLS is often misunderstood.⁹

The question is whether such an approach is translatable in countries and legal systems where neither legal realism nor liberal democracy were experienced or even widely known. We need to ask whether CLS's ideas are applicable in Central and Eastern Europe, a space with a relatively long experience of real socialism. CLS proclaims a politically oriented approach to law, more specifically a left-oriented approach to law and legal science.¹⁰ In communist and later post-communist countries such an approach is complicated. It could seem to be a paradox to use the CLS point of view in a situation where we can provide our own critical point of view based on our own (often more profound, practical, and 'existential' in Havel's terminology) opinion. A non-critical use of CLS theory in non-Western and non-Common Law legal systems would be absurd in the same sense as in Havel's plays.¹¹

Probably the best example of this paradox is described in Tom Stoppard's play *Rock'n'roll*.¹² In this play at the beginning, one of the main characters Max, the English professor living his personal life and also his academic career for Communism, explains the geniality of Marxist ideology to Jan, another main character of the play and most importantly a Czech student. At the end of the play, after facing Jan's own tragic experience with real socialism, Max has to admit his mistake about this point. This description provides a clear analogy to the use of CLS's ideas in a Czech context.

There are a number of important differences between Western critical legal thinking and critical legal thinking in Central and Eastern Europe. Havel himself presents the example of Czech dissidents and Western activists.¹³ Dissidents in a totalitarian regime are in permanent danger because of the power of a totalitarian state. Such dissidents risk their personal lives, their careers, and often their freedom. On the other hand, activists in democratic systems may face some difficulties but usually not so severe. Critical legal thought may have a similar legal, philosophical, or political basis in every country in the world but conditions are different—the risks of this approach are much higher in totalitarian states than in democracies.

The CLS movement was officially absent in Czech discourse during the communist era because of its Western origin. On the other hand, the situation in Czechoslovakia in the 1960s and 1970s coincided with the Western experience in several aspects.¹⁴ The reasons for the emergence

---

⁹ Adam Gearey, '"Change is Gonna Come": Critical Legal Studies and the Legacies of the New Left' *Law and Critique* 24 (2013), 211.
¹⁰ Přibáň, 'Kritická,' 1212.
¹¹ Václav Havel, *Hry* (Prague: Torst 1999).
¹² Tom Stoppard, *Rock'n'roll* (Prague: Maťa 2007).
¹³ Havel, 'The Power of the Powerless.'
¹⁴ Unger, 'The Critical,' 564–7.

of the CLS movement are comparable in complexity to the emergence of critical legal thought in Czechoslovakia before, during, and after the Prague Spring.[15] There is the same feeling of necessity for social change based on a critical approach to the connection between law and politics. There is also the same orientation towards leftist ideas serving as a critique of an official system of power. As a result of this, Czech critical legal thought has much in common with Western critical legal thought which evolved through the CLS movement. Nevertheless, social and political differences also resulted in the development of another contrasting tradition of critical legal thought within Czech discourse.

10.4 Václav Havel as the Main Figure of Czech Dissent

As already stated, each country has its own characteristic features of law based on its historical experience and on the socio-cultural system present or at work in that particular country. The Czech Republic is no different in this respect regardless of its communist past. Nevertheless, the aspect in which the Czech Republic differs from Western discourse is this direct connection to communist era practices. The situation of Czech critical legal thought is complicated in view of this completely different political basis.[16]

The legal criticism of law is a mirror of law itself. But law is a mirror of the whole society. It is no coincidence that William Shakespeare often used law in this sense and Havel did the same.[17] This connection works also in the opposite direction so we are able to examine complex legal discourse through non-legal critical thought. The fact that such critical thought is not formally legal does not mean that it is not essentially legal because the purely legal critique of law does not alone constitute a legal environment.

During the period of actually existing socialism there were dissidents who influenced legal discourse even more than the official legal opinion of the state. Havel was probably the most important of them.[18] There were other dissidents who represented critical thought in Czechoslovakia during the communist era,[19] but it is necessary to focus on Havel for one precise reason. Havel influenced Czech social and legal discourse before the Velvet

---

[15] Mark Tushnet, 'Critical legal studies: A political history' *Yale Law Journal* 100 (1991), 1515; Charles Sabatos, 'Criticism and Destiny: Kundera and Havel on the Legacy of 1968' *Europe-Asia Studies* 80 (2008), 1827.

[16] Přibáň, 'Kritická,' 1212.

[17] Theodore Ziolkowski, *The mirror of justice: literary reflections of legal crises* (Princeton: Princeton University Press 2003).

[18] John Keane, *Václav Havel: politická tragedie v šesti dějstvích* (Prague: Volvox Globator 1999).

[19] Petr Blažek, ed., *Opozice a odpor proti komunistickému režimu v Československu 1968–1989* (Prague: Dokořán 2005).

Revolution and possibly even more after it.[20] Though not strictly legal in the usual sense, Havel's critical ideas as contained in his dramas or essays are highly important because in communist Czechoslovakia,[21] critique both of the state as well as the law was simply abandoned.[22]

10.5 Havel's Texts

10.5.1 Český úděl? (The Czech Lot?)

Firstly, we should mention a quite famous set of polemical essays from 1968 that straddle the border between artistic and political texts, namely Milan Kundera's *The Czech Lot* and Havel's *The Czech Lot?* These essays are probably the most impressive examples of critical thinking in Czechoslovakia during the era of real socialism. They define Havel's and Kundera's points of view at the point of the Prague Spring (among other authors such as Milan Uhde or Karel Kosík).[23] The CLS movement started at a very similar time to the Prague Spring. Both of these movements were intended to criticize the 'old' system (including politics) and to invent a 'better' one. Both were connected with a left-wing political sphere. While Kundera and Havel were 'original' critical thinkers of Central Europe, this polemic also highlighted their fundamental disagreement.

Charles Sabatos sees the 1968 Prague Spring as the most radical social experiment in the communist Eastern Bloc. He points out the personal and artistic differences between Havel and Kundera as the reason for their difference in opinions on the Prague Spring.[24] This is true in part, but the main reason for their disagreement should be seen in their different philosophical and political points of view. Kundera's attitude is a result of critical thinking but it is Havel who can be considered to be critical of socialism with a human face.

In his essay, Kundera defends the importance of the Czechoslovakian role in world politics and history and for this purpose he chooses the term 'Czech national destiny.' He introduces the Czech nation as the nation of brave innovators of the old system.[25] On the contrary, Havel criticizes the

---

[20] Adam Michnik and Agnieszka Marczyk, 'When Socrates Became Pericles: Václav Havel's "Great History," 1936–2011,' *Common Knowledge* 18 (2012), 387.

[21] Olga F. Chtiguel, 'Without Theatre, the Czechoslovak Revolution Could Not Have Been Won,' *The Drama Review* 34 (1990), 88.

[22] Jan Kavan, 'Czechoslovakia 1968: Revolt or Reform? 1968—A Year of Hope and Non-Understanding,' *Critique* 36 (2008), 289.

[23] Jan Zouhar, 'O českém údělu,' *Musicologica brunensia* 46 (2011), 159.

[24] Sabatos, 'Criticism and Destiny,' 1827.

[25] Milan Kundera, 'Český úděl,' *Listy* (1968), 19.

idea of the uniqueness of 'Central Europe' as a form of cultural identity.²⁶ Despite the fact that it was Kundera's essay 'The Tragedy of Central Europe'²⁷ which became a turning point in Western perceptions of the communist bloc,²⁸ it was Havel who provided a critique of the situation in Central Europe, both before and after 1968.

If Kundera is more like an 'old-fashioned' critical thinker speaking in political terms, Havel can be seen as a critical thinker similar to CLS thinkers insofar as he evaluates the Prague Spring from an existentialist 'postmodern' viewpoint. Havel explains that Prague's Spring was merely a political attempt to restore a 'normal'/traditional democratic state, rather than a brave new event or a world-breaking discovery. Indeed he criticized Kundera's romantic interpretation of the Czech role in world political history.²⁹ Analogically, it is the same situation as with the CLS movement where the postmodern approach of Foucault and Lyotard replaced the ideas of the Frankfurt School.³⁰ Together with his advocacy of the 'power of the powerless' and his reluctance to view the situation merely as an historical moment of the Prague Spring, Havel's comprehensive 'postmodern' critique is, as we shall in the following analysis of his plays, the reason why he influenced critical thought in Czechoslovakia before the Velvet Revolution the most.³¹

10.5.2 *Plays*

The most influential part of Havel's critique of the system can be found in his plays.³² Havel himself explained his dramatic goal as one of forcing the audience to see the misery of Czechoslovak reality.³³ In his plays, he tried to warn society and highlighted fundamental questions by manifesting their absence.³⁴ He confronted his audience with three types

---

[26] Václav Havel, 'Český úděl?' in *Z dějin českého myšlení o literatuře: antologie k dějinám české literatury 1945–1990* (Ústav pro českou literaturu AV ČR 2005), 470–5, accessed 12 December, http://www.ucl.cas.cz/edicee/data/antologie/zdejin/3/havel-1.pdf.

[27] Milan Kundera, 'The Tragedy of Central Europe,' *The New York Review of Books* 18 (1984), 33.

[28] Sabatos, 'Criticism and Destiny,' 1827.

[29] Havel, 'Český úděl,' 4715.

[30] Přibáň, 'Kritická,' 1211. Furthermore, the instantaneous influence of Kundera¢s influence on Czech critical thought was interrupted by his emigration.

[31] Robert Pirro, 'Václav Havel and the political uses of tragedy,' Political theory 30 (2002), 228.

[32] Christopher D. Brooks, 'The art of the political: Havel's dramatic literature as political theory,' *East European Quarterly* 39 (2005), 491.

[33] Václav Havel, *Disturbing the Peace*, trans. Paul Wilson (New York: Alfred A. Knopf, 1990).

[34] James Pontuso, *Václav Havel: Civic Responsibility in the Postmodern Age* (New York: Rowman and Littlefield, 2004).

of dramatic interventions: the early absurdist comedies (*The Garden Party* and *The Memorandum*), the Vanek morality plays (*Audience, Private View*, and *Protest*), and the psychological prison plays.[35] In his early absurdist comedies Havel criticized the state and the law that reminds of Derrida's thinking of law as play.[36] In these plays Havel refuses to accept the rules of the system; to live within a lie. There is a also strong link to Havel's essay 'The Power of the Powerless' through the use of meaningless words as the result of the emptiness of the system.

The Garden Party—In this play Havel criticizes human behaviour within the totalitarian system with the example of an ordinary but ambitious young man.[37] The main character, Hugo Pludek, is sent by his parents to meet Mr Kalabis at the garden party of the liquidation office. During the party Hugo faces many absurd situations and finally learns how to survive in this crazy world. In the end he becomes the head of the newly created Central Inauguration and Liquidation Committee. Unfortunately, he loses his own identity because of this adaptation to his new environment.[38]

Trensky observes that not only are the theatrical qualities of this play apparent, but also its great political and critical potential . He explains that:

> The great originality of Havel's talent finds its full expression especially in the subsequent acts, when the play acquires the character of a political satire. All the features of the avant-garde dramaturgy are retained, but, while continuing to be a general critique of modern mechanized society, the play goes on to expose the absurdities of the socialist system in particular. The second act is an easily recognized allegory of the institutionalization of private life in present-day Czechoslovakia, while the third act lampoons the monstrous bureaucratic machinery of the country.[39]

Later he points out that there cannot be any doubt that this play in general contains 'a parody of Marxian dialectics, referring to the thesis of permanent change.'[40]

The Memorandum—In this next play, Havel deals with the idea of an artificial bureaucratic language.[41] The main character, Gross, has to use

---

[35] Phyllis Carey, 'Living Lies: Václav Havel's Drama,' *Cross Currents* 42 (1992), 200.
[36] Jacques Derrida, *Writing and difference* (Chicago: University of Chicago Press, 1978) 196-250.
[37] Václav Havel, 'The Garden Party' in Václav Havel, *The garden party and other plays* (New York: Grove Press 1993), 1–62.
[38] Havel, 'The Garden Party,' 47.
[39] Havel, 'The Garden Party,' 55.
[40] Havel, 'The Garden Party,' 55.
[41] Václav Havel, 'The Memorndum' in Václav Havel, *The garden party and other plays* (New York: Grove Press, 1993), 63–130.

a synthetic language called Ptydepe in order to create a better scientific modern world. At the end of the first part of the play, Ptydepe causes Gross's downfall. In the second part of the play problems with using Ptydepe are described. Its role is central for the whole drama, as well as the disillusionment caused by the loss of enthusiasm for the socialist ideal after the fall of the Stalin cult.[42] Moreover, a critique of the bureaucratic machinery in Czechoslovakia is also apparent.[43]

The Power of the Powerless—This is probably Havel's most important work dealing with law.[44] This essay refers to the world of a ritually reproduced lie which is, according to Havel, common to the post-totalitarian system as well as to the liberal democratic system. Havel criticized the consumer value system of Eastern Europe in the similar way as CLS did in relation to the Western world.[45] The difference was in the reason for this critique. Havel simply refused each such failure of modern humanity, both in Western and communist Europe. In this essay, which is well-known both in the Czech Republic and abroad,[46] Havel asserts that dissent is an inevitable consequence of the post-communist system, a natural expression of the 'power of the powerless.'

The main part of this critique relates to the term 'post-totalitarian system.' On the one hand, Havel sees ideology positively as a dignified way to legitimize what is above, below, and on either side. Accordingly, he deems ideology necessary in the post-totalitarian system. On the other hand, he also considers ideology to be its main weakness. Before explaining why, it is worth pausing here to note that Havel's explanation of the principle of the post-totalitarian system is crucial for the understanding of legal discourse in Czechoslovakia. He explains that conformity, uniformity, and discipline were obligatory for each citizen. He argues that this system serves people only to the extent necessary to ensure that people will serve it. This means that the law of this system serves people only to the extent necessary to ensure that people will serve the system. Ideology creates a bridge between the system and individuals. According to Havel, these individuals confirm the system in the way that they fulfil it and *de facto* make it. Havel thus concludes that they *are* the system.

Havel further affirms that in the post-totalitarian system, living in truth has several dimensions. There is an existential dimension which includes

---

[42] Havel, 'The Memorandum,' 63.
[43] Havel, 'The Memorandum,' 64–5.
[44] Havel, 'The Power of the Powerless.'
[45] Richard W. Bauman, *Ideology and Community in the First Wave of Critical Legal Studies* (University of Toronto Press, 2002).
[46] Mark A. Mattaini and Kristen N. Atkinson, 'Constructive non-cooperation: Living in truth,' *Peace and Conflict Studies* 18 (2011), 3.

returning humanity to its inherent nature; a noetic dimension, which reveals reality as it is; a moral dimension of setting an example to others; and, most importantly, an unambiguous political dimension of living in truth. When an opposite—living a lie—is supposed to be the main pillar of the whole system, the fundamental threat to the system is living in truth. It must be emphasized that living truth is the fundamental critique of the system and so the system's interest in its suppression is far greater than anything else.

Havel exposes the absence of truth in every aspect of a person's life, and does the same for the law. Indeed law is the most important part of the critique of a post-totalitarian system, so important that it probably inspired other critiques that ultimately led to the Prague Spring. Havel asserts that the Prague Spring is usually understood as a clash between two groups. This clash lies on the level of real political power. The first group includes those who wanted to maintain the system without any changes; the second group consisting of people who wanted to reform the rigid system. However, Havel also argues it is frequently forgotten that the Prague Spring was merely a consequence of the long-term political process. Metaphorically, it can also be seen as the inevitable final act of a long drama originally played out in the theatre of the conscience of society. And that somewhere at the beginning of this drama there were individuals who were willing to live in truth, even when things were at their worst.

10.6 Dissidents

Living in truth was the main concept of critical thinking in the former Czechoslovakia and the consequent ethics of dissent still lives on in critical thinking in the Czech Republic. Therein lies the answer to the question concerning the signatories to Charter 77 and how they influences critical legal thought in Czechoslovakia and in the Czech Republic.[47] These Chartists were the infamous drop in the ocean that caused the flood. Havel demonstrates the power of this flood by stressing the confrontation between a thousand Chartists and the post-totalitarian system. He confesses that this confrontation would appear to be politically hopeless but this is only from a traditional point of view. Through the traditional lens of the open political system where each political force is measured on the level of real power, such confrontation does indeed seem hopeless. However, from the perspective of the post-totalitarian system, it appears

---

[47] In the late 1970s, Charter 77 was created by the Committee for the Defence of the Unjustly Prosecuted (VONS). It was an activity lying somewhere on the border between dissidence and opposition as the signatories requested that the State comply with human rights standards, see Michael Bernhard, 'Civil Society and Democratic Transition in East Central Europe,' *Political Science Quarterly* 108 (1993), 307.

fundamentally different.

In Havel's opinion, Charter 77 was the most important political event in Czechoslovakia because it was not merely a coalition of communists and non-communists, it was also a community *a priori* open to anyone. Moreover, it had a special political significance that cannot be overestimated because of the moral aspect of its pledges. An opposition in the post-totalitarian system does not exist. In fact, even Charter 77 cannot be considered an opposition. On the contrary, dissidents and especially 'Chartists,' in Havel's words, simply decided to live in truth.

10.7 Living in Truth

Living in truth means to frankly and loudly speak your opinion. According to Přibáň to live in truth refers not just to the rule of law but essentially to the true and just individual legal consciousness. Though the Chartists officially demanded compliance with human rights law, living in truth is more connected with the Radbruch formula than with the rule of law.[48] Havel argued for dissidents to express their solidarity with their fellow citizens in order to find a harmony with their conscience. By doing so, they cannot be deemed to be any kind of opposition. Their authentic attitude cannot be simply defined negatively as people who are against something. It constitutes, rather, a foundational critical attitude toward a political system, not a political programme.[49]

Žižek has also repeatedly stressed this point and most explicitly in his review of John Kean's biography of Havel where Žižek portrays Havel as a tragic figure of European politics, theatre, and philosophy.[50] He denies evaluating Havel's life in terms of an unrivalled success story and declares Havel to have been the Philosopher-King. Moreover, Žižek criticizes Havel's political work after the Velvet Revolution. For Žižek, Havel's approach including living in truth is primarily philosophical, not political. That is the reason for Havel's tragedy for both Žižek and Kean. Žižek adds that Havel's philosophy is an inevitable consequence of the post-communist system which cannot survive in the absence of the regime it opposed.[51]

Nevertheless, all of Havel's theoretical interventions are based on the most important legal critique in Czechoslovakia: Charter 77. Havel

---

[48] Gustav Radbruch, *O napětí mezi účely práva* trans. Libor Hanuš (Wolters Kluwer Česká republika 2012).

[49] Havel, 'The Power of the Powerless.'

[50] Slavoj Žižek, *Did somebody say totalitarianism?* (London: Verso Books, 2001).

[51] Slavoj Žižek, 'Attempts to escape the logic of capitalism,' *The London Review of Books* (1999), 7.

explained that dissidents were not 'renegades' or 'backsliders' and they were not primarily denying or rejecting anything. So it is natural that the 'dissident' movement would takes the form of a defence of human and civil rights. This fact is connected to a principle of legality, a milestone of the legal discourse in post-totalitarian systems. Dissidents just insist on respecting the law. As Havel argues:

> On the primary level, this stress on legality is a natural expression of specific conditions that exist in the post-totalitarian system, and the consequence of an elementary understanding of that specificity. If there are in essence only two ways to struggle for a free society—that is, through legal means and through (armed or unarmed) revolt—then it should be obvious at once how inappropriate the latter alternative is in the post-totalitarian system.[52]

The everyday work of dissidents was connected with this legal way of criticizing the post-totalitarian system. This is natural because conditions in the post-totalitarian system were static and stable and society was not sharply polarized on the level of actual political power. Post-totalitarian society was not able to accept any critique other than this peaceful one. On the other hand, Havel pointed out that

> all of this, however, is not the main reason why the 'dissident' movements support the principle of legality. That reason lies deeper, in the innermost structure of the 'dissident' attitude. This attitude is and must be fundamentally hostile toward the notion of violent change—simply because it places its faith in violence.[53]

10.8 Conclusion

This chapter has sought to demonstrate that Havel influenced Czech critical legal thinking and that critical (legal) thought was also present in the former Czechoslovakia. The analysis has also shown that living in truth is the main concept of Czech tradition of critical thinking.

Living in truth is not synonymous with legality. The content of this concept is much deeper. In Havel's own words:

> Of course, one need not be an advocate of violent revolution to ask whether an appeal of legality makes any sense at all when the laws—and particularly the general laws concerning human rights—are no more than a façade, an aspect of the world of appearances, a mere game behind which lies total manipulation.[54]

---

[52] Havel, 'The Power of the Powerless.'
[53] Havel, 'The Power of the Powerless.'
[54] Havel, 'The Power of the Powerless.'

That living in truth can lead to constructive non-cooperation is perhaps the most important lesson that can be drawn from Havel and the power of critique in the post-totalitarian system.

The generalizability of these conclusions is subject to certain limitations. For instance, Havel's thoughts are famous and important, but they represent only a small sample of such ideas in Czechoslovakia during the era of real socialism. And of course the works analyzed are only a partial selection from his oeuvre. Nevertheless, this selection may be considered a kind of manifesto for Czech critical thinking. It does not constitute critical thought in the Western sense. It was, rather, the only possible way to think critically in the post-totalitarian system. It responded to the basic problems specific to Czech society just as critical legal thought in the West responds to the specific problems of its social and legal orders.

Afterword

Law Between the Specters of the Past and the Impossible Object of Desire

Leszek Koczanowicz

I AM VERY FLATTERED and happy to be invited to write an afterword to this superb volume examining the situation of law in post-communist countries. I am flattered because, though a non-jurist, I was accepted by a rather hermetic circle of legal scholars to share my reflections on law during and after transformation. As I have done some work on transformation and its relevance to the theory of democracy, I feel to some extent justified to comment on the role of law during the transition to democracy. The invitation also gives me an opportunity to address a subject that I have always felt is missing in my work. It has been missing because I could not find any good description of the role of law that would transcend the professional jargon and show law in the social and cultural contexts of post-communist societies. This collection is an obvious exception; the chapters convincingly portray the problems encountered in the implementation of the new legal order. Before I discuss the relationship between law and the cultural dimension of transformation, let me start with some personal reflections on law.

I must confess that, like many other ordinary citizens, I am afraid of any contact with the legal apparatus. I have always preferred to stay away from lawyers even if I felt that in some situations I was perfectly validated in my claims. Nevertheless, I was wary of entering the labyrinth of legal procedures which are as a rule described in a truly esoteric language. I think that this 'fear of law' is a common experience in our society, and my first guess as to the sources of this feeling was the communist past. Law in communist countries was a very awkward issue. So far it has not been adequately investigated, and I was gratified to find some interesting insights on the topic in the chapters of this volume. As I remember, law in communist countries was dreaded because the central or regional bureaucracy could use it rather arbitrarily. Sometimes, however, legal procedures could be employed as a weapon against oppression as attested by Vladimir

Bukovsky's memoir *To Build a Castle: My Life as a Dissenter*,[1] where he describes a peculiar strike he organized in prison. Bukovsky encouraged his fellow inmates to write several petitions a day complaining about the dismal conditions of prison life. As, according to the Soviet law, each petition had to be answered, the prison administration had most of its time taken up by writing formal responses. Eventually, the administration had to accept at least some of the prisoners' demands. This anecdotal reference exemplifies what was probably a common perception of law under communism: the unpredictability of law. Despite efforts of many decent lawyers, law found itself in a grey zone produced by the dualistic structure of power, in which the party apparatus competed with the state and regional administration. That peculiar structure of power generated many exceptions to 'the rule of law,' with the ordinary citizens most annoyed at the special privileges for the *nomenklatura*.

Therefore, it does not come as a surprise that one of the axes the utopian visions of a better world revolved around was the idea of the just society, a society where law would become a real regulator of social relations without any exceptions. In a sense, just law and the rule of law became, to use psychoanalytical categories, an object of desire. More importantly still, people came to identify the rule of law with social justice and even, to some extent, with social and economic equality. As I argued elsewhere, the critique of the communist state had an ethical character that subsumed all spheres of society, the economy included.

> The economy thus was to express the moral values appreciated in the private lives of the people. Trust and justice should lead social reform and penetrate all spheres of social and political activity.[2]

When it turned out that such utopia was unrealizable, we felt dejected; and, to tell the truth, this sense of disappointment still permeates our public sphere. The mood is, of course, largely attributable to the gross mistakes committed in transformation. As many authors show, the first stage of transformation was characterized by uncontrolled privatization and the neglect of workers' rights.[3]

What I found in this volume is an excellent description of how a 'new law' was created. The chapters clearly show that the transformation of law was no exception to the general rule—that the process unfolded rather as a palimpsest of different layers and intentions than as a straightforward progression from one system to another. Law, thus, did not evade the fate

---

[1] Vladimir Bukovsky, *To Build a Castle: My Life as a Dissenter* (Viking Adult, 1979).
[2] Leszek Koczanowicz, *Politics of Time: Dynamics of Identity in Post-Communist Poland* (Berghahn Books: 2008), 46.
[3] David Ost, *The Defeat of Solidarity: Anger and Politics in Postcommunist Europe* (Ithanca and London: Cornell University Press, 2005).

of the general transformation even though some lawmakers have made considerable efforts to prove that post-transformation law rests exclusively on the premises of logical necessity and integrity. Even if such a vision of law dovetails with the common people's desire to live in a just country, law itself fails the test of reality. It is commonly perceived as convoluted, incoherent, and ill-executed. Of course, the reasons informing public perceptions are complex, but in public discourse the failures of law are ascribed rather to factors external to the functioning of law than to the construction of law itself. This volume provides a useful point of departure for rational discussion of post-transformation law as it demonstrates its genealogy and reveals its incoherencies. Such discussion can foster a better understanding of the problems of the transition to democratic society and possible ways of rectifying them.

But beyond this particular context, the volume is an important contribution to social theory. If social theory is preoccupied with the political anthropology of modernity, i.e. the relationship between the individual and power, law is certainly one of its essential factors. Given this, 'the fear of law' is not so much connected with law's specific manifestation, but rather with law as an overall expression of the hegemony of certain social groups. In conclusion to his seminal essay 'Critique of Violence,' Walter Benjamin sketches a utopian way out of the vicious circle of consecutive forms of law:

> The law governing their oscillation rests on the circumstance that all law-preserving violence, in its duration, indirectly weakens the lawmaking violence represented by it, through the suppression of hostile counter-violence. ... This lasts until either new forces or those earlier suppressed triumph over the hitherto lawmaking violence and thus found a new law, destined in its turn to decay. On the breaking of this cycle maintained by mythical forms of law, on the suspension of law with all the forces on which it depends as they depend on it, finally therefore on the abolition of state power, a new historical epoch is founded.[4]

One can of course ruminate on the impossibility of Benjamin's solution, but the central question which he seems to pose about the possibility of law in an unjust society cannot be erased.

---

[4] Walter Benjamin, 'Critique of Violence,' in *Reflections: Essays, Aphorisms, Autobiographical Writings*, ed. Peter Demetz, trans. Edmund Jephcott (New York: Schocken Books, 1986), 300.

Index

abortion 22, 101, 107, 114–6, 117, 119, 121, 125, 127, 128, 130, 132, 141, 151, 199
actually existing socialism 6, 66–78, 80, 84, 86–9, 206, 208
Adorno, Theodor 27
Agamben, Giorgio 45
ancien régime 61, 87, 88

Bakhtin, Mikhail Mikhailovich 37
Barlett, Katherine T. 91
Bator, Andrzej 30
Baudrillard, Jean 38
Benjamin, Walter 36, 45, 46, 65
Berger, Peter 107
Bérier, Franciszek Longchamps de 177, 190
biopolitics 50, 58
Bolsheviks 75, 81, 88
Borkowski, Andrew 177
Bourdieu, Pierre 25, 107, 108, 110, 118, 122
Bradley, Harriet 122

Camus, Albert 43
Catholic Church 115, 116, 152
capitalism 4, 10–12, 14, 17–18, 45–6, 48–9, 60, 62, 66–7, 74, 92, 115, 161, 202
Central Europe
  periphery 2–4
  sources of legal critique 7–10
Cercel, Cosmin 1–15
communism 58, 59

Communist
  government 66, 69
  Party 18, 24, 27, 39, 167
Critical Legal Studies (CLS) 32, 36, 92, 93, 206–9, 210–14
Croatian legal education 90, 93
Czech legal
  critique 15
  legal culture 206

Dębiński, Antoni 177
Dębska, Hanna 13, 106–130
democracy 10, 18, 22, 27, 52, 54, 55–6, 63, 99, 136, 160, 193, 203, 208–9, 219
Derrida, Jacques 27, 180, 205
Dissescu, Constantin 62
dissident(s) xvi, 8, 206, 209–10, 216–17
Djuvara, Mircea 58
Douzinas, Costas xii–xvi, 2, 9, 10, 11
Durkheim, Émile 120

EU accession 53, 94, 102
European legal tradition 178, 180, 181, 204, 205

Farmer, Paul 133
feminism 91, 94, 98, 99, 100, 101, 103, 105, 114, 116, 122, 134, 135
feminist jurisprudence 12, 14, 91, 92, 97, 99, 101, 105, 134, 135
Foucault, Michel 27, 28, 36, 39
Frankfurt School 8, 11, 16, 212
free market 102, 160–4, 169, 170, 175

French Revolution 51
Freud, Sigmund 4
Fuszara, Malgorzata 145

Galtung, Johan 133
Gardocki, Lech 203
Geertz, Clifford 33
Gender 12, 93, 97, 103, 106, 114, 119, 122, 131, 134–6, 138, 144, 146–7, 153
Giaro, Tomasz 68
Gilligan, James 134
Girard, René 56
Graff, Agnieszka 130

Hall, Stuart 40
Havel, Václav 4, 15, 206–13
Hoetink, Hans R. 191
Honoré, Tony 190
Horkheimer, Max 27
Human Rights 33, 90, 97, 99, 101–2, 125–7, 138, 170–1, 190–1

ius commune 181–82, 185, 198, 201, 205

Jhering, Rudolf von 191
Justinian 176, 180–1, 183, 188–9, 190, 192, 199, 200

Kantorowicz, Hermann 184
Kašić, Biljana 102
Kelman, Mark 36
Kennedy, Duncan 41
Klusoňová, Markéta 15, 206–218
Koczanowicz, Leszek 219–21
Kuhn, Thomas S. 86
Kühn, Zdeněk 2
Kukovec, Damjan 4
Kundera, Milan 38, 39

Lacan, Jacques 49
language & hegemony 32–43

legal
  education 12, 14, 25, 90–4, 103–4, 154, 162–3, 165
  interpretation 35, 41, 120, 143
  profession 13–4, 104, 154, 163, 168–70, 173
Letowska, Ewa 146
Liszcz, Teresa 129
Lukmann, Thomas 107
Lyotard, Jean-Francois 28, 30, 180

Mańko, Rafał 1–15, 66–89, 195, 202
Marx, Karl 49, 75
Milan Kundera 38, 211–12
Minda, Garry 34–5
modernism 46, 179, 188
modernity v, 27, 45, 47, 50–1, 59, 61–2, 221

Negulescu, Paul 58
nineteen eighty-nine (1989) 6, 10, 12, 21, 24–5, 52–3, 55, 63, 67–8, 70, 72, 74, 79, 80, 82, 86, 89, 91–2, 112, 114–16, 132, 134, 147, 151, 154, 160–1, 167, 170, 180–2, 197, 202, 208, 210
Noelle-Neumann, Elisabeth 32
non-official law 14, 132, 149, 153
Novalis 36

October Revolution 88
Orestano, Riccardo 195
Ortner, Sherry B. 118

picnolepsy 45–50
Polish
  Civil Code 88
  Constitution 137
  Constitutional Court 16, 106
    genealogy of 17–23
  jurisprudence 144
  law 71, 75, 81, 124, 132, 137, 141, 145–6, 171, 195, 197, 201,

204–5
Polish legal
  community 71, 87, 168, 202
  culture 67, 72–3, 88, 89, 197
  history 67, 73, 189
  practice 198, 202
  scholars 23, 24, 25
  science 194
  system 171, 172, 196
  tradition 204
Polish private law 85, 87
positivism 7, 13, 62, 94, 99, 106, 158, 166–8
postcoloniam(ism) xiv, 3, 28
postmodern(ism) 27, 30, 43, 255, 159, 106, 188, 212
Prague Spring 210–12, 215
Přibáň, Jiří 32
property law, socialist 75

Radačić, Ivana 12, 90–105
Rajski, Jerzy 72
relativism 106, 169
resistance 8, 15, 45, 58, 206
Rhode, Deborah L. 91
Rodak, Lidia 13, 131–153
Revolution
  anti-modern 28
  anti-positivistic 6
  global 193
  legal 202
  pro-Western 27
  See also French Revolution; nineteen eighty-nine (1989), October Revolution; Velvet Revolution
Romanian
  Constitution 53
  constitutional law 44
  legal history 56
  legal theorists 58
Roman law 14, 51, 74, 176–8, 180–3, 184–97, 199, 2005

Sadurski, Wojciech 69
Safjan, Marek 70
Schmitt, Carl 64
Siscar, Gregorio Mayáns y 183
Sitek, Bronisław 196
Škop, Martin 11, 32–43
Slavoj, Žižek 60, 160, 207, 216
socialism. *see* actually existing socialism
socialist
  law 86, 193
  property law 75
Solidarność (Solidarity) 19, 115
Soviet Union 3, 18, 81, 89, 193, 194
Srokosz, Jacek 14, 154–175
Stroiński, Rafał T. 71
structural violence 14, 131–6, 138, 140–2, 146, 148, 153
sublimation 178
Sulikowski, Adam 1, 1–15, 16–31
Supreme Court 3, 6, 8, 14, 20, 29, 75, 82, 84, 85–6, 88, 96, 144, 198–99, 200–3
Święcicka, Paulina 14, 176–205
symbolic violence 4, 5, 109, 112, 118

Tamás, Gáspár Miklós 61
technicism 154–157
translation 34, 36–7, 42, 61

Velvet Revolution 208, 210, 212, 216
Virilio, Paul 45

Warczok, Tomasz 13, 106–130
Watson, Alan 188
Western legal science 184
West, the 3, 18, 23–4, 28, 69, 155, 203, 208, 218
White, Hayden 179
Wojtyczek, Krzysztof 26–7
women's rights 97, 100–1, 103, 105, 132, 140, 150–2

www.ingramcontent.com/pod-product-compliance
Lightning Source LLC
Chambersburg PA
CBHW031105080526
44587CB00011B/829